Second Edition

# Introduction to
# Social Research

Second Edition

# Introduction to Social Research

Quantitative and Qualitative Approaches

**KEITH F PUNCH**

**SAGE** Publications
London • Thousand Oaks • New Delhi

SAGE Publications Ltd
1 Oliver's Yard
55 City Road
London EC1Y 1SP

SAGE Publications Inc.
2455 Teller Road
Thousand Oaks, California 91320

SAGE Publications India Pvt Ltd
B-42, Panchsheel Enclave
Post Box 4109
New Delhi 110 017

**British Library Cataloguing in Publication data**

A catalogue record for this book is available from the British Library

ISBN 978-0-7619-4416-4


**Library of Congress Control Number 2004099537**


Typeset by C&M Digitals (P) Ltd., Chennai, India
Printed in Great Britain by The Cromwell Press Ltd, Trowbridge, Wiltshire

# Contents

# Figures

# Tables

# Examples

# Preface to Second Edition

The second edition of *Introduction to Social Research: Quantitative and Qualitative Approaches* retains the structure and rationale of the first edition, but there are also several changes:

- At the end of each chapter, the main concepts covered in the chapter are brought together as review concepts.
- At the end of the book, a glossary of terms has been added. This is not a full-scale glossary of all terms used in social science research, but focuses on those terms which are prominent in this book, aiming in each case to give conceptual rather than technical descriptions. As noted on page 289, several of the terms in this glossary are also dealt with in the *Key Research Terms* booklet from the Open University course EK310 ('Research with Children and Young People'). Cross referencing those terms offers readers an alternative interpretation.
- In Chapter 8, a new section on action research has been added, and the section on discourse analysis has been expanded. I want to thank Wayne McGowan for his assistance with these sections.
- In Chapter 12, the discussion of ethical issues in research has been broadened.
- The appendices have been re-done, and reduced from three to two. Appendix 1 now deals with computer software, concentrating on SPSS for quantitative research, and N6 for qualitative research. I want to thank John West for his contribution on SPSS, and Roger Vallance for his contribution on N6. Appendix 2 deals with the Miles and Huberman material for drawing and verifying conclusions in qualitative analysis, and now includes their list of six 'fairly classic analytic moves' used by most approaches in qualitative analysis.

In addition to these changes, the text has been reworded and reduced in various places throughout the book and new tables and/or diagrams have been added, with a view to improving the clarity of the material.

I want to thank Myra Taylor for her help in re-doing the index for this second edition, and Robyn Wilson for her continued clerical and secretarial assistance. As always, it has been a pleasure to work with Patrick Brindle and the editorial team at Sage Publications.

Keith F Punch
Graduate School of Education
University of Western Australia
January, 2005
email: keith.punch@uwa.edu.au

# Preface to First Edition

In the last few years especially, I have felt that there is an increasing need for researchers to have a basic understanding of both main approaches to social research, the quantitative and the qualitative. Several books have appeared in the last 10 years, which are helpful in dealing with this problem. Examples are those written (or edited) by Bryman (1988), Brannen (1992), Creswell (1994), Neuman (1994) and Gilbert (1996). But while these books are valuable, it seems to me they are not aimed primarily at the introductory level – not written to give a comprehensive overview and a basic understanding of the main ideas, before getting into more complex and technical (and sometimes philosophical) issues.

Because of these perceptions, this book is written for the introductory level, and aims to cover the basics of both quantitative and qualitative research in a balanced way, setting both within a common framework for research and stressing the logic and ideas involved. 'Balanced' here means that the two approaches are given equal weight. Thus, roughly equal space is devoted to the two approaches, and they are discussed using the same general headings. The quantitative approach occurs first in the book merely as a reflection of the history of the last 30 or so years. In preparing the book, I have tried to keep the content grounded in the problems I encounter when working with research students (especially beginning research students), and when consulting about research in the wider community. I explain this approach in more detail in Chapter 1.

In line with this, my main debt is to the many research students (and researchers) I have worked with and learned from over the years, in several countries. I am also grateful to the following people at the Graduate School of Education of The University of Western Australia for their help in compiling this book: Sandra Carrivick for her careful reading and helpful comments and suggestions; Brad Hicks for his help in surveying computer programs for qualitative analysis; Shane Langsford for similar help with computing in quantitative analysis; Robyn Wilson, and especially Dianne Pitschel, for their tireless work in helping to prepare the manuscript; and Graham Douglas and Tom O'Donoghue who both provided helpful reactions to earlier drafts of chapters. Felicity Haynes and Roger Slee were supportive as Heads of the Graduate School of Education at The University of Western Australia while this book was being written.

My thanks also go to John Hattie, who provided facilities at the University of North Carolina (Greensboro) while a first draft of the book was written and for helpful comments on its content, and to the Faculty of Economics,

Commerce, Education and Law at The University of Western Australia for a period of study leave while the first draft was written, and for financial support to enable me to complete the work.

I want to thank Simon Ross at Sage Publications (UK) for his help and encouragement, the editorial team at Sage and the reviewers. I am sure they will recognize the influence they have had.

Lastly on this list, but not in fact, I want to thank my wife, Rosie-Amatul, for her constant support and understanding during the preparation of this book.

# 1
# Introduction

This book is about empirical research in social science. It covers both quantitative and qualitative approaches, and focuses on the essential elements of each. It places both approaches within the same framework for organizing research, and it deals with them under the same main headings. The stress is on the logic of what is done in research, rather than its technical aspects. Therefore it is not a 'how to do it' book, but aims instead to develop a basic understanding of the issues involved and of the ideas behind the main techniques.

In selecting material for the book, and presenting it, I have been guided by two central questions:

* What should be the content of an introductory course in social research, before any methodological specialization?
* How can that content be presented in a way which shows 'how research works', and which gives enough tangible and practical understanding of issues, methods and techniques to get a project under way?

The book is written primarily for upper-level undergraduate and beginning graduate students in different areas of social science, but I hope it will also be suitable for other researchers who want to overview the logic of social research and the main ideas behind its methods, quantitative and qualitative.

Given the widespread use of both quantitative and qualitative methods today, and an increasing tendency to combine them,[1] it is important for a researcher to have an understanding of both approaches, whatever specialization of method that researcher may also subsequently develop.

This first chapter sets the context for the material to be covered, and gives more detail about the book's approach and its rationale. The chapter outline of the book is shown in Section 1.6.

## 1.1 Background

A brief overview of developments in social science research over the last 30 years or so can set the background for the contents of this book, and for the approach that it takes. Beginning in the 1960s, the traditional dominance of quantitative methods, as *the* way of doing empirical research in social science, was challenged. That challenge accompanied a major growth of interest in using qualitative methods, and this in turn produced a split in the field, between quantitative and qualitative researchers.[2] A prolonged quantitative–qualitative debate ensued, sometimes described as the 'paradigm wars'. Much of that debate was characterized by either–or thinking. Some thought that only quantitative approaches should be used to study human behaviour. Others were just as emphatic that only qualitative approaches are appropriate. More recently, however, there have been moves towards a détente, and an increased interest in the combination of the two approaches (Bryman, 1988; 1992; Hammersley, 1992).[3]

The full story of these developments, and of the important debates which accompanied them, is much more complex than this. I have focused here only on one main dimension of it, the quantitative–qualitative distinction, since these remain the two central approaches in social research today, and since this distinction is a central organizing principle for this book. A major consequence of these developments is that qualitative research methods have moved much more into the mainstream of social science research, compared with their marginalized position of some 30 years ago. As a result, the field of social science research methodology is now bigger and more complex than it used to be. The context in which research operates is now also more complex.

The history briefly outlined above also has a deeper level, a level which is not just about the quantitative–qualitative debate, or about research methods. Both of these matters are connected to underlying paradigm issues.[4] On this deeper level, a major rethinking began some time ago, and is ongoing. It has brought a questioning of all aspects of research (its purposes, its place and role, its context, and conceptualizations of research itself) as well as the techniques it uses. It has also brought the development of new perspectives, and of new approaches to data and to the analysis of data, within qualitative research especially. Prominent features of that rethinking are the detailed critique of positivism,[5] and the emergence and articulation of several different paradigm perspectives, as alternatives to positivism. As a result, paradigm issues are in a state of change and development, and many matters are still contested.

With respect to these paradigm questions, my view is that we should be aware of the issues involved, and of the areas of debate. These are indicated in several places throughout the book. But we can proceed to do research, and to train researchers, mindful of those debates yet not engulfed by them, and without necessarily yet being able to see their resolution. In other words, we can acknowledge the connections of methods to these deeper issues, and discuss them from time to time as they arise, without making them the major focus of this book, or of our research. This is to take a pragmatic approach, consistent with the view that not all questions for social research are driven by paradigm considerations, and that different sorts of questions require different methods for answering them. Both of these points are elaborated in later chapters.

To choose the pragmatic approach is to start by focusing on what we are trying to find out in research, and then to fit methods in with that. A different choice would be to start with the theoretical and philosophical considerations involved in the discussion and analysis of paradigms. To do that, and to engage fully with paradigm issues, would produce a different sort of book. Because this book aims to give an overview of both approaches set within a common view of research, and because it is aimed at the introductory level, it takes the pragmatic approach of focusing on research questions. But such a pragmatic choice does not dispense with paradigm issues. They are always present to some extent, even if implicitly: any research makes assumptions, especially about how questions are answered and knowledge is developed, and about the nature of data. Those assumptions are connected to paradigm issues.

Acknowledging the paradigm issues, but not making them a central focus, is a simplifying device which helps in organizing the contents of this book. The book uses some other simplifying devices, whose function is to make it easier to see what is essential in the content of both approaches, and easier to understand the main ideas of that content.

## 1.2 **Some Simplifying Devices**

The first follows from the fact that the book deals with empirical research methods.[6] Empirical research involves data, and data are of two main types: quantitative data, in the form of numbers, and qualitative data, not in the form of numbers. We deal here with methods for both quantitative empirical research and qualitative empirical research. Thus, as used here:

Quantitative research is empirical research where the data are in the form of numbers.

Qualitative research is empirical research where the data are not in the form of numbers.

These simplified definitions get us started and they are at the heart of the distinction between quantitative and qualitative research. Later, we will broaden the definitions to include differences in paradigms and methods as well as data.[7]

Second, a sharp distinction is made in the early part of this book between the pre-empirical and empirical stages of research. It is stressed in Chapters 3 and 4 that empirical research has an important pre-empirical stage, where careful analysis of the problem and the questions clarifies the empirical, technical and methodological considerations. Question development may be the best term to describe this pre-empirical work, which is important in setting up the research. It essentially comes down to clarifying and disentangling the different issues, and to restating the original problem as a series of empirical research questions. This question development work is often underemphasized, but the pre-empirical stage is important, since the issues involved in doing empirical research are as likely to be conceptual and analytical as they are to be technical and methodological. While this distinction is made sharply, in order to stress the importance of conceptual and analytical issues, these issues do not always precede the methodological issues. Sometimes the two are intertwined.

Third, research questions are strongly highlighted, and a model of research is used which stresses their central role. They are the goal of the pre-empirical stage of the research; they provide the backbone of the empirical procedures; and they are the organizing principle for the report. This model is stressed in order to clarify and illustrate the research planning process, and it is set up as a useful goal for that process. At the same time, actual research situations may require this model to be modified, in two ways. Research questions worked out in advance may change as the empirical work proceeds: there is no requirement that they be 'set in concrete'. Again, it may not be desirable or possible to plan certain types of studies in terms of prespecified research questions. Rather, the strategy in those cases is to identify and clarify the research questions as the study proceeds. When that happens, research questions retain a central role, but emerge at a different stage of the study. This points ahead to the contrast between prespecified and emerging research questions, designs and methods – an important distinction and a theme which is discussed in Chapter 2.

Fourth, the book stresses that methods should follow from questions. How we do something in research depends on what we are trying to find out. This point is stressed because, too often in the past teaching of research methods, we have put the methodological cart before the substantive (or content) horse. This has been called 'methodolatry', the idolatry of method, and has been particularly characteristic of (though not exclusive to) the quantitative approach. Many previous research methods books have taught methods 'in the abstract'. They are only about methods, and there is little connection between methods, on the one hand, and defining and analysing research problems, on the other. I think research methods texts at the introductory level now need to be more eclectic, and stronger in connecting methods to problem and question identification, definition and analysis. This book aims to do both of these things. Therefore, before it covers quantitative and qualitative methods, it deals with identifying, defining and analysing research questions, with the phrasing of research questions, and with connections between questions, data, and techniques for their collection and analysis.

In other words, the book, especially in the early chapters, stresses the influence of research questions on research methods as a useful teaching/learning device. In actually doing research, methods can constrain and influence the questions that can be asked. These influences are recognized in later chapters, and the reciprocal interaction between question and method is discussed. But the question-to-method influence is deliberately stressed, because of its value in ensuring a close fit between the research questions and the methods. In the end, a main objective of the planning is to maximize the fit between questions on the one hand, and design and procedures on the other. This point is also an important theme, and is discussed in Chapter 2.

Fifth, in several places, models are used for thinking about research, and some sharp distinctions are drawn. Simplified models to represent aspects of the research process are useful in teaching and learning about research. At the same time, actual research is often quite messy, and clear-cut textbook models have to be modified, but the models help in building understanding. Similarly, it is helpful to draw some contrasts very sharply, to illustrate the points involved. Once understood, those sharp distinctions can be relaxed, as they often must be in actual research. An example is the central distinction in the book between quantitative and qualitative research. That distinction is made sharply in the early chapters, and is relaxed somewhat in Chapter 11.

## 1.3 Research Methods Training

The main audience for this book is beginning research students in different social science areas, who need to learn about research methods, and who may be required to carry out a piece of research. Writing the book with this context in mind is intended to provide a comprehensive coverage of the stages of research, but it can easily be adapted by readers to other contexts for research.

Because it is written with the project (or dissertation) student in mind, I make some assumptions about students' work. In particular, I assume that students are responsible for identifying their own research areas and topics, and for developing their ideas for presentation in a formal research proposal. After carrying out the research, I assume the project will be reported in written form. This book deals with the general question of research writing in Chapter 12. These assumptions stress the scholarly context of the research, which is dealt with in Chapters 11 and 12.

In my experience, there has been a considerable change in research methodology training from 30 years ago. Then, when most research was quantitative, it was generally true that research students would get their methods training before doing their project. The idea was that they would master the techniques (usually quantitative design, measurement and statistics) before doing the research. Now, it seems that much more methods training goes on at the same time as the dissertation, during the research work. I do not see this as a problem, but it means we need to think about research methods training on two levels.

The first is a basic level of understanding, dealing with the logic of research, and covering both quantitative and qualitative approaches. The second level is more technical and more specialized, dealing with the different techniques of quantitative and qualitative research. This book is about the first level, and it aims to provide the foundation for more advanced training in research methods. The ideal course structure, in my view, would show these two levels. The first level is a comprehensive introduction to the main ideas of research, covering both approaches. The second level is more detailed and technical, and probably subdivides into a number of specialized courses, dealing with different aspects and techniques of quantitative and qualitative methods.

This two-level structure would also accommodate the contextualization of research methods. The issue here is between the common elements in research methods across all social science areas, on the one hand, and the specialized elements which characterize different social science areas, on the other. There is an important body of common knowledge about methods, which is generally applicable to empirical research in social science. There is also specialized contextual knowledge and perspectives about research methods, which is not so generally applicable. The two-level course structure deals with this. The first course deals with the common elements in research methods across the social sciences. The second-level courses deal with the contextually different and more specialized material.

## 1.4 Essentials and Logic

The full field of research methods, especially across both the quantitative and qualitative approaches, is very big – far too big for one book. Therefore selection of material is necessary. In making that selection, I have tried to concentrate on what a reader is most likely to need, in order to understand the logic of research, and in order to get the process of planning and developing research under way. In both approaches, my focus is therefore on the basics and the essentials. Whether the project will use quantitative methods, qualitative methods, or both, the guiding question has been: what are the basic and essential ideas and techniques the researcher needs to know? Compiling the book has thus involved identifying and distilling the core essentials of quantitative and qualitative methods. At the same time, as well as being selective, the book also aims to be both comprehensive and ambitious. While introducing research, it also aims to take readers a long way into empirical research in the two approaches, by focusing on essentials.

For quantitative research, the selection of material has seemed less problematic than for qualitative research. That reflects the agreement that I think would be found on what constitutes the essentials of quantitative methods. For qualitative research, by contrast, selection of both material and perspective has been less straightforward, as has distilling the material selected. Here I think there would be much less agreement on what constitutes 'essentials'. This is because of the paradigm diversity and the variety of perspectives and approaches within qualitative research, especially to the analysis of qualitative data. In the face of these choices about what to include and what to emphasize in qualitative research, it is presented in this book (in Chapters 8, 9 and 10) in a way that emphasizes its logical similarities with quantitative research. Thus the same main headings are used for both (design, data collection, data analysis). And, in the analysis of qualitative data, where the range of methods and perspectives is greatest, I have emphasized two approaches (the Miles and Huberman approach and, especially, grounded theory) which are most similar in logic to quantitative research. But I do not intend to imply that all qualitative research proceeds this way, and Chapter 10 includes a number of the other approaches which are important in current qualitative research.[8]

The book also aims to be more than just a collection of methods, by presenting a view of research (given in Chapters 3 and 4) and using that view to guide the selection and presentation of material. This means that the chapters are interconnected and that there is considerable cross-referencing of material between chapters. It also means that technical and methodological issues, which are discussed in logical terms, are related back to the analytical framework for research presented in the earlier chapters. That framework depends heavily on research questions. New approaches and perspectives, especially within qualitative research, have opened up both new types of research questions, and a much wider range of research questions. There are now many more things that we might be interested in finding out than research had previously considered. But even with this wider range, the need for clear research questions, and for close question–method fit, still applies.

The description of research as 'organized common sense' is useful. It supports the idea that good research is within the reach of many people. It is also consistent with the view that we can simplify the more technical aspects of research methods, and enhance understanding, by showing the logic behind them. This book therefore concentrates on the logic behind techniques, in an effort to avoid obscuring that logic behind technical considerations. I do not advocate a formula approach to doing research, since I do not believe that research can be reduced to a set of mechanical steps. On the contrary, I try to stress understanding rather than 'how to do it'. I like the idea that method should be seen not as a codification of procedures, but rather as information about actual ways of working (Mills, 1959). This means that principles and guidelines are stressed throughout the book, rather than sets of mechanical rules. It also means that common sense is needed at all stages of the research process, a point which comes up many times in the different chapters.

## 1.5 Science, the Social Sciences and Social Research

Already, the terms 'science' and 'social science' have been used several times. What is science, and what are the social sciences? What does it mean to study something scientifically? Much has been written on the topic of the scientific method, and today, especially, there are different definitions and points of view. As a starting point in learning about research, however, I suggest a simple and traditional conception of the method of science.[9]

In that conception, the essence of science as a method is in two parts. The first part concerns the vital role of real-world data. Science accepts the authority of empirical data and ideas have to be tested against data. The second part is the role of theory, particularly theory which explains. The aim is to explain the data, not just to collect the data and not just to use the data to describe things. Explanatory theory has a central role in science. The two essential parts to science are therefore data and theory. Put simply, it is scientific to collect data about the world, to build theories to explain the data, and then to test those theories against further data. Whether data come before theory, or theory comes before data, is irrelevant. It only matters that both are present. This point about the irrelevance of the order of theory and data has implications later in this book. There is nothing in this definition of science about the nature of the empirical data, and certainly nothing about whether the data are quantitative or qualitative. In other words, it is not a requirement of science that it involve numerical data, or measurements. It may well do so, but it is not necessary that it do so. This point is also relevant to later chapters of this book.

The general term 'social science' refers to the scientific study of human behaviour. 'Social' refers to people and their behaviour, and to the fact that so much of that behaviour occurs in a social context. 'Science' refers to the way that people and their behaviour are studied. If the aim of (all) science is to build explanatory theory about its data, the aim of social science is to build explanatory theory about people and their behaviour. This theory about human behaviour is to be based on, and is to be tested against, real-world data.

Human behaviour can be studied from many different perspectives. The basic social sciences can be distinguished from each other according to the perspective they take on the study of human behaviour. Many would agree that there are five basic social sciences: psychology, sociology, anthropology, economics and political science. These mainly differ from each other in the perspective they take: thus, psychology typically focuses on the individual person, whereas sociology is more concerned with groups and the social context of behaviour, and so on. We should not try to take these distinctions too far, because of the variety of perspectives that exists within the basic areas, and because some would want to include other areas as basic social sciences. Also, there are fields at the intersections between these basic social sciences (for example, there is social psychology, social anthropology, and so on), but it is useful to keep these basic areas in mind. They can be thought of as disciplines, which can be applied to a variety of different areas.

The applied social sciences can now be distinguished from the basic social sciences by the setting or area of behaviour they focus on. There are many of these areas: some of the main ones are education, organization studies, government studies, administration and management, social work, nursing studies and health research, certain areas of medicine and public health, family studies, child development, marketing and market research, recreation and leisure studies, communication studies, justice, legal and clinical studies, policy analysis, programme evaluation, and research for social and economic development.

Within these areas, there are also specialized approaches. One way to see this is to think of disciplines applied to areas. For example, with education as the area, and psychology, sociology, anthropology, economics and political science as the basic disciplines, we have five specialized areas within education: the psychology of education, the sociology of education, and so on. Thus, to see education as an applied social science means to apply one or other of the basic social sciences to the study of behaviour in the educational setting. The same applies to other areas. We do not need to worry greatly about precise classifications, and the exact borders between these areas. Rather, the point of this sketch is to indicate the reach of the applied social sciences.

Together the social sciences, basic and applied, cover a very wide domain. What unifies them is their focus on human behaviour, and the central role of empirical research in the way they are studied. Because of this central role of empirical research, a premise of this book is that there is a great deal of similarity in research methods across the various areas shown above. Of course, there are also differences in methodological emphasis in different social sciences, and there are affinities for (and hostilities towards) some methods in some disciplines.[10] But the similarities in the general logic of inquiry, and in the basics of designs and empirical procedures, are very strong. This means that we can apply that logic, and those designs and procedures, in many different areas.

## 1.6 Organization of the Book

After this introductory chapter, the book is presented in 11 chapters, as follows:

Chapter 2 ('Some Central Issues') deals with three themes which occur frequently throughout the book, and which are therefore brought together in Chapter 2 for reference purposes. Some readers may want to skim this chapter on a first reading, and to return to it for reference as the themes come up in relation to different topics.

Chapters 3 and 4 deal with the pre-empirical stage of research, focusing on research questions. Chapter 3 ('Research Questions') deals with identifying and developing research questions, and with the role of hypotheses and the literature in doing that. Chapter 4 ('From Research Questions to Data') continues the consideration of research questions, but concentrates more on linking the questions to data.

Chapters 5, 6 and 7 give an overview of quantitative research methods. Chapter 5 ('Quantitative Research Design') describes the main ideas involved in the design of quantitative studies. Chapter 6 ('Collecting Quantitative Data') considers what is involved in collecting quantitative data, and the central role of measurement in that process. Chapter 7 ('The Analysis of Quantitative Data') describes the logic behind the main statistical techniques used in quantitative social science. These three chapters would be suitable, as a unit, for the reader who only wants an overview of quantitative methods.

Chapters 8, 9 and 10 give a similar overview of qualitative research methods, using the same general headings. Chapter 8 ('Design in Qualitative Research') discusses the main strategies for use in qualitative research, and before that notes the complexity and diversity of contemporary qualitative research and two of its important perspectives (feminism and postmodernism). Chapter 9 ('Collecting Qualitative Data') deals with the main methods of data collection in qualitative research. Chapter 10 ('The Analysis of Qualitative Data') discusses issues involved in analysing qualitative data, focuses on two of the main approaches which have been developed, and overviews several recent and more specialized approaches. Again, these three chapters would be suitable, as a unit, for the reader who wants an overview of qualitative methods.

Chapter 11 ('Mixed Methods and Evaluative Criteria') is in two parts. The first part deals with combining the two approaches. The second part presents general evaluative criteria for assessing empirical research. Chapter 12 ('Research Writing') deals with the general topic of research writing, discusses proposals in some detail, and notes some of the ethical issues involved in social research.

Two appendices contain additional material. Appendix 1 deals with computing software for quantitative and qualitative analysis, and Appendix 2 deals with Miles and Huberman's (1994) tactics for drawing and verifying conclusions in qualitative analysis.

## 1.7 Suggestions for Further Reading

Because this book concentrates on the essentials and main ideas of research, with the aim of providing a comprehensive foundation for doing empirical research in the social sciences, detailed technical treatment of topics is not given. For those who want to go further into more technical aspects of the material, or who want to study techniques not dealt with in detail here, suggestions for further reading are given at the end of each chapter throughout the book.

## 1.8 The Use of Examples

Examples have constituted a special problem in compiling the book, partly because of the breadth of material covered in relation to space available, partly because the book is about social research in general (including basic and applied areas), and partly because it stresses essentials and logic rather than technical matters. After considerable deliberation, a threefold approach has been taken to the use of examples.

First, for main topics of research design and strategy in both approaches, a selection of prominent examples is included in boxes. Thus, in Chapter 5, examples of experiments, quasi-experiments and correlational surveys are given; in Chapter 8, examples of case studies, ethnographies and grounded theory studies are given; and in Chapter 11, examples of mixed-method studies are given. The selection of these examples was guided by the desire to cover a range of areas and topics, and by a preference for studies which are well known and likely to be easily located.[11] The selection is intended to be illustrative rather than comprehensive, and the examples are briefly annotated.

Second, for topics in qualitative analysis especially, and for some other topics in different chapters, other examples are boxed and placed in the text. Again, the effort has been made to identify easily accessible examples, and placing them in boxes is intended to make them easy to locate in the text, without breaking up the text too much.

Third, where appropriate, examples are also discussed occasionally in the text.

The intention of presenting examples in the first two of these ways is that they can be read in conjunction with different sections of the book, to illustrate and broaden understanding of the material presented. At the same time, the main examples cited give a flavour of the scope and breadth of research areas, topics and approaches in social research, which is particularly appropriate in this book. The examples are not critically assessed here, though they can of course be read in the light of the evaluative criteria discussed in Chapter 11.

## 1.9   REVIEW CONCEPTS

Empirical research: data ⟨ numbers (quantitative)
not numbers (qualitative)

Quantitative empirical research: data as numbers
Qualitative empirical research: data as (mostly) words

Questions ⟶ Methods
Research questions ⟶ Research methods

The scientific method in the social sciences

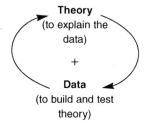

**Theory**
(to explain the data)

+

**Data**
(to build and test theory)

See also Figure 2.1

Research as organized common sense

## NOTES

1   This statement is about social research in general, not necessarily all social science areas.
2   More accurately, it exacerbated a split which had already long existed (Hammersley, 1992).
3   The 'paradigm wars' were especially vigorous in the field of educational research. A good record of those 'wars', including the moves towards reconciliation and détente, can be found in a series of articles in *The Educational Researcher*, beginning in the 1970s.
4   The term 'paradigm' is discussed in Section 2.4.
5   Positivism is discussed in Section 2.4.
6   The term 'empirical' is discussed in Section 2.4.
7   There are broader definitions than this, especially for qualitative research. Thus Patton (1990: 88), for example, lists 10 forms of qualitative inquiry. The definition I have is deliberately very empirical. 'Not in the form of numbers' is itself a broad category, and includes words, pictures and visual material, audio material, and so on. In this book, however, the focus is on qualitative data as words. The value of this sharp distinction between quantitative and qualitative data has been questioned in the literature (for example, Hammersley, 1992: 41–3). Here its value is pragmatic in providing a clear starting point to distinguish the two approaches. Later, as I have done elsewhere (Punch, 2000: 3–4), the definitions can be broadened to match their use by Bryman (1992: 58), who points out that each approach is associated with a 'certain cluster of methods'. In Chapter 11, the sharp distinction used here is relaxed.

8   At the start of Chapter 8, where the focus moves from quantitative to qualitative research, the diversity of perspectives and methods within qualitative research is discussed in more detail. This point occurs again at the start of Chapters 10 and 12.

9   Conceptions of 'science' and the 'scientific method' are contested today, and recent work has shown how such conceptions (including this one) are part of a discourse about what science is and does (see, for example, Gilbert and Mulkay, 1984; Wooffitt, 1996). Despite this, the traditional view of the scientific method is a good starting point in research training, even if it is later modified. Also, there is resistance today to the term 'science' itself when applied to the study of human behaviour. That resistance is most closely associated with some recent perspectives in qualitative research, and especially with postmodernism (see Chapter 8), and extends to the term 'social science'. Many prefer the broader term 'social research', which leaves behind some of the modernist connotations of science. Because this book deals with both quantitative and qualitative approaches, the terms 'social science' and 'social research' are both used.

10  Some affinities are natural – for example, the use of qualitative fieldwork and ethnography in anthropology. Others seem based more on tradition – for example, the use of quantitative methods in psychology. But a trend, across social research in general in recent years, has been towards a broader and more eclectic view of methods.

11  For this reason, many good examples in dissertations are not included.

# 2
## Some Central Issues

The first three sections in this chapter (description versus explanation, question–method connections, and structure which is prespecified versus structure which unfolds) discuss issues which come up frequently throughout the rest of the book. They are issues familiar to researchers who have worked with both approaches, but they are not often written about as separate topics in the research methods literature. The reason for this may be that most of the research methods literature has been written from within either the quantitative or the qualitative approach. These three issues emerge as central when the two approaches are brought together, as in this book. They are examples of the way the options in planning a piece of research broaden when both approaches are considered. Whereas each issue might have been taken for granted in the previously dominant quantitative approach, the emergence of the qualitative approach has opened up other possibilities. This applies especially to the second and third themes, question–method connections and prespecified versus unfolding structure.

## 2.1 Description versus Explanation

In Chapter 1, a brief description of the scientific method was given, stressing that it has the two central parts of data and theory, and that the objective of scientific inquiry is to build explanatory theory about its data. In this view, the aim is to explain the data, not just to use the data for description. This distinction between description and explanation is particularly relevant to the purposes of a piece of research.

The description–explanation distinction is easy to understand on one level, and difficult to understand on another.[1] Fortunately, it is on the easier level that the practical value of the distinction lies. Description and explanation represent two different levels of understanding. To describe is to somehow draw a picture of what happened, or of how things are proceeding, or of what a situation or person or event is like. To explain, on the other hand, is to account for what happened, or for how things are proceeding, or for what something or someone is like. It involves finding the reasons for things, events and situations, showing why and how they have come to be what they are. Description is a more restricted purpose than explanation. We can describe without explaining, but we can't really explain without describing. Therefore explanation goes further than description: It is more than just description: it is description plus something else.

Description focuses on *what* is the case, whereas explanation focuses on *why* something is the case.[2] Science as a method of building knowledge has, in general, pursued the objective of explanation, not just of description. There is a good reason for this. When we know why (or how) something happens, we know much more than just what happens. It puts us in a position to predict what will happen, and perhaps to be able to control what will happen. Thus explanatory knowledge is more powerful than descriptive knowledge. But descriptive knowledge is still important, since explanation requires description. To put it around the other way, description is a first step towards explanation. If we want to know why something happens, it is important to have a good description of exactly what happens. There are often clues to explanation in a full description, and it is hard to explain something satisfactorily until you understand just what the something is (Miles and Huberman, 1994: 91).

This distinction comes up mainly when the purpose of a piece of research is being considered. Is the purpose to describe, to explain or both? Descriptive studies are sometimes given a lower status than studies which aim to explain. That is why we sometimes hear the expression 'it is only a descriptive study'. But while this judgement may sometimes have merit, it has to be made carefully. There are situations where a thorough descriptive study will be very valuable, For example:

- A new area for research is being developed, and exploratory studies are planned. It is very sensible then to focus on systematic description as the objective of the research.
- Careful description of complex social processes can help us to understand what factors to concentrate on for later explanatory studies.

Whether description or explanation is the appropriate purpose for a piece of research depends on the particular situation. Here, as elsewhere, blanket rules are not appropriate. Rather, each research situation needs to be analysed and understood in its own context. It is useful to raise this question of whether the objective of a study is description and/or explanation, especially during the planning stages of research. A good way to do it is to ask 'why' about the things being studied, as well as 'what'.

In scientific work, explanation is tied to theory, as in the term 'explanatory theory'. Theory is also elusive to define, but a fairly basic definition works quite well for many projects, and is the one used here. The essential idea of theory is the attempt to explain whatever is being studied, with the explanation being couched in more abstract terms than the terms used to describe it. We will return to this idea of theory in two places later in the book. The first is in Chapter 3, where we consider the role of hypotheses in relation to research questions. There we will see that theory stands behind the hypothesis, in an inductive–deductive relationship with it (Nagel, 1961; Brodbeck, 1968). Studies which use this approach are *theory verification* studies. The second is in Chapter 10, where we discuss grounded theory analysis in studies which aim to develop theory. These are *theory generation* studies.

This distinction between theory verification and theory generation research is important. A project which has explanation as its objective can set out to test theory or to build theory – to verify theory or to generate it. For Wolcott (1992), this is the distinction between 'theory first' and 'theory after'. In theory-first research, we start with a theory, deduce hypotheses from it, and design a study to test those hypotheses. This is theory verification. In theory-after research, we do not start with a theory. Instead, the aim is to end up with a theory, developed systematically from the data we have collected. This is theory generation.

Quantitative research has typically been more directed at theory verification, while qualitative research has typically been more concerned with theory generation. While that correlation is historically valid, there is no necessary connection between purpose and approach. That is, quantitative research can be used for theory generation (as well as for verification) and qualitative research can be used for theory verification (as well as for generation), as pointed out by various writers (for example, Hammersley, 1992; Brewer and Hunter, 1989). However, while the connection is not necessary, it is nonetheless likely that theory generation research will more often be qualitative. Research directed at theory generation is more likely when a new area is being studied, and exploration of that new area is more likely to use the less structured fieldwork techniques of qualitative research.

Is theory verification research better than theory generation research? This book does not favour one research purpose over the other, since both are needed and both have their place. Either purpose can be appropriate in a research project, and sometimes both will be appropriate. It depends on the topic, on the context and practical circumstances of the research, and especially on how much prior theorizing and knowledge exist in the area. As with other aspects of a project, the researcher needs to consider the alternatives, select among them according to sensible criteria, and then articulate that position.

Theory generation research was given new legitimacy in social science by the development of grounded theory. Grounded theory is an explicit theory generation research strategy, developed in reaction against the overemphasis on theory verification research in the American sociology of that time. Glaser and Strauss stated this clearly in their original grounded theory publication:

> Verification is the keynote of current sociology. Some three decades ago, it was felt that we had plenty of theories but few confirmations of them – a position made very feasible by the greatly increased sophistication of quantitative methods. As this shift in emphasis took hold, the discovery of new theories became slighted and, at some universities, virtually neglected. (1967: 10)

Glaser and Strauss argued that the emphasis on verification of existing theories kept researchers from investigating new problem areas, prevented them from acknowledging the necessarily exploratory nature of much of their work, encouraged instead the inappropriate use of verificational logic and rhetoric, and discouraged the development and use of systematic empirical procedures for generating as well as testing theories (Brewer and Hunter, 1989).

This gives us a useful general guideline for when each purpose might be appropriate. When an area has lots of unverified theories, an emphasis on theory verification research seems a good thing. On the other hand, when an area is lacking in appropriate theories, it is time for the emphasis to shift to theory generation. Also, when research is directed mostly at the verification of existing theories, looking at new problem areas is discouraged, and the logic and techniques (usually quantitative) of verification research are seen as more important. When it is important to look at new areas in research, theory generation appeals as the appropriate purpose. This aspect of grounded theory research is taken up again in Chapter 8.

The description–explanation distinction fits in with the structure of scientific knowledge. In line with the conception of science given in Chapter 1, we can distinguish three levels of knowledge. At the lowest level, there are discrete facts. At the next level, there are empirical generalizations which group those facts together. At the highest level are theories, whose function is to explain the generalizations. This structure is summarized in Figure 2.1. The first two levels (facts and empirical generalization) focus on description, while the third level focuses on explanation.

This model of the structure of scientific knowledge comes primarily from a positivistic perspective, and stresses a nomothetic view of knowledge. It can be

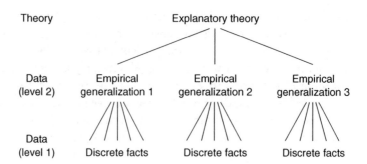

**Figure 2.1** *The structure of scientific knowledge (nomothetic view)*

contrasted with an idiographic view of knowledge, a more appropriate aspiration for social research in the eyes of many qualitative researchers.[3] But while its nomothetic bias is acknowledged, this model is very useful as a starting point in learning about social science research. Much research is based on this model, and it can often help in organizing an individual project. It is clear and easy to understand, so the researcher who wishes to diverge from this model can see where and why the divergence occurs. In other words, when researchers argue about paradigms and knowledge, this model helps to see what the argument is about.

There is another reason for stressing this model here. It shows the hierarchical structure of knowledge, with higher levels of abstraction and generality at the top and lower levels at the bottom. This is similar to the hierarchical structure which links data indicators to variables and concepts, and which is central to latent trait measurement theory in quantitative research, and to the concept–indicator model behind grounded theory coding in qualitative research. These topics are described in Chapters 6 and 10 respectively. This hierarchical structure of increasing levels of abstraction and generality, shown here with respect to scientific knowledge in general, and shown in later chapters with respect to concept–data links in both quantitative and qualitative research, is thus fundamental to much empirical research. An example of it is indicated in Example 2.1.

A well known example of this way of structuring knowledge is Durkheim's work on the social aetiology of suicide, described in Durkheim (1951) and summarized in Greenwood (1968). Durkheim theorizes 'upwards' from a series of empirical generalizations to a law of suicide.[4]

Example 2.1
*The hierarchical structure of knowledge*

## 2.2 Question–Method Connections

One of the simplifying devices mentioned in Chapter 1 was the influence of research questions on research methods. The point here is that the matching or fit between the research questions and research methods should be as close as possible, and that a very good way to do that is for methods to follow from questions.

Different questions require different methods to answer them. The way a question is asked has implications for what needs to be done, in research, to answer it. Quantitative questions require quantitative methods to answer them, and qualitative questions require qualitative methods to answer them. In today's research environment, with quantitative and qualitative methods often alongside each other, the matching of questions and methods is even more important. Since this book deals directly with both approaches, it is inevitable that this issue should be a recurrent concern. The wording of questions is also important, since some words and wording carry methodological implications. Thus 'variables', 'factors which affect' and 'the determinants or correlates of ', for example, imply a quantitative approach, while 'discover', 'seek to understand', 'explore a process' and 'describe the experiences' might imply a qualitative approach. Creswell (1994: 71) links these last four terms to grounded theory, ethnography, case study and phenomenology respectively.

An example of different research questions and their implications for methods is given by Shulman (1988: 6–9), from educational research. He takes the study of reading, suggests a number of different questions, and shows the methods that would be required to answer each. Thus, a first question might be: what makes some people successful readers and other unsuccessful? (Or, how can we predict what sorts of people will have difficulty learning to read?) Such questions would be answered using a correlational study which examined relationships between variables. A second question might be: what are the best possible methods for teaching reading to youngsters, irrespective of their backgrounds or attitudes? This question would involve an experimental study comparing different teaching methods. A third question might be: what is the general level of reading performance across different age, sex, social or ethnic groups in the population? This would require a survey of reading performance and reading practices. A fourth set of questions might be quite different from the previous ones: how is reading instruction carried on? What are the experiences and perceptions of teachers and students as they engage in the teaching and learning of reading? How is this complex activity accomplished? Here, a case study involving observation and interview might be used, perhaps using the perspective of ethnomethodology. Shulman goes on to suggest philosophical and historical questions as well. Other examples of question–method corrections are indicated in Example 2.2.

- Shulman (1988: 6–9) shows connections between questions and methods with the topic of reading research in education; similar examples are noted by Seidman (1991: 5).

  Example 2.2
  *Question–method connections*

- Marshall and Rossman (1989: 78) show, in a table, the links between research purposes, research questions, research strategy and data collection techniques.
- Maxwell (1996: 81–5) adapts a table from LeCompte and Preissle (1993) to show the links between 'What do I need to know?' and 'What kind of data will answer the questions?' and illustrates these links with actual research questions.
- Maxwell (1996: 80) gives the example of a mismatch between questions and method, whereby, in a study of how historians work, the 'right answer' is found to be to the 'wrong question'.

A good way to achieve a fit between questions and methods is to ensure that the methods we use follow from the questions we seek to answer. In other words, the content of the research (the research questions) has a logical priority over the method of the research. To say that content precedes method is to say that we first need to establish what we are trying to find out, and then consider how we are going to do it. On a practical level, this is often a good way to get a research project off the ground. Sometimes it is difficult to know where and how to start, in planning research. If so, asking 'What are we trying to find out?' usually gets our thinking going, and ensures that we start with the content, not with the method. Putting questions before methods is also a good defence against overload when developing a research proposal. To delay consideration of methods until it is clear what the questions are helps in managing the inevitable complications which accompany a full examination of the possibilities for research in any area. It helps in keeping the question development stage systematic, and under control. It also helps achieve good question–method fit, a central criterion in the validity of research.

I am stressing this point here to counteract a previous unfortunate tendency in social science research. In Chapter 1, the term 'methodolatry' was used:

> I use the term *methodolatry*, a combination of *method* and *idolatry*, to describe a preoccupation with selecting and defending methods to the exclusion of the actual substance of the story being told. Methodolatry is the slavish attachment and devotion to method that so often overtakes the discourse in the education and human service fields. (Janesick, 1994: 215)

Methodolatry thus means putting method before content. It is first learning the research method, then finding research questions that can fit into the method. It is looking for research questions guided by methods.

This is a danger when we overstress the teaching of research methods for their own sake. Because of that, this book concentrates on the logic and rationale behind empirical research and its methods. Once this logic is mastered, we can focus on research questions, and then fit the techniques and methods to the questions. In my opinion, the best sequence of learning activities for research is to start by learning the logic of research, then to focus on identifying and developing the research questions, and then to fit methods and techniques to the questions.

I am using the concept of methodolatry to argue for minimizing the direct influence of methods on research questions, which we can do by first getting the research questions clear, and then focusing on the methods required to answer them. But methods can also indirectly influence research questions, by constraining what can be studied. There are limits as to what can be designed in research, and to what data can be obtained and analysed. While taking that into account, the advice is nonetheless to focus on questions first, as much as possible. In the above example, after showing how different methodological approaches fit different questions, Shulman emphasizes the same point: 'we are advised to focus first on our problem and its characteristics before we rush to select the appropriate method' (1988: 15). Thus, when misfit between the parts becomes apparent during the planning of the research, it is a matter of adapting the parts to each other. Since I see methods primarily as tools, for use in answering research questions, I think it is better to adapt design and methods to questions, rather than to adapt the questions to the design and methods.

Question–method fit is an aspect of conceptual clarity in a piece of research. Conceptual clarity involves the precise and consistent use of terms, internal consistency within an argument, and logical links between concepts, especially across different levels of abstraction. The pre-empirical question development work described in Chapter 3 is directed at this conceptual clarity. Developing specific research questions is a good way of achieving clarity and matching questions and methods.

It is also part of a larger fit between all components of a research project. A full list of component parts would include the paradigm, the research questions, perhaps also the conceptual framework, the study design, the data collection procedures and the data analysis procedures. Questions and methods are just two of those parts, and all parts should fit together. The fit is about the overall validity of a piece of research. While validity is a technical term, this point can also be seen on a common-sense basis. A research project, from one point of view, is a story or an argument. That argument does not stand up well if its parts do not fit together. A project whose components do not fit together therefore has questionable validity. Specifically, we can have little confidence in the answers put forward to research questions on the basis of a design and methods which do not fit with the questions: the argument behind the research falls down.

The different perspectives within qualitative research open up many new and different types of research questions. Thus ethnographic questions might focus on cultural and symbolic aspects of behaviour; grounded theory questions might focus on understanding social processes, and how people manage different types of situations; a conversation analysis study might focus on conversational structure and on the role of conversation in taken-for-granted everyday activities; discourse analysis questions might focus on the way an institution (for example) presents itself to the world, the symbols and language it uses, and the connection of those with its ideology, knowledge, power and so on. Perspective can thus be important in generating research questions. Within qualitative research especially, the range of questions of interest is now very broad. But it remains important, even with this broader range of questions, that the methods we use should follow from and fit in with the questions we seek to answer.

## 2.3 Prespecified versus Unfolding: Structure in Research Questions, Design and Data

How much the research questions, design and data should be preplanned in a piece of research, and how much they should emerge as the research develops, is another recurring theme in this book.

There is a continuum we can set up for thinking about research questions and methods, with the dimension of interest being the amount of prespecified structure in the research strategy that is used. The central comparison is between research which is prespecified (or preplanned, or prefigured, or predetermined) on the one hand, and research which is unfolding (or emerging, or open-ended) on the other. Prespecified here refers to how much structure is introduced ahead of the empirical work, as opposed to during the empirical work. This continuum applies to three areas: to research questions, to research design, and to data.

Miles and Huberman (1994: 16) discuss this idea in the context of qualitative research under the heading of 'tight versus loose'. Those terms are equivalent to the terms used here: tight means prespecified, and loose means unfolding. The key questions are: to what extent are the research questions, the design and the data focused, specified and structured ahead of the actual empirical work? To what extent does the focus in the research questions, and the structure in the design and the data, unfold and emerge as the empirical work proceeds? The continuum of possibilities is shown in Figure 2.2. This diagram shows that quantitative research typically falls towards the left-hand end of the continuum, whereas qualitative research typically occupies a much greater range along the continuum.

The word 'structure', as used here, means showing what the different parts of the research are, how they connect with each other, what will be done in the research, and in what sequence. It means knowing what we are looking for, and how we are going to get it – knowing what data we will want, and how

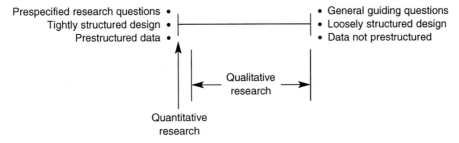

**Figure 2.2**    *Prespecified versus unfolding: the timing of structure*

they will be collected. It also means knowing what structure the data will have and how they will be analysed.

At the extreme left-hand end of the continuum, everything is prespecified: the research questions, the design and the data. It is all worked out in advance; a set of steps is laid down, and the researcher proceeds through those steps. At the other end, we can envisage a project where very little structure is determined in advance, with a relatively open-ended and unstructured approach to the research questions, the design and the data. The strategy is that these will unfold as the study is carried out. Let us see what this contrast means for each of the three areas.

### Research questions

At the left-hand end of the continuum, specific research questions are set up in advance to guide the study. It is quite clear, in advance, exactly what questions the study is trying to answer. At the right-hand end, only general questions are set up in advance. The argument is that, until some empirical work is carried out, it is not possible (or, if possible, not sensible) to identify the specific research questions. They will only become clear as the research unfolds, and as a specific focus for the work is developed. Wolcott (1982) has a nice description for this contrast: 'looking for answers' versus 'looking for questions'. As we will see in Chapter 4, there is often a close connection between the research questions and the conceptual framework in a study. The issue described here in terms of research questions applies to conceptual frameworks as well: they can be developed and specified in advance of the research, or they can emerge as the research proceeds. The more tightly developed and prespecified the research questions are, the more likely it is that there will be a well developed conceptual framework as well.

### Design

At the left-hand end, the design is tightly structured. The clearest examples come from quantitative research: experimental studies, and non-experimental quantitative studies with carefully developed conceptual frameworks. Research questions, design and conceptual framework come together here, since a tightly structured design requires that variables be identified, and that their conceptual status in the research be made clear. At the right-hand end, the design is indicated in general terms only (for example, as in an unfolding case study, or an ethnography). Like the research questions, it will take detailed shape as the research progresses, and as the specific focus for the study is developed.

### Data

At the left-hand end, data are structured in advance. A very clear example is quantitative data, where measurement is used to give the data numerical structure. Using numbers is the most common way of structuring data in advance, but there are other ways as well. Whether numerical or other categories are used, the point is that those categories are pre-established, or set up *a priori*. At the right-hand end, the data are unstructured at the point of collection. No pre-established categories or codes are used. The structure of the data, the categories and codes, emerge from the data during the analysis: they are developed *a posteriori*. Thus the comparison is between starting with categories for the data, and getting to them during the analysis of the data – between precoding the data and postcoding the data. This point about data has implications for instrumentation in data collection, not only in quantitative research, but in qualitative research as well.

The continuum shown in Figure 2.2 can now be described more accurately. It is really about when in the research process the structure is introduced. The structure can be introduced in the planning or pre-empirical stage, when the research is being set up, before data are collected; or, it can be introduced in the execution stage of the research, as the study is being carried out, as data are being collected. Either way, structure is needed. A research project will be difficult to understand, and will lack credibility as a piece of research, without structure in its research questions, its design, especially in its data, and also in its report. So this contrast is not about having structure or not having structure, but about when in the research process the structure occurs. In other words, this continuum is about the timing of structure in the research – whether that structure is introduced ahead of the empirical research, or is introduced during and as a result of the empirical research. Another way of saying this is that the structure might be imposed on the research (and especially on the data) ahead of the empirical processes; or that the structure might emerge during the research, in terms of the specific questions on which to focus, the design to follow, and the categories to use in representing the data.

The possibilities along this continuum represent different possible research styles. As the diagram shows, there is a correlation between these styles, on the one hand, and the typical quantitative and qualitative research approaches, on the other. The typical quantitative study is much more likely to have specific research questions and a clear conceptual framework and design for its variables, and to use measurement as its way of structuring the data. It is harder to talk about typical qualitative studies, and they may cover a wider range along the continuum. Many of them fall towards the right-hand end, with general rather than specific questions set up in advance, with a general design, and with data not coded at the point of collection. This is well captured by Miles and Huberman, discussing field research as a central part of the qualitative approach:

> The conventional image of field research is one that keeps prestructured designs to a minimum. Many social anthropologists and social phenomenologists consider social processes to be too complex, too relative, too elusive, or too exotic to be approached with explicit conceptual frames or standard instruments. They prefer a more loosely structured, emergent, inductively 'grounded' approach to gathering data: the conceptual framework should emerge from the field in the course of the study; the important research questions will become clear only gradually; meaningful settings and actors cannot be selected prior to fieldwork; instruments, if any, should be derived from the properties of the setting and its actors' views of them. (1994: 17)

This general correlation between style and approach also extends to theory verification versus theory generation research, the distinction noted in Section 2.1. Theory verification research, by definition, is more likely to have clear-cut research questions leading to hypotheses, a tightly structured design, and pre-established categories for data. Theory generation research, by contrast, will more likely use an approach where specific research questions unfold as the study develops, and where codes and categories for the data are empirically derived.

It is not a question of which strategy is best, since a large part of the answer to that question is 'it depends'. The question interacts with the overall approach to the research. Is it a quantitative study, a qualitative study or one which combines the two approaches? If quantitative, it is more likely to be towards the left-hand end of the continuum in Figure 2.2. If qualitative, there is likely to be a greater range of possibilities. Nor is it a dichotomous choice between two extreme positions: it is a continuum. For clarity, the description in this section has been given in terms of the ends of the continuum. In practice, there are many points along the continuum, and any study may combine elements of either strategy, the prespecified one or the unfolding one.

How much predetermined structure is desirable in a project is a matter for analysis in each particular situation. Structure is necessary. But the timing of the structure – when is the appropriate point to introduce that structure – depends on such factors as the topics and goals of the research, the availability of relevant knowledge and theory about the topic, and the researcher's familiarity with the situation being studied (Miles and Huberman, 1994). Other factors to be considered are the preferred style of the research, the resources (including time) available to the researcher, and to what extent the researcher is interested in explanation versus interpretation. Depending on these factors, there can be merit in either approach. As Huberman and Miles (1994) point out, what is required is a careful analysis of each situation where research is proposed. The research strategy should then be custom built, as far as is possible, on the basis of that analysis.

The discussion in this section has treated research questions, design and data together. Subsequent chapters deal with questions, design and data separately, before bringing them back together in Chapters 11 and 12. Without wishing to advise against exploratory unfolding studies, it is worth noting some of the benefits in having at least a reasonable level of specificity in the research questions. For example, they give guidance during initial data collection, thereby saving time and resources and helping to avoid confusion and overload, an especially valuable benefit for the beginning researcher. In addition, research questions which are at least reasonably focused make it easier to communicate about the research, which can be important in the presentation of a research proposal. Brewer and Hunter (1989) point out that, once a study is published, it is irrelevant whether the research questions initiated the study or emerged from it – but it can matter at the proposal stage. Finally, it is very often the case that the researcher does have knowledge about the proposed research problems, even in a relatively unexplored area ('experiential data' and 'experiential knowledge': see Strauss, 1987; Maxwell, 1996). There is great benefit in getting that knowledge out on to the table, and working carefully to develop research questions in advance of the empirical work is a good way to do that.

Developing specific research questions to a point where they are stable, and connecting them to the design, data collection and data analysis parts of the research, requires careful work. The question being considered here is whether that work is done in advance of the research or during it. That brings us back to fitting the various parts of a project together, as discussed in Section 2.2. This fitting together can be done ahead of the research, or during the research, but either way it needs to be done. Just as Section 2.2 stressed the pragmatic benefits of 'questions first, methods later' in maximizing that fit, so this section stresses the pragmatic benefits of beginning with research questions which are at least reasonably well developed.

To summarize: there is a continuum of possibilities, which is about pre-specifying versus unfolding structure in the research. It applies to research questions, design and data. The issue is structure and its timing: when in the research is structure introduced? Prespecified research does it ahead of the empirical procedures. Unfolding research does it during them. As a general rule, at least a reasonable level of specificity in the initial research questions is desirable, though various factors need to be taken into account in particular situations. Chapter 3 will describe a model of research where considerable effort is invested in developing research questions ahead of the empirical work. But that is not the only model, and when research questions come later, they still require both the analytical development described in Chapters 3 and 4, and the matching with methods, design and data described in Section 2.2.

## 2.4 Some Important Terms

Many of the terms we use in discussing research are self-explanatory, and require no special consideration. Others are technical, and will be dealt with as they arise in the following chapters. A third group of terms is not entirely technical, but is part of a somewhat specialized vocabulary of research. They are discussed here, to clarify their usage. A separate glossary of some 90 important researcher terms is given on pp. 289–95.

*Empirical* is a central term in this book and in scientific research generally. It means that something (or its impact) is observable (Ragin, 1994), where 'observation' is broadly interpreted. The essential idea is to use observable, real-world experience, evidence and information as the way of developing and testing ideas.[5] Like other writers, I prefer the general term 'data' to describe this evidence and information in a research context. Sometimes there is a misconception that 'empirical' applies only to quantitative data, but the term applies equally to data in both approaches. Strictly speaking, this means that the expressions 'quantitative empirical data' and 'qualitative empirical data' are both redundant, since 'data' implies 'empirical'. Despite that, the latter phrase 'qualitative empirical data' is sometimes used in this book for emphasis.

*Paradigm* is a complex term which occurs very frequently in the research methods literature. As used in social science, it means a set of assumptions about the social world, and about what constitute proper techniques and topics for inquiry. In short, it means a view of how science should be done. It is a very broad term, encompassing elements of epistemology, theory and philosophy, along with methods. Paradigms have been the subject of vigorous debate, as in the phrase 'paradigm wars' which has been used to describe the arguments between quantitative and qualitative researchers. Sometimes the term 'paradigm' is used to describe quantitative research or qualitative research, as in 'the quantitative paradigm' or 'the qualitative paradigm' (for example, Creswell, 1994). This book prefers the term 'approaches' for that, as noted below.

I do not go deeply into paradigm issues in this book, for reasons given in Chapter 1. There is a short section on the diversity of paradigms in present-day qualitative research at the start of Chapter 8, but aside from that, the term is not used very much. *Positivism* is a frequently noted paradigm position in the literature, being at the centre of the paradigm debates. It is not easy to define, and it has several different (and confusing) varieties: thus Halfpenny (1982) lists 12 varieties, but Blaikie (1993: 16) reduces those to three. The term was invented by Comte, a founding father of sociology, and it has a long history in philosophy, reaching its peak with the logical positivists of the 1930s and 1940s. Numerous attempts have been made to identify its central tenets, and Blaikie suggests they are seven.[6] For our purposes, the main ideas are the belief that objective accounts of the world can be given, and that the function of science is to develop explanations in the form of universal laws – that is, to develop nomothetic knowledge. Positivism is commonly associated with quantitative methods, and, as noted in Chapter 1, much of the development in qualitative methods has been associated with the wide-ranging critique of positivism.[7]

The overall conceptual framework used in this book for thinking about research has three main parts: paradigms, content and methods. Methods subdivide into design, data collection and data analysis.

*Content* refers here both to the overall area for research, and to the topic within that area. In setting up the research, the topic may be broken down into general and specific research questions, as shown in Chapters 3 and 4, and together these describe the content of the research. The word 'substantive' is often used to describe the content, and to contrast content with method. Substantive refers to the substance of the research, and is a synonym for content.

*Method* is used here as a general term, to include design, data collection and data analysis. Data collection and data analysis come together as the empirical procedures for the research. Design is discussed in both Chapter 5 (quantitative) and Chapter 8 (qualitative). 'Methodological' is sometimes used as the adjective derived from method.[8] The terms 'substantive' and 'methodological' are often used in contradistinction to each other, to describe different main parts of a research study. Substantive refers to its content, methodological to its method. However, the noun 'methodology' is more ·problematic. Technically, it refers to the study of method(s), the overall analysis of how research proceeds, and that is how it is used in this book. It is often used more loosely, as in the phrase 'the research methodology of this study'. In such a case, 'research method(s)' would be a more accurate term.

The central terms 'quantitative' and 'qualitative' are called here *approaches* to research. As noted, paradigm is sometimes used in this way, as is tradition, but approach is preferred here, to describe the configuration of assumptions and ideas that characterize quantitative research on the one hand, and qualitative research on the other. They are distinctive approaches, but they also have similarities and overlaps, and can be brought together in various ways. This point is taken up in Chapter 11.

The simplified definitions of quantitative and qualitative research given earlier can now be broadened. Chapter 1 described quantitative research as empirical research where the data are numerical, and qualitative research as empirical research where the data are not numerical. These definitions focus on data, and this is the heart of the matter, but they can now be expanded to include research questions and methods as well. Quantitative research, therefore, uses numerical data and, typically, has structured and predetermined research questions, conceptual frameworks and designs. Qualitative research not only uses non-numerical and unstructured data but also, typically, has research questions and methods which are more general at the start, and become more focused as the study progresses. However, qualitative research is harder to characterize with these sorts of descriptions than is quantitative research, since it is more variable. It may come from a range of positions along the continuum shown in Figure 2.2.

At the conclusion of a piece of research, we have its *results, findings* and *conclusions*. Various writers use these terms in different ways, but here 'results' refers to what comes directly from the analysis of the data. Examples are 'the results of the regression analysis' or 'the results of the open coding'. 'Findings' refers to the answers to research questions, and 'conclusions' refers to what can be concluded on the basis of the answers to the research questions.

The term *validity* requires special comment, even at this early stage. It is a common term in everyday language, but also a technical term in research. As such, it has several different meanings, the common thread of which is the isomorphism (or otherwise) between the reality studied and the reality reported. Its main technical meanings are as follows:

- *Validity of data.* This is usually expressed as a question: how well do these data represent the phenomena for which they stand? In developing ways to deal with this question, quantitative researchers have used the more specialized ideas of content validity, criterion-related validity and construct validity. But the issue is in fact similar in both approaches, because of the hierarchical nature of abstraction in the link between data indicators and variables (quantitative) and concepts (qualitative). This topic is dealt with in Chapters 6 and 11.
- *Overall validity of the research.* This is about the piece of research as a whole, and refers to the extent to which the different parts of the study fit together. It was discussed in Section 2.2, and is discussed again in Chapter 11.
- *Internal validity.* This is about the study's research design. The question here is whether it is a true reflection of the reality studied. This question has slightly different versions for quantitative and qualitative research, as is discussed in Chapter 11.
- *External validity.* This refers to the generalizability of the study's findings. The question here is how far the study's findings can be generalized, or transferred to other settings.

Still other meanings of validity are specific to qualitative research (Miles and Huberman, 1994: 36):

- *Descriptive/contextual validity.* This refers to whether the account of the research is complete and thorough.
- *Interpretive validity.* This asks whether the account given in the research connects with the lived experience of the people studied.

Because of these various specialized meanings, 'validity' is a term which needs careful usage in social science research.

---

## 2.5   REVIEW CONCEPTS

Description :   what?         Purpose of research is to describe.
Explanation :   why? how?     Purpose of research is to explain.

Explanatory theory:
*theory verification research*          versus          *theory generation research*

- theory before                                         - theory after
- concepts before                                       - concepts after
- structure before                                      - structure after

Views of knowledge:

- nomothetic
- ideographic

**Research questions ⟶ Research methods**

$$\begin{bmatrix} \text{Research questions} \\ \text{which meet} \\ \text{the empirical} \\ \text{criterion} \end{bmatrix} \rightarrow \begin{bmatrix} \text{What data will} \\ \text{answer these} \\ \text{questions: quantitative;} \\ \text{qualitative; both?} \end{bmatrix} \rightarrow \begin{bmatrix} \text{What methods will} \\ \text{give these data} \\ \text{and answer these} \\ \text{questions?} \end{bmatrix}$$

**Question–method fit**

The timing of structure:

- research questions
- design
- data

Terms:

- empirical
- paradigm
- content, method
- results, findings, conclusions, validity

---

## NOTES

1   The 'difficult' level is about precise definitions of the two terms, and about philosophical investigations into the concept of explanation. See, for example, Little (1991), Lewins (1992).

2   There is a third question along with what and why: how? The 'how' question can also be part of description as well as explanation.

3   A nomothetic view sees generalized knowledge, universal laws and deductive explanations, based mainly on probabilities derived from large samples, and standing outside

the constraints of everyday life. An idiographic view sees nomothetic knowledge as insensitive to local, case-based meanings, and directs attention rather to the specifics of particular cases. It prefers to see knowledge as local and situated (Denzin and Lincoln, 1994: 99–104). The idiographic view thus points towards understanding and interpretation as possible goals of research, alongside description and explanation.

4   Note also Atkinson's (1978) critique of that work, focusing on how suicide rate statistics are constructed, and what they mean.

5   *Empiricism* refers to a philosophical position which sees observation as the foundation of scientific knowledge.

6   Unity of method, phenomenalism, nominalism, atomism, general laws, separation of facts and values, and against metaphysics: see Blaikie (1993: 14–16).

7   This is not meant to imply that all quantitative research is positivistic, or that qualitative research is necessarily non-positivistic. This is far too simple, since (a) the term positivism is open to many interpretations; (b) some quantitative researchers would reject the description that quantitative work is positivistic (see, for example, Marsh, 1982); and (c) some qualitative research is similar in logic and methods to positivism (see, for example, discussions of naturalistic ethnography in Roman, 1992; and participant observation in Willis, 1981; Bryman, 1988).

8   It is not the only adjective derived from method. 'Methodical' is the more common adjective in everyday use, but it is not so often used in a research context.

## *Further Reading*

Babbie, E. (1992) *The Practice of Social Research*. 6th edn. Belmont, CA: Wadsworth.

Bailey, K.D. (1987) *Methods of Social Research*. 3rd edn. New York: Free Press.

Creswell, J.W. (1994) *Research Design: Qualitative and Quantitative Approaches*. Thousand Oaks, CA: Sage.

Lewins, F. (1992) *Social Science Methodology*. Melbourne: Macmillan.

Little, D. (1991) *Varieties of Social Explanation: An Introduction to the Philosophy of Social Science*. Boulder, CO: Westview.

Marshall, C. and Rossman, G.B. (1989) *Designing Qualitative Research*. Newbury Park, CA: Sage.

Maxwell, J.A. (1996) *Qualitative Research Design: An Interactive Approach*. Thousand Oaks, CA: Sage.

Miles, M.B. and Huberman, A.M. (1994) *Qualitative Data Analysis*. Thousand Oaks, CA: Sage.

Neuman, W.L. (1994) *Social Research Methods: Qualitative and Quantitative Approaches*. Boston: Allyn and Bacon.

Wolcott, H.F. (1994) *Transforming Qualitative Data: Description, Analysis, and Interpretation*. Thousand Oaks, CA: Sage.

# 3
# Research Questions

As a finished product, a piece of empirical research needs to demonstrate both conceptual clarity and a good fit between its different component parts, especially between its questions and its methods. For the report of the completed research, the order in which things were done does not matter, only that there is this conceptual clarity and good fit. They can be achieved in different ways: the questions can be developed first, and the methods aligned; or, the research might begin with only a general approach to its topic, and then develop focus in the questions and methods as things proceed; or there might be a mixture of these two, where the researcher cycles backwards and forwards between questions, methods and some initial data.

The next two chapters describe a model of research with well developed research questions 'up front'. This is a good model for learning about research, making it easy to see the connections between questions, concepts and data, and thereby promoting fit and conceptual clarity. As a model, it is worth aiming at; if it is rejected as not appropriate, the reasons for that rejection are helpful in understanding the area, and in tailoring a more suitable approach. This helps clarify where on the continuum of structure the researcher wants to be. That position can then be articulated to ensure that the approach to design and data fits with it.

Miles and Huberman (1994: 55) point out that developing research questions is a valuable defence against the confusion and overload that are possible in the early stages of research. Often, also, the researcher can make considerable progress towards identifying specific research questions, particularly when considerable knowledge is brought to the research. However, when research questions emerge during the project rather than in advance of it, the need for conceptual clarity and for fit still arises, and therefore the issues in these next two chapters remain relevant. They do not disappear, they simply come up later.

## 3.1 General and Specific Research Questions

Empirical research is driven by research questions. One way to get to research questions is to identify a research area and topic, and then develop questions within that area and topic, working deductively from general to specific questions. Another is more inductive: to begin with some specific questions, and to work from these back to more general questions.

General research questions guide our thinking, and are of great value in organizing the research project, but they are not themselves specific enough to be answered. Specific research questions ideally follow from the general question(s). They direct the empirical procedures, and they are the questions which are actually answered in the research. It is useful in planning to identify and separate the general and the specific research questions.

It is also important to distinguish both of these from the research area and topic. This difference can be a source of confusion. When asked the key question 'What are you trying to find out?', students will often respond by identifying an area or a topic. But a research area, a research topic and research questions are different things. An area identifies a general field of inquiry, within which we can identify different topics. A topic is a theme within the area, but is still very general. Within a topic, therefore, we can identify many research questions, general and specific. Thus there is a hierarchy of concepts:

- research area
- research topic
- general research question(s)
- specific research question(s)
- data collection question(s).[1]

The first general way of proceeding identified above is to begin with a research area, move to a topic within that area and then identify questions. Sources and types of research areas and topics are discussed by Marshall and Rossman (1989), Campbell et al. (1982) and Zuckerman (1978), and seven ways of selecting topics are suggested by Neuman (1994: 110): personal experience, curiosity based on something in the media, the state of knowledge in a field, solving a problem (often associated with professional experience), 'social premiums',[2] personal values and everyday life. Whatever the method of selection, identifying an area and a topic enables the researcher to connect the work to the research literature.[3] But identifying the area and topic are only the first steps, and the researcher needs to go further, by developing both general and specific research questions.

The second way of proceeding is to begin with some specific question of interest. Again, this may come from any source at all: personal or professional experience, 'real-world observations, dilemmas and questions' (Marshall and Rossman, 1989: 28), the literature, or somewhere else. When beginning with a specific question, it will be necessary to move upwards in generality and abstraction to more general research questions and then to the research area. It does not matter which of these ways is used, or if they are mixed up. What matters is the development of the questions, their location in a research area, and their ordering into general and specific research questions.[4]

Example 3.1 shows quantitative and qualitative examples of general and specific research questions. It is often easier to develop this sort of question structure in quantitative projects, because of established patterns of thinking in quantitative design, as is described in Chapter 5. But it is helpful in planning qualitative research too, as the Miles and Huberman example shows. In ethnographic research also, Spradley (1980) suggests a taxonomy of specific research questions which can follow general questions. The general questions are sometimes called 'grand tour' questions; the specific questions would then be 'mini tour' questions, though the taxonomy has other sorts of specific questions as well. In addition to these examples, the monograph by Campbell et al. (1982) contains many general and specific research questions generated by applied psychological research into organizations and their behaviour, and Miles and Huberman (1994: 24) cite Smith's example of different types of specific research questions and their general form, used in a study evaluating reading instruction.

---

*Quantitative*

**Example 3.1**
*General and specific research questions*

- De Vaus (1991: 27–44) starts with the broad topic of divorce, and then (guided by a conceptual model) frames general and specific research questions to guide a survey to study increases in divorce rates.
- Jaeger (1988: 308–11) shows the hierarchical approach to defining research questions in designing a survey of teacher 'burnout'. Three broad areas are identified, and general and specific research questions are developed within each area.

*Qualitative*

- Miles and Huberman (1994: 24) show the use of general and specific research questions in their case study of the adoption of innovations. Four general questions are shown, and several specific questions are derived from each.

## 3.2 Developing Research Questions

Sometimes the more abstract concepts of research area and topic, and general and specific research questions, are not enough to get the process of identifying and developing research questions started. When that happens, it is good to focus on the question 'What are we trying to find out?' The focus on this question almost always shows that there is 'much more here than meets the eye'. The topic expands, and many questions are generated. What perhaps seemed simple and straightforward becomes complicated, many-sided and full of possibilities. This can happen whether the researcher proceeds deductively or inductively. On the one hand, any research area, when fully analysed, will yield many research questions, general and specific. On the other, any research question, when carefully considered, will generate others, and they in turn will generate more.

What sort of work is this, in the question development stage? First, it is generating possibilities. Answers to the question 'What are we trying to find out?' are provisional at this stage. We do not want to get to a final set of questions too quickly, because we might overlook possibilities. Generating possibilities is not endless, but we do want to allow enough time to see what the possibilities are. Second, it is a mixture of question subdivision, where we split a general question into its component parts, and of disentangling the different questions from each other. Third, it is ordering these questions, and progressively developing focus.

It is usually an iterative process to get a stable view of what one is trying to find out. There are benefits to doing some of this work with others: another student, or a small group, which might include supervisor(s), colleagues or other researchers. Others will often see possible questions that the individual researcher might miss, and discussion with others can also be a stimulus to think more deeply, and perhaps differently, about the topic.

What generally happens after a period of question development is that the whole thing has expanded, sometimes greatly. This can cause anxiety, but for most projects it should happen. In fact, if it doesn't, we should probably be concerned, since it may be a sign of insufficient question development work. Therefore, it is to be encouraged, within reason, as an important stage. Probing, exploring, and seeing other possibilities with a topic can be valuable before reaching closure on the specific directions for a project.

When a small set of starting questions has multiplied into a larger set, disentangling and ordering are required. Disentangling is necessary because one question will often have other questions within it. Ordering involves categorizing, and the grouping of questions together. This will soon become hierarchical, and general and specific research questions begin to be distinguishable from each other.

The final stage then involves bringing the project down to size, since it has usually become too big. In fact, it probably suggests a research programme with several research projects by now. How is this trimming done? It is important to decide which questions are manageable within the practical constraints of this project, and which seem the most important. There are of course limits around any project – even if that project involves a grant and a team of researchers. The principle here is that it is better to do a smaller project thoroughly than a larger project superficially. Trimming a project down to size is a matter of judgement, and experience in research has a big role to play here. Once again, therefore, this stage is best done in collaboration with others.

How many research questions should there be? There are practical limitations on any one project, and it is better to have a small job done thoroughly than a large job done only superficially. More than about three or four general research questions, assuming that each is subdivided into (say) two or three specific questions, is testing the upper limit of what can be done in one study.[5]

This question development stage is pre-empirical, in the sense that we are not yet really focusing on questions of method, which come later. As far as possible, we are following the rule to put substantive or content issues before methodological issues. Method questions will always intrude to some extent, but there is value during this stage in keeping them at arm's length. The questions 'How will I do this?' or 'Should I use this method or that method?' are important, but the point here is that they can come too early.

During this planning stage, there is benefit to 'hastening slowly'. Since research questions do not usually come out right the first time, several iterations are often required, and we only reach an answer to the question 'What are we trying to find out?' after careful thought. This question development stage needs time – time to see the possible questions buried in an area and to see related questions which follow from an analysis of particular questions. The set-up stage of the research is important, for the decisions taken here will influence what is done in later stages. This does not mean that the decisions cannot be varied, as when iteration towards the final research questions goes on during the early empirical stages of the project. But varying them should not be done lightly if considerable effort has been invested in reaching them during the set-up stage.

Focusing on what we are trying to find out is useful not only at this stage, but at all stages of research, including research which unfolds. It helps to keep things focused during planning, design and execution of the project – especially during data analysis – and it helps in the writing up of the research report.

## 3.3 The Role of Research Questions

Research questions are central, whether they are prespecified or whether they unfold during the project. They do five main things:

- They organize the project, and give it direction and coherence.
- They delimit the project, showing its boundaries.
- They keep the researcher focused during the project.
- They provide a framework for writing up the project.
- They point to the data that will be needed.

The third point (keeping focused during the project) requires a comment. Research can get complicated, and it is therefore easy for any of us to get lost on the way through a project. Clearly stated research questions have great value in bringing the research back on track in those situations when complications or side issues threaten to take it off course. Being able to step back from the complications and details, and to refer again to research questions, can be of great assistance.

The last point above, indicating what data will be necessary in the project, is the empirical criterion, to be discussed in Chapter 4. The idea is that a well asked question indicates what data will be necessary to answer it. This brings up again the distinction between a research question and a data collection question (see note 1 to this chapter). A research question is a question which guides the project, and which the research is designed to answer. A data collection question is more specific again, and is a question which is asked (perhaps in a survey questionnaire or interview) to provide data relevant to a research question.

Chapter 4 also discusses conceptual frameworks. The conceptual framework shows the conceptual status of the factors, variables or phenomena we are working with, usually in diagram form. Developing the research questions often involves developing a conceptual framework for the research as well. These two things do not have to go together, but it can be very useful when they do. This is because developing the questions often brings into focus the (implicit) conceptual framework we are using in our thinking about the topic. When that is the case, it is a good idea to make that framework explicit. The research questions then operationalize that conceptual framework, pointing ahead to the data. In quantitative research, that is usually very clear, and it is taken for granted that the conceptual framework for the study will be shown. Developing a conceptual framework can be very useful in qualitative research as well, focusing and delimiting the study, and giving direction to the sampling decisions which will be required. Examples of conceptual frameworks are given in Chapter 4.

To this point, this chapter has dealt with identifying and developing the research questions, and with their central role in a project. It is time now to consider the hypothesis, and what role it has in research.

## 3.4 **Hypotheses**

Complicated definitions of the hypothesis can be found in some of the older research methodology literature (Nagel, 1961; Brodbeck, 1968; Kerlinger, 1973), but these will not be used here. Instead, I will use the simple definition of the hypothesis as a predicted answer to a research question. To say we have a hypothesis is to say we can predict what we will find in answer to a question. We make this prediction before we carry out the research – *a priori*. A specific research question states what we are trying to find out. The hypothesis predicts *a priori* the answer to that question.

This now raises a question about the basis for that prediction. On what basis can we make such a prediction? Why do we expect to find this (what we predict), rather than something else? In general, there are only two answers to this last question. One is: because another researcher did some similar research and this is what was found. While this answers the question, it does not explain the prediction. The other answer to 'Why predict this?' involves an explanation. Propositions are put forward which explain why the predicted answer (the hypothesis) can be expected. We can call this set of propositions a 'theory'.

In this case, we have a theory, which explains the hypothesis, and from which the hypothesis follows, by deduction, as an if–then proposition. If the theory is true, then the hypothesis follows. So, in executing the research and testing the hypothesis, we are actually testing the theory behind the hypothesis. This is the classical hypothetico-deductive model of research. In passing, we should note that it shows why theories cannot be proved, only disproved. We cannot prove the if-part (the theory) by validating the then-part (the hypothesis).[6] This is why it is often pointed out that scientific knowledge develops by disproving its theories (Popper, 1959).

Two points follow from viewing the structure of inquiry in this way. The first concerns the role of hypotheses in empirical research. We should only have hypotheses when it is appropriate to do so. When is that? When we do have an explanation (a theory) in mind behind our hypotheses. If this is the case, we should by all means formulate hypotheses as predicted answers to research questions, and test them. If not, we can ignore hypotheses and proceed with research questions. After all, there is no logical difference between research questions and research hypotheses, when it comes to their implications for design, data collection and data analysis.

Therefore there is a simple procedure for determining whether it is appropriate to have hypotheses. Once we have specific research questions, we can routinely ask, of each one, and before carrying out the research: 'What answer do we expect to this question?' If we cannot predict with any confidence, we need go no further into the matter of hypotheses, and we can proceed instead with research questions. If we can predict, we next ask: 'Why do we predict this (and not something else)?' If the only answer to that question is 'Because some other researcher found it to be true', again we do not need to propose hypotheses. If, however, we really do have some explanation in mind, from which the predicted answer(s) follow, then there is value in proposing hypotheses, and exposing and analysing the theory behind them. In testing the hypotheses, we are then testing the theory. The hypothesis has a central role in the testing of theories, and it should not be divorced from that role. This means that there is no point in putting forward hypotheses for testing unless we can also put forward the theory behind them.

The second implication of this way of seeing the hypothesis concerns the overall structure of scientific knowledge, and takes us back to the diagram shown in Figure 2.1. The structure shown in that diagram illustrates the point made above: that a hypothesis is derived from, and explained by, the higher-order theory above it. It also shows the hierarchical structure of knowledge, with increasing levels of power, abstraction and generality towards the top of the diagram, and the central role of empirical generalizations. This view of the hypothesis, its relationship to research questions and to the theory behind it, shows, in microcosm, the same structure. This underlines the point that there are concepts and propositions at different levels of abstraction in a research project, and therefore that there need to be logical links between these different levels of abstraction.

Hypotheses are given a very prominent place in some research methods books, especially quantitative ones (for example, see Burns, 1995), but that is not the case here. The sequence of ideas shown above helps in understanding the role and place of the hypothesis, and enables judgements about the appropriateness of hypotheses in a study. If appropriate, we can use them. If not, the study is better kept at the level of research questions. There is no point in simply having hypotheses, for their own sake. What is useful in all cases is to go through the above questioning sequence, once the research questions are settled, asking whether the answer to each research question can be predicted, and, if so, on what basis.

## 3.5 A Simplified Model of Research

Whether or not hypotheses are appropriate, organizing research around research questions, and insisting that each question conforms to the empirical criterion given in the next chapter, leads to a simple but effective model of the research process. It can be diagrammed as shown in Figure 3.1.

This simplified model of research stresses:

- framing the research in terms of research questions
- determining what data are necessary to answer those questions
- designing research to collect and analyse those data
- using the data to answer the questions.

The model in the upper part of the diagram shows research questions without hypotheses. The model in the lower part shows research questions with hypotheses.

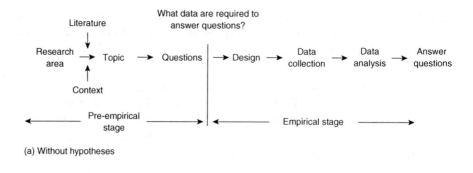

(a) Without hypotheses

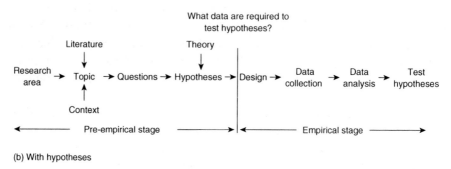

(b) With hypotheses

**Figure 3.1**   *Simplified model of research*

Based on this model of research, we can see that two overall questions guide the research planning process. They are also the questions around which the research proposal can be written, and, later and with some additions, the research report. The questions are the straightforward ones of:

• What? What questions is the research trying to answer? What is it trying to find out?
• How? How will the research answer these questions?

This chapter and the next deal with the ways of answering the 'what' question. Chapters 5 through 10 concentrate on the 'how' question. There is also a third question:

• Why? Why are these questions worth answering? Why is this research worth doing?

This concerns the justification for doing the research, and is discussed in Chapter 12.

This model of research helps to organize the planning, execution and writing up of the research. Especially during planning, it also helps to counter overload and possible confusion. It is effective with quantitative, qualitative and mixed-method research. It needs modification where prespecified research questions are not possible or desirable, and where the plan is that they will be developed as the early empirical work provides focus. In those cases, as noted earlier, it is still worth keeping this model in mind, in order to see where and why it is not appropriate. When research questions are developed as the research becomes focused, the analytic process described in this chapter is delayed. It comes after some empirical work, not before. When that happens, question development will be influenced by the initial data. Otherwise, it is much the same process, and just as important for ensuring the fit between the parts of the research.

## 3.6 The Role of the Literature

The appropriate point in the planning process at which to concentrate on the literature is something which may well vary in different styles of research. In a traditional model of research, the literature is reviewed (often comprehensively) as part of the research planning and question development stage. The literature itself becomes an input to the analysis and planning during this stage. This is the recommended way to proceed in many research situations, and it has been the model typically followed in quantitative research and in some types of qualitative research. At the other end of the scale, we might have, for example, a grounded theory study, where the literature coverage is deliberately delayed until directions emerge from the early analysis of data. The literature is brought in later, and treated as further data for analysis. The reason for this, as explained in Chapter 8, is that the researcher wants categories and concepts to emerge from the data – to be fully grounded in the data – rather than to be brought to the data from the literature. If these two examples are the two ends of a scale, there are obviously points in between, which combine elements of the two approaches.

It is a matter of judgement at what point to concentrate on the literature. Factors involved in this judgement include the style of the research, the overall research strategy, what the objectives of the proposed study are, the nature of the substantive problem and how much is known about it, how well developed the literature in the area is, and how closely this study wants to follow the directions established by that literature. A further important factor is the knowledge that the researcher already has, especially when the research topic comes from practice or experience.

In applied social research, many topics and questions come from the world of professional practice, and are often set in organizational, institutional, community or public settings. Often, also, the researcher is a professional practitioner, or closely connected with professional practice, in that setting. In such a situation, the researcher has considerable knowledge about the topic before commencing the research. This knowledge can be used as a starting point for the question development work described earlier. This involves exploring and articulating that knowledge, an activity which will often be valuable to the individual in encouraging reflection about the issue. For the research itself, this knowledge is a valuable input to the research planning process. Maxwell (1996: 27–9) offers some specific suggestions for dealing with 'experiential knowledge', and gives the example (1996: 30–1) of an 'experience memo' on the topic of diversity.

In such cases, there is often some benefit in delaying for a while the use of the literature, during the question development stage. There is benefit, in other words, to doing a certain amount of work on developing the questions (and perhaps the conceptual framework) before consulting the literature. This is because the literature will influence that process, and we may want to minimize or delay that influence. Of course, the literature can be a fruitful source of concepts, theories and evidence about a topic, but it can also influence how we look at a topic, thereby precluding the development of some new way. Guidelines for dealing with the literature in developing a research proposal are given in Punch (2000: 42–5).

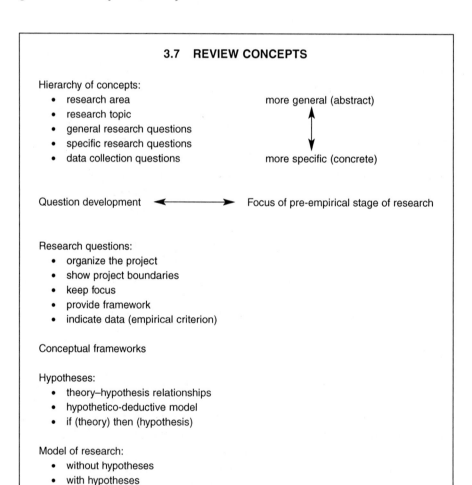

### 3.7 REVIEW CONCEPTS

Hierarchy of concepts:
- research area
- research topic
- general research questions
- specific research questions
- data collection questions

more general (abstract)

↑
↓

more specific (concrete)

Question development ←——————→ Focus of pre-empirical stage of research

Research questions:
- organize the project
- show project boundaries
- keep focus
- provide framework
- indicate data (empirical criterion)

Conceptual frameworks

Hypotheses:
- theory–hypothesis relationships
- hypothetico-deductive model
- if (theory) then (hypothesis)

Model of research:
- without hypotheses
- with hypotheses

## NOTES

1   A specific research question is a question the research itself is trying to answer. A data collection question is a question which is asked in order to collect data to help answer the research question. It is more specific still than the research question (see Punch, 2000: 27).

2   This term means that some topics are 'hot', and offer an opportunity: 'for example, you read that there is a lot of money available to conduct research on nursing homes, but few people are interested in doing so. Your need of a job suggests nursing homes as a topic' (Neuman, 1994: 110).

3   A fruitful source of research topics is also a university (or departmental) dissertation or project library. It is common practice in these projects for the writer to suggest avenues and areas for further research, making a collection of such projects a valuable resource.

4   Sometimes the literature will talk about research problems rather than research questions. The distinction is academic, and has no practical significance in planning research. A problem requires a solution, and can always be phrased as a question. A question requires an answer, and can always be phrased as a problem.

5   Miles and Huberman are more ambitious: they suggest that more than a dozen or so general questions is 'looking for trouble' (1994: 25).

6   To claim to do so is to commit the logical fallacy of 'affirming the consequent'.


## *Further Reading*

Babbie, E. (1992) *The Practice of Social Research*. 6th edn. Belmont, CA: Wadsworth.

Brewer, J. and Hunter, A. (1989) *Multimethod Research: A Synthesis of Styles*. Newbury Park, CA: Sage.

Campbell, J.P., Daft, R.L. and Hulin, C.L. (1982) *What to Study: Generating and Developing Research Questions*. Beverly Hills, CA: Sage.

Clark, A.W. (1983) *Social Science: Introduction to Theory and Method*. Sydney: Prentice-Hall.

Marshall, C. and Rossman, G.B. (1989) *Designing Qualitative Research*. Newbury Park, CA: Sage.

Maxwell, J.A. (1996) *Qualitative Research Design: An Interactive Approach*. Thousand Oaks, CA: Sage.

Miles, M.B. and Huberman, A.M. (1994) *Qualitative Data Analysis*. Thousand Oaks, CA: Sage.

Neuman, W.L. (1994) *Social Research Methods: Qualitative and Quantitative Approaches*. Boston: Allyn and Bacon.

Punch, K.F. (2000) *Developing Effective Research Proposals*. London: Sage.

Zuckerman, H. (1978) 'Theory choice and problem choice in science', in J. Gaston (ed.), *Sociology of Science*. San Francisco: Jossey-Bass. pp. 65–95.

# 4

# From Research Questions To Data

## 4.1 The Empirical Criterion

The essential idea of the empirical criterion for research questions is that a well stated research question indicates what data will be necessary to answer it. It is useful to apply this criterion to all research questions, as they are developed. Another way of saying this is that 'a question well asked is a question half answered': the way a well asked question is stated shows what data will be necessary to answer it. Since empirical research means collecting data, we will not know how to proceed if the research questions do not give clear indications of the data needed to answer them.

This criterion applies most clearly to prespecified research questions. What about when there are no clearly prespecified research questions – where, instead, the research strategy is for the questions to emerge? There still has to be a close fit between questions and data, but now, rather than questions leading to data, we may have data leading to questions. In fact it is more likely that there will be a 'reciprocal interaction' between the questions and the data. In this sort of unfolding situation, the question identification and question development processes are delayed. Instead of before the research, they come in later, with the data influencing the way the questions are identified and developed. But it is still important that the questions and the data fit with each other, so the criterion is applicable whether the research questions are prespecified or whether they unfold.

## 4.2 Linking Concepts and Data

Empirical research requires the linking of data to concepts, the connecting of a concept to its empirical indicators.[1] In quantitative research, this idea is described as operationalism. Variables have conceptual definitions, where they are defined using abstract concepts, and operational definitions, where they are connected by means of empirical operations to data indicators. The same idea applies in qualitative research, but comes up in the analysis of data.

The empirical criterion stresses the link between research questions and data, or between concepts and their empirical indicators. This link is an important part of the fit between the different parts of a research project. It is also part of the overall logical chain within a piece of research. Tight logical connections are needed between all levels of abstraction in that chain. Figure 2.1 shows the different levels of abstraction in theories, empirical generalizations and first-order facts. First-order facts are very concrete; empirical generalizations use abstract concepts; and theories use even more abstract concepts. There must be firm connections between concepts at each level of abstraction in this hierarchical structure.

We can illustrate these points using Charters's example in his discussion of the hypothesis, remembering that a hypothesis is a predicted answer to a research question. Charters (1967) shows propositions at different levels of generality, and demonstrates the need for logical links between those levels:[2]

* *Theoretical proposition.* Aggression occurs when a person is frustrated in getting to his goals. That is, whenever a person is prevented from getting something he wants, an aggressive urge arises within him that induces him to behave aggressively toward the party responsible for his frustration.
* *Conceptual hypothesis.* Elementary school children who are prevented by their teacher from going to recess on a sunny day will express greater hostility in their remarks to the teacher during the remainder of the school day than elementary school children who are not prevented by the teacher from going to recess, other things being equal.
* *Operational hypothesis.* The ratio of 'hostile' to 'non-hostile' remarks made by pupils and classified as 'directed towards teacher', based upon the observation of classroom interaction by a trained observer between 2.00 and 3.30 in the afternoon of sunny days, will be significantly lower under condition A (27 second-grade pupils in Hawthorne School whose teacher said, 'You may go to recess now') than under condition B (36 second-grade pupils in Hawthorne School whose teacher said, 'Instead of going to recess today, I think we had better work some more on spelling').

In a tightly prefigured quantitative study such as is used in this example, the linking of concepts and data is done ahead of the empirical work of data collection and analysis. The link is made *from concepts to data*. In the language of quantitative research, the variables are operationally defined. In a more 'open-ended' qualitative study, say a grounded theory study, that linking is done during the empirical work. In fact, one purpose of such a study is to develop concepts linked to, or grounded in, the data. In that sort of study, the link is made *from data to concepts*. Earlier, in the comparison between theory verification and theory generation research, I used Wolcott's theory-first or theory-after description. Here, it is concepts-first or concepts-after. Whenever it is done, before or during the empirical part of the research, the careful linking is necessary, and the principles are the same. These same points are stressed by Lewins (1992).

It is useful to apply the empirical criterion to all research questions. When all questions satisfy this criterion, we are ready to move from content to method. When research questions fail the test of this criterion, one of two situations will usually apply. Either we have more conceptual-analytic question development work to do, which means that the questions are most likely still not specific enough. This is typical of questions which are being developed deductively, from the general to the specific. Or we have research questions which are faulty in some way. This leads to the topic of good and bad research questions.

## 4.3 Good and Bad Research Questions

It follows from Chapter 3 that good research questions are:

- *Clear*. They can be easily understood, and are unambiguous.
- *Specific*. Their concepts are at a specific enough level to connect to data indicators.
- *Answerable*. We can see what data are required to answer them, and how the data will be obtained.
- *Interconnected*. They are related to each other in some meaningful way, rather than being unconnected.[3]
- *Substantively relevant*. They are interesting and worthwhile questions for the investment of research effort.

Bad research questions fail to satisfy one or more of these criteria. Mostly, this is because either they are unclear and not specific enough, or they fail on the test of the empirical criterion, which is expressed in the second and third points above. If we cannot say how we would answer each research question, and what evidence would be required to answer it, we cannot proceed.

While there are many different ways in which research questions can be inappropriate or unsatisfactory, there are two types of problems which often occur. The first concerns value judgements, the second concerns causation. Both are important philosophical issues, and both have been prominent in the paradigm discussions referred to earlier.

## 4.4 Value Judgements

Value judgements are moral judgements or statements. They are statements about what is good or bad, right or wrong (or any synonyms of these words), not in the sense of instrumental values (means) but in the sense of terminal values (ends). They are often described as statements of 'ought' (or 'should'), and are contrasted with statements of 'is'.[4] The problem is that it is not clear how (or whether) we can use empirical evidence to make such value judgements. There are two main positions on this important issue.

One position is that we cannot use empirical evidence in the making of value judgements because of the so-called 'fact-to-value gap'. The fact-to-value gap maintains that there is a fundamental difference between facts and values, and that, because of that difference, there is no logical way to get from statements of fact to statements of value. If this is true, it means that evidence is irrelevant to the making of value judgements, and that value judgements cannot be justified by evidence. Some other basis will be required for their justification. For proponents of this view, science must remain silent on value judgement questions, since scientific research, being based on empirical data, can deal only with the facts. This is not a small problem, since value judgements are among the most important judgements people must make. In this view, science has no role in making those value judgements. Nor do value judgements have any place in scientific inquiry. This is the conventional, positivist, 'science-as-value-free' view, and it has a long history.[5]

The other main view is that this gap is based on a mistaken dualism which sees facts and values as quite different things. In this view, that distinction is invalid, and the fact-to-value gap is therefore a misleading fallacy. The reasoning behind this view is not easy to summarize, but it is described by Lincoln and Guba (1985: Chapter 7). They indicate the many possible meanings of values, they show why the fact–value dualism is discredited, they stress the value-ladenness of all facts, and they show the four main ways in which values have a direct impact on the research. They end the chapter with this plea that we discontinue the fallacious dichotomy between facts and values, and stop trying to exclude values from research:

> At this point, *at a minimum*, we should be prepared to admit that values do play a significant part in inquiry, to do our best in each case to expose and explicate them ... and, finally, to take them into account to whatever extent

we can. Such a course is infinitely to be preferred to continuing in the self-delusion that methodology can and does protect one from their unwelcome incursions. (1985: 186)

This rejection of the positivist view comes from several quarters. Feminist scholars, for example, have repeatedly challenged the 'persistent positivist myth' (Haig, 1997) that science is value free, and critical theorists and feminists alike regard the distinction between facts and values as simply a device which disguises the role of conservative values in much social research. Instead of value-free research, critical theorists especially argue that research should be used in the service of the emancipation of oppressed groups: in other words, that it should be openly ideological (Hammersley, 1993).

> The attempt to produce value-neutral social science is increasingly being abandoned as at best unrealisable, and at worst self-deceptive, and is being replaced by social sciences based on explicit ideologies. (Hesse, 1980: 247)

While the positivist value-free position has a long history, opposition to it has grown strongly in the last 20 years. Ironically, the positivist position is itself a statement of values, and many see it as discredited in maintaining that inquiry can be value free. The problem with the rejection of the value-free position, however, is that it is not clear where it leads.[6] This can complicate the development of research questions, since the area of value judgements is controversial. In the face of that, I suggest three points to keep in mind. First, we should be aware that there are different positions on this issue, and therefore not be surprised if we encounter different reactions to it. Second, we should recognize when value statements are being made, and be careful about phrasing research questions in value judgement terms.[7] We should be aware of synonyms for 'good–bad' and 'right–wrong', which may camouflage the value judgements, but do not remove the issue.[8] Third, if value judgement terms are used in questions, we can first determine whether they are being used in the instrumental or the terminal sense. If instrumental, we can rephrase the question to get rid of the value judgement term(s). If the terms are being used in the terminal value sense, we should indicate how the evidence will be used in conjunction with the value judgements.

## 4.5 Causation

Scientific research has traditionally sought the causes of effects, events or phenomena. Indeed, a useful definition of scientific research in any area is that it seeks to trace out cause–effect relationships. In this sense, science reflects everyday life. The concept of causation is deeply ingrained in our culture, and saturates our attempts to understand and explain the world. On the everyday level, we find it a very useful way to organize our thinking about the world:

the word 'because', for example, is one of the most central in our language, and in our world view. As Lincoln and Guba (1985) point out, our preoccupation with causation may be related to our needs for prediction, control and power. Whether that is true or not, the concept of causation is deep seated, and perhaps built into the way we think about the world.

But causation is also a difficult philosophical concept. What does causation mean, and how do we know when we have a cause (or the cause, or the causes) of something? The definitional question about causation has no easy answer. For example, Lincoln and Guba (1985: Chapter 6) review six main formulations of the concept of causation. Similarly, Brewer and Hunter (1989) discuss different types of causes. Without going into the definitional details, one way to simplify this complicated issue is to see the difference between the constant conjunction view of causation and the necessary connection view.

In the *constant conjunction* view, to say that $X$ (for example, watching violence on television) causes $Y$ (for example, the development of antisocial attitudes) is to say that every time $X$ occurs, $Y$ occurs. This means simply that $Y$ always follows $X$, that there is a constant conjunction between them. This view is clear enough, but it has a problem. Night always follows day, yet we don't want to say that day causes night. Therefore constant conjunction alone does not seem to be enough to define causation.

On the other hand, in the *necessary connection* view, to say that $X$ causes $Y$ is to say not only that $X$ is followed by $Y$, but that $X$ must be followed by $Y$. In this view causation means that the variables are necessarily connected. The problem with this view is that we cannot observe that $X$ must be followed by $Y$. We can only observe whether or not $X$ is followed by $Y$. We cannot observe the necessity part. Since we cannot observe it, we must infer it. Thus causation, in this view, is not observable, it can only be inferred. It is, in other words, not an empirical concept.

The necessary connection view of causation therefore leads to this question: under what conditions is it plausible to infer that an observed relationship is a causal one? This is a difficult question, precisely because the world is full of relationships we can observe, but most of them are not causal. It is a question to which many answers have been proposed (see, for example, Lincoln and Guba, 1985; Rosenberg, 1968; Brewer and Hunter, 1989). Without attempting here a full treatment of this question, the main conditions for inferring that $X$ (watching violence on television) causes $Y$ (the development of antisocial attitudes) are:

- The variables $X$ and $Y$ must be related.[9]
- A time order between the variables must be demonstrated, with the cause $X$ preceding the effect $Y$.[10]
- There must be a plausible theory showing the links by which the variables are causally related: that is, the missing links which bring about the causal connection must be specified.
- Plausible rival hypotheses to the preferred causal one must be eliminated.

**Table 4.1** *Substitute terms for cause and effect*

| Cause | Effect |
|---|---|
| Independent variable | Dependent variable |
| Treatment variable | Outcome variable |
| Predictor variable | Criterion variable |
| Antecedents | Consequences |
| Determinants | |

'Correlates' is sometimes used for both causes and effects. Sometimes 'cause–effect relationship' is replaced by 'functional relationship'.

Perhaps no topic has received more attention in quantitative research design than this. For a long time, and in some quarters still, the experiment has been the preferred empirical research design, because, by systematically eliminating rival hypotheses, it is the safest basis we have for inferring causal relationships between variables. We will see this in Chapter 5. More recently, there have been advances in designs for inferring causation, both in quantitative research through the development of quasi-experimental and non-experimental designs, and also in qualitative research (see, for example, Miles and Huberman, 1994: 143–71).

Different researchers have different views of causation (Huberman and Miles, 1994: 434), and the credibility of causal claims depends on the view one holds. Despite the resistance to the concept and terminology of causation among some qualitative researchers, and despite the view of Lincoln and Guba (1985) that the concept may have outlived its usefulness, it seems a safe assumption that many researchers will continue to want to think causally about the world. But it is important to be careful about the way we use the word 'cause(s)'. In particular, we need to remember that causation can only be inferred, according to the necessary connection view described above. This is one reason that the word 'cause(s)' itself is not often used among experienced researchers. Other words are substituted. We therefore need to be careful about such statements in a proposal as 'In this research we will find the cause(s) of ...'. Still more must we be careful of statements in a finished report that 'In this research we have found the cause(s) of ...'.[11]

On the assumption that we retain the idea of causation, I suggest that we proceed as follows. First, when we are thinking causally, we replace the words 'cause' and 'effect' by other terms, choosing from those shown in Table 4.1, especially in quantitative studies. Second, we proceed to study the extent to which and the ways in which things are interconnected and variables are interrelated, according to whatever design we have chosen. Third, we reserve any causal description of observed relationships until it is time to interpret the results. It is one thing to observe, describe and report the relationship; it is another to interpret it, to say how it came about. If the interpretation we prefer is a causal one, we are on safe ground if we point out that this interpretation is an inference, and then argue for it on the basis of the sorts of conditions mentioned earlier.

The distinction in the third point just made is important, and will come up again later in this book. It is the difference between observing and describing a relationship between variables (or a connection between things), on the one hand, and interpreting that relationship or explaining it and saying how it came about, on the other. The difficulty in research is not normally in showing that a relationship exists. The difficulty is more likely to lie in interpreting that relationship.[12] Later chapters will show that there has been much work done on this issue in both the quantitative and qualitative approaches. For now, it is important to see clearly this distinction between describing a relationship and interpreting it.

What terms can we substitute for cause and effect? In a quantitative context, instead of cause, we use the term 'independent variable'. Instead of effect, we use 'dependent variable'. Other synonyms for these are 'treatment' or 'predictor' variable for independent variable, and 'outcome' or 'criterion' variable for dependent variable. In still other contexts, 'antecedents' and 'determinants' are used for causes, 'consequences' for effects, and 'correlates' for both. The main thrust of these terms is to get away from the metaphysical part of the term 'cause' itself.

Two other points are made before leaving this topic of causation. The first is more applicable to quantitative research, the second to qualitative research. Both have implications for research design, and the analysis of data.

### Multiple causation

The discussion in this section has been simplified by talking basically about one cause and one effect, and by talking about only one direction for causation (from X to Y). In social research today, especially quantitative research, thinking about a single cause and a single effect is uncommon, and multiple causation is seen as much more realistic. Multiple causation means that there will likely be more than one cause, and probably several causes, for any particular effect. Effects are thought to have several causes, and these causes can act together in various ways, and can fluctuate in importance in how they bring about the effect. The terms 'multiple causes', 'conjunctional causes' and 'conjectural causes' express these ideas. While the discussion in this section has been simplified, and put in terms of one cause and one effect, everything we have said about the nature of causes and the logic of causation holds for the more complicated case of multiple causation.

The same point also applies to effects. Much research has moved from a single effect to multiple effects. Multiple effects means that there will likely be several effects of any given cause, or set of causes. This move from single to multiple causes and effects has important consequences for research design, as shown in Table 4.2. This diagram shows the various combinations of single and multiple causes and effects. In the top left-hand cell, there is the

**Table 4.2** *Cause–effect combinations and designs*

|  | | Causes (independent variable, IV) | |
|---|---|---|---|
|  | | **Single** | **Multiple** |
| **Effects (dependent variable, DV)** | **Single** | One cause, one effect<br><br>$IV \rightarrow DV$ | Multiple cause, one effect<br><br>$\begin{bmatrix} IV \\ IV \\ IV \\ IV \end{bmatrix} \rightarrow DV$ |
| | **Multiple** | One cause, multiple effects<br><br>$IV \rightarrow \begin{bmatrix} DV \\ DV \\ DV \\ DV \end{bmatrix}$ | Multiple causes, multiple effects<br><br>$\begin{bmatrix} IV \\ IV \\ IV \\ IV \end{bmatrix} \rightarrow \begin{bmatrix} DV \\ DV \\ DV \\ DV \end{bmatrix}$ |

one-cause/one-effect design, now rather outmoded in social science research. In the top right-hand cell, there is the multiple-causes/one-effect design, the most common design in quantitative research, and the basis of the important multiple regression approach to be described in Chapters 5 and 7. The bottom left-hand cell shows the one-cause/multiple-effects design, while the bottom right-hand cell shows the multiple-causes/multiple-effects design.[13]

### Causation in qualitative research

The second point concerns causation in qualitative research. The term 'causation' has positivist connotations (Hammersley and Atkinson, 1995: 233), and this, combined with the difficulty of assessing causal claims, makes some qualitative researchers reluctant to use the concept. Some postmodernists, for example, as pointed out by Neuman (1994), reject the search for causation because they see life as too complex and rapidly changing. Thus causation has typically been a preoccupation of quantitative research.

However, as Hammersley and Atkinson (1995) point out, causal theories and models are common in ethnographic work, even if they are used implicitly. Similarly, Miles and Huberman (1994) make clear the importance of causation in qualitative research. Indeed, they claim that qualitative studies are especially well suited to finding causal relationships. Qualitative studies can

> look directly and longitudinally at the local processes underlying a temporal series of events and states, showing how these led to specific outcomes and ruling out rival hypotheses. In effect, we get inside the black box; we can

understand not just that a particular thing happened, but how and why it happened. (Huberman and Miles, 1994: 434)

And again:

> We consider qualitative analysis to be a very powerful method for assessing causality ... Qualitative analysis, with its close-up look, can identify *mechanisms*, going beyond sheer association. It is unrelentingly *local*, and deals well with the complex network of events and processes in a situation. It can sort out the *temporal* dimension, showing clearly what preceded what, either through direct observation or *retrospection*. It is well equipped to cycle back and forth between *variables* and *processes* – showing that 'stories' are not capricious, but include underlying variables, and that variables are not disembodied, but have connections over time. (Miles and Huberman, 1994: 147)

In *Qualitative Data Analysis*, Miles and Huberman show how causal networks can be developed to model qualitative data, just as causal path diagrams model quantitative data.

## 4.6 Conceptual Frameworks

A conceptual framework is a representation, either graphically or in narrative form, of the main concepts or variables, and their presumed relationship with each other. It is usually best shown as a diagram. Some sort of conceptual framework is often implicit as the question development stage described in Chapter 3 proceeds. Often it helps in the development of the research questions to make this conceptual framework explicit. In those cases, development of the research questions and the conceptual framework goes hand in hand. The direction of thinking may be from the conceptual framework to the research questions, or vice versa, or they may interact with each other in some reciprocal way. Developing both together, like the questions themselves, is usually an iterative process.

Whether or not it is appropriate to have a predetermined conceptual framework depends on how much prior knowledge and theorizing are brought to the research. In discussing the development of research questions, it was pointed out that there is often considerable prior knowledge, and the same point applies to the conceptual framework. It is useful to get our prior knowledge and theorizing out on to the table, and organizing that into a conceptual framework as research questions are developed can bring several benefits:

- It brings clarity and focus, helping us to see and organize the research questions more clearly.
- It helps to make explicit what we already know and think about the area and topic.

- It can help considerably in communicating ideas about the research; therefore it can simplify the preparation of the research proposal, and can also make it more convincing.
- It encourages selection, and assists in focusing and delimiting thinking during the planning stage.

In quantitative research, where well developed research questions are typical, the conceptual framework is common, usually in diagram form. The diagram(s) will typically show the variables, their conceptual status in relation to each other, and the hypothesized relationships between them. In qualitative research, there is, as usual, more of a range. Conceptual frameworks have generally been less common in qualitative research, but, as Miles and Huberman (1994) and Maxwell (1996) make clear, a strong case can be made for their usefulness there too. Example 4.1 refers to conceptual frameworks for both quantitative and qualitative studies.

---

*Quantitative*

- Neuman (1994: 47) shows five conceptual frameworks to represent possible causal relationships between variables.
- Rosenberg (1968: 54–83) shows numerous conceptual frameworks to represent intervening and antecedent variable relationships.
- Calder and Sapsford (1996) show a variety of multivariate conceptual frameworks.

**Example 4.1**
*Conceptual frameworks*

*Qualitative*

- Miles and Huberman (1994: 18–20) show conceptual frameworks for their studies on disseminating educational innovations, and on school improvements.
- Miles and Huberman (1994: 21) also show two conceptual frameworks used by other qualitative researchers: one an ethnographic study of minority children's school experience, the other an emergent conceptual framework for the study of the creation of a new school.

---

## 4.7 From Research Questions to Data

Once we have stabilized our research questions, and ensured that they are satisfactory in terms of the empirical criterion and the other criteria presented in Section 4.3, we can move from content to method. The connection from content to method is through data: what data will be needed, and how will they be collected and analysed? Before we get down to details of method, therefore, we need to consider the nature of data.

What are data? As noted earlier, synonyms for data are evidence, information, or empirical materials. The essential idea is first-hand observation and information about (or experience of) the world. Obviously, that could include all sorts of things, so 'data' is a very broad term, and is subdivided into quantitative and qualitative. Both are empirical.

### 4.7.1 Quantitative data

The key concept here is quantity, and numbers are used to express quantity. Therefore quantitative data are numerical: they are information about the world, in the form of numbers.

Information about the world does not occur naturally in the form of numbers. It is we, as researchers, who turn the data into numbers. We impose the structure of the number system on the data, bringing the structure to the data. This means there is nothing 'God-given' about the numerical structure we impose; on the contrary, that structure is very much man made. It is therefore not inevitable, or essential, that we organize our empirical data as numbers. The question is whether we find it useful to impose this structure on the data. If we find it useful (and if it is feasible), we should do it. If not, we are not at all bound to do it.

Measurement is the process by which we turn data into numbers. Measurement involves assigning numbers to things, people, events or whatever, according to particular sets of rules, as will be discussed in Chapter 6. Therefore to collect quantitative data is to collect measurements. By definition, quantitative data collected with measuring instruments are prestructured, falling at the left-hand end of the structuring continuum presented in Figure 2.2. The numerical structure is imposed on the data, ahead of the research.

Two types of operations produce numbers: counting and scaling. Counting is such a common everyday occurrence that we don't think twice about it. We do it automatically, it is straightforward and not problematic, and we find it extremely useful in dealing with the world. When we count, we are counting with respect to something. There is a dimension of interest, some scale or quantity we have in mind, which gives meaning to the counting.

Scaling[14] is rather different, though again we do it all the time. The basic idea here is that we have in mind some characteristic, or property, or trait – we will use trait – and we envisage a continuum, or scale, ranging from a great deal (or perhaps 100%) of that trait, to very little (or perhaps 0%) of that trait. Further, we envisage different locations along that continuum, corresponding to different amounts of that trait. We use this sort of thinking and describing very frequently in everyday language, and it is not difficult to find many examples. Nor do we normally consider it a problem to do that. In other words, the idea of scaling (though we do not normally call it that) is deeply ingrained into our world view and into our language. This needs stressing because of the controversies which can arise with this same operation in a research situation. As a final step, in actual measurement, we assign numbers to represent those different locations along the scaled continuum. We do not normally make this last step in everyday life, and it seems to be here that the controversies arise. The idea of a scale is useful to us in everyday life because it helps us to be systematic in our thinking, and because it helps us to compare things (or events, or people) in a standardized way. Making standardized comparisons is something we often want to do, and measurement formalizes those comparisons, enabling us to make them more precise and systematic.

To summarize, quantitative data are data in the form of numbers, from either counting, or scaling, or both. Measurement turns data into numbers, and its function is to help us make comparisons. Although measurement is a technical tool, it is a technical tool with very great similarities to what we do with great frequency in everyday life. It is important to stress this point because the process of measurement itself has been at the centre of much of the debate between quantitative and qualitative researchers. Measurement seems also to have fostered entrenched positions in that debate. One entrenched position is slavishly devoted to measurement, and believes only in research where the data are quantitative. The other is just as slavishly anti-measurement, distrusting all quantitative research. In this book, I want to avoid such entrenched positions about measurement, which we can do by asking two questions. First, will it help us to measure what we want to study: that is, will it be useful for the comparisons we wish to make? Second, if it is helpful, is it in fact possible to measure in this particular situation? We will return to this question in Chapter 6.

Counting and scaling are part of measurement, and it is variables which are measured, produced by measurement. The concept of a variable (something which varies) is central to quantitative research. Quantitative research design shows how the variables are seen and organized with respect to each other. Quantitative data collection is about how the variables are to be measured, and quantitative data analysis is about how the measurements of the variables are to be analysed. Thus the concept of a variable, and the measurement of variables, are essential to the way quantitative research proceeds.

### 4.7.2 Qualitative data

We have defined quantitative data as empirical information in the form of numbers, produced by measurement. Qualitative data can therefore be defined as empirical information about the world, not in the form of numbers. Most of the time (but not always: see note 7 in Chapter 1) this means words.

This definition covers a very wide range, and qualitative data do indeed include many different types of things. Denzin and Lincoln (1994) use the term 'qualitative empirical materials', and point out that it includes interview transcripts, recordings and notes, observational records and notes, documents and the products and records of material culture, audiovisual materials, and personal experience materials (such as artefacts, journal and diary information, and narratives). The qualitative researcher thus has a much wider range of possible empirical materials than the quantitative researcher, and will typically also use multiple data sources in a project. For some qualitative researchers, literally everything is data. In this book, we concentrate on qualitative data from observation (and participant observation), interviews or documents – or, as Wolcott (1992) puts it, on qualitative data from 'watching, asking or examining'.

We saw that quantitative data have a predetermined structure, being at the left-hand end of the structure continuum in Figure 2.2. What about qualitative data? As with research questions and research designs, qualitative data can fall anywhere along this continuum. Thus, they can be towards the left-hand end, and well structured, as in the case of standardized interview questions with response categories, or observations based on a predetermined observation schedule.[15] On the other hand, qualitative data can be totally unstructured at the point of collection, as in the transcript of an open-ended interview, or field notes from participant observation. In this case, there would be no predetermined categories or codes. Rather, the structure in the data will emerge during the analysis. The basis of this structure is codes and categories, and they are typically derived from the data in the initial stages of analysis, as is described in Chapter 10.

Earlier, we saw comparisons between theory-before and theory-after, between concepts-before and concepts-after, and between research-questions-before and research-questions-after. Here it is a case of structure-before or structure-after in the data. But here, with data, another point emerges. 'Structure-before' means that the researcher imposes codes, categories or concepts on the data: these are researcher-imposed concepts. Measurement in quantitative research is a clear example of concepts and structure imposed on the data by the researcher. By contrast, 'structure-after' allows respondents in research to 'tell it in their own terms' to a much greater extent.[16] This is often a big issue in a research project. A common criticism of prestructured data is on this very point: that prestructuring the data does not permit people to provide information using their own terms, meanings and understandings. On the other hand, when we collect data using people's own terms and meanings, it is difficult to make standardized comparisons. This is an example of the sort of choice often facing the researcher. Like all other such choices, it needs to be analysed, and there are advantages and disadvantages in each way of doing it. Thus, it will often seem good to begin with the data in respondents' own terms and concepts. But the systematic comparisons which structure and measurements permit are also valuable, and they require that the same terms and concepts be used across different respondents – that they be standardized. That suggests combining the two approaches in such a way as to retain the advantages of each. Some specific suggestions for doing that are given in Chapter 11.

Open-ended qualitative data are often appealing to researchers who are keen to capture directly the lived experience of people. But unstructured qualitative data require some processing to prepare them for analysis. Therefore the data themselves represent a text constructed by the researcher. It is one thing to experience (some aspect of) the world. It is another thing to represent that experience in words. Once data are put into words, it is the researcher-constructed text which is used in the analysis. It is inevitable that the words we use to record data from the field will reflect, to some extent, our own concepts. Thus, as Miles and Huberman (1994: 10) write, behind the apparent simplicity of qualitative data there is a good deal of complexity,[17] requiring care and self-awareness from the researcher. In this sense, too, qualitative research is similar to quantitative: in both, the researcher brings something to the data.

## 4.8 Combining Quantitative and Qualitative Data

We can now summarize these sections on the nature of data. Quantitative data are information about the world in numerical form, whereas qualitative data are (essentially) information about the world in the form of words. Quantitative data are necessarily structured in terms of the number system, and reflect researcher-imposed constructs. Qualitative data may range from structured to unstructured, and may or may not involve researcher-imposed constructs. The basic difference between the two types of data lies in the process of measurement, which has often engendered rigid positions about research, and which has been at the centre of debates between proponents of the two approaches.

To move past these rigid positions does not of course mean that we must combine the two types of data – only that we can do so when appropriate. Thus there are three possibilities for any empirical study. It can have all quantitative data, it can have all qualitative data, or it can combine both types in any proportions. Which of these three should apply is not a matter for rules. The type of data we finish up with should be determined primarily by what we are trying to find out, considered against the background of the context, circumstances and practical aspects of the particular research project. Concentrating first on what we are trying to find out means that substantive issues dictate methodological choices. The 'substantive dog' wags the 'methodological tail', not vice versa.

This topic of combining quantitative and qualitative data is discussed again in Chapter 11. Before that, we have to look in detail at each of the two different types of data: the designs which produce them, the methods for collecting them, and how they can be analysed. For ease of presentation, we now separate out the quantitative and qualitative approaches, and deal with them separately. Thus the next three chapters, Chapters 5, 6 and 7, deal with quantitative research, and Chapters 8, 9 and 10 deal with qualitative research. In both cases, we deal first with design, second with the collection of data and third with the analysis of data. The two approaches are brought together again in Chapters 11 and 12.

---

### 4.9   REVIEW CONCEPTS

The empirical criterion for research questions:
- 'A question well asked is a question half answered.'

Linking concepts to data:
- quantitative research (typically): from concepts to data
- qualitative research (typically): from data to concepts

Value judgements:
- fact–value gap: important distinction or misleading fallacy?

Causation:
- constant conjunction view versus necessary connection view
- substitute terms for cause–effect: independent–dependent variables
- multiple causation
- causation in qualitative research

Quantitative data: numbers produced by measuring
- counting
- scaling

Qualitative data: words (mostly) produced by
- watching
- asking
- examining

Should I measure?
- Will it be possible?
- Will it be helpful?

Will my study have:
- quantitative data only?
- qualitative data only?
- both quantitative and qualitative data?

---

## NOTES

1  In quantitative research, the key concepts are variables, so the link is between variables and data, as in the operational definition of variables.
2  The paper by Charters (1967) is a valuable discussion of the functions, anatomy and pathology of the hypothesis. However, to my knowledge it has never been published.

3   They should form a coherent whole, rather than being a 'random collection of queries about the topic' (Maxwell, 1996: 107).

4   Terminal values are ends in themselves. Instrumental values are means towards achieving these ends. For a discussion of value judgements in science, see Broudy et al. (1973: 502–48), and Brodbeck (1968: 79–138).

5   See, for example, O'Connor (1957), especially Chapter 3.

6   Thus different writers reach different conclusions about how values are to be involved in empirical inquiry.

7   To admit the value-ladenness of facts does not justify the making of sweeping value judgements.

8   Examples are 'worthwhile–worthless', 'effective–ineffective' and 'efficient–inefficient'.

9   For convenience, the ideas are expressed here quantitatively, in terms of variables. The ideas generalize to the qualitative situation.

10  If the time order cannot be established, the 'relative fixity and alterability' of the variables must support the proposed causal inference: see Rosenberg (1968).

11  Sometimes words other than 'cause' are used, but the causal connotations remain. Some examples are 'due to', 'affects', 'contributes to', 'has an impact on', 'is a function of', and 'determines'.

12  A well known example of this is 'correlation is not causation'. Correlation is about showing the relationship. Causation is about interpreting it.

13  Quantitative research also accommodates more than one direction for causal influences. The ideas of mutual causation and reciprocal influences between variables can be built into causal path models, which specify the networks of causal influences among a set of variables (see, for example, Davis, 1985; Asher, 1976).

14  Scaling is used here to mean placing on a scale, or continuum. In Chapter 6, the more general term 'measurement' is used. Here scaling, along with counting, is seen as one type of measurement. In general, the term 'scaling' is used more often in psychology, the term 'measurement' more often in educational research.

15  Highly structured interview responses or observational data are often described as quantitative. Retaining the sharp distinction given in Chapter 1, they would not be described as quantitative here unless they are actually turned into numbers.

16  But not necessarily totally, since questioning already introduces some structure. However, some questions are more structured than others.

17  This complexity has another aspect too, centring on the use of language and the analytic status of qualitative data, discussed in Section 9.1.4.

## *Further Reading*

Blalock, H.M. Jr (1982) *Conceptualization and Measurement in the Social Sciences.* Beverly Hills, CA: Sage.

Brewer, J. and Hunter, A. (1989) *Multimethod Research: A Synthesis of Styles.* Newbury Park, CA: Sage.

Charters, W.W. Jr (1967) 'The hypothesis in scientific research'. Unpublished paper, University of Oregon, Eugene.

Davis, J.A. (1985) *The Logic of Causal Order.* Beverly Hills, CA: Sage.

Guba, E.G. and Lincoln, Y.S. (1989) *Fourth Generation Evaluation*. Newbury Park, CA: Sage.

Hage, J. and Meeker, B.F. (1988) *Social Causality*. Boston, MA: Unwin Hyman.

Lieberson, S. (1985) *Making it Count: The Improvement of Social Research and Theory*. Berkeley, CA: University of California Press.

Miles, M.B. and Huberman, A.M. (1994) *Qualitative Data Analysis*. Thousand Oaks, CA: Sage.

Rosenberg, M. (1968) *The Logic of Survey Analysis*. New York: Basic.

# 5
## Quantitative Research Design

This chapter deals with the main ideas behind quantitative research design. One theme of the chapter is the broad division in the logic of quantitative design between comparing groups, on the one hand, and relating variables, on the other. We can see this by looking briefly at some methodological history. Three main types of design follow from that broad division: experiments, quasi-experiments and correlational surveys. A second theme is the shift from comparison between groups to relationships between variables, as a way of thinking, and the use of regression analysis as a design strategy for implementing that shift. Running through both themes are the ideas of independent, control and dependent variables. We begin the chapter by looking at research design in general, in order to set a context both for quantitative design in this chapter and for qualitative design in Chapter 8.

## 5.1 What is Research Design?

Three uses of the term 'research design' can be distinguished in the literature, roughly ordered from general to specific. At the most general level, it means all the issues involved in planning and executing a research project – from identifying the problem through to reporting and publishing the results. This is how it is used by Ackoff (1953) and Miller (1991), for example. By contrast,

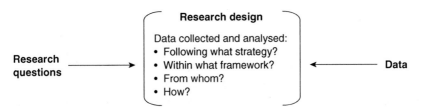

**Figure 5.1**   *Research design connects research questions to data*

at its most specific level, the design of a study refers to the way a researcher guards against, and tries to rule out, alternative interpretations of results. Experimental design, for example, has grown into a sophisticated field of study, based on the numerous strategies developed to counter the various possible threats to the valid interpretation of results. Between these two, there is the general idea of design as situating the researcher in the empirical world, and connecting research questions to data (Denzin and Lincoln, 1994). The first view is too broad for our purposes in this chapter, and the second will come up as we go through the chapter. Here, we will focus on the third use of the term, since we need a way of thinking about design which is general enough to accommodate both quantitative and qualitative approaches.

In this view, research design situates the researcher in the empirical world, and connects the research questions to data, as shown in Figure 5.1. The research design is the basic plan for a piece of research, and includes four main ideas. The first is the strategy. The second is the conceptual framework. The third is the question of who or what will be studied. The fourth concerns the tools and procedures to be used for collecting and analysing empirical materials. Research design thus deals with four main questions, corresponding to these ideas. The data will be collected (and analysed):

* Following what strategy?
* Within what framework?
* From whom?
* How?

These questions overlap, especially the first two. Also the second question, in particular, is more typical of quantitative designs, although it does apply in some qualitative research. We will now look briefly at each of the four questions.[1]

### Following what strategy?
At the centre of the design of a study is its logic or rationale: the reasoning or the set of ideas by which the study intends to proceed in order to answer its research questions. The term 'strategy' refers to that. Thus, in quantitative

research, the experiment includes a strategy designed to achieve certain comparisons. So does the correlational survey. Similarly, in qualitative research, a multiple case study involves a strategy for setting up certain comparisons. Ethnography and grounded theory are different sorts of strategies the qualitative researcher might use. Answers to the question 'Following what strategy?' will differ according to whether the approach is quantitative or qualitative. If quantitative, is the strategy experimental, quasi-experimental, or non-experimental? If qualitative, is the strategy case study, ethnography, or grounded theory, or some combination of these? If there is a combination of quantitative and qualitative approaches, what is the mixture of strategies? Associated with this question of strategy is another important question: to what extent will the researcher manipulate or organize the research situation, as against studying it naturalistically? In other words, to what extent will the researcher intervene in the research situation, contriving it and constructing it for research purposes, as against studying it as it occurs? Quantitative research design can vary from extremely interventionist to non-interventionist. Qualitative research design is generally non-interventionist.

### Within what framework?

Framework here means conceptual framework: the conceptual status of the things being studied, and their relationship to each other. In Chapters 3 and 4 we saw that prespecified research questions are often accompanied by a clear conceptual framework, and that developing and describing that framework can help in clarifying the research questions. The structure continuum (Figure 2.2) applies to the conceptual framework as well: it may be developed ahead of the study, or it may emerge as the study progresses. Quantitative designs typically have well developed prespecified frameworks, whereas qualitative designs show much more variability. Together with the strategy, it is the conceptual framework which determines how much prespecified structure a study will have.

### From whom will the data be collected?

This question concerns sampling for the research. In this form, the question is biased towards quantitative studies. The more general question 'Who or what will be studied?' (Denzin and Lincoln, 1994) covers both quantitative and qualitative approaches.

### How will the data be collected and analysed?

This question asks about the tools and procedures to be used in data collection and analysis, topics dealt with in Chapters 6 and 7 for quantitative research, and Chapters 9 and 10 for qualitative research.

Together, these four components of research design situate the researcher in the empirical world. Design sits between the research questions and the data, showing how the research questions will be connected to the data, and what tools and procedures to use in answering them. Therefore it needs to follow from the questions, and fit in with the data. Because strategy is central to design, I will sometimes use the term 'design strategy' in what follows; but, as used here, design is a broader term than strategy.

In quantitative studies, where variables are central, the design and conceptual framework tend to come together. The design shows how the variables are arranged, conceptually, in relation to each other. The conceptual framework therefore also shows the structure of the proposed study. While quantitative research design tends to fall towards the tightly structured left-hand end of the structuring continuum, it varies in terms of how much the situation is contrived for research purposes, as this chapter will show.

## 5.2 Some Background

A brief sketch of some aspects of the methodological history of quantitative research can provide background both for this chapter and for Chapter 7, on quantitative data analysis.

Empirical social science research, as we know it today, began some 150 years ago.[2] The early social scientists, especially in psychology and sociology, were impressed by the progress of the natural sciences, especially physics and chemistry, and set out to imitate their use of the scientific method in building knowledge. They saw the core of the scientific method as two things: the experiment and measurement. We describe the experiment later, but its central idea involves the artificial manipulation of some treatment variable(s) for research purposes, setting up controlled comparison groups. In the simplest case, the comparison groups are alike in all respects, on all other variables, except for their differential exposure to the treatment variable. The other variables are controlled by the design. The aim is to relate the treatment variable(s) to outcome variable(s), having controlled the effects of other variables. The experiment was seen as the basis for establishing cause–effect relationships between variables, and its variables had to be measured. Thus a great deal of early social science research was characterized by experimental design and by measurement.

In the 1950s to 1960s, quantitative researchers began to broaden the scope of the experiment, partly because of its limitations. There was no questioning the logic of the experiment, but limitations to its applicability, both practical and ethical, forced this development. The logic of the experiment was extended first to quasi-experimental and then to non-experimental situations. These terms are explained in Section 5.5. This happened because many of the most important questions in social science research could not be studied by experimental design. Yet there were many examples of naturally occurring treatment groups (see Section 5.5), where the comparisons of interest were possible, but where they had not been set up specifically for research purposes.

The development was therefore to apply the principles of experimental design in these quasi-experimental situations, studying these naturally occurring treatment groups. Since these comparison groups had not been set up for research, other (extraneous) variables were not controlled in the design. Therefore, it was necessary to develop techniques for controlling extraneous variables in the analysis of data, since, with the impossibility of true experimentation, they could not be controlled in the design. In other words, what was developed was a statistical approximation to the desired experimental situation where the groups were alike in all respects, on these other variables. This was done through the statistical control of extraneous variables in data analysis, rather than through the physical control of these variables in the design. These ideas are more fully described in Sections 5.4 through 5.9. In these developments, measurement continued to be central: the introduction of more variables only accentuated the need for measurement.

These developments left two strands within the fields of quantitative design and data analysis. The first was the strand of comparison between groups, based on the experiment, and with the *t*-test and analysis of variance as its main statistical features. The second was the strand of relationships between variables, based on non-experimental reasoning, with correlation and regression as its main features. I will call this second strand the correlational survey strand.

Comparing the direction of thinking behind these two strands is interesting. The true experiment looks 'downwards' or 'forwards', as it were, from the independent variable to the dependent variable, from causes to effects. The central question here is: what is the effect of this cause? The correlational survey looks 'upwards' or 'backwards', from the dependent variable to the independent variable, from effects to causes. The central question here is: what are the causes of this effect? Because this approach takes the world as a given, studying it after things have happened, it is sometimes called *ex post facto* research – research which occurs after the fact. Mapping the variance in the dependent variable, and accounting for that variance, become central notions in this way of thinking, and they are important themes in this and the next two chapters.

The above description is most typical of applied social science areas, especially those with a sociological bias. The two strands developed in a different way in psychology, as Cronbach (1957) has pointed out. However, the end result is much the same. Cronbach called the two strands the 'experimentalists' and the 'correlationists'. The experimentalists create variation in the treatment variable, in order to study the consequences of doing that. They study how nature is put together, not through taking nature as it is, but through changing it and understanding the consequences of those changes. The correlationists, on the other hand, study the natural correlations occurring in nature. There is no manipulation to introduce changes, but rather the study of nature as it is (Shulman, 1988).

The two strands – comparison between groups, and relationships between variables – are related to each other, particularly when it comes to the analysis of data. But they are also important distinct emphases, and a convenient way to present the material of this chapter. We will deal with the experiment first, and then move to the correlational survey. This is because it is important to understand the logic of experimental design, and the developments which have flowed from it. Before that, however, we have to deal with some terminology.

## 5.3 Independent, Dependent and Control Variables

Discussing causation in Chapter 4, I pointed out that technical language avoids the use of the terms 'cause' and 'effect'. The most common terms substituted, and those that will mostly be used here, are independent variable (for cause) and dependent variable (for effect). They are not the only terms used, as shown in Table 4.1. In experimental design, common terms are also treatment variable and outcome variable, and the treatment variable is often also called the experimental variable. But independent variable and dependent variable are the most widespread terms, and apply in both the experimental and non-experimental (survey) situations. In addition to independent and dependent variables, we need now to introduce the idea of control variables.

The term 'control variable(s)' signifies a variable whose effects we want to remove or control. We want to control the variable because we suspect that it might confound, in some way, comparisons we want to make, or relationships we want to study. It is extraneous to the variables that we really want to study but, at the same time, may influence those variables, and the relationship between them (Rosenberg, 1968). Therefore we want to remove its effects. Technical synonyms for 'remove its effects' are 'partial it out' or 'control it'. In addition, the term 'covariate(s)' is often used as a synonym for control variable(s), and analysis of covariance is the most general of the techniques for controlling variables. A description of ways of controlling these extraneous variables is given later in this chapter, and in Chapter 7. For the moment, we are thinking only of the conceptual role of control variables in a research design. Now we have three general categories or types of variables:

independent variable(s) ⟶ control variable(s) (covariates) ⟶ dependent variable(s)

This shows the conceptual status of different variables in our thinking about research design. It is a general conceptual framework, showing the structure of a study in terms of these variables. The conceptual status for any variable may change from study to study, or from part to part within the one study. Thus, any particular variable may be an independent variable in one study, a dependent variable in another, and a control variable in a third. The researcher must of course make clear the conceptual status of each variable at each stage of the study.

## 5.4 The Experiment

As noted in Section 5.2, one main strand in quantitative research design is that of comparison between groups. The clearest case of this is the experiment. In research design, 'experiment' is a technical term with a precise meaning, which is made clear shortly. In discussing the logic of the experiment, we will use the simplest possible case of only two comparison groups.

The basic idea of an experiment, in social science research, is that two comparison groups are set up. Then we, as researchers, will do something (administer a treatment, or manipulate an independent variable) to one of the groups. We call that the experimental group or the treatment group. We do something different, or nothing at all, to the other group (the control group). We then compare the groups on some outcome or dependent variable. Our intention is to say that any differences we find in the outcome variable between the groups are due to (or caused by) the treatment or independent variable. In technical terms, we aim to attribute dependent or outcome variable differences between the groups to independent or treatment variable differences between the groups. This attribution is based on the important assumption that the groups are alike in all other respects. We will discuss this assumption shortly.

The experiment is based on comparisons between the groups. In the simplest case described above, the objective is to have the two groups alike in all respects, except that they receive different treatments, or differential exposure to the independent variable. We then test for differences between them in the outcome (dependent) variable. If the only difference between the groups is in the treatment they received, then, because the independent variable occurs before the dependent variable, we have the strongest possible basis for inferring that differences in the dependent variable are caused by the independent variable. This is why the experiment has traditionally been the preferred design among so many quantitative researchers, especially in psychology and applied psychology fields.

The 'alike in all respects' criterion is the important assumption referred to earlier. How can this be achieved? How can the comparison groups be set up to be identical, except for differential exposure to the independent variable? Historically, different methods have been tried for achieving this. At one time, matching was favoured, whereby there was a deliberate effort to match the group members, one by one, in terms of relevant characteristics. However, one does not need many characteristics before that turns out to be impractical. Modern experimental design favours the random assignment of participants to comparison groups, as the way of meeting the 'alike in all respects' criterion.

This solution demonstrates a fundamental principle of quantitative reasoning. Random assignment of participants to treatment (or comparison) groups does not guarantee alikeness or equality between the comparison groups. Rather, it maximizes the probability that they will not differ in any systematic way. It is an ingenious way to control for the many extraneous variables which could differ between the groups, and which therefore could invalidate conclusions about relationships between the independent and dependent variables based on comparisons between the groups. Random assignment of participants to treatment groups is a form of physical control of extraneous variables. When physical control of these variables by random assignment of participants to treatment groups is not possible, researchers will resort to the statistical control of variables. This is where true experimental design gets modified into various quasi-experimental designs. This is described in Section 5.5.

To summarize, then, we have a true experiment if there is:

* the manipulation of one or more independent variables for the purposes of the research, and
* the random assignment of participants to comparison groups.

This description gives the essential logic of the experiment, but it is only an introduction to the topic of experimental design. Because situations in the real world are so variable, and because extraneous variables can influence results in so many different ways, it has been necessary to modify and embellish this basic experimental design a great deal (see, for example, Kirk, 1995). Thus a wide variety of experimental designs have been developed, in order to ensure greater internal validity in different sorts of research situations. 'To ensure internal validity' here means to ensure better control of extraneous variables, or to eliminate rival hypotheses to the proposed causal one linking the independent and dependent variables. As a result of these developments, experimental design is a specialized topic in its own right. An important reference for the topic is the classic work by Campbell and Stanley (1963), in which they list the most common designs and the threats to the internal validity of those designs. Example 5.1 shows a number of experiments from different social science areas.

In 'Opinions and social pressure', Asch's (1955) classic experiment on compliance, male undergraduate students were recruited for a study of visual perception. Seven subjects were shown a large card with a vertical line on it and then asked to indicate which of three lines on a second card matched the original. Six of the group were accomplices of the researcher and gave false responses. The one 'real' subject was exposed to the subtle pressure of the other participants who presented a unanimous verdict.

**Example 5.1**
*Examples of experiments*

'Universals and cultural differences in the judgments of facial expressions of emotion', Ekman et al.'s (1987) study, found that people from 10 disparate societies showed considerable cross-cultural agreement in the judgement of facial expressions.

Gordon's (1992) research 'Treatment of depressed women by nurses' utilized a comparative design to test the hypothesis that traditional treatment carried out by male therapists tends to perpetuate passivity and negative self-image in women. The findings suggest that nurse-facilitated groups provide therapeutic value to moderately depressed women.

Milgram's *Obedience to Authority*, written in 1974, attempted to discover how the Holocaust could have occurred by examining the strength of social pressure to obey authority. Subjects were duped into thinking that they were administering increasingly severe electric shocks to learners in a memory experiment.

In 'Cognitive, social and physiological determinants of emotional state', Schachter and Singer (1962) tested a theory of emotion by independently manipulating autonomic arousal and situational factors to see whether they jointly determined subjects' emotions.

Sherif et al. (1961) conducted a classic field experiment, *Intergroup Conflict and Cooperation: The Robber's Cave Experiment*, in which pre-adolescent American boys were brought into a summer camp in order to control and study the relations that developed among them.

In Zimbardo et al.'s (1974) study 'The psychology of imprisonment: privation, power and pathology', volunteer male students were divided into two role-playing groups: guards and prisoners. In a simulated prison in the basement of the university building prisoners were 'deindividualized' and guards were 'militarized'.

Where it is possible to experiment, this design clearly provides the strongest basis for inferring causal relationships between variables. However, there are two problems, which severely limit the applicability of the experiment in social research. The first is practicality. It is simply not possible to investigate experimentally many of the questions of real interest and importance. Even with substantial funding, these questions remain out of reach, just on practical grounds. The second is ethics. Very often, questions of research interest are beyond the reach of the experiment, for a variety of ethical reasons.[3]

However, despite these limitations, it is often still possible to make many of the comparisons we want to make, even if they are not set in a tight experimental design. There are situations where the comparisons that we want to make (and that we would have structured into an experiment were that possible) occur naturally, in the sense of not having been set up artificially for research purposes. These are called 'naturally occurring treatment groups'. The question now arises as to how we can capitalize on these situations for research purposes. This leads us to consider first quasi-experimental and then non-experimental designs. Both involve the extension of experimental reasoning to the non-experimental situation.

## 5.5 Quasi-Experimental and Non-Experimental Design

We can summarize the essential ideas here as follows:

- In the quasi-experiment, comparisons are possible because of naturally occurring treatment groups. The naturally occurring treatment groups are fairly clear-cut, though not set up for research purposes. Therefore the experimental treatment is not controlled by the researcher, but the researcher has some control over when to measure outcome variables in relation to exposure to the independent variable. (Examples of quasi-experiments are shown in Example 5.2.)
- In the non-experiment, because the comparison groups are not at all clear-cut, the concept of naturally occurring treatment groups is broadened to naturally occurring variation in the independent variable. The researcher has little control over when to measure outcome variables in relation to exposure to the independent variable. The non-experiment is really now equivalent to the correlational survey.

---

In 'The influence of physical attractiveness and manner of dress on success in a simulated personnel decision', Bardack and McAndrew (1985) investigated the effects of physical attractiveness and appropriate dress on the decision of participants to hire someone.

**Example 5.2**
*Examples of quasi-experiments*

Campbell and Ross's classic study 'The Connecticut crackdown on speeding: time-series data in quasi-experiment analysis' (1968) used naturally occurring treatment groups. The Connecticut 'crackdown' of the 1950s was a public programme in one American state to reinforce police action to curb excessively fast driving.

---

(Continued)

In 'Comparison of feminist and non-feminist women's reactions to variants of non-sexist and feminist counseling', Enns and Hackett (1990) addressed the issue of matching client and counsellor interests along the dimension of attitudes towards feminism. The hypothesis tested was that feminist subjects would be more receptive to a radical feminist counsellor whereas non-feminist subjects would rate the non-sexist and liberal feminist counsellor more positively.

*Example 5.2 (Continued)*

Glass's (1988) 'Quasi-experiments: the case of interrupted time series' described a number of quasi-experiments utilizing time-series designs across several research areas: psychotherapy, road traffic accidents and fatalities, the stock market, self-esteem, anxiety, crime statistics and state school enrolments.

In *Experimental and Quasi-Experimental Designs for Research*, Campbell and Stanley (1963) described the formal characteristics, and the strengths and weaknesses, of 10 different types of quasi-experimental designs.

In *Big School, Small School*, Barker and Gump (1964) studied the effects of school size on the lives of high-school students and their behaviour, using samples of US schools of different sizes.

In *School Class Size*, Glass et al. (1982) reviewed studies of the effect of class size on pupil achievement, demonstrating that better learning occurs in smaller classes.

Thus there is a continuum of quantitative research designs here, where the true experiment is at the left-hand end, the non-experiment at the right-hand end, and the quasi-experiment in between. The continuum, shown in Figure 5.2, is about two things:

- The researcher's ability to control exposure to the independent variable, and therefore how clear-cut the comparison groups are. In the experiment, the researcher manipulates the independent variable, and has control over the groups' exposure to it. In the quasi-experiment and the non-experiment, the researcher has no such control.
- The researcher's ability to control when to take measurements on the dependent variable(s) in relation to exposure to the independent variable. Again, in the experiment the researcher can control this, taking dependent variable measurements at the most appropriate time. In the non-experiment, there is little opportunity to control this.

Thus, in both cases, control is high at the left-hand end of this continuum, and low at the right-hand end.

| Experiment | Quasi-experiment | Non-experiment (correlational survey) |
|---|---|---|
| • Manipulation of independent variable(s) | • Naturally occurring treatment groups | • Naturally occurring variation in independent variable(s) |
| • Random assignment to treatment groups | • Statistical control of covariate(s) | • Statistical control of covariate(s) |

**Figure 5.2**   *Continuum of quantitative research designs*

We want to take advantage of these naturally occurring treatment groups in a research situation. They provide the comparisons we want. But there is a logical difficulty in doing this, a clear threat to internal validity. It relates to the 'alike in all respects' criterion of the experiment. We may well find exactly the comparisons we want in naturally occurring treatment groups, and we can certainly make the comparisons between these groups with respect to one or more outcome variables. But how can we be sure that there are not other differences between these naturally occurring comparison groups, over and above their differential exposure to the independent variable – differences that may themselves be responsible for any differences between the groups on outcome variables? We have not been able to assign people randomly to these groups, to control variables physically, through the design. Therefore there is the real possibility of extraneous variable influences – of systematic differences between the groups on factors relevant to the outcome variable.

The strategy to deal with this problem is to remove the influence of such possible extraneous variables by identifying them, measuring them, and extracting their effects statistically. We control them statistically, in the analysis, using the rationale shown in Chapter 7. Logically, controlling variables in this way achieves a statistical approximation to the desired physical situation of the experiment, where the comparison groups are alike in all respects except for their differential exposure to the independent variable. These extraneous factors become the control variables, or the covariates mentioned earlier. A covariate is thus an extraneous variable which is likely to be related to the outcome variable, and to differ between the comparison groups. The analysis of covariance (ANCOVA) is the technical name given to statistical techniques for controlling covariates. Control variable analysis is the more general term for the statistical control of extraneous variables.

Control variable analysis, and covariance analysis in particular, represent an important and widely used quantitative research design strategy. Such analysis applies when there are one or more extraneous variables whose effects we want to remove, in order to get a clearer picture of relationships between independent and dependent variables. All control variables have to be identified and measured before the implementation of the treatment(s). We cannot control a variable, or covary out its effects, during the analysis of data unless we have measurements on that variable. And we won't have measurements on it unless we have anticipated its possible effects, and designed its measurement into the study. This is another example of the benefits of the careful question development work recommended in Chapters 3 and 4.

Random assignment of subjects to treatment groups, as in the true experiment, is the strongest design for demonstrating causality. But, given the great difficulty of doing this in real-world research, control variable analysis in general and covariance analysis in particular are valuable in many research situations. Covariance analysis is therefore a major concept in quantitative design and analysis. It will come up again in Chapter 7, but its essential idea can be expressed in a few sentences:

> To covary out one or more variables from a comparison between groups is to reach a statistical approximation to the (desired) physical situation where the groups are the same on the covariate(s). If they are the same on the covariates, the covariates cannot be responsible for differences on the outcome variables. Therefore outcome variable differences are more likely to be due to independent variable differences.

I have put this in terms of comparison between groups, in order to see it clearly. It applies just as well in studying relationships between variables. This is taken up again in Section 5.9 on the physical and statistical control of variables.

What sorts of variables should be seen as covariates? As always, logical considerations prevail. Following the above description, a variable should be controlled or covaried out if it:

- is known or suspected to differ between the comparison groups, and
- is related to either the independent variable or, more likely, the dependent variable.

As Chapter 7 will show, the logic of the statistical technique of covariance analysis is to extract from the dependent variable the variance it holds in common with the covariate(s), and then to see if the remaining variance in the dependent variable is related to the independent variable. Thus, covariance analysis, like everything else in quantitative design and analysis, works on relationships between variables. It is time now to deal directly with this theme.

This means we move from the first main strand in quantitative design (comparison between groups) to the second main strand (relationships between variables).

## 5.6 Relationships between Variables: the Correlational Survey

In the quasi-experiment, treatment groups are reasonably clear-cut. In the non-experiment, we move from the concept of discrete comparison groups to the broader concept of naturally occurring variation in the independent variable. That is, instead of talking about separate comparison groups who differ on some variable of interest, we are now talking about a whole range of differences on that same variable. Discrete comparison groups, whether two or more, are simply a special case of this more general situation.[4] I will now use the term 'correlational survey' instead of 'non-experiment' for this research design.

The word 'survey' has different meanings. It is sometimes used to describe any research which collects data (quantitative or qualitative) from a sample of people. Another meaning, common in everyday language, is a simple descriptive study, usually concerned with different pieces of information, which are studied one piece at a time. Variables as such may not be involved, and continuous variables, as will be described in Chapter 6, are unlikely. This is sometimes called a 'status survey' or a 'normative survey' or a 'descriptive survey', and its purpose is mainly to describe some sample in terms of simple proportions and percentages of people who respond in this way or that to different questions. Such surveys are common today, especially in market research and political research.[5]

The term 'correlational survey' is used here to stress the study of relationships between variables; some of these surveys are shown in Example 5.3. Those relationships are often studied using conceptual frameworks similar to those used in experimental design. Thus, in this sort of survey, we will conceptualize variables as independent, control (or covariate) and dependent, as shown earlier. This illustrates the point already made: the logic behind correlational surveys is based on the logic behind experimental design. Because we can only rarely experiment, research methodologists have applied the principles of experimental reasoning to the non-experimental research situation, developing logically equivalent non-experimental designs for those situations where variation occurs in the independent variables of interest, but where it is not possible to manipulate or control that variation for research purposes.[6] For this reason, it is important for researchers to understand the basic principles of experimental design, even if they are unlikely to design experiments.

Bean and Creswell's (1980) study 'Student attrition among women at a liberal arts college' investigated factors affecting student dropout rates at a small religious coeducational liberal arts college in a Midwestern American city.

Example 5.3
*Examples of surveys*

Blau and Duncan's (1967) influential book *The American Occupational Structure* looked at the movement from 'particularism' and 'ascription' to 'universalism' and 'achievement' by surveying occupational mobility in American society. The book included considerable material on the role of education in the intergenerational transmission of inequality. This was one of the first studies to use path analysis.

*Equality of Educational Opportunity* (Coleman et al., 1966) undertook the most comprehensive survey of the US school system, focusing mainly on the relationship between school characteristics and student achievement. Using a series of regression analyses, it produced the finding that school characteristics had little effect on student achievement. This led to the controversial conclusion that family background was more important than school characteristics in explaining differential achievement.

DeCasper's (1988) 'Use of the Georgia eighth grade criterion-referenced test: reports by ninth grade teachers' surveyed a representative sample of ninth-grade teachers in the state schools of Georgia. Information was sought about teachers' use of and opinions on test results provided by the state department of education.

De Vaus and McAllister (1987) explored, in 'Gender differences in religion: a test of structural location theory', the observation in the sociology of religion literature that on whatever measure is used, women seem to be more religious than men. While the descriptive data show this, no-one has explained empirically why this is so. Hence the research questions investigated were: why are women more religious than men? And does gender have a sociological basis?

Peaker (1971) in his report *The Plowden Children Four Years Later* described a follow-up national survey of 3000 school age children in the United Kingdom. Combined evidence from home and school from 1964 and 1968 is analysed and displayed.

*Fifteen Thousand Hours: Secondary Schools and their Effects on Children* (Rutter et al., 1979) is a large-scale study of 12 London secondary schools carried out over a three-year period. The study investigated whether schools and teachers have any effect on the development of children in their care.

The aim of the survey 'The consumption sector debate and housing mobility' (Savage et al., 1990) was to examine the satisfaction of public housing tenants with a range of services provided by a local authority in south-east England. The hypothesis tested was that mobility of public sector housing was associated with labour market position.

We will now look at the quantitative design strand of relationships between variables, and see how that can be developed into a research design strategy of accounting for variance.

## 5.7 Relationships between Variables: Causation and Accounting for Variance

To say that two variables are related is to say that they vary together, or covary, or share common variance. What variance means, and the different ways in which variables can vary together, will be explored in Chapter 7, but the essential idea of covariance is that the variables hold some of their variance in common. When two variables hold some of their variance in common, we can use the concept of accounting for variance and say that one variable accounts for (some of the) variance in the other. We can also say that one variable explains some of the variance in another, but accounting for variance is the more common description.

In Chapter 4, we took a brief philosophical look at the concept of causation, single and multiple. We saw how important that concept is in science, since we want to find the cause(s) of events or effects. But we saw that we cannot do this directly, because of the metaphysical element in the concept of causation. Therefore we may start with ideas of causation in mind, but we need to 'translate' those ideas to make them suitable for empirical research, rephrasing our research questions to replace causal language.

One way to do that is to change questions of the form 'What causes $Y$?' into 'What causes $Y$ to vary?' and then into 'How can we account for variance in $Y$?' The first rephrasing introduces the term 'vary'. To vary means to show differences, so now we are looking for and focusing on differences in $Y$, on variance in $Y$. This is important: our strategy of inquiry in order to learn about $Y$ is to look for variance in $Y$, for differences in $Y$. This simple conceptual step is fundamental to a great deal of empirical inquiry, and underlines the key importance of the concept of variance in research. This same point comes up again in different ways in measurement in Chapter 6 (see especially Section 6.8) and in data analysis in Chapter 7 (see Section 6.4). Now we almost have a form of the question that we can operationalize, but we still have to get rid of the troublesome word 'cause'. So we rephrase a second time, and now the question is in terms of accounting for variance.

Thus accounting for variance becomes a crucial step in the way we proceed in empirical research, especially *ex post facto* research.[7] Since variance means differences, this is why it is often said that the scientific method works on differences. A main strategy of science is to find out how something varies, and then to account for that variance. The idea of learning about a phenomenon by studying its variation and accounting for that variation applies also in qualitative research, as can be seen in some approaches to the analysis of qualitative data, and especially in grounded theory. These matters are taken up in Chapter 10.

Returning to quantitative research, we now have a research strategy we can operationalize. This is because, if two variables are related, one can be said to account for variance in the other. This is the crux of the matter. The way we account for variance in a dependent variable is to find the independent variables to which it is related.

As pointed out in Chapter 4, we have moved well past simple one-variable causation, accepting the idea of multiple causation for any particular dependent variable. This is the commonly occurring design shown in the top right-hand cell of Table 4.2. We accept that several (maybe many) factors will be necessary to give us a full causal picture for that dependent variable. In the language of this chapter, we have several independent variables and one dependent variable. If we can account for something close to 100% of the variance in our dependent variable with a particular set of independent variables, and if we know the importance of each of the independent variables in accounting for that dependent variable variance, then we understand the dependent variable very well – how it varies and how to account for that variance. Just as important, we would also have clear indications about which independent variables to concentrate on, in order to bring about changes in the dependent variable.

Multiple linear regression (MLR) is a research design which addresses these issues directly – which tells us how much of the variance in a dependent variable is accounted for by any group of independent variables, and which also tells us how important each independent variable is in accounting for that variance. In this chapter, we look at MLR as a general design strategy. In Chapter 7, we look at MLR as a general data analysis strategy.

## 5.8 Multiple Linear Regression as a General Design Strategy

Multiple linear regression (MLR) is basically a statistical technique for the analysis of data, but here I want to consider it as a design strategy, as a way of conceptualizing and organizing quantitative research. It fits situations where we want to focus on a dependent variable, and to study its relationship with a number of independent variables. Regression analysis is important because we want to do that sort of investigation very often. The conceptual framework is shown in Figure 5.3, and covariates may or may not be included. Of course, the conceptual framework is not limited to four independent variables. The general objective in the research is to account for variance in the dependent variable, and to see how the different independent variables, separately or in combination, contribute to accounting for that variance.

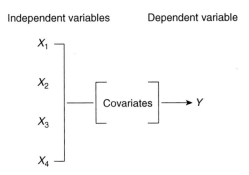

**Figure 5.3**   *Conceptual framework for multiple linear regression*

With MLR we can:

- Estimate how much of the variance in a phenomenon we can account for using a particular set of independent variables. When most of the variance is accounted for, we are well on the way to understanding the dependent variable. Conversely, if only a small proportion of the variance is accounted for, we still have a long way to go in understanding it.
- Determine the effects of the different independent variables on the dependent variable, by estimating the unique variance each independent variable accounts for. We can say which independent variables are of most and least importance in accounting for variance in the dependent variable, and therefore in bringing about change in the dependent variable. This is important knowledge when it comes to recommending strategies for changing the dependent variable.

Many quantitative research problems fit into this design, and many other studies can be designed in this way. Whenever a researcher is interested in relationships between variables, a regression analysis design can be used. There are also benefits to thinking this way about an overall research area. When (as often) the focus is on some major dependent variable, MLR provides a coordinated overall approach to the topic, as well as a ready-made conceptual framework and design. The requirements are that the researcher must be able to specify, define and measure the independent variables, in addition of course to the dependent variable.

Sometimes, the focus in research may be more on a detailed study of the relationship between variables than on accounting for variance. That is a strategic decision to be made in planning the research, but it is also a matter of emphasis in how we think about the question, since these are two sides of the same coin. We account for variance by studying relationships with other variables. Therefore, even when the focus is on relationships, we do well to use a regression analysis design, for two reasons: all aspects of the relationship can be studied within that design, as noted in Chapter 7; and knowing how much variance we can account for gives us a strong indication of how important the relationship is.

To sum up, the conceptual framework which goes with MLR is useful because it addresses directly questions of key substantive significance. It deals with central questions of interest, those which derive directly from causation. It also has two other advantages. First, it is flexible, in being able to accommodate different conceptual arrangements among the independent variables, including their joint effects on a dependent variable. This applies particularly to covariance analysis, interaction effects, and non-linearity. As Chapter 7 will show, these are three important areas of research interest. Second, it is not a difficult approach to understand, conceptually or operationally. In this chapter, we have been stressing its relevance to designing research in a particular area, and noting that it comes with a ready-made set of research questions and a conceptual framework. That is why it is described here as a general design strategy. In Chapter 7, we look at MLR as a general data analysis strategy.

## 5.9 Controlling Variables

The term 'control' has already come up a number of times and it is another central concept in research design. As noted, it is extraneous variables we want to control – variables which may either confound the relationship we want to study or cause spurious interpretations of that relationship. To control such a variable means to remove its effects, or not to let it have any influence. There are two general ways variables are controlled in research – physical ways and statistical ways. In physical control, variables are controlled in the design. In statistical control, variables are controlled in the analysis of data. We will discuss each, in turn, and they are summarized in Table 5.1. Physical control is characteristic of experimental designs, whereas statistical control is more characteristic of correlational survey designs.

Physical control means that the variable is actually physically controlled, in the design of the study. There are three types of physical control. First, in *randomization*, a variable can be controlled by having it vary randomly, or non-systematically. The logic here is that the variable can have no systematic effect if it does not vary in a systematic way. Its effects will cancel each other out, because its variance is random. This idea is used when people are randomly assigned to treatment groups in an experiment. As pointed out, this does not guarantee that the treatment groups will not differ from each other. Rather, it maximizes the probability that they will not differ in any systematic way.

Second, in *restriction*, a variable is controlled by physically restricting its variance and holding it constant in a study. Holding it constant means it has no

**Table 5.1**  *Strategies for controlling variables*

| In the design | In the analysis |
| --- | --- |
| Randomization | Stratification |
| Restriction | Partial correlation |
| Matching | Analysis of covariance |

variance in this piece of research. If it has no variance, it cannot have any covariance with other variables. This is the same as saying that it cannot show any relationship with other variables in the study, and therefore can have no effect on them. This second form of physical control is done in sample design and selection. For example, if gender was thought to be a possible extraneous or confounding factor in a study, one strategy would be to include in the study only either males or females. Because there is no variance in gender, it is controlled. The gain is clear: if only one sex group is included, then gender cannot be a factor in the relationships between other variables. But the loss is clear too: if only males are included, the study can have nothing to say about females (or vice versa). This sort of trade-off occurs frequently in research. In this case, a more complete answer might be possible. Both sexes could be included, and then the sample could be partitioned into sex groups during the analysis of the data. This would achieve both control of gender and generalizability to both sex groups. It also shifts control of the variable from physical to statistical.

Third, in *matching*, group members are matched, one by one, on relevant characteristics. The problem, as noted, is that this quickly becomes impractical as the number of characteristics increases.

Statistical control means that the variable is controlled not in the design, but rather in the analysis of the data. The facility for statistical control has to be designed into the study, in the sense that the variable to be controlled has to be measured. The logic of statistical control is that the analysis achieves a statistical approximation to the desired (but unattainable) physical situation where the comparison groups are the same on the control variable. There are three types of statistical control:

* stratification, or test factor elaboration (Rosenberg, 1968), where the control variable, the test factor, is partitioned, and the analysis into the relationship between variables is conducted within each level of the control variable, as described in the case of gender above
* partial correlation, where the variable to be controlled is partialled out of the relationship between the other two variables; this is a suitable technique when all variables are continuous, and is discussed in Chapter 7
* the analysis of covariance, where the control variable (the covariate) is extracted or covaried out first, before the mainstream analysis is done.

The third of these ways, covariance analysis, has been described already, and is covered in more detail in Chapter 7, where it is incorporated into the MLR approach to data analysis. This third way is stressed here because it reflects the situation described in Sections 5.7 and 5.8 – the very common situation in research where there are several independent variables, one or more control variables, and a dependent variable. While analysis of covariance is stressed, these three methods are logically equivalent to each other, in the sense that they are all designed to achieve the same thing – controlling the effects of unwanted or extraneous variables. To control an extraneous variable is also logically equivalent to eliminating alternative or rival hypotheses.

---

### 5.10   REVIEW CONCEPTS

Quantitative research:
- reality as variables
- measure the variables
- study relationships between the variables

Research design
data collected and analysed:
- following what strategy?
- within what framework?
- from whom?
- how?

Main quantitative designs:
- experiments
- quasi-experiments
- correlational surveys (non-experiments)

Comparisons between groups:
- *t*-test
- analysis of variance (ANOVA)

Relationships between variables:
- correlation
- regression

Independent variable(s):   cause(s)
Dependent variable(s):   effect(s)
Control variable(s):   covariate(s)

Experiment:
- manipulation of independent variable
- random assignment of participants to treatment groups

Quasi-experiment:
- naturally occurring treatment groups
- statistical control of covariate(s)

Non-experiment (correlational survey):
- naturally occurring variation in independent variable
- statistical control of covariate(s)

## 5.10 REVIEW CONCEPTS (CONTINUED)

Surveys:
- status, normative, descriptive
- correlational
- longitudinal

Variance:
- covariance
- correlation
- accounting for variance
- from causation to accounting for variance

Multiple linear regression

Controlling variables:
- physical control (randomization, restriction, matching)
- statistical control (stratification, partial correlation, analysis of covariance)

## NOTES

1 It is easier in quantitative than in qualitative research to separate the strategy and framework parts of design (the first two questions) from the data collection and analysis parts (the second two questions). We will see this again in Chapter 8.
2 With the exception of economics, which has a much longer history.
3 Shulman (1988: 16) shows that the experiment is even less possible today, on ethical grounds, than it was a generation ago.
4 This conceptual move, from discrete comparison groups to a continuum of variation, is actually an important and recurring theme in quantitative research. It comes up again in the discussion of measurement in Chapter 6.
5 The data for such surveys might be collected by interviewing (structured or unstructured), giving rise to the term 'survey interview'.
6 Both simple descriptive surveys and correlational surveys are cross-sectional, with data collected from people at one point in time. Cross-sectional surveys need to be distinguished from longitudinal surveys, in which data are collected from people at different points over a period of time. Longitudinal research is an important specialized area: see Menard (1991).
7 This is the 'looking backwards' strategy noted in Section 5.2, in situations where we cannot experiment.

## *Further Reading*

Babbie, E. (1990) *Survey Research Methods.* 2nd edn. Belmont, CA: Wadsworth.

Blalock, H.M. (1969) *Theory Construction: From Verbal to Mathematical Formulations.* Englewood Cliffs, NJ: Prentice-Hall.

Brown, S.R. and Melamed, L. (1990) *Experimental Design and Analysis.* Newbury Park, CA: Sage.

Campbell, D.T. and Stanley J.C. (1963) *Experimental and Quasi-Experimental Designs for Research*. Chicago: Rand McNally.

Cook, T.D. and Campbell, D.T. (1979) *Quasi-Experimentation: Design and Analysis Issues for Field Settings*. Chicago: Rand McNally.

Creswell, J.W. (1994) *Research Design: Qualitative and Quantitative Approaches*. Thousand Oaks, CA: Sage.

de Vaus, D.A. (1991) *Surveys in Social Research*. 3rd edn. London: UCL Press.

Fowler, F.J. (1988) *Survey Research Methods*. Newbury Park, CA: Sage.

Keppel, G. (1991) *Design and Analysis: A Researcher's Handbook*. 3rd edn. Englewood Cliffs, NJ: Prentice-Hall.

Kerlinger, F.N. (1973) *Foundations of Behavioural Research*. New York: Holt, Rinehart and Winston.

Marsh, C. (1982) *The Survey Method: The Contribution of Surveys to Sociological Explanation*. London: Allen and Unwin.

Sapsford, R. and Jupp, V. (1996) 'Validating evidence', in R. Sapsford and V. Jupp (eds), *Data Collection and Analysis*. London: Sage. pp. 1–24.

# 6
# Collecting Quantitative Data

Quantitative data are in the form of numbers, and measurement is the process by which data are turned into numbers. This chapter describes the main ideas in measurement, and the application of those ideas in research situations. It was pointed out in Chapter 4 that data about the world do not occur naturally in the form of numbers, that measuring something involves imposing a structure on it, and that there is a choice in research about whether to structure data quantitatively or not. This chapter therefore includes some comments on the general question of when measurement is appropriate in social science research. To simplify, the discussion throughout this chapter assumes that we are measuring the characteristics (or traits) of people. It generalizes to measuring the characteristics of things or events, instead of people.

## 6.1 Types of Variables

Variables can be classified in several ways. One fundamental way is to distinguish between discrete and continuous variables.

*Discrete variables* (also called categorical variables and discontinuous variables) vary in kind rather than in degree, amount or quantity. Examples include eye colour, gender, religious affiliation, occupation, and most kinds of treatments or methods. Thus, if an educational researcher wants to compare computerized and non-computerized classrooms, the discrete variable involved is the presence or absence of computers (Wallen and Fraenkel, 1991). For a discrete variable, the variance is between different categories, and there is no idea of a continuum or scale involved. People are classified into mutually exclusive categories, of which there may be any number. A dichotomous variable has two categories, a trichotomous variable has three, and so on.

*Continuous variables* (also called measured variables) vary in degree, level or quantity, rather than in categories. With differences in degree, we have first rank ordering, and then placing on a continuum.[1] Ordering people into ranks means identifying the first, second, third and so on among them, according to some criterion, but it does not tell us how far apart the rankings are. Introducing an interval of measurement tells us that, and lifts the level of measurement from ordinal to interval. When this is done, the variable is continuous: we have a continuum, with intervals, showing less and more of the characteristic. Examples of such differences in degree are height, weight and age. As another example, we can assign numbers to students to indicate how much interest they have in a subject, with 5 indicating a great deal, 4 indicating quite a lot, and so on. In this case, we have constructed a continuous variable 'degree of interest' (Wallen and Fraenkel, 1991).

This distinction between discrete and continuous variables is important, and is discussed in many places in the literature, usually in the context of levels of measurement (see, for example, Kerlinger, 1973).[2] It has historical significance and also practical significance, particularly in influencing how quantitative data are analysed. Because of this, we need to know always what sort of a variable we are dealing with.

Both types of variable are common in research. Sometimes there is no difficulty (or choice) in which type is involved, as when a variable has only categories and no continuum. Sometimes, however, the researcher has a choice as to how a particular variable will be used. Here, the question is whether to use discrete categories or a measured continuum to make the desired comparisons. The historical development, which had important consequences, was to prefer the measured continuum rather than discrete categories, wherever possible. We express the same preference when we use 'varying shades of grey' to describe something, rather than using simply 'black versus white'.

To see something in discrete categories is to sharpen the comparisons, which is sometimes what we want. On the other hand, seeing that thing as a measured continuum is more flexible, which is also sometimes what we want. We saw an example of this same shift in the case of research design, when we moved from comparison between groups to relationships between variables.

We will see the same shift again in the analysis of quantitative data. One implication now is that, while differences in degree can always be turned into differences in kind (as when we convert a set of continuous educational achievement scores into dichotomous comparison groups such as 'pass' or 'fail'), we often do better in research to retain them as differences in degree. We preserve information that way, which is valuable as long as the information is reliable. While each research situation should be assessed on its merits, a useful point to keep in mind is that continua or scales, rather than simple dichotomies or trichotomies, provide more information.[3]

## 6.2 The Process of Measurement

Measurement can be seen as the process of using numbers to link concepts to indicators, when a continuum is involved.[4] We can illustrate this process using the measurement of self-esteem as described by Rosenberg (1979), and summarized by Zeller (1997: 823–4) in three tasks:

1   *Defining self-esteem.* Rosenberg (1979: 54) defines self-esteem as a positive or negative orientation toward oneself. An individual of low self-esteem 'lacks respect for himself, considers himself unworthy, inadequate, or otherwise seriously deficient as a person'. On the other hand, persons of high self-esteem consider themselves to be persons of worth. High self-esteem carries no connotations of 'feelings of superiority, arrogance, conceit, contempt for others, overweening pride'.
2   *Selecting measures of self-esteem.* That is, selecting indicators to provide empirical representations of the concept. Having defined self-esteem theoretically, Rosenberg (1979: 291) then constructs indicators that he considers measure the concept. The indicators are statements about oneself, and subjects respond to these indicators by expressing strong agreement, agreement, disagreement, or strong disagreement. Some indicators are written with a positive description of self: 'On the whole, I am satisfied with myself', and 'I feel that I'm a person of worth, at least on an equal plane with others.' Other indicators are written with a negative description of self: 'I feel I do not have much to be proud of', and 'I wish I could have more respect for myself.' Rosenberg constructed five positive and five negative indicators of self-esteem.
3   *Obtaining empirical information for those indicators.* Rosenberg then obtains data for these indicators by asking adolescents to respond to each indicator in terms of the response categories.

A fourth task involves evaluating the validity of the indicators, assessing to what extent the indicators represent the concept of self-esteem empirically. We discuss validity in Section 6.8.

This view of the process shows that we actually construct a variable when measuring it, and anticipates the question of validity, which involves the inference from indicators to concepts. This description of measurement also helps in clarifying the question of when measurement is appropriate in social research. That question is important because measurement has been at the centre of debates between quantitative and qualitative researchers, and because beginning researchers are sometimes puzzled about whether a study should be done quantitatively or qualitatively. Keeping this view of measurement in mind, I suggest the following ideas as a guide to thinking about when measurement might be appropriate:

- We have in mind a characteristic or construct or trait of some sort, which we can define unidimensionally (or in terms of its unidimensional components).[5]
- We envisage a continuum with greater and lesser amounts of this trait, giving different locations along the unidimensional continuum, based on different quantities of the trait.
- We can find reliable ways of identifying the different locations along the continuum: that is, we can identify the indicators which will provide empirical representation of those locations. Then we can assign numbers to these locations to calibrate the continuum.
- We believe that the trait shows observable regularities, and that it is reasonably stable over time – or, if it varies, it varies in a systematic instead of a random way. To put it another way, we do not think the trait we want to measure is in a constant state of change (or of 'becoming').

If these ideas apply, we have a situation where we can construct a measure of the trait. Given situations where we *Can* measure, when in research *Should* we measure, and when not? The approach taken in this book is that we need to assess each research situation and make a considered decision, case by case.

On the one hand, making comparisons is essential to research, and measurement is a way of making comparisons systematically, formalizing and standardizing those comparisons. We can therefore consider measuring whenever we want to make systematic comparisons, and whenever the conditions shown above apply. Recognizing that this can occur very often in research, including in qualitative research, enables measuring instruments to be employed alongside qualitative data in appropriate situations.

On the other hand, however, the advantages we might gain through measurement need to be weighed against possible disadvantages. For example, there may be paradigm objections to measurement, in a particular piece of research, whereby the researcher may reject the assumptions on which measurement is based – and especially the assumption that the reality to be studied can be conceptualized as variables and measured. This is a complicated matter, and full discussion of it is beyond the scope of this book.

Second, measurement involves the disentangling and some simplification of concepts. To see complex phenomena as unidimensional variables is to disentangle and simplify. There are some research situations where we would not want to do that – where, on the contrary, we want a more holistic approach to the phenomenon. The implication of this is that we often cannot get the full picture about something just by measuring it. However, we can often get part of the picture, and often a very valuable part, by measuring aspects of it. In these situations, it is not appropriate that measurement should be the only tool for collecting data. It suggests again the complementarity of quantitative and qualitative data, combining the measurement data with more holistic qualitative data.

Third, the nature of the reality being studied, and the approach being taken to it, may not make it appropriate to measure. This may be particularly true of some aspects of social reality. It was mentioned above that the reality being measured is seen as stable, rather than in a constant state of becoming. However, seeing social reality as in a constant state of becoming (and never of 'being') is exactly the view that is central to some qualitative perspectives. These perspectives stress the social construction of reality and its constantly negotiated and renegotiated meanings (for example, Berger and Luckman, 1967). If the research wants to focus on those aspects, measurement is not a good tool. Measurement involves a snapshot, taken at one point in time. This does not fit well if process and constant change are the focus in the research. However, here again complementary approaches may be valuable. The one-point-in-time still photograph can provide a good background against which to look at the situation's more dynamic and processual aspects.

Fourth, measurement necessarily involves imposing a numerical structure on the data. To design the research in terms of measurement is to use researcher-imposed constructs, rather than constructs which might emerge from the people being studied. The extent to which this is a problem depends on the purposes of the research, but here again, combining approaches might make sense. As a first step, people's own constructs can be elicited. Then measurements for them can be constructed, to take advantage of the comparisons that measurement permits.

These are some of the points which arise when considering the use of measurement in research. We should also note the distinction between established measuring instruments, on the one hand, and shorter *ad hoc* researcher-constructed measures (rating scales: Andrich, 1997), on the other. There is a role for both. The former would normally only be used in a highly quantitative context, and most likely when relatively complex variables are seen as the main focus of the research. These established instruments are discussed in Sections 6.5 and 6.7. The latter (the rating scales) might well have a role in any research situation, including a qualitative one. They are discussed in the section on survey questionnaire construction, later in this chapter. In some projects, full-scale measurement might not be appropriate, but the use of rating scales might well be.

## 6.3 Latent Traits

In social and psychological measurement the characteristic or trait that we want to measure is not directly observable. It is hidden, or latent. We can only measure something which cannot be observed by inference from what can be observed.

The basic idea of latent trait theory is that, while the trait itself is not observable, its interaction with the environment produces surface-level, observable indicators (often called 'items') which can be used to infer the presence or absence of the trait – or, more accurately, to infer the level or degree of the trait which is present. A measuring instrument can therefore be constructed using these items as the basis for making an inference about the unobservable trait. There is, theoretically, an infinite set of these observable indicators. In order to provide a stable inference, the measuring instrument needs to have a reasonable sample of them. To put it more formally, the measuring instrument samples from among this theoretically infinite set of observable indicators to produce a set of items from which a reliable inference can be made to the unobservable trait beneath. This is the essential idea of latent trait measurement, and it is shown in Figure 6.1. It explains why there are many items, instead of just one, on a typical social-psychological measuring instrument. Clearly one item is not enough to provide a stable inference. In fact, the more items the better, within reason.

We should note three things about latent trait measurement. First, it requires that we define the trait, and specify the indicators from which we will make the inference, showing the relationship of these indicators to the trait. This points again to the question of measurement validity, to be discussed in Section 6.8. Second, we will use multiple indicators or items, on the grounds that the more indicators we have the better the inference we can make. We will then need somehow to aggregate the responses to these multiple items. In practical terms, we will need to add up the responses. This raises the issue of adding like with like, making sure that the items whose responses we add up are measuring aspects of the same thing.[6] Third, the different items are interchangeable, in the sense of being equally good indicators of the trait. In

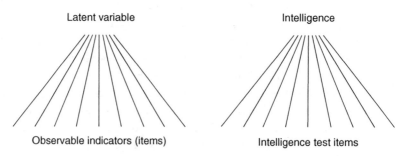

**Figure 6.1**   *Latent trait measurement*

Chapter 10, we will see the similarity between these ideas and grounded theory analysis in qualitative research.

## 6.4 Measuring Techniques

We can look at some basic ideas involved in measuring techniques by reviewing the scaling of attitudes as an example. Measuring attitudes emerged as an important research area in social science in the 1920s and 1930s, and has continued to attract research attention. The size of this research effort means that attempts have been made to measure almost anything one can think of, in the way of social and psychological variables. That does not mean that all attempts have been equally successful, and each has to be reviewed critically before being adopted in research. But it does mean that we should keep this point in mind when we are planning research. We return to this point in Section 6.7.

Three of the main names in this brief history of attitude scaling are Thurstone, Guttman and Likert. They took different approaches to the scaling of attitudes, but their central ideas can be briefly summarized.[7]

Thurstone's technique was called the 'equal appearing interval scale'. Recognizing that different attitude items fall at different points along a unidimensional attitude continuum, he devised a method of calculating the scale value of each attitude item, and then used those scale values to scale people with respect to the attitude. Guttman similarly saw the different attitude content of different items, but used this information in a different way. He proposed a form of scaling whereby the ordering of items according to their attitude content could be used, in conjunction with a dichotomous response format, to determine the location of people along the attitude continuum. This method came to be called 'cumulative scaling'. Some years later, Likert proposed a simpler format, whereby a respondent would respond to each item according to a simple response scale, rather than a dichotomy, and responses to the items could be summed. This method is called the 'method of summated ratings', or, more commonly, the 'Likert method'.

Studies comparing these three methods seemed to indicate that they produced similar results (Edwards, 1957). This being so, the simpler procedures of Likert came, over time, to be preferred. As a result, the Likert summated rating procedure is widely used in social research today, and is the form of scaling most often seen on questionnaires and instruments used in research. However, the gains in ease of construction and administration in moving from Thurstone and Guttman to Likert come at a cost. Thurstone and Guttman recognized that different statements, or items, carry different amounts of the attitude being measured. This is the idea of the scale value of the item. They developed ways to formalize and make use of this property in their procedures. With Likert, the scale value of the item has disappeared. Important recent work has been done on this point, bringing together the methods of attitude scaling, and calibrating both people and items onto the same scale of interest. This is Rasch measurement, a specialized development beyond the scope of this book (Andrich, 1988).

The basic ideas involved in measurement can now be made more concrete by considering the steps to use in constructing a measuring instrument for use in research. This discussion is directed towards the measurement of major variables. What is said can be adjusted as required for use with shorter *ad hoc* rating scales.

## 6.5 Steps in Constructing a Measuring Instrument

This section outlines a general set of steps by which a measuring instrument can be constructed, based on the description of measurement just given. The question of using an already existing measuring instrument, or constructing one specifically for a project, is discussed in Section 6.6.

For simplicity, let us assume that we are measuring some attitude-type variable. If we are constructing a descriptive, fact-gathering questionnaire, we have a simpler task, though it is along these same general lines: Section 6.9 deals with that. We may of course be combining the two – some fact-gathering and some attitude-type scaling. We can describe the construction of a measuring instrument under six main steps:

1. The first step is a definitional one. We must define clearly what we are setting out to measure. In technical terms, we need to produce a conceptual definition of the variable. The measuring instrument will then become its operational definition.
2. Next, we select a measuring technique. There are several possibilities here, but most likely some type of Likert response format will be used. The actual words to be used in the scaled item responses will depend on the subject matter we are dealing with, and may require some pilot testing.[8]
3. Items now need to be generated: how many, and where do they come from? Since latent traits are involved, the draft form of the scale will need many items – as many as can be practically administered in a pilot test. When it comes to the final length of the scale, practical considerations will be important, especially the question of how many items respondents can deal with. Within reason, there should be as many items for each dimension as respondents can respond to validly. The items can come from anywhere at all: from analysis of the definition, from discussion and reading, from the literature, or from other measures.
4. We now have a draft form of the measure. It is a good idea to go through this with a small group of people (say five or six) who are typical of the people we want to measure. We go through the items and the procedures for answering the questionnaire, and have them discuss each item. This enables us to see what meaning they give to each item, and to compare this with the

meaning we had in mind when we generated the item. We also want to see to what extent they are easily able to respond to each item. During this stage, we are interested not so much in their actual responses as in their interpretations, and whether they can easily respond to each item. A good item is (among other things) one people can respond to easily, and with conviction. One characteristic of a poor item is that people have difficulty placing their response on the scale. This step will often produce numerous modifications, and will likely show us things we had not thought of.

5    We pretest this modified second-draft scale more formally now, with a group of 25 or so typical respondents, and analyse their responses in the light of the criteria in Section 6.8.

6    We then modify and reduce the scale in the light of the results of this analysis, selecting the best items for each dimension.[9]

The sixth step may or may not finalize the scale. If necessary, therefore, we repeat steps 5 and 6 until a satisfactory final version is available. This description shows that considerable detailed work is involved in achieving good measurement. For this reason, the decision whether to construct a measuring instrument or to use an already existing one is important.

## 6.6 To Construct an Instrument or to Use an Existing Instrument?

This is a common question in research: should we use an already existing research instrument, or should we construct our own? No blanket rules apply, and we have to assess each case, but we can make some general comments. Of course, we will assume that the measure we have located is a good one, in terms of the criteria to be discussed in Section 6.8.

First, as noted, good measurement is achievable, but considerable development work is involved. If the variable is complex and multidimensional, the amount of work is increased. The more complex the variable, the more work, time and resources are required to achieve good measurement. This is an argument for using what already exists. A second argument for using what already exists is that the more an instrument is used in research, the more we learn about its properties. If the variable involved is a central variable in an area, this is an important consideration. A third argument is that research results from different studies are more easily compared, and integrated and synthesized, if the same measuring instrument for a central variable has been used.

However, as a fourth point, we need to think about the construct validity of the instrument, in relation to the study we are proposing. Any measuring instrument represents one operational definition of a variable, and operational definitions differ, just as measuring instruments do. In any particular study, it may be that the operational version in the existing instrument does not fit well enough with the conceptual definition preferred. In such a case, it might be preferable to develop a new measure. That of course must be set against the effort and resources involved in developing a new measure.

On balance, therefore, we would need good reason for passing over an already existing instrument, particularly if the variable is a central variable in a research area. For this type of variable, I would not recommend developing a new measure, especially if a reasonable instrument is already available. I would modify this conclusion, however, for the common research situation where *ad hoc* quantitative data can be obtained with rating scales: attitudes towards specific issues are a good example. If the procedures described in Section 6.5 are followed, perhaps in truncated form, effective data can be produced which will add to the precision and value of the research. That is, there is an important role for short rating scales, tailor-made to the purposes and context of a particular project. They can be used in a variety of research situations, including qualitative ones, and for a variety of research purposes. They have great flexibility, and they can assist in making the comparisons we want.

### 6.7 **Locating Existing Measuring Instruments**

As mentioned, literally hundreds of measuring instruments have been developed by social science researchers over many years. The first problem is to locate them, and the second is to assess their value in a particular research situation. Help in locating them comes from collections of research instruments which have been compiled, numerous examples of which are shown in the further reading suggestions at the end of this chapter.

The *Mental Measurements Yearbook* series is produced by the Buros Institute of Mental Measurements at the University of Nebraska. This is a particularly distinguished series, which includes not only collections of research instruments, but expert critical reviews of them and their psychometric characteristics. It is therefore helpful in both locating and assessing instruments. The volume *Tests in Print* includes a comprehensive index to the *Mental Measurements Yearbooks*. The publication edited by Goldman and Mitchell (1996) concentrates on tests which are not commercially available.

Older collections of instruments are also available (Shaw and Wright, 1967). Some of these cover attitudes in general, and others, such as those from the Institute of Social Research at the University of Michigan, concentrate on particular attitudes, such as political attitudes, or occupational attitudes (Robinson et al., 1969; Robinson and Shaver, 1973). Though older, they may still be useful to the researcher reviewing measurement attempts in an area, or looking for ideas for items in constructing an instrument.

It is worthwhile to spend some time browsing these collections, especially the *Yearbooks*. They give an idea of the vast amount of work that has been done in developing measuring instruments, and they are also a good starting point in the search for instruments. Despite these collections, however, the search may need to go further, because current research may use and report new scales well before they appear in these collections. 'Going further' means reading research journals and dissertations. It is unusual for a journal to publish a new scale, because of space limitations, even though it will report research using that scale. In such a case, the author(s) can be contacted directly, using information provided in the journal. Dissertations are harder to keep up with, because they are not published. Regular reading of *Dissertation Abstracts International* and national dissertation indexes can help here. Again, while a scale will not be published in an abstract, contact details for the author are normally provided.

## 6.8 Reliability and Validity

If we find a measuring instrument in the literature, how do we assess its quality for use in research? Similarly, if we are developing our own measuring instrument, what qualities should we try to build into it? For both questions, the two main technical criteria are reliability and validity. These are sometimes called psychometric characteristics of an instrument.

### 6.8.1 Reliability

Reliability is a central concept in measurement. It basically means consistency. There are two main aspects to this consistency: consistency over time (or stability) and internal consistency. We will deal with each briefly.

First, consistency over time, or stability of measurement over time, is usually expressed in the question: if the same instrument were given to the same people, under the same circumstances, but at a different time, to what extent would they get the same scores? To the extent that they would, the measuring instrument is reliable. To the extent they would not, it is unreliable. Stability over time can be directly assessed, under certain circumstances, by administrations of the same instrument (or by parallel forms of the instrument)[10] at two points in time. This is called test–retest reliability and requires two administrations of the measuring instrument.[11]

Second, internal consistency relates to the concept–indicator idea of measurement described earlier. Since multiple items are used to help us infer the level of the latent trait, the question concerns the extent to which the items are consistent with each other, or all working in the same direction. This is the internal consistency of a measuring instrument. Various ways have been devised to assess the extent to which all items are working in the same direction. The best known are the split-half techniques, the Kuder–Richardson formulas, and coefficient alpha (Cronbach, 1951; Anastasi, 1988). Internal consistency reliability estimation requires only one administration of the instrument.

These two different methods (test–retest reliability and coefficient alpha) tap the two different meanings of consistency. Either or both can be used to estimate the reliability of a measuring instrument. Why is reliability important? Intuitively, we would want consistency of measurement, but there are important technical reasons too, which involve a little more basic measurement theory.

Any actual (or observed) score can be thought of as having two parts: the true score part and the error part. As an example, take the measurement of weight. When we step on the scales, we get a particular (observed) measurement. We know that any one observed measurement is not perfectly accurate. We know that it contains some error. We also know that the smaller the error the more accurate the measurement, and the larger the error the less accurate the measurement. Intuitively, we control for the error and estimate the true score by taking several readings, and averaging them. We regard that average of several readings as a better estimate of the true score, the measure we really want.

These ideas are formalized in the concept of reliability. Observed scores are made up of the true scores, which we want to estimate, and error. The smaller the error, the closer the observed scores are to the true scores. Reliability enables us to estimate error, and reliability and error are related reciprocally: the larger the reliability, the smaller the error, and conversely, the smaller the reliability, the larger the error. Measures which have high reliability produce observed scores which are close to true scores.

Now we can relate reliability to variance, distinguishing between reliable variance and error variance. A good measuring instrument for research purposes picks up differences between people, producing variance in the scores. We can divide the total variance in a set of scores into reliable variance and error variance. This is the reciprocal relationship between the two: when reliability is high, error variance is low; when reliability is low, error variance is high. The reliability of a measure tells us how much error variance is in the scores. Reliable variance produced by a measuring instrument is true variance. That is, the differences in scores between people produced by a measure with high reliability are real differences. This is important, because what is not true variance is error variance. Error variance is spurious variance, or random variance, or 'noise'; it is variance which proceeds purely from the fact that the measure itself is not 100% reliable. When a measure has low reliability, some of the differences in scores between people which it produces are spurious differences, not real differences. Error variance, by definition, cannot be accounted for by relationships with other variables. This is important, because, as discussed earlier, a central strategy in research is that of accounting for variance through relationships with other variables.

We should note that all measures have some unreliability. Even physical measurement does not produce exactly the same measures of the same object at two different points in time. Therefore social measurement is not unique in having some unreliability, or error variance. It is harder to reduce error variance in social and psychological measurement than in (say) physical measurement, but error variance is present wherever measurement is used. Because one of our central strategies in research is accounting for variance in a dependent variable, it is necessary that we have estimates of the reliability of all measures, especially of the dependent variable. We want to know how much of the variance is able to be accounted for, after measurement error is estimated.

### 6.8.2 Validity

A second central concept in measurement is validity. Validity is a technical term with specific meanings: here, we are focusing on measurement validity.[12] Its meaning can be shown in this question: how do we know that this measuring instrument measures what we think it measures? Measurement validity means the extent to which an instrument measures what it is claimed to measure; an indicator is valid to the extent that it empirically represents the concept it purports to measure.

Because of the latent nature of the variables we want to study, there is an inference involved between the indicators we can observe (or the items people respond to) and the construct we aim to measure. Validity is about that inference. So the validity question is: how reasonable is the inference from indicator(s) to concept? The measuring instrument or procedure itself is not valid or invalid. The validity question only applies to the inference we make from what we observe. Among the various approaches to the validation of instruments, the three main ones are content validity, criterion-related validity, and construct validity.

Content validity focuses on whether the full content of a conceptual definition is represented in the measure. A conceptual definition is a space, holding ideas and concepts, and the indicators in a measure should sample all ideas in the definition (Neuman, 1994). Thus the two steps involved in content validation are to specify the content of a definition, and to develop indicators which sample from all areas of content in the definition.

In criterion-related validity, an indicator is compared with another measure of the same construct in which the researcher has confidence. There are two types of criterion validity. Concurrent validity is where the criterion variable exists in the present: for example, a researcher might wish to establish the awareness of students about their performance in school during the past year. In this situation, each student could be asked the question: 'What was your grade point average last year?' The response could then be concurrent-criterion validated by correlating it with the grade point average obtained from the school's records office. Predictive validity is where the criterion variable will not exist until later: the researcher might wish to have students anticipate their performance in school during the next year, asking each student the question: 'What do you think your grade point average will be next year?' The response could then be predictive-criterion validated by correlating it with the grade point average obtained from the school's records office after a year (Zeller, 1997).

Construct validity focuses on how well a measure conforms with theoretical expectations. Any measure exists in some theoretical context, and should therefore show relationships with other constructs which can be predicted and interpreted within that context. An example would be validating a measure of alienation by showing its relationships with social class (de Vaus, 1991). Zeller (1997) gives a detailed description of the six steps involved in establishing construct validity.

There is no foolproof procedure to establish validity, and the validation methods used should depend on the situation. Because all methods have limitations, Zeller believes that inferences about validity cannot be made solely on the basis of quantitative or statistical procedures. He advocates a validation strategy which combines quantitative and qualitative methods. 'A valid inference occurs when there is no conflict between messages received as a result of the use of a variety of different methodological procedures' (1997: 829). We will see in Chapter 10 that this same issue of validation runs through approaches to the way qualitative data are analysed.

Reliability and validity are the two main psychometric characteristics of measuring instruments. One other characteristic is mentioned here, because it fits in with the research strategy outlined in Chapter 5. 'Sensitivity' here means the ability of a measuring instrument to pick up differences between people – to discriminate between them and produce variance. Other things being equal, the best measuring instruments for research purposes (and the best items) are those which spread people out and produce the greatest variance. But it must be true or reliable variance, in the sense discussed above.[13]

This criterion can be used in assessing and selecting individual items and subscales in developing a measuring instrument. It is also consistent with the overall research strategy based on variance and accounting for variance. This strategy will not work if there is no variance (or little variance). A measuring instrument which does not differentiate between people produces little or no variance.[14] We can use this idea to develop a three-part research strategy, based around a central variable in an area. The first part requires developing a measure of the variable which produces good variance. The second part involves accounting for this variance, investigating the factors which produce or influence that variance, using the question: what accounts for these differences? This is about identifying independent variables which relate to the dependent variable. The third part asks about the effects of this variance, or the outcomes which follow from it, using the questions: what difference does it make that people differ on this variable? What are the results or consequences of this variance? In the second part, the variable we are considering is the dependent variable, and independent variables are related to it. In the third part, it is the independent variable and it is related to dependent variables. This general strategy is useful when we are organizing research in a new area. We come to understand a variable through understanding how it varies and the antecedents and consequences of that variance, and this strategy formalizes that. We will see a similar strategy in qualitative analysis in Chapter 10.

## 6.9 Developing a Survey Questionnaire

In Chapter 5, we focused on the correlational survey as a major quantitative design. Its centrepiece is the survey questionnaire, the subject of this section. The correlational survey is not a simple descriptive survey, but rather a multi-variable survey, seeking a wide range of information, and with some conceptual framework of independent, control and dependent variables. It is likely, there-fore, that the questionnaire will seek factual information (background and bio-graphical information, knowledge and behavioural information) and will also include measures of attitudes, values, opinions and beliefs. One useful frame-work for developing such questionnaires distinguishes between cognitive, affec-tive and behavioural information; another divides it up into knowledge, attitudes and behaviours (or behaviour intentions). Any of these areas may use, in whole or in part, already existing measures, or may develop them specifically for this research, as outlined in Section 6.5.

The development of the survey questionnaire can proceed along the lines sug-gested in Section 6.5. In this case, definitional questions are perhaps even more important. Because a wide range of information is usually sought in a major survey questionnaire, a clear conceptual map of the questionnaire is the first step in its development, and this is often best done in diagram form. The map should work from the general to the specific, first showing the general type of variable and then translating that down to specific variables, with the dimensions and subscales as appropriate. Then specific questions and items can be developed.

Development of its specific parts then depends on the types of measure-ments involved. In some respects, developing the factual-type questions will be easier, but here again we should aim to build on previous work, in two ways. First, extensive consideration has been given to the whole topic of ask-ing factual questions for research purposes. Of course, there are many ways to ask even a simple factual question, and some ways are better than others. We do not have space to go into that topic here, but a number of books deal with it (for example, Moser and Kalton, 1979; Sudman and Bradburn, 1982; Oppenheim, 1992; Lewins, 1992). Second, many excellent survey question-naires have been developed, and can be useful in various ways. Help in locat-ing them comes from Converse and Presser (1986), who list nine sources of survey questions which they have found useful. In addition, survey question-naires are often included in the published reports of large surveys; Jaeger (1988) reviews a number of important social and educational surveys in the United States, and Thomas (1996) indicates 10 major surveys which are carried out regularly in the UK.

Mention should also be made of the semantic differential, often a useful and efficient way to collect affective information in a survey questionnaire. The semantic differential was an outcome of research, conducted in the 1950s, into the way people organize and use semantic space. That research suggested that we use bipolar adjective pairs, in three main dimensions (evaluative, potency, activity), to organize our thinking about the world. Therefore the semantic differential asks people to respond to different concepts using rating scales running between bipolar adjective pairs. Sometimes, mapping the semantic space will be the focus of the research in its own right. Here, the semantic differential is seen more as a tool in developing a survey questionnaire. Mostly it is used to get affective responses, focusing on the evaluative dimension. The original work is reported in Osgood et al. (1957). Other useful references are Kerlinger (1973) and the semantic differential sourcebook by Snider and Osgood (1969).

### 6.10 Collecting the Data: Administering the Measuring Instrument

So far, this chapter has been about measurement and measuring instruments. This section is about procedures for data collection, since these too affect the quality of the data. Empirical research is only as good as the data on which it is based, so the checkmark responses to questionnaire items (which become the quantitative researcher's data), and the frame of mind and conscientiousness of the respondent when they were made, are all-important. It is worth taking every precaution possible to ensure that the data are as good as they can be, whatever the mode of administration of the instruments.[15] Two general points to keep in mind are the following.

First, it is necessary to ensure that respondents have been approached professionally and, within limits, fully informed about the purpose and context of the research, about confidentiality and anonymity, and about what use will be made, and by whom, of the information they provide. It helps also to point out that this sort of research is not possible without their cooperation, and they should know clearly what they are being asked to do. Experience shows that when this is done properly and professionally, people will cooperate, and the quality of the data is improved.

Second, as far as possible, the researcher should stay in control of the data collection procedure, rather than leave it to others or to chance. Thus, if face-to-face administration (single or group) is possible instead of a mailed questionnaire, it is to be preferred, despite the additional work. Again, if it is a choice between the researcher administering the questionnaire, and somebody else on the researcher's behalf, the former is better. If others have to do it, they need training in the procedures to follow. These things may involve trade-offs, especially with sample size, but it is better to have a smaller data set of good quality than a larger one of lower quality.

It is unfortunate in research when an excellent job has been done of developing a data collection instrument, but the same thought and effort have not been put into the data collection procedures. Both are important in determining the quality of the data. One particular aspect of this, and a hurdle for all survey research, is the issue of response rates. Very low response rates are both disappointing and troublesome, since they carry the possibility of biased results. If response rates are given due importance in the data collection planning stage, there are often procedures which can be used to maximize them. It is important, therefore, to include the issue of response rates in the planning for the research, ahead of the data collection, rather than have it occur as an afterthought following the administration of the questionnaire.

## 6.11 Sampling

Sampling has been an important topic in the research methodology literature, with well developed and mathematically sophisticated sampling plans (see, for example, Cochran, 1977; Jaeger, 1984). That does not seem so true today, probably because of three trends: the growth of interest in qualitative methods, a swing away from large samples in quantitative studies, and, as social research has proliferated, the growing practical problem of obtaining access to the large and neatly configured samples required by sophisticated sampling plans. Very often indeed, the researcher must take whatever sample is available, and the incidence of convenience samples (where the researcher takes advantage of an accessible situation which happens to fit the research context and purposes) is increasing.

Despite this, the basic ideas involved in sampling remain important. In some quantitative research situations we may still need to use sophisticated sampling plans. Also, sampling models are the basis of statistical inference, and statistical inference remains a key decision-making tool in quantitative research. Finally, these ideas give us a useful model to keep in mind when planning actual sample selection in a study. Therefore we need to look at the basic ideas involved in sampling. This section should be read in conjunction with Section 7.7 on the logic of statistical inference.

All research, including qualitative research, involves sampling. This is because no study, whether quantitative, qualitative or both, can include everything: 'you cannot study everyone everywhere doing everything' (Miles and Huberman, 1994: 27). Sampling in quantitative research usually means 'people sampling'.[16] The key concepts therefore are the population (the total target group who would, in the ideal world, be the subject of the research, and about whom one is trying to say something) and the sample (the actual group who are included in the study, and from whom the data are collected).[17]

The logic of quantitative sampling is that the researcher analyses data collected from the sample, but wishes in the end to make statements about the whole target population from which the sample is drawn. That logic is

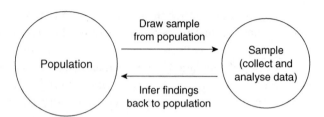

**Figure 6.2**   *Populations and samples*

shown in Figure 6.2. The data are collected from the sample, and analysed to produce the study's findings. But the findings are still about the sample, so the next step is generalizing the findings from the sample to the population. This involves a sample-to-population inference, the central question in which is: how representative is the sample of the population? Representativeness is a key concept, though, as noted below, it is more applicable to some studies than to others. Sampling to achieve representativeness is usually called probability sampling, and while different strategies have been designed to achieve it, the main one is some type of random selection. This is a quite different meaning of 'random' from that used in experimental design in Chapter 5. There, the idea was random allocation to treatment groups, and this was done to ensure control of extraneous variables. Here, the idea is random selection, which is done to ensure representativeness. In random selection, each element in a population has an equal chance or equal probability of being chosen. Stratifying the population along different dimensions before random selection produces stratified random samples.

A sampling plan is not independent of the other elements in a research project, particularly its research purposes and questions. This is another instance of the fit between a project's parts, as discussed in Chapter 2. The sampling plan should have a logic which fits in with the logic of the research questions. Thus, if the research questions require representativeness, some form of representative sampling should be used. On the other hand, if the research questions highlight relationships between variables, or comparisons between groups, some sort of deliberate or purposive sampling may well be more appropriate, since it makes sense to select the sample in such a way that there is maximum chance for any relationship to be observed. Similarly, if the design is experimental or quasi-experimental, the sample should be selected to make comparisons as clear-cut as possible.[18] Deliberate or purposive sampling resembles theoretical sampling as used in qualitative research, and as discussed in Chapter 10. We will see there that sampling strategies are equally important in qualitative research.

Whatever sampling strategy is used, the research proposal and report need to address three questions:

- How big will the sample be, and why?
- How will it be chosen and why?
- What claims will be made for its representativeness?

The first two questions tie the sampling plan to the overall logic of the study. The third question becomes especially important in those cases where convenience samples are used in the research. There is nothing wrong with that, and valuable knowledge can be gained by studying these samples, but the researcher needs to assess the extent to which the sample is typical of some larger population.

## 6.12 Secondary Analysis

Secondary analysis is the term used for the reanalysis of previously collected and analysed data. It is important in quantitative work (especially in surveys), and is growing in importance in qualitative research as well, as noted in Chapter 9. There are some clear advantages to working with an existing body of data, including cost (for many survey researchers, there is little chance of obtaining funding to carry out large-scale data collection), time (the researcher can begin analysis soon, rather than investing large amounts of time in data collection), quality (an existing data bank is likely to have higher-quality data than the lone, inexperienced researcher can hope to obtain), and making difficult populations accessible (Procter, 1996). It is increasingly important also for students to be aware of the possibilities of secondary analysis and the data banks which support it,[19] and it has special attractions given the cost and time limits involved in student project work (including dissertations).

However, these attractions do not mean that secondary analysis is always straightforward. There can be both methodological difficulties and difficulties of interpretation of the raw data (Reeve and Walberg, 1997), and the possibility always exists that the original questions and data are not relevant to the present problem: 'The real challenge in secondary analysis lies in finding ways of forcing the data, collected by someone else, quite often with entirely different theoretical and analytical orientations, to answer your questions' (Procter, 1996: 262). While important and appealing, therefore, it is necessary that a proposed secondary analysis be accompanied by careful planning and consideration of the data in the light of the proposed research. Procter's advice (1996: 257) is valuable: by all means to explore the possibility of secondary analysis, but not to commit oneself to it without discussing its pitfalls with an experienced adviser. Useful references on secondary analysis are Hakim (1982), Stewart (1984), Kiecolt and Nathan (1985), Dale et al. (1988) and Procter (1996).

## 6.13   REVIEW CONCEPTS

Variables:
- discrete (categorical, discontinuous)
- continuous (measured)

Measuring a variable:
- defining the variable
- selecting indicators
- getting empirical information about indicators

Latent traits:

latent variable

observable indicators (items)

Measuring techniques:
- Thurstone (equal appearing intervals)
- Guttman (cumulative scaling)
- Likert (summated ratings)

Reliability:
- consistency over time (test–retest)
- internal consistency (coefficient alpha)
- high reliability = low error variance (and vice versa)

Validity:
- content validity
- criterion-related validity (concurrent, predictive)
- construct validity

Frameworks for variables in correlational surveys:
- cognitive–affective–behavioural
- knowledge–attitudes–practices
- the semantic differential

Sample versus population:
- a sample is drawn from a population

Sampling strategy:
- how big and why?
- how chosen and why?
- how representative?

Representative sampling:
- generalizability

Deliberate sampling:
- purposive
- theoretical

Secondary analysis

NOTES

1  This was called scaling in Chapter 4, and is central to the discussion of measurement in this chapter.

2  Most discussions identify four levels of measurement: nominal, ordinal, interval and ratio.

3  This point has implications for constructing data collection questions in a survey. For example, many questions are asked with a dichotomous yes/no or true/false response, when a scaled response to the same question would be better, and would produce more information.

4  This is a slight modification of Zeller's (1997) definition. He uses, as an 'adequate' definition, the process of linking concepts to indicators. He describes the earlier well known definition of Stevens (1951) – 'the assignment of numbers to objects or events according to rules' – as 'inadequate', and gives reasons.

5  There may be more than one trait, but each one needs to be defined unidimensionally.

6  This is the question of dimensionality, and is captured in the expression 'We can't add oranges and battleships'. But we could add, for example, their weight, showing that it is the trait that is being measured, not the object itself.

7  A detailed description of their work is given in Edwards (1957).

8  Probably the most common form of words is 'strongly agree, agree, disagree, strongly disagree', but other forms are possible.

9  Item analysis gives criteria for selecting the best items for a scale (see Oppenheim, 1992; Friedenberg, 1995).

10  Parallel forms are different forms of the instrument constructed to be equivalent. This indicates a third (more technical) form of consistency – consistency of the instrument over item content sampling.

11  The assumption made here is that the trait being measured would not have changed substantially in the time period between the two administrations.

12  See Section 2.4 for other technical meanings of validity.

13  In other contexts than research, it may not be important for a measuring instrument to spread people out, and to produce variance. An example would be testing for mastery learning in education.

14  To put it in different terms: we are studying relationships between variables. Relationships mean correlation. Conceptually, correlation is the same as covariation. If there is no variation, there can be no covariation. One of the factors influencing the size of the correlation is the amount of variance in the scores of each variable. The relationship between variables may be underestimated if measures produce little variance.

15  Individual or group administration (face to face), by telephone, or by mail (Jaeger, 1988). Internet surveys are now also being conducted.

16  Though in fact it means more than this. Bracht and Glass (1968), writing about the external validity of experiments, distinguish between population validity (or people sampling) and ecological validity (dealing with the 'environment' of the study and generalizing results to other environments).

17  The terms 'sample' and 'population' are therefore technical terms which should be used accurately. In particular, the confused term 'sample population' should be avoided.

18  Kerlinger (1973) expressed these ideas in his 'maxmincon' principle of design: maximize experimental variance, minimize error variance, control extraneous variance.

19  Examples of existing survey data archives include the General Social Survey in the USA, the International Social Survey Programme covering some 12 countries (mostly European), and the General Household Survey in the UK (see Procter, 1996; Neuman, 1994).

## *Further Reading*

Allen, M.J. and Yen, W.M. (1979) *Introduction to Measurement Theory*. Monterey, CA: Brooks/Cole.

Carley, M. (1981) *Social Measurement and Social Indicators*. London: Allen and Unwin.

Converse, J.M. and Presser, S. (1988) *Survey Questions*. London: Sage.

Cronbach, L.J. (1990) *Essentials of Psychological Testing*. 5th edn. New York: Harper and Row.

de Vaus, D.A. (1991) *Surveys in Social Research*. 3rd edn. London: Allen and Unwin.

Edwards, A.L. (1957) *Techniques of Attitude Scale Construction*. New York: Appleton-Century-Crofts.

Fink, A. and Kosecoff, J. (1985) *How to Conduct Surveys: A Step-by-Step Guide*. Beverly Hills, CA: Sage.

Henry, G.T. (1990) *Practical Sampling*. Newbury Park, CA: Sage.

Jaeger, R.M. (1988) 'Survey methods in educational research', in R.M. Jaeger (ed.), *Complementary Methods for Research in Education*. Washington: AERA. pp. 301–87.

Kalton, G. (1983) *Introduction to Survey Sampling*. Beverly Hills, CA: Sage.

Moser, C.A. and Kalton, G. (1979) *Survey Methods in Social Investigation*. 2nd edn. Hants: Gower.

Oppenheim, A.N. (1992) *Questionnaire Design, Interviewing and Attitude Measurement*. London: Pinter.

Rossi, P.H., Wright, J.D. and Anderson, A.B. (1983) *The Handbook of Survey Research*. New York: Academic.

### Collections of measuring instruments
Bearden, W.O. (1999) *Handbook of Marketing Scales.* Chicago: American Marketing Association.

Bonjean, C.M., Hill, R.J. and McLemore, S.D. (1967) *Sociological Measurement.* San Francisco: Chandler.

Bowling, A. (1991) *Measuring Health: A Review of Quality of Life Measurement Scales*. Philadelphia: Open University Press.

Bruner, G.C. and Hansel, P.J. (1992) *Marketing Scales Handbook: A Compilation of Multi-Item Measures*. Chicago: American Marketing Association.

Conoley, J.C. and Impara, J.C. (eds) (1995) *Twelfth Mental Measurements Yearbook*. Buros Institute of Mental Measurements. Lincoln, NB: University of Nebraska Press.

Frank-Stromborg, M. (ed.) (1988) *Instruments for Clinical Nursing Research*. Norwalk, CT: Appleton & Lange.

Goldman, B.A. and Mitchell, D.F. (eds) (1996) *Directory of Unpublished Experimental Mental Measures*. Vol. 6. Washington, DC: American Psychological Association.

Hersen, M. and Bellack, A.S. (eds) (1988) *Measures for Clinical Practice*. New York: Free Press.

Maddox, T. (ed.) (1997) *Tests: A Comprehensive Reference for Assessments in Psychology, Education and Business*. 4th edition. Austin, TX: Pro Ed.

McDowell, I. and Newell, C. (1987) *Measuring Health: A Guide to Rating Scales and Questionnaires*. Oxford: Oxford University Press.

Miller, D.C. (1991) *Handbook of Research Design and Social Measurement*. 5th edn. Newbury Park, CA: Sage.

Murphy, L.L., Conoley, J.C. and Impara, J.C. (1994) *Tests in Print IV: An Index to Tests, Test Reviews, and the Literature on Specific Tests*. Vol. 1. Buros Institute of Mental Measurements. Lincoln, NB: University of Nebraska Press.

Price, J.M. and Mueller, C.W. (1986) *Handbook of Organizational Measures*. Marshfield, MA: Pitman.

Shaw, M.E. and Wright, J.W. (1967) *Scales for the Measurement of Attitudes*. Ann Arbor, MI: Institute of Social Research.

Stewart, A.L. and Ware, J.E. (eds) (1992) *Measuring Functioning and Well-Being*. Durham, NC: Duke University Press.

Straus, M.A. and Brown, B.W. (1978) *Family Measurement Techniques: Abstracts of Published Instruments, 1935–1974*. Rev. edn. Minneapolis: University of Minnesota Press.

Streiner, D.R. and Norman, G. (1995) *Health Measurement Scales: A Practical Guide to their Development and Use*. Oxford: Oxford University Press.

Sweetland, R.C. and Keyser, D.J. (1986) *Tests: A Comprehensive Reference for Assessments in Psychology, Education, and Business*. 2nd edn. Kansas City, MO: Test Corporation of America.

# 7

# The Analysis of Quantitative Data

Quantitative data are analysed using statistics. There are scores of books written for this field, perhaps more than for any other topic in research, and there is no point in producing another. This chapter therefore takes a different approach. This book is not about statistics but about doing research, and its intention is to show the logic behind each stage of empirical research. This point applies particularly to statistics. Statistics is one of the many tools the researcher needs.

Like other tools, it can be used very effectively without the user having a full knowledge of how it works. What is needed, however, is an understanding of the logic behind the various statistical tools, and an appreciation of how and when to use them in actual research situations. Thus I stress here the logic of quantitative data analysis, but there will be very few equations or formulas. Those are dealt with in the statistical literature, to which directions are given.

In Chapter 5, the two main strands of quantitative research design were identified. These strands continue into this chapter. One strand sits in the tradition of the experiment, and is based on the idea of comparison groups. Its main statistical expression is the analysis of variance, which includes the $t$-test, and which extends to the analysis of variance (univariate and multivariate). As we saw in Chapter 5, this strand looks from the top down, from independent variables to the dependent variable, guided by the question: what are the effects of this cause? The other is the correlational survey strand, and is based more on the idea of relationships between variables in the non-experimental setting. Its main statistical expression is correlation and regression. This strand looks from the bottom up, from the dependent variable back to the independent variable, guided by the question: what are the causes of these effects?

These two strands are related, but they also represent different ways of thinking, and different emphases. The logic of data analysis in both strands is described in this chapter, but the strand emphasized most is the correlation-regression strand. This is because it is the easier of the two to interpret, because it is the more widely applicable across many social science areas, and because it connects directly with the research strategy of accounting for variance outlined in Chapter 5. In that chapter, multiple linear regression (MLR) was proposed as a general research design strategy. In this chapter, MLR is proposed as a general data analysis strategy.

Two other points should be stressed, one general, one specific. The general point is that, in any project, the way the data are analysed is governed by the research questions. Thus, while this chapter describes the logic of quantitative data analysis, the actual techniques and the way they are used in a project follow from the research questions. The specific point is that the level of measurement of the variables influences the way we do some of the quantitative analysis. The most important distinction is between nominal and interval levels of measurement, or between discrete and continuous variables. The quantitative researcher needs to keep that distinction constantly in mind. When a variable is continuous, we can add and average scores. When it is categorical, we cannot.[1]

## 7.1 Summarizing Quantitative Data

Quantitative research involves measurements, usually of a number of variables, across a sample. Therefore, for each variable, we have scores for each member of the sample. We call this a distribution and we need ways of summarizing it. The two main concepts we use are central tendency and variation. This is modelled on what we do in everyday life. If you ask someone what London is like in summer, you might hear 'the temperature averages about 25 degrees (central tendency), but it changes a lot (variation)'.

### 7.1.1 Central tendency: the mean

There are three common measures of central tendency: the mean, the mode and the median. While there are technical issues in deciding which is the most appropriate,[2] the mode and the median are much less used in research than the mean. Therefore we will deal with the mean here. It is familiar to everyone, and to obtain it we simply add up the scores and divide by the number of scores. The more common term is the average; the more technical term, used here, is the mean.

Two features of the mean should be mentioned. The first is technical: it is the point in a distribution about which the sum of the squared deviations is at a minimum. This makes it important for estimating variance, and for least squares analysis.[3] The second feature is that the mean is a very effective statistic where scores within a distribution do not vary too much, but it is not so effective when there is great variance.[4] Therefore it is important to know how much spread or variability there is in a set of scores, in order to interpret the mean correctly.

### 7.1.2 Variation: standard deviation and variance

Like central tendency, statisticians have developed several ways to measure the variance in a set of measurements. For example, one simple but useful concept is the range: the highest score in the sample minus the lowest score. But the most common measure of variability is the standard deviation. It goes with the mean, because the deviations involved are deviations of individual measurements from the mean of the distribution. Those deviations are calculated and standardized to give us the standard deviation. In one number, it summarizes the variability in a set of data. The more spread out the scores, the larger the standard deviation.

From the standard deviation, we can easily obtain the variance. The variance is the square of the standard deviation; or, the standard deviation is the square root of the variance. Like the standard deviation, the variance gives us a numerical estimate of the amount of spread in the data. While the standard deviation is commonly used in descriptive statistics, the variance is more commonly used in statistical inference (see Section 7.7). But we can always obtain one from the other.

Interpreting the standard deviation together with the mean tells us something about how much spread there is in the scores in a distribution, and

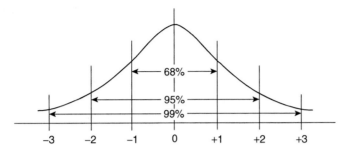

**Figure 7.1**    *The normal distribution curve*
*Source*: Jaeger, 1990: 55

important properties of the distribution relate to how far away from the mean
we move in terms of standard deviations. In particular, if the distribution is
normal or bell shaped, we know that, as shown in Figure 7.1, approximately:

- 68% of all cases fall within one standard deviation either side of the mean
- 95% of all cases fall within two standard deviations either side of the mean
- 99% of all cases fall within three standard deviations either side of the
  mean.

The figures will not vary too much from these, even when the distribution is
not bell shaped.

   Thus, knowing the mean and the standard deviation tells us a great deal
about the distribution of a set of scores. Both the standard deviation and the
variance give us numerical estimates of the variability in the distribution.
While the standard deviation is helpful in interpreting that variability, variance
is the more general concept, and is central both to the analysis of quantitative
data and in the overall quantitative research strategy. As shown in Chapter 5,
much of our thinking is based on accounting for variance – on finding out how
much people (or things) differ, and then accounting for those differences using
relationships with other variables. We will return to this theme in Section 7.4.

### 7.1.3 Frequency distributions

In addition to the mean, standard deviation and variance, simple frequency
distributions are a useful way to summarize and understand data. Their calcu-
lation is straightforward. The individual scores in the distribution are tabulated
according to how many respondents achieved each score, or gave each
response, or fell into each category. Absolute numbers and/or percentages may
be used. Depending on the overall score range, it will sometimes be useful to
group scores in ranges, so that we can see more easily the distribution of the
frequencies. We can show results as frequency distribution tables, or as graphs.

Histograms and frequency polygons are the most usual, but other graph forms, such as pie charts or horizontal bar charts, are possible.

Frequency distributions of responses can tell, at a glance, something about the shape of the distribution, and this can be important in determining subsequent steps in the analysis. They also help the researcher to stay close to the data, at least in the initial stages of the analysis. There is great benefit to getting a 'hands-on feel' of the data, especially when the availability of computerized programs makes it so easy for the researcher to be removed from the data.

## 7.2 Relationships between Variables: Cross-Tabulations and Contingency Tables

Quantitative research is based on relationships between variables, and many different ways have been developed to study these relationships. Different ways are needed because of variables at different levels of measurement, the distinction between discrete and continuous variables being especially important. In this section we will deal with basic cross-tabulations, and show how the logic of chi-square can be combined with it. Because they are so flexible, these methods cover many of the situations encountered in quantitative research. They can also be used for variables at any level of measurement. The important case of relationships between two continuous variables is not considered in this section, but is described in Section 7.4.

The basic cross-tabulation or contingency table[5] is easy to construct and read, applicable to a wide range of situations, and the foundation for more advanced analyses. A good treatment of the topic is given by Rosenberg (1968) in *The Logic of Survey Analysis*. He shows how sophisticated analysis of quantitative survey data is possible with nothing more than simple contingency tables. The example given in Table 7.1 comes from this book. The table contains data about two variables. In its simplest form, each variable has two categories, and the $2 \times 2$ table has four cells. But other forms are possible, and each variable can have any number of categories. As Rosenberg's example shows, percentages are a convenient way to show the data, but actual numbers can be used as well.

The contingency table is used in Rosenberg's work basically as a descriptive tool. It can easily be extended to hypothesis testing and inference with chi-square. We can usually learn a lot about the relationship between the cross-tabulated variables just by inspection of the contingency table. If there is a pattern in the table (that is, if the two variables are related) this will be visible in the distributions shown in the cross-tabulation. But often we will also want a more formal test of that relationship. We can use chi-square to do this, and we will now look briefly at its logic.

**Table 7.1** *Age and listening to religious programmes*

| Listen to religious programmes | Young listeners | Old listeners |
|---|---|---|
| Yes | 17% | 26% |
| No | 83% | 74% |
| Total | 100% | 100% |

*Source*: Rosenberg, 1968: 25

To use chi-square to see if the two variables are related, we begin with the actual cross-tabulations. These are called the observed frequencies in each cell. Then we calculate what the cross-tabulations would look like if there were no relationship between the variables. This gives a second set of entries in each cell, called the expected frequencies. Now we compare the observed and expected frequencies in each cell of the cross-tabulation. Some simple calculations allow us to summarize this comparison into the statistic called chi-square. We can then use the chi-square statistical inference table to decide on the importance of the difference between observed and expected distributions, and to decide whether the variables are related. Of course, the observed distribution will always differ to some extent from the expected one; they will never be identical. The question, here as elsewhere in statistical analysis, is: how much of a difference makes a difference? Or, in statistical terms: is the difference significant? This is a matter for statistical inference, which we will deal with in Section 7.7.

## 7.3 Comparisons between Groups: the Analysis of Variance

### 7.3.1 Analysis of variance

The basic idea here is that we want to compare groups on some dependent variable of interest. The groups may be formed in the design of the study, as in an experiment, or they may be naturally occurring and formed by partitioning of the sample in data analysis.[6] The simplest form of comparison between groups is when there is only one way of classifying the people, only one way of forming the groups. This is one-way analysis of variance, or one-way ANOVA.[7] While there may be any number of groups, the simplest form of ANOVA is when there are only two groups. In this case, ANOVA becomes equivalent to the *t*-test. Since the *t*-test is a special case of one-way analysis of variance, we will deal with the more general case. The logic is the same.

#### One-way ANOVA

In one-way ANOVA, we are comparing groups on some dependent variable. Imagine three comparison groups, with the people in them measured on some dependent variable of interest. The question is: do the groups differ on their scores? We have to be careful with this question. People, of course, will not all have the same score on the variable; not even all the people in one group will have the same score. So the question really is: on average, taken overall, do the three groups score differently? There are two possible sources of variance in our scores. There is variance of scores within the groups, and variance of scores between the groups. Our problem is to decide whether the variance between the groups is larger than the variance within the groups. If it is, we can conclude that the groups differ; if not, we can conclude that the groups do not differ.

That is the basic logic of analysis of variance. We partition the total variance of a set of scores into that part due to individuals' membership in the different groups (called treatment variance, or systematic variance, or between-group variance) and that part due to variation within the groups (called error variance[8] or within-group variance). This is done by first finding the mean score for each group; then finding out how much individual scores within groups vary around the group means; then finding the overall mean for the whole sample irrespective of groups (the grand mean); and then finding out how much group means vary around the overall mean. This enables us to calculate two quantities, the between-group variance and the within-group variance. We then form a ratio, called $F$, to compare the two, such that:

$$F = \text{(between-group variance)}/\text{(within-group variance)}$$

When $F$ is large, between-group variance is much greater than within-group variance, and there are 'significant' differences between the groups. When $F$ is small, between-group variance is not much bigger than within-group variance, and group differences are not significant.

What do we mean by saying that $F$ is large or small? This is a recurrent question in quantitative data analysis.[9] As with chi-square, statistical inference helps here by providing a decision-making rule. The $F$-ratio summarizes information about the two sorts of variances, the variance between groups and the variance within groups, into one value. This calculated value can then be referred to a statistical table to decide whether it is large or small. Technically, the calculated $F$-ratio is compared with a critical value, stored in a statistical table, to determine the likelihood that it could have come about by chance. The logic of statistical inference, for this and other cases, is explained further in Section 7.7.

### Two-way ANOVA

When the people can simultaneously be classified in two ways to form comparison groups, we move from one-way ANOVA to two-way ANOVA. The basic logic is the same, in that we compare between-group variance with within-group variance, but now we have a more complicated situation. In the example shown in Table 7.2, the dependent variable is educational achievement, and students are jointly classified by gender and by socio-economic status (SES).

**Table 7.2** *Two-way ANOVA: gender × SES with educational achievement as dependent variable*

|  | **Boys** | **Girls** |
|---|---|---|
| High SES | Average score for boys, high SES | Average score for girls, high SES |
| Medium SES | Average score for boys, medium SES | Average score for girls, medium SES |
| Low SES | Average score for boys, low SES | Average score for girls, low SES |

We cannot now simply ask about differences between groups. Which groups? There are possible differences between sex groups (the main effect due to gender) and possible differences between SES groups (the main effect due to SES). But there is another possibility also: the *interaction* between the two classifications. While 'interaction' is a term used very commonly (and often loosely), the meaning of it in this context is precise, technical and important.

### 7.3.2 Interaction

Interaction is, apparently, ubiquitous in our world, including the world we research. It is one of the reasons for some of the complications of quantitative research design. The essential idea is that the effect of one independent variable on the dependent variable is influenced by (or interacts with, or depends on) another independent variable. This is shown in Figure 7.2.

Do boys score higher than girls in the results shown in this diagram? The answer is that it depends on what level of SES we are talking about: yes for high SES, no for low SES. Similarly, do students from high SES backgrounds perform better than those from low SES backgrounds? Again, it depends on whether we are talking about boys or girls: yes for boys, no for girls. The key

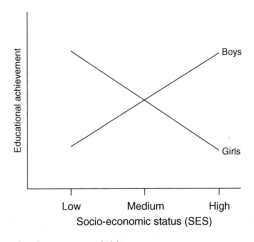

**Figure 7.2** *Interaction between variables*

phrase is 'it depends on …': whenever we use that phrase, we have interaction. Given how often we need to use that phrase, it is not surprising that interaction is described as 'ubiquitous'.

The point about interaction is that it invalidates our attempts to make simple and sweeping generalizations. With the results as above, we cannot generalize about gender differences in achievement. That is, we cannot say that boys achieve better than girls, or vice versa. Nor can we generalize about social class differences.

Thus, in two-way ANOVA, we have three different questions we need to ask. Using the above example, the three questions are:

- Is there interaction between gender and SES with respect to achievement?
- If not, do girls and boys score differently? (That is, is there a main effect due to gender?)
- And do students from different SES levels score differently? (That is, is there a main effect due to SES?)

We would not investigate the main effects of gender and social class until we have investigated interaction effects. It is logical that we first find whether or not there is interaction between the independent variables. Only if there is no interaction do we proceed to talk about main effects. The situation of no interaction is shown in Figure 7.3.

This example of interaction is from educational research. Another well known educational example is the treatment-by-aptitude interaction, whereby the effectiveness of a method of instruction (the treatment) depends upon the level of ability of the student (the aptitude). We can easily imagine that a teaching method that works very well with highly able students would not work so well with less able students. Which teaching method works best depends on the ability level of the student. There is interaction between the two.

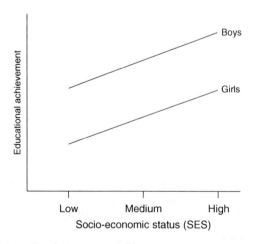

**Figure 7.3** *No interaction between variables*

### 7.3.3 Analysis of covariance

Analysis of variance (ANOVA) and analysis of covariance (ANCOVA) are closely related and use the same set of ideas. In Chapter 5, ANCOVA was described as the most general of the three ways of controlling a variable in the analysis.[10] To control in this sense means to remove the influence of. We can now briefly describe the logic of analysis of covariance, to see how this is done. For simplicity, we assume there is only one covariate. Because we want to remove the effects of the covariate before we do the comparison between the groups, we first use the relationship between the covariate and the dependent variable to adjust the dependent variable scores. This is equivalent to removing its effects from the dependent variable. Then we perform the standard analysis of variance, as described above, on the adjusted dependent variable scores. If between-group differences on the adjusted scores are significantly larger than within-group differences, we know that the independent variable is related to the dependent variable after controlling the effects of the covariate. Thus analysis of covariance is really analysis of variance performed on the adjusted dependent variable scores. The adjustment has been to remove the effects of the covariate, and we can covary out more than one variable at one time. We will see in Section 7.4.7 that we can also do ANCOVA using the regression analysis framework.

### 7.3.4 From univariate to multivariate

An important development in quantitative research methods in the last 30 years has been the trend from univariate studies to multivariate studies. Again, these terms have technical meanings. 'Univariate' means only one dependent variable. 'Multivariate' means more than one dependent variable.

This trend developed because we want to know about several possible differences between our comparison groups, not just one difference. Or, in experimental situations, we want to know about several effects of some treatment variable, not just one effect. When there is more than one dependent variable, univariate analysis of variance (ANOVA) becomes multivariate analysis of variance (MANOVA). If we are using covariates as well, univariate analysis of covariance (ANCOVA) becomes multivariate analysis of covariance (MANCOVA). These analyses required the development of multivariate statistical techniques.

Why is there a problem here which required new techniques? Why could the several dependent variables not just be treated sequentially, one at a time, requiring simply several ANOVAs? The answer is because the dependent variables are likely to be related to each other. The problem, in other words, is correlated dependent variables. This means that errors of inference in the statistical testing are likely to be compounded if the correlations between the dependent variables are not taken into account. Therefore, if we are planning between-group comparisons on more than one variable, either within or outside an experimental design framework, and if those variables are related to each other, we will need multivariate techniques for the analysis of the data. ANOVA will have to become MANOVA, and ANCOVA will have to become MANCOVA.

## 7.4 Relationships between Variables: Correlation and Regression

We move now to the second strand of data analysis – relationships between variables – and we begin with the case of simple correlation between two continuous variables. This is Pearson product-moment correlation, the most important (but not the only) type of correlation analysis. It tells us the direction and strength of relationships between variables – both how the variables are related, and how much they are related.

### 7.4.1 Simple correlation

In this situation, we are concerned with the relationship between two continuous variables. The basic idea is best illustrated with a simple example. If a sample of people (say 100) has been measured on two continuous variables, we can plot their scores on a two-dimensional graph. Each of the 100 points is plotted in the two-dimensional space formed by the $X$ and $Y$ axes, and together these points make up a scatter diagram. We can tell a great deal about the relationship between these two variables from the shape of that scatter diagram. Figure 7.4 shows the three main possibilities.

In Figure 7.4a, the shape of the scatter is oval or elliptical, and points upwards to the right. We can see that higher scores on $X$ tend to go with higher scores on $Y$, and lower scores on $X$ tend to go with lower scores on $Y$. These variables are said to be positively (or directly) correlated. The two variables go up or down together. We can also see that a reasonably good prediction is possible, from $X$ to $Y$ or vice versa. If we know a person's score on $X$, we can estimate with reasonable precision (that is, with not too much scatter) that person's score on $Y$.

In Figure 7.4b, the exact reverse is true. The scatter is still oval or elliptical in shape, but now it points downwards to the right. Higher scores on $X$ tend to go with lower scores on $Y$, and lower scores on $X$ tend to go with higher scores on $Y$. These variables are said to be negatively correlated (or inversely or indirectly correlated). The two variables go up and down in opposition to each other. A reasonably good prediction is still possible, from $X$ to $Y$ or vice versa. As before, if we know a person's score on $X$, we can estimate with reasonable precision that person's score on $Y$.

In Figure 7.4c, the scatter has a very circular shape. A high score on $X$ might be associated with any level of score on $Y$, and vice versa. In this case, the

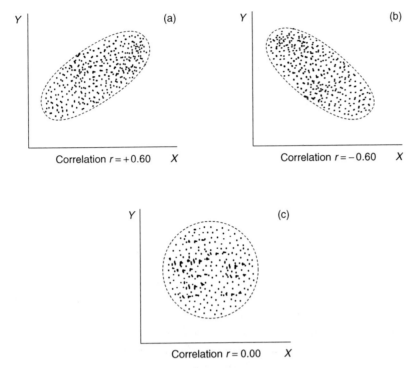

**Figure 7.4**   *Scatter diagrams associated with Pearson
product-moment correlation coefficients of various magnitudes*
*Source*: Jaeger,1990: 65

variables are uncorrelated: there is no relationship between them. Clearly, prediction here is not possible.

In Figures 7.4a and 7.4b, we can summarize and simplify things by placing a 'line of best fit' through the points, sloping as the scatter diagram slopes. This is done by finding the mean of each interval and connecting the means across the different intervals. This line of best fit can then be smoothed into a prediction line between the two variables. The tighter the points in the scatter diagram cluster around such a line, the stronger the relationship and the better the prediction. This line of best fit is also called the *regression* line of Y on X.[11]

We have just described simple correlation and regression geometrically. It can also be done algebraically. The algebraic formalization of these ideas is known as the Pearson product-moment correlation coefficient $r$, the most widely used measure of correlation. The computation formula ensures that $r$ varies between 0 and 1, positive or negative as the case may be. That is, it can range from $-1.00$ to $+1.00$. The closer numerically the coefficient is to 1 (positive or negative), the stronger the relationship. This is very convenient, for it means that the correlation coefficient can tell us at a glance both the direction and the strength of the relationship. A number close to 0 tells us that the variables are not substantially related: it describes Figure 7.4c.

Conceptually, correlation is the same as covariation.[12] When two variables are related, positively or negatively, they vary together. This means they share common variance, or covary. This points to an important property of the correlation coefficient. If we square it, we get a numerical estimate of the proportion of the variance in one variable which is held in common with, or accounted for by, the other. Thus, a correlation of $+0.50$ between two variables tells us that approximately 25% of the variance is held in common between them. Similarly, if $r = -0.70$, $r^2 = 0.5$, and this tells us that some 50% of the variance in one variable can be accounted for by the other. This concept is important as we move from simple to multiple correlation, and fits in very well with our strategy of accounting for variance.

### 7.4.2 Multiple correlation and regression

Simple correlation and regression has one independent and one dependent variable. Multiple correlation and regression has more than one independent variable, and one dependent variable. Reflecting the multiple causation concept we discussed in Chapter 4, a common situation in research is where we have several independent variables and one dependent variable. We wish to study factors affecting the dependent variable. We wish to account for variance in it, by studying its relationship with the independent variables.

The logic and the algebra of simple correlation generalize to multiple correlation, but multiple correlation now involves solving simultaneous equations. Assume we have four independent variables, and one dependent variable measured across a sample of people. Our input is now five sets of actual scores,[13] one for each independent variable and one for the dependent variable, for each person. We use these actual scores to see how much the variables are related. Specifically, we use them to see how well the independent variables are able to predict the dependent variable. We first estimate the relationship between the independent variables and the dependent variable, using the logic described in simple correlation above. Then we use that knowledge to predict people's scores on the dependent variable, and we compare the predicted dependent variable scores with the actual dependent variable scores. We summarize that comparison with the correlation coefficient already described. That is, the simple correlation coefficient between the predicted dependent variable scores and the actual dependent variable scores is in fact the multiple correlation between the four independent variables and the dependent variable. The multiple correlation coefficient is written $R$. When we square it, $R^2$ tells us how much of the variance in the dependent variable is accounted for.

This is the logic of multiple correlation analysis, and the output from the analysis is of two kinds. First, the squared multiple correlation coefficient $R^2$ is estimated. This gives a direct estimate of the amount of variation in the dependent variable which is explained or accounted for by the independent variables.

Second, the weights (called regression weights) attaching to each independent variable are estimated, telling us how important each independent variable is in predicting the dependent variable.

### 7.4.3 Squared multiple correlation coefficient

The squared multiple correlation coefficient $R^2$ is a particularly important statistic, especially in the research strategy of accounting for variance outlined in Chapter 5. It tells us how much of the variance in the dependent variable is accounted for by this group of independent variables. Thus it provides a direct answer to the central question in the strategy of accounting for variance. Like the simple correlation coefficient, $R$ is normalized to vary between 0 and 1, so that $R^2$ also varies between 0 and 1. The closer it is to 1.00 (or 100%), the more of the variance in the dependent variable can be accounted for. The squared multiple correlation coefficient $R^2$ also tells us how good our prediction of the dependent variable is, with this set of independent variables. These two ideas are linked. The more variance we can account for, the more accurate the prediction we can make. Conversely, the less variance we can account for, the less accurate is our prediction. This means that the squared multiple correlation coefficient measures for us the predictive efficiency of any particular regression model.

### 7.4.4 Regression weights

It is important to know how good our prediction is, by knowing how much of the variance we can account for. But we also need to know how important each independent variable is in accounting for this variance. This is the concept of the relative importance of predictor variables. The regression weights in our regression equations give a direct estimate of this. The computations produce two types of weights: raw weights, suitable for use with the raw scores as input to the analysis, and standardized weights, for use with standardized scores. We will use the latter since, unlike the former, they can be directly compared with each other. Their full name is standardized partial regression coefficients, usually abbreviated in the literature to beta (ß) weights. Their technical interpretation is important. The ß weight for (say) independent variable $X_1$ tells us how much of a change we would make in the dependent variable by making a one-unit change in the variable $X_1$, while keeping all other variables constant.

### 7.4.5 Stepwise regression

Stepwise regression means dropping out variables from the regression equation, usually one at a time or stepwise, to see what difference this makes to how much variance we can account for in the dependent variable.[14] It is another way we can assess how important an independent variable is. The basic idea is this. First, we use all the independent variables in our regression equation, to see how much of the dependent variable variance we can account for. That is measured by $R^2$, which tells us the predictive efficiency of that regression equation. Then we drop out an independent variable, recompute the regression equation, and see what change there has been in how much variance we can account for. This gives us a second $R^2$. Comparing the two $R^2$ tells us how important the variable was that we dropped out, in accounting for variance in the dependent variable.

Stepwise regression is very useful and a widely used technique. In fact, it is a special case of a more general procedure we can use, to test the predictive efficiency of regression models. We can think of each regression equation as a regression (or prediction) model. Each model produces a squared multiple correlation coefficient, which tells us how well that model predicts the dependent variable (or how much of the variance in the dependent variable we can account for). Therefore we can compare the predictive efficiency of different models by comparing their squared multiple correlation coefficients. In this way, MLR can be used to investigate many different questions about the effects of different independent variables on the dependent variable, and about how those effects come about. Stepwise regression analysis looks at one particular question: whether or not dropping this particular independent variable reduces the predictive efficiency of our model. But there are many other types of questions we can investigate, using the logical framework of MLR, and comparing squared multiple correlation coefficients.

### 7.4.6 Review: MLR as a general data analysis system

We have covered a lot of material in this section, so it is appropriate that we pause for review. We first covered simple correlation and extended that to multiple correlation. We linked that to the strategy of accounting for variance directly through the squared multiple correlation coefficient. We then linked correlation to regression, through prediction. This gives us prediction equations, or regression models. We then considered regression weights in those equations, and the logic of stepwise regression. Finally, we generalized that to the comparison of different regression models, through their predictive efficiency.

As presented here, MLR falls within the strand of relationship between variables in quantitative design and data analysis, and focuses mainly on continuous variables. It provides us with a way of dealing with all types of such continuous variable relationships, from simple to complex. The investigation of all those can be done within the one regression analysis framework.

However, the technique of MLR also has the flexibility to deal with the strand of comparison between groups in design and data analysis. That is, the same logical framework of MLR can be used to deal with $t$-tests, analysis of variance (including interaction) and analysis of covariance. This is because these analyses depend on group membership, and variables to express group

**Table 7.3**   *Quantitative research design and statistics*

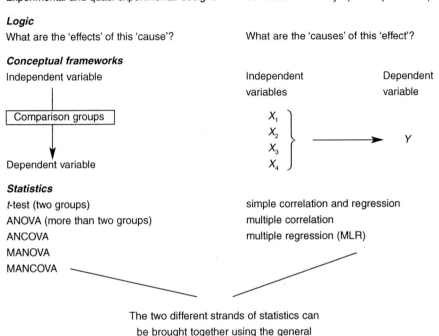

| Comparing groups | Relating variables |
|---|---|
| **Designs** | |
| Experimental and quasi-experimental designs | Correlational surveys (non-experiments) |
| **Logic** | |
| What are the 'effects' of this 'cause'? | What are the 'causes' of this 'effect'? |

**Statistics**

| | |
|---|---|
| *t*-test (two groups) | simple correlation and regression |
| ANOVA (more than two groups) | multiple correlation |
| ANCOVA | multiple regression (MLR) |
| MANOVA | |
| MANCOVA | |

The two different strands of statistics can
be brought together using the general
linear model (Section 7.4.6)

membership can be formulated and used in regression equations. In other words, MLR can deal with discrete variables as well as continuous variables. Discrete variables to express group membership are called 'binary' or 'dummy' variables in regression analysis (Hardy, 1993).

With straightforward dummy variables we can do *t*-tests, and one- and two-way analysis of variance, using these regression techniques. This also includes interaction questions in two-way ANOVA. And because categorical and continuous variables can be included in the same regression models, we can do analysis of covariance this way as well, as shown below. In short, this one approach can cover all of the main data analysis ideas we have dealt with in this chapter, as shown in Table 7.3.

Thus MLR provides one analytic framework and one set of steps which can be used to investigate a very wide range of data analysis questions from both of the main strands identified in this chapter. Because the one analytic framework can handle both categorical and continuous variables, MLR is a tool of great power and flexibility, with application to a wide range of situations. It is also easy enough to understand and apply. Since the same steps can be used to investigate such a wide range of questions, it means that researchers can build their own statistical models for the analysis of data, guided by the specific questions they want to investigate, instead of being limited only to the conventional models routinely described in statistics books. Building these models requires the researcher to make an exact statement of the research questions.

### 7.4.7 Analysis of covariance using MLR

In Section 7.3.3 we saw the logic of ANCOVA in the analysis of variance framework. We can now use the same logic here. In the example used earlier, we want to know whether the independent variable affects the dependent variable after removing the effects of the covariate. When done by MLR, this requires the comparison of two regression models. The first uses the covariate only to predict the dependent variable, and produces its $R^2$. The second uses the independent variable (in the between-group comparison assumed here, the independent variable is a set of binary vectors representing group membership) together with the covariate to predict the dependent variable. Its $R^2$ is compared with the first model's $R^2$ to see if its predictive efficiency is better. If it is, group membership adds to knowledge of the dependent variable over and above the covariate. That means there are between-group differences after controlling the covariate. If not, group membership adds nothing to prediction of the dependent variable, over and above the covariate. That means that between-group differences are not significant, over and above the effects of the covariate.

## 7.5 The Analysis of Survey Data

The correlational survey is the central strategy in the strand of relationships between variables in quantitative research, so there are likely to be many variables involved, some discrete and some continuous, and many different questions of interest. To simplify what can become a complicated analysis, we will look at it here in three main stages (simple descriptive analysis, two-variable relationships, joint and multivariable[15] relationships), which together provide a useful analytic framework. Of course, these stages need to be used in conjunction with the research questions guiding the study.

### Descriptive analysis

With complex survey data sets, an initial descriptive analysis of the data is useful. This would be done on a variable-by-variable basis, and would use the techniques described in Section 7.1 in this chapter: means, standard deviations (or variances), and frequency distributions. If there are scales involved, there might also be some item analysis, and, whether or not there are scales, there might also be some data reduction (see Section 7.6). One benefit of an initial descriptive analysis is keeping the researcher close to the data; another is understanding the distribution of each variable across the survey respondents.

### Two-variable relationships

As a next step, some two-variable relationships in the survey might be singled out for special analysis, guided again by the research questions. Any of the techniques of association might be used, but two approaches are strongly recommended. First, as noted earlier, the approach detailed by Rosenberg (1968) provides a useful framework for working through this stage, stressing the logic of the analysis. A feature of his approach is his clarification of the meaning of relationships between variables (1968: 3–22), and then of the conceptual status of variables in a relationship, systematically extending two-variable relationships into three- and four-variable relationships (1968: 22–158).[16] Second, multiple linear regression analysis can be used to investigate all questions of two-variable relationships and group comparisons, as we have just seen. The same logic lies behind these two approaches.

### Joint and multivariable relationships

Here the value of the MLR approach becomes apparent, since it can easily be extended past two-variable relationships. It is difficult to extend the cross-tabulation approach of Rosenberg to analysis which simultaneously involves many variables, but MLR, on the other hand, extends easily to situations involving many variables. Most of the joint and multivariable questions of interest can be answered using this approach, including detailed questions about relationships between variables, and questions involving comparisons between groups. It requires specification of the conceptual status of variables in the survey (some as independent, some as control variables or covariates, and some as dependent), in accordance with the research questions. Many other questions, including interaction and non-linear and polynomial relationships, can be investigated using the MLR approach. As noted, a benefit of this approach is that it forces the researcher to be specific in formulating research questions, and in translating them into data analysis operations.

## 7.6 Data Reduction: Factor Analysis

Quantitative social science research, especially non-experimental research, is characterized by multivariable studies. Having many variables often makes it difficult to understand the data. This difficulty has led to the development of techniques to reduce the number of variables, but without losing the information the original variables provide. Factor analysis is the name given to a group of related techniques developed for this purpose.

The idea behind factor analysis is based on the correlation between variables, as shown in Figure 7.5. When two variables are correlated, we can propose the

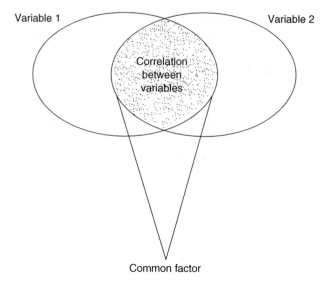

**Figure 7.5**    *Factor analysis diagram*

existence of a common factor, which both variables share to some extent, and which therefore explains the correlation between them. This idea generalizes to any number of variables.

In factor analysis, therefore, we are aiming to reduce the number of variables by finding the common factors among them. We begin the analysis with the original observed variables which we have measured. We then find the correlations between them, and factor analyse these correlations. We end the analysis with a smaller number of derived or unobserved variables, called factors.

Consider the example of six educational tests – three in arithmetic, algebra and geometry, and three in English, French and history. We can easily imagine that, if we measured a sample of students with these tests, we would find two clusters of correlations among the tests. The first cluster would show the overlap between arithmetic, algebra and geometry, while the second would show the overlap between English, French and history. If this were the case, factor analysis of the correlations among the six tests would produce two main factors, one corresponding to the mathematical variables ('mathematical ability') and one to the language variables ('language ability'). Based on that factor analysis, we can therefore reduce the number of variables we have to deal with, from six to two. The six were the original measured variables; the two are the extracted or derived factors. These two factors effectively summarize the information contained in the original six tests, so that we have reduced the number of variables without loss of information. As a result, it is now easier for us to talk about just two factors instead of six variables. We can next calculate scores on the two derived factors for each student, for use in subsequent analysis.

These are called factor scores, and we can use them to simplify the subsequent analysis.

Thus the input into a factor analysis is the set of correlations between the original variables. Once the computer has performed the mathematical calculations, the solution will show the derived factors, and the relationship of each factor to the original variables. It shows this through factor loadings – the loading of each original variable on each derived factor. The researcher interprets the meaning of each extracted factor by means of those loadings, usually after rotation.

Geometrically speaking, factor analysis can be thought of as placing axes through the space described by the original variables. The objective of rotation is to place those axes in the best possible place for interpretation of the factors. The 'best possible place' can be defined mathematically, and set up as a criterion to guide the analysis. The first factor analysis solution from the computer is arbitrary, in terms of the placement of the axes. Therefore the axes can be rotated until this criterion is realized. The original axes are at right angles to each other, in this space. This is called orthogonal factor analysis. If this property is preserved, the factor scores which are calculated will be uncorrelated with each other. However, this property can also be relaxed in rotation, if a non-orthogonal or oblique solution seems preferable. Correlated factor scores would then result.

We should note one other aspect of factor analysis which will come up again in the analysis of qualitative data. It concerns levels of abstraction. In factor analysis we begin with observed variables, and we end with unobserved or extracted factors. The variables are at a lower level of abstraction or generality than the factors. Thus algebraic ability, for example, is more specific than mathematical ability. Mathematical ability is a more general concept, at a higher level of abstraction.

Actually, this is the second time we have raised the level of abstraction in the analysis of quantitative data. The first time was from items to variables. This second time is from variables to factors. This is shown in a level of abstraction diagram, as on the right-hand side of Figure 7.6. It is useful to see clearly these levels of abstraction, and especially to see factor analysis this way. When we discuss the analysis of qualitative data in Chapter 10, we will see that a very similar process of raising the level of abstraction is involved, as indicated on the left-hand side of Figure 7.6.

## 7.7 Statistical Inference

Until now in this chapter we have been looking at the logic behind different techniques in the analysis of quantitative data. We have actually been doing *descriptive statistics*,[17] which is concerned with summarizing and describing data. The topic of statistical inference, or *inferential statistics*, is different. It is not a technique for summarizing and describing data. Rather, it is a tool to

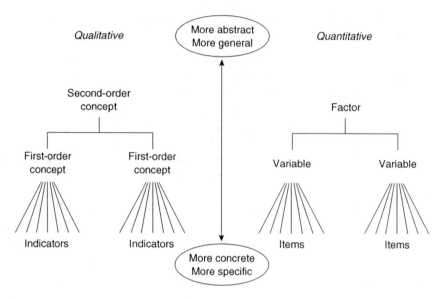

**Figure 7.6** *Levels of abstraction in data analysis*

assist in making decisions based on the analysis of data using the descriptive statistical techniques already discussed. Statistical inference is one of the many tools needed in research. This section considers the logic behind statistical inference and how it is applied, and should be read in conjunction with Section 6.11 on sampling.

First, what is the problem which gives rise to statistical inference? In our research, we select some sample, and we collect data only from that sample. We do this because we cannot study the whole population. But after the research, we wish nonetheless to make statements about some larger population from which the sample was drawn. In other words, we are faced with an inference, from the sample back to the population. There is a symmetry here, as we saw in Figure 6.2. We draw a sample from the population, and we study the sample. But then, after studying the sample, we wish to infer back to the population. The inference question therefore is: how likely is it that what I found to be true in my sample is also true in my population?

In order to answer that question, we have to rephrase it in probabilistic terms. It becomes: how likely am I to be wrong, if I infer that what I found to be true of my sample is also true of my population? Since the question is phrased in terms of the likelihood of being wrong, the answer will also be in terms of the likelihood of being wrong, expressed as 'times per 100' or as 'times per 1000'. This leads to statements such as: 'I will be wrong less than 5 times in 100 if I make that inference' (or less than 5 times in 1000, or whatever). These are the familiar confidence levels, or statistical significance levels, or probability levels. They are usually shown in research reports as $p < 0.05$, $p < 0.001$, and so on.[18]

How do we work out this likelihood of being wrong? We calculate some statistic(s) from our sample data and then we use statistical inference tables to determine that likelihood. Those tables are in most statistics books, and now in computers. In the analysis of our sample data, we calculate a statistic which summarizes some aspect of the data we are interested in: it might be chi-square, comparing observed and expected distributions; or $r$, showing the level of association between two variables; or $F$, comparing the predictive efficiency of two regression models. We then refer that statistic to its distribution as shown in statistical inference tables, in order to see how likely it is that a value of this size would be obtained for this statistic by chance.

This gives us another perspective on how statistical inference works. We are really asking: how likely is it that my calculated statistic, which of course is based on data obtained from the sample, came about by chance, as an 'accident' of the particular sample I happened to study? As before, the answer is in terms of a probability level. It takes the form: 'A value of this size, for this statistic, would come about by chance (say) 5 times in 100 ($p = 0.05$) with a sample of the size used in this research.' Now, if this value would come about by chance only 5 times in 100, it would be a non-chance occurrence 95 times in 100. In other words, if I am likely to be wrong less than 5 times in 100, in making the inference that what I found to be true in my sample is also true in my population, then I am likely to be right more than 95 times in 100. These seem like good odds. It seems that it is not a chance result, and not an accident of this particular sample. It seems real, and we call it 'statistically significant'. The term 'significance' therefore has a special meaning in quantitative analysis.

The above example used 5 times in 100 as the cutoff point. This is the so-called 5% confidence level, or 5% significance level. By convention, this is a widely accepted cutoff level in social research. But if a particular research result had a probability of (say) 7% of occurring by chance ($p = 0.07$), we should not dismiss it as unimportant just on the grounds that it does not reach statistical significance. Statistical significance levels are useful in guiding our decisions about when results are 'real' or not. But we should use them intelligently, based on an understanding of what they mean.

This question of inference arises whenever we wish to generalize from a sample to some larger population, whatever descriptive statistics we are using. The question does not arise if we do not wish to generalize, or if we have somehow studied the whole population we are interested in. Sample size is important in determining the outcome of a statistical significance test. The bigger the sample size, the smaller the numerical value of the statistic required in order to reach significance. Conversely, the smaller the sample size, the bigger the numerical value of the statistic required in order to reach significance.

## 7.8 Computer Software for the Analysis of Quantitative Data

Among the many computer packages which have been developed for the analysis of quantitative data, the most widely used in social science research is the Statistical Package for the Social Sciences (SPSS). Now in its 11th release, SPSS is an extremely comprehensive package which can perform highly complex data manipulation and analysis with simple instructions. SPSS has a vast number of statistical and mathematical functions, scores of statistical procedures, and a very flexible data handling capability.

SPSS can read data in almost any format (e.g. numeric, alphanumeric, binary, dollar, date, time formats) and version 6 onwards can read files created using spreadsheet or database software. This makes SPSS even more versatile, since many researchers already use spreadsheets (such as Excel), and since almost every computer now carries a spreadsheet program. Thus the statistical analysis power of SPSS can be combined with the flexibility, and other advantages, of spreadsheets.

In addition to its widespread popularity – and contributing to it – several useful guides and workbooks have been written to assist students and researchers learning to use SPSS. They include *SPSS Survival Manual* (Pallant, 2001), *SPSS Analysis without Anguish* (Coakes et al., 2003), and *Doing Statistics with SPSS* (Kerr et al., 2002). Appendix 1 contains a step-by-step guide to analysing quantitative data using SPSS.

---

### 7.9 REVIEW CONCEPTS

Strands of statistical analysis:
- comparison between groups
- relationships between variables

Summarizing data:
- central tendency: mean (mode, median)
- variance: standard deviation, variance
- frequency distribution
- the normal curve
- cross-tabulation, contingency table

Chi-square ($\chi^2$)

Univariate analysis of variance (one dependent variable):
- *t*-test
- one-way ANOVA
- two-way ANOVA
- interaction
- the *F*-ratio
- analysis of covariance (ANCOVA)

## 7.9    REVIEW CONCEPTS (CONTINUED)

Multivariate analysis of variance (more than one dependent variable):
- multivariate analysis of variance (MANOVA)
- multivariate analysis of covariance (MANCOVA)

Simple correlation and regression:
- scatter diagram
- positive correlation
- zero correlation
- negative correlation

Multiple correlation and regression:
- squared multiple correlation coefficient ($R^2$)
- regression weights ($\beta$)
- stepwise regression
- accounting for variance
- relative importance of independent variables

Analysing survey data:
- descriptive analysis
- two-variable relationships
- joint and multivariable relationships

Factor analysis:
- correlation as common variance
- levels of abstraction

Statistical inference:
- sample versus population
- confidence levels, significance levels, probability levels ($p < 0.05$ etc.)

## NOTES

1   As a general rule, parametric statistics are appropriate for interval-level data, and non-parametric statistics for nominal- and ordinal-level data (see Siegel, 1956; Kerlinger, 1973).

2   Mainly, the level of measurement, the shape of the distribution, and the stability of the scores.

3   Least squares analysis is one of the foundations of statistics.

4   When variance is large, the median is a better measure of central tendency.

5   Cross-tabulation means that two variables will be cross-tabulated against each other. Contingency table means that the purpose of the cross-tabulation is to see if the distribution on one of the variables is related to, or contingent on, the other.

6   Examples of groups formed by partitioning are males versus females, old people versus young people, people born in the UK versus people not born in the UK, and so on.

7   The term 'ANOVA' is used a great deal in psychology and education, but not so much in other social science fields.

8   This use of error variance is different from its use in connection with the reliability of measurements in Chapter 6.

9   It is really the same question as: how much of a difference makes a difference?

10  The others were stratification (or test factor elaboration) and partial correlation.
11  There is also the regression line of $X$ on $Y$.
12  Correlation can be defined as standardized covariation.
13  This is slightly inaccurate. 'Scores' implies continuous variables, but independent variables can be discrete as well as continuous.
14  Stepwise can also mean adding in variables, rather than dropping them out. The 'steps' can be done forwards or backwards. We will talk here about dropping variables out, sometimes called 'backward stepping regression analysis'. But the whole idea also works the other way around.
15  As noted, 'multivariate' is a technical term meaning more than one dependent variable. 'Multivariable' is a more general term, simply meaning many variables.
16  Rosenberg's book *The Logic of Survey Analysis* is recommended for building a foundation in quantitative data analysis, largely because it stresses the logic of the analysis.
17  With the exception of chi-square, and comparing the predictive efficiency of regression models.
18  $p < 0.05$ actually means that I will be wrong less than 5 times in 100, if I conclude that what was true of my sample is also true of my population. Similarly, $p < 0.001$ would mean being wrong less than 1 time in 1000; and so on.


## *Further Reading*

Berry, W.D. (1984) *Nonrecursive Causal Models*. Beverly Hills, CA: Sage.

Comfrey, A.L. and Lee, H.B. (1992) *A First Course in Factor Analysis*. 2nd edn. Hillsdale, NJ: Erlbaum.

Glass, G.V. and Stanley, J.C. (1970) *Statistical Methods in Education and Psychology*. Englewood Cliffs, NJ: Prentice-Hall.

Jaeger, R.M. (1983) *Statistics as a Spectator Sport*. Beverly Hills, CA: Sage.

Kerlinger, F.N. and Pedhazur, E.J. (1973) *Multiple Regression in Behavioral Research*. New York: Holt, Rinehart and Winston.

Kish, L.D. (1987) *Statistical Design for Research*. New York: Wiley.

Lipsey, M. (1990) *Design Sensitivity: Statistical Power for Experimental Research*. Newbury Park, CA: Sage.

Rosenberg, M. (1968) *The Logic of Survey Analysis*. New York: Basic.

Tatsuoka, M.M. (1988) *Multivariate Analysis: Techniques for Educational and Psychological Research*. 2nd edn. New York: Macmillan.

# 8
## Design in Qualitative Research

In this book, the quantitative and qualitative approaches are both presented under the same three main headings: design, data collection and data analysis. Before considering these for qualitative research, the first part of this chapter looks at the more complex nature of this field. This overview notes the diversity within qualitative research, and looks briefly at two of the important perspectives which inform contemporary qualitative research – feminism and postmodernism. The second part of the chapter then considers designs in qualitative research. The theme of diversity in qualitative research continues in Chapters 9, 10 and 12.

## 8.1 Overview

### 8.1.1 Diversity in qualitative research

In sharp contrast with quantitative research, which seems relatively methodologically unidimensional despite its internal technical debates, a dominant feature of present-day qualitative research is its diversity. Early in their *Handbook*, Denzin and Lincoln write:

> It did not take us long to discover that the 'field' of qualitative research is far from a unified set of principles promulgated by networked groups of scholars. In fact, we have discovered that the field of qualitative research is defined primarily by a series of essential tensions, contradictions and hesitations. These tensions work back and forth among competing definitions and conceptions of the field. (1994: ix)

Qualitative research methods is a complex, changing and contested field – a site of multiple methodologies and research practices. 'Qualitative research' therefore is not a single entity, but an umbrella term which encompasses enormous variety.

Three aspects of this diversity concern paradigms, approaches to data, and methods for the analysis of data. The last two are dealt with in this book in Chapters 9 and 10 respectively. This section comments on the diversity of paradigms and perspectives in qualitative research. We need to be aware of the differences between quantitative and qualitative research on this issue.

Paradigm debate and diversity have not been a typical feature of quantitative research. In general, quantitative research has been mainly based on positivism: as Tesch (1990) points out, the whole approach of constructing concepts and measuring variables is inherently positivistic.[1] The situation in qualitative research is quite different, with several different paradigm positions, and much paradigm discussion and debate. By comparison with quantitative research, qualitative research is multidimensional and pluralistic with respect to paradigms. The main alternative paradigms within qualitative research are positivism, postpositivism, critical theory and constructivism, but there are finer distinctions than these and more detailed subdivisions (especially under critical theory). Furthermore, paradigm developments within qualitative research continue, so that we do not yet have a final picture (Denzin and Lincoln, 1994). It is important to be aware of this range of paradigm possibilities within qualitative research, especially when reading the literature.

One effect of these developments within qualitative methodology has been to highlight the political nature of social research – the recognition that social research, like other things people do, is a human construction, framed and presented within a particular set of discourses (and sometimes ideologies), and conducted in a social context with certain sorts of social arrangements, involving especially funding, cognitive authority and power. Both the substantive concepts and the methods research uses are ways of describing the social world for particular purposes, not just abstract and neutral academic tools. In other words, social science research is a political process, and always has been. Thus Apple (1991: vii) stresses the inescapably political contexts in which we speak and work, and points out that all of our discourses are politically uninnocent. Or, as Punch (1994) puts it, politics suffuses all social science research, from the micropolitics of personal relations in a research project, to issues involving research units, universities and university departments, and ultimately government and its agencies.

Some aspects of the political nature and context of research are discussed by Sapsford and Abbott (1996), and by the various writers in *Beyond Methodology* (Fonow and Cook, 1991). A collection of readings edited by Hammersley (1993) considers the politics of research in relation to development studies in the Third World, feminism, critical theory, evaluation studies, and methodology and data themselves. Hammersley (1995) also presents a comprehensive review of the changes in the nature of ideas about social research, with reference to political issues and concerns. In Chapter 6 of that book, he undertakes a detailed analysis of the question 'Is social research political?'

Research methods and styles themselves can be seen from this 'politicized' perspective. Sapsford and Abbott (1996) note the argument that choices about research styles are choices which have political elements. Research styles are not neutral, but embody implicit models of what the social world is or should be like, and of what counts as knowledge and how to get it. A consequence of this is that a large area of knowledge is suppressed as 'non-scientific' by the limitations of prevailing research methodologies. Research methods themselves, as a field of study, can be analysed and understood using the approaches and techniques developed within the field to study other things. The politics of research methods, and the university contexts in which choices about methods often occur, are discussed by Jayaratne and Stewart (1991) and by Eisner (1991).

Feminism and postmodernism are two perspectives from which the political aspects of research have received a great deal of attention. The former stresses the role of power in research, especially in the traditional hierarchical relationship between researcher and researched.[2] Like critical analysis, and some types of class, race and ethnic studies, feminism also often has emancipation as its goal.

The latter perspective often 'foregrounds' power directly, insisting that social science is no more immune from the power–knowledge connection than any other human activity (Lather, 1991). Such perspectives apply to virtually every part of the research process: the conception of research itself, the purposes of research, the role of the researcher, approaches to design, data collection and analysis, ethical considerations and evaluative criteria.

### 8.1.2 Feminism

Feminist thinking has been making an important contribution to social science research methods since the 1960s, playing a particularly significant role in reshaping qualitative research practices. Despite this, it is difficult, at this time, to describe a distinctive feminist methodology. Olesen (1994) and Roman (1992) both point out that there are different feminisms, and therefore different feminist approaches to research methods. The field is complex and changing: 'labile' is the term Olesen uses. But the theme running through this complexity is that 'it is important to centre and make problematic women's diverse situations and the institutions and frames that influence those situations, and then to refer the examination of that problematic to theoretical, policy, or action frameworks in the interests of realizing social justice for women' (Olesen, 1994: 158, quoting Eichler, 1986).

For Blaikie (1993), the core feminist criticism is that all science is based on a masculine way of viewing the world. It is androcentric, and omits or distorts women's experiences (Oakley, 1974; Smart, 1976; Stanley and Wise, 1983). The argument has been presented as follows:

> What counts as knowledge must be grounded on experience. Human experience differs according to the kinds of activities and social relations in which humans engage. Women's experience systematically differs from the male experience upon which knowledge claims have been grounded. Thus the experience on which the prevailing claims to social and natural knowledge are founded is, first of all, only partial human experience only partially understood: namely, masculine experience as understood by men. However, when this experience is presumed to be gender-free – when the male experience is taken to be the human experience – the resulting theories, concepts, methodologies, inquiry goals and knowledge-claims distort human social life and human thought. (Harding and Hintikka, 1983: x)

Although it may be difficult to define a distinctive feminist methodology, there are clear themes in feminist thinking about research methods. Haig (1997) identifies five common features of feminist methodology: the rejection of positivism, the pervasive influence of gender relations, the value-ladenness of science, the adoption of a liberation methodology and the pursuit of non-hierarchical research relationships. Some of these are shared with other perspectives, especially critical theorists and postmodernists: for example, this list is similar to the five basic assumptions Lather uses in linking feminism with postmodernism.[3] What is different about the feminist viewpoint, however, is that each of these points is seen as contributing to the subordination and oppression of women. It is the second of these – the pervasive influence of gender relations, and the view of traditional orthodox research methods as having a patriarchal basis (Roman, 1992) – which most identifies the feminist position.

Attempts to summarize and categorize feminist views on research methods vary, but three common categories which are used are feminist empiricism, feminist standpoint epistemology, and feminist postmodernism (Olesen, 1994; Haig, 1997). *Feminist empiricism* aims to modify the norms and procedures of traditional social science to remove its biases, especially its sexist biases. In this view, traditional science can be reshaped to serve feminist ends, and the full range of methods, quantitative and qualitative, can be employed to study feminist issues. *Standpoint epistemologists*, by contrast, reject traditional research methods, however modified. They see the characteristics of researchers as important determinants of the way they see and interpret reality. Some standpoint epistemologists go further, and hold that the subjugated position of women is a privileged vantage point from which to view social reality. While that particular viewpoint attracts criticism, relations of ruling are seen as inherent in conventional research methods. In this respect, standpoint epistemologists are close to critical theorists. *Feminist postmodernism*, like other postmodernist thinking,

> rejects the epistemological assumption of modernist, Enlightenment thought. Thus, it stands opposed to the foundationalist grounding of knowledge, the universalizing claims for the scope of knowledge, and the employment of dualistic categories of thought. By contrast, postmodern feminism is an epistemology that is nonfoundationalist, contextualist, and nondualist, or multiplist, in its commitments. (Haig, 1997: 182)

For some, the commitment to feminism implies a commitment to action. Thus Hammersley (1995) sees emancipation as a main theme of feminist methodology, and Lather believes that research is feminist only if linked to action:

> I [engage in] feminist efforts to empower through empirical research designs which maximize a dialogic, dialectically educative encounter between researcher and researched … What I suggest is that our intent more consciously be to use our research to help participants understand and change their situations. (quoted in Reinharz, 1992: 175)

Action research in general highlights the political and politicizing nature of the research process. It brings with it a different role for the researcher, and it is frequently the preferred strategy in research for empowerment. While feminist action research exemplifies these points, not all action research is feminist. Section 8.6 looks at action research in general.

Reinharz (1992: 180–94) identifies five types of feminist research with an explicit action connection. In *action research*, projects attempt directly to change people's behaviour, and gather and analyse data concurrently. They intervene and study in a continuous series of feedback loops. Action and evaluation proceed simultaneously. In *participatory or collaborative research*, the people studied make decisions about the study design and procedures, and distinctions between the researcher(s) and those on whom the research is done disappear. Participants make decisions about the research during the research, rather than function as passive 'subjects'. *Needs assessment or prevalence research* seeks to determine how many people have a particular experience or need. Needs assessment research usually relies on surveys[4] to determine how widespread the problem or need is. *Evaluation research* aims to assess the effectiveness of different actions in meeting needs or solving problems. It is used to evaluate individual and organizational behaviour, and to evaluate evaluation research itself. Finally, in what Reinharz calls the *demystification framework*, researchers believe that the act of obtaining knowledge creates the potential for change because the lack of research about certain groups accentuates and perpetuates their powerlessness. Because the needs and opinions of certain groups are not known, they have little influence on the conditions under which they live. The study of such groups is political because it demystifies, and feminist research can 'raise consciousness'. Demystification here means the change in consciousness that occurs among the relatively powerless, when they consider their situation in a new light.[5]

The action orientation of some feminist research, and specifically its 'emancipatory impulse', is shared with other traditions of social thought, such as black studies, Marxism, and gay and lesbian studies (Fonow and Cook, 1991). We noted earlier that feminist research typically involves the pursuit of non-hierarchical relationships, and a radical redefinition of research roles. Associated features are its refusal to ignore the emotional dimension in the conduct of inquiry, and its acknowledgement of the role of affect in the production of knowledge (Mies, 1991). We will see this again when we look at feminist approaches to interviewing in Chapter 9.

### 8.1.3 Postmodernism

Postmodernism is difficult to define. Denzin and Lincoln's (1994: 15) definition is in only the most general terms: a contemporary sensibility, developing since World War II, that privileges no single authority, method or paradigm. Lather's (1991: 159) is more revealing: postmodernism[6] is the code name for the crisis of confidence in Western conceptual systems. It has arisen against the background of a loss of faith in the power of reason and the shattering of traditional religious orthodoxies; it is linked to feminism and postcolonialism; it has been validated by the collapse of communism (the socialist grand narrative); and it draws inspiration from cyberspace and the 'virtual world of hyperreality'. For Hammersley (1995), postmodernism involves the critique of a corrupt and oppressive modernity, though it is not a single coherent body of argument. Postmodernism is prominent in discussions of contemporary culture, and it is hard to find an area of study where it has not had an impact (Apple, 1991). Our interest here is in its impact on the context of present-day social inquiry.

A central idea in postmodernism is the disbelief in and debunking of all 'grand narratives',[7] including those of Western civilization. For our purposes, the most relevant metanarrative being debunked is the Enlightenment 'myth' of the gradual but steady progress of reason and freedom (Lyotard, 1984). Emancipation through reason is seen to have failed, and the flaws in rationality are increasingly exposed:

> The program of making everything knowable through the supposedly impersonal norms and procedures of 'science' has been radically questioned. The hope of constructing a 'grand narrative', either intellectual or political, that will give us the ultimate truth and will lead us to freedom has been shattered in many ways. (Apple, 1991: vii)

Thus there is a rejection of the assumptions of rationality, of traditional Western epistemology, or of any supposedly secure representation of reality that exists outside of discourse itself (Kincheloe and McLaren, 1994). This rejection has profound consequences for views of knowledge. Out goes the view of knowledge as disinterested and based on secure foundations, in favour of a conceptualization of knowledge as 'constructed, contested, incessantly perspectival and polyphonic' (Apple, 1991: xx). Truth is a destructive illusion, and a complete rethinking of science is involved, including confronting our 'Cartesian anxiety', with its lust for absolutes and for certainty in ways of knowing. In postmodern thinking, reality is a text, subject to multiple interpretations, multiple readings, multiple uses. And knowledge is not at all disinterested, but is inextricably bound up with power (Foucault, 1980).

Postmodernism is informed by such intellectual movements as structuralism and poststructuralism, psychoanalysis, semiotics and deconstructionism. It also shares much with feminist perspectives. Like feminism, it changes the way research is viewed. In this book, we will consider mainly its impact on approaches to the analysis of qualitative data. Those most commonly associated with postmodernism are deconstruction, discourse analysis and semiotics, the last two of which are discussed in Chapter 10.

The displacement of Western metanarratives of truth is grounded in deconstruction: not a method, according to Derrida (1984: 124), but a disclosure of how a text functions as desire. Some (for example, Parker et al., 1995) use deconstruction to look for suppressed and/or multiple meanings in a text (or conversation or event), and to expose the ideology inevitably present in all forms of communication. Feldman (1995) uses deconstruction in this way, and points out the assumptions behind it: that ideology imposes limits on what can and cannot be said, and that writers write and actors act from within an ideology, bounding their texts and their actions by the limits of their ideology. Deconstruction, as an analytical tool, aims to expose those ideological limits.

'Text' and 'discourse' are central terms in the postmodernist perspective; narratives and metanarratives are texts with discourses. In general terms, discourse signifies the 'system of relations between parties engaged in communicative activity', a view which stresses the inescapably political context of communication. Discourse and politics are coupled, just as knowledge and power are coupled (Apple, 1991: vii). Since a discourse is beneath the writer's awareness, discourse analysis and semiotics are both involved in exposing the deeper meanings of communication, and their connections with power and ideology. Haig (1997), writing about feminist postmodernism, notes that the postmodernist emphasis on language underwrites a discourse analysis approach to research, where the study of texts is substituted for the broader study of social reality.

Postmodernism emphasizes the ways we create our worlds by means of language. Language is seen as both carrier and creator of a culture's epistemological codes. The innocent view of language as the transparent representation of external reality is replaced by the view of language as centrally implicated in the construction of knowledge in its inevitably political context. We will see this point again in Chapter 9, when we look at the centrality of language.

Feminism and postmodernism are two of the more prominent features of the contemporary context for social research, but they are not the only ones. Others include the various critical perspectives (see, for example, Hammersley, 1995: Chapter 2), racial and ethnic perspectives, and the interdisciplinary perspectives of cultural studies (Denzin and Lincoln, 1994). There is cross-cut and overlap between all of these, but taken together they stress the political dimensions of research and contribute to the diversity in qualitative research. An implication of this diversity for us, in the next three chapters, is that such perspectives may change the way different topics are viewed and techniques are used. But the topics and techniques themselves represent some of the common elements within the diversity of qualitative research.

### 8.1.4 Common themes within the diversity

The prespecified versus unfolding continuum discussed in Chapter 2 applies to research questions, to designs, and to data (see Figure 2.2). Quantitative research is more likely to fall towards the left-hand end of this continuum, with well developed research questions, conceptual frameworks and tight designs linking the variables, and highly structured data. Qualitative research is more diverse than this. It is more likely to fall away from the left-hand end of the continuum, and much of it towards the right-hand end. There, the structure of the design and data is not organized in advance, but develops as the empirical work proceeds. Qualitative research is also much more eclectic, in using multiple strategies and methods, than quantitative research. For the qualitative researcher, the range of what can count as useful data, and of ways of collecting them, is very wide indeed. Together with the pluralism of paradigms and the multiple perspectives of qualitative research, these points mean that qualitative designs and data collection and analysis techniques cannot be as neatly described as their quantitative counterparts.

While qualitative research is much more diverse than quantitative research, there are at the same time important recurrent features in qualitative research. To finish this section, and to complete the transition to qualitative research, we will note these recurrent features.

The first is that a major characteristic of qualitative research, reflected in its designs, is that it is naturalistic, preferring to study people, things and events in their natural settings. While much quantitative research (for example, an experiment) is not at all naturalistic, quantitative research can be naturalistic also, in studying people in their natural settings without artificially contriving situations for research purposes. Some observational studies and correlational surveys fall into this category, but they are likely to have a prefigured conceptual framework and design, with prestructured data. Qualitative designs are more likely to delay conceptualizing and structuring of the data until later in the research. They are also less likely to contrive or create a situation for research purposes.

Beyond this main characteristic, there are several attempts to classify the many varieties of qualitative research by identifying its common features (for example, Tesch, 1990; Wolcott, 1992). A summary of the recurrent elements in qualitative research is given by Miles and Huberman and is reproduced here:

- Qualitative research is conducted through an intense and/or prolonged contact with a 'field' or life situation. These situations are typically 'banal' or normal ones, reflective of the everyday life of individuals, groups, societies, and organizations.
- The researcher's role is to gain a 'holistic' overview of the context under study: its logic, its arrangements, its explicit and implicit rules.
- The researcher attempts to capture data on the perceptions of local actors 'from the inside', through a process of deep attentiveness, of empathetic understanding, and of suspending or 'bracketing' preconceptions about the topics under discussion.
- Reading through these materials, the researcher may isolate certain themes and expressions that can be reviewed with informants, but that should be maintained in their original forms throughout the study.

- A main task is to explicate the ways people in particular settings come to understand, account for, take action, and otherwise manage their day-to-day situations.
- Many interpretations of this material are possible, but some are more compelling for theoretical reasons or on grounds of internal consistency.
- Relatively little standardized instrumentation is used at the outset. The researcher is essentially the main 'instrument' in the study.
- Most analysis is done with words. The words can be assembled, subclustered, broken into semiotic segments. They can be organized to permit the researcher to contrast, compare, analyze, and bestow patterns upon them. (1994: 6–7)

Many of these features will come up in different ways in the next three chapters. They provide a good background against which to look at main qualitative research designs.

## 8.2 Design in Qualitative Research

In Chapter 5, research design in general was described as the overall plan for a piece of research, including four main ideas: the strategy, the conceptual framework, the question of who or what will be studied, and the tools to be used for collecting and analysing empirical materials. Design situates the researcher in the empirical world. When research questions are prespecified, the design sits between the research questions and the data, and it shows how the research questions will be connected to the data. When research questions are developed as the study unfolds, the design still needs to connect the questions to the data, and to fit in with both.

Thus, as in Chapter 5, in considering design we are moving from what data will be needed to how and from whom they will be collected. The same four questions can be used. That is, the data will be collected: following what strategy? Within what framework? From whom? How? Against this background, this chapter describes two main qualitative research designs – case studies and ethnographies. In addition, a separate section will consider grounded theory as an important and distinctive strategy in qualitative research.[8] There will often be overlap between these three: any particular qualitative study will not necessarily be one thing or the other. While recognizing that, it is still useful to consider each separately.

## 8.3 Case Studies

In this section, case studies are discussed under four headings: the general idea of case studies, some main characteristics, case studies and generalizability, and preparing a case study. Some case studies are summarized in Example 8.1.

*Beachside Comprehensive: A Case Study of Secondary Schooling* (Ball, 1981), a study of mixed-ability teaching in a comprehensive school, utilized comparisons of lesson observations between those of the researcher and those provided by teachers.

Example 8.1
*Examples of case studies*

In *The Administrative Behavior of Federal Bureau Chiefs,* Kaufman (1981) presented a case study of six federal bureau chiefs. Kaufman spent intensive periods of time with each chief, interviewing them, attending meetings with them and sitting in on discussions in their offices.

*Tally's Corner* (Liebow, 1967) is a book about a single group of black men, living in a poor, inner-city neighbourhood. By befriending these men the author was able to learn about their lifestyles, their coping behaviour, and in particular their sensitivity to unemployment and failure.

'Case study interviews: caring for persons with AIDS' (Matocha, 1992) used a multiple case study approach to discover the effects of AIDS on family members responsible for the care of relatives with the disease. A grounded theory approach was incorporated in the study.

Neustadt and Fineberg's (1983) study *The Epidemic That Never Was: Policy-Making and the Swine Flu Affair* provides a comprehensive analysis of a mass immunization campaign. It was originally published as a government report, *The Swine Flu Affair: Decision-Making on a Slippery Disease.*

*In Search of Excellence: Lessons from America's Best-Run Companies* by Peters and Waterman (1982) is based on more than 60 case studies of large-scale successful American businesses. The text contains cross-case analyses with each chapter dealing with characteristics associated with organizational excellence.

*TVA and the Grass Roots: A Study of Politics and Organization,* a classic study by Selznick (1949) of the Tennessee Valley Authority (TVA), describes the political behaviour and organizational decentralization that occurred as a result of the TVA Act. Under this Act the TVA was charged with the duty to plan for the proper use, conservation and development of the natural resources of the Tennessee River drainage basin and its adjoining territory.

*Street Corner Society: The Social Structure of an Italian Slum* (Whyte, 1955) is a classic example of a descriptive case study. It describes an Italian-American subculture, 'Cornerville', covering one neighbourhood in Boston in the 1940s. Issues of career advancement of low-income youths and their ability (or inability) to break with neighbourhood ties are discussed.

### 8.3.1 The general idea

What is a case study? The basic idea is that one case (or perhaps a small number of cases) will be studied in detail, using whatever methods seem appropriate. While there may be a variety of specific purposes and research questions, the general objective is to develop as full an understanding of that case as possible. We may be interested only in this case, or we may have in mind not just this case we are studying, but others like it. That raises the question of generalizability, which we will look at later.

In keeping with other approaches in qualitative research, the case study aims to understand the case in depth, and in its natural setting, recognizing its complexity and its context. It also has a holistic focus, aiming to preserve and understand the wholeness and unity of the case. Therefore the case study is more a strategy than a method. As Goode and Hatt pointed out many years ago: 'The case study then is not a specific technique; it is a way of organizing social data so as to preserve the unitary character of the social object being studied' (1952: 331). This strategy for understanding contrasts strongly with the reductionist approach of some quantitative research.

What then is a case? It is difficult to give a full answer to this question, since almost anything can serve as a case, and the case may be simple or complex. But, with Miles and Huberman (1994), we can define a case as a phenomenon of some sort occurring in a bounded context. Thus, the case may be an individual, or a role, or a small group, or an organization, or a community, or a nation. It could also be a decision, or a policy, or a process, or an incident or event of some sort, and there are other possibilities as well. Brewer and Hunter (1989) list six types of units which can be studied in social science research: individuals; attributes of individuals; actions and interactions; residues and artefacts of behaviour; settings, incidents and events; and collectivities. Any of these may be the focus of case study research.

If there are different types of cases, there are also different types of case study. Stake (1994) distinguishes three main types:

- the intrinsic case study, where the study is undertaken because the researcher wants a better understanding of this particular case
- the instrumental case study, where a particular case is examined to give insight into an issue, or to refine a theory
- the collective case study, where the instrumental case study is extended to cover several cases, to learn more about the phenomenon, population or general condition.

The first two of these are single case studies, where the focus is within the case. The third involves multiple cases, where the focus is both within and across cases. It is also called the multiple case study, or the comparative case study.

Because of the great variation, it is not easy to define the case study. Stake gives a 'pretty loose definition': a case study is 'a study of a bounded system, emphasizing the unity and wholeness of that system, but confining the attention to those aspects that are relevant to the research problem at the time' (1988: 258). Yin (1984: 23) stresses that a case study is an empirical inquiry that:

- investigates a contemporary phenomenon within its real-life context, when
- the boundaries between phenomenon and context are not clearly evident, and in which
- multiple sources of evidence are used.

A dictionary of sociological terms defines a case study as:

> a method of studying social phenomena through the thorough analysis of an individual case. The case may be a person, a group, an episode, a process, a community, a society, or any other unit of social life. All data relevant to the case are gathered, and all available data are organized in terms of the case. The case study method gives a unitary character to the data being studied by interrelating a variety of facts to a single case. It also provides an opportunity for the intensive analysis of many specific details that are often overlooked with other methods. (Theodorson and Theodorson, 1969)

These definitions together highlight four main characteristics of case studies.

### 8.3.2 Four characteristics of case studies

First, the case is a 'bounded system': it has boundaries. Yin points out that the boundaries between the case and the context are not necessarily clearly evident. Nonetheless, the researcher needs to identify and describe the boundaries of the case as clearly as possible.

Second, the case is a case of something. This may seem obvious, but it needs stressing, to give focus to the research, and to make the logic and strategy of the research clear. Identifying what the case is a case of, is also important in determining the unit of analysis, an important idea in the analysis of data.

Third, there is an explicit attempt to preserve the wholeness, unity and integrity of the case. The word 'holistic' is often used in this connection. At the same time, since not everything can be studied, even about one case, specific focus is required. Research questions help to define this focus.

Fourth, multiple sources of data and multiple data collection methods are likely to be used, typically in a naturalistic setting. Many case studies will use sociological and anthropological field methods, such as observations in natural settings, interviews, and narrative reports. But they may also use questionnaires and numerical data. This means that the case study is not necessarily a qualitative technique, though most case studies are predominantly qualitative.

### 8.3.3 Case studies and generalizability

A common criticism of the case study concerns its generalizability: 'This study is based on only one case, so how can we generalize?' Because this reaction is so common, we need to take this question seriously.

The first point is to ask whether we would want to generalize from a particular case study. There are two types of case study situations where generalization would not be the objective. First, the case may be so important, interesting, or misunderstood that it deserves study in its own right. Or it may be unique in some very important respects, and therefore worthy of study. These are examples of Stake's (1994) intrinsic case study. The intention of such a study is not to generalize, but rather to understand the case in its complexity and its entirety, as well as in its context. Second, a strong argument can often be made about studying the 'negative case'. This is where a particular case seems to be markedly different from the general pattern of other cases, perhaps even completely opposite to them, creating the need to understand why this case is so different. The logic is that we can learn about the typical by studying the atypical, as when we study disease in order to learn about health. This is Stake's second type of case study, the instrumental case study. Therefore, whether a case study should even seek to generalize, and claim to be representative, depends on the context and purposes of the particular project. Generalization should not necessarily be the objective of all research projects, whether case studies or not (Denzin, 1983).

Aside from these two situations, however, there are many case studies where we do have in mind more than just the case being studied, and where we do want to find something more broadly applicable. How can a case study produce something that might be generalizable? There are two main ways that a case study can produce generalizable results. Both depend on the purposes of the case study, and especially on the way its data are analysed. The first is by conceptualizing, the second is by developing propositions. In both instances, the findings from a case study can be put forward as being potentially applicable to other cases.

To conceptualize means that, on the basis of the disciplined study of this case, and using methods for analysis which focus on conceptualizing rather than on describing (for example, those described in Chapter 10 under grounded theory), the researcher develops one or more new concepts to explain some aspect of what has been studied. Indeed, to develop such new concepts may require the sort of in-depth study that is only possible in a case study. To develop propositions means that, based on the case studied, the researcher puts forward one or more propositions – they could be called hypotheses – which link concepts or factors within the case. These can then be assessed for their applicability and transferability to other situations. This turns the traditional model of research around. In traditional quantitative research, we often begin with propositions or hypotheses: they are inputs into the research. In this view of case study research, we end with them: they become outputs of the research.

In neither of these instances will the one case study have proved generalizability of its findings. But it can certainly suggest such generalizability, putting forward concepts or propositions for testing in further research. Clearly, every case that can be studied is in some respects unique. But every case is also, in some respects, similar to other cases. The question is whether we want to focus on what is unique about a particular case, or on what is common with other cases. At different times we need to do each of these, and we need to be aware of when we are doing each. This is a matter to be addressed in the purposes and research questions which are developed to guide a case study. When generalizability is a goal, and we are focusing on the potential common elements in a case, it is necessary for the analysis of the case study data to be conducted at a sufficient level of abstraction. The more abstract the concept, the more generalizable it is. Developing abstract concepts and propositions raises the analysis above simple description, and in this way a case study can contribute potentially generalizable findings.

The generalization process is not mechanical, though this is more freely recognized in qualitative research than in quantitative research. There have been some attempts to see the complexity of generalization in the quantitative context (for example, Bracht and Glass, 1968), but it is still widely regarded there as generalization from a sample to a population. In fact, however, as Firestone (1993) points out, there are three levels of generalization: generalization from sample to population, analytic or theory-connected generalization, and case-to-case transfer. Similarly, Stake (1988: 260) distinguishes between scientific generalization, arrived at by experimentation and induction, and naturalistic generalization, where general understandings are furthered by case studies and experience in individual events.[9] The two types of case study generalization described above are examples of analytic or theory-connected or theoretical generalization.

While on this 'lack of generalizability' criticism of case study research, which is often a 'kneejerk' reaction to the case study, we should note the central role given to the case method of teaching in professional schools of business, medicine and law, as well as nursing, public administration, social work and psychoanalysis (Reinharz, 1992). In these training situations, historical cases are studied in great detail, and are used to train managers, doctors, lawyers and so on, to deal with situations they will encounter in the future. This clearly underlines the potential generalizability of knowledge built from case studies. If every case were totally unique, there would be no transferability of knowledge from one case to another, and little point in the case method of training.

Case studies have had an ambiguous place in social science (Reinharz, 1992), and historically there has often been a disapproving attitude towards the case study. This attitude is usually based on the generalizability criticism, and is expressed in the condescending remark 'that's only a case study'. This book takes a different view. Properly conducted case studies, especially in situations where our knowledge is shallow, fragmentary, incomplete or nonexistent, have a valuable contribution to make, in three main ways.

The first is what we can learn from the study of a particular case, in its own right. As noted, the case being studied might be unusual, unique or not yet understood, so that building an in-depth understanding of the case is valuable. This might cover all of the three types of case study described by Stake. Second, only the in-depth case study can provide understanding of the important aspects of a new or persistently problematic research area. This is particularly true when complex social behaviour is involved, as in much social research. Discovering the important features, developing an understanding of them, and conceptualizing them for further study, are often best achieved through the case study strategy. Following this line of argument, it may be that too much research has tried to go straight to measurement and quantitative mapping, without the fuller understanding of the phenomena and processes involved that is best achieved by case studies.[10] Third, the case study can make an important contribution in combination with other research approaches. For example, a case study ahead of a survey can give direction to that survey not possible without the understanding built from the case study. Similarly, a survey could be followed by, or done in conjunction with, one or more case studies. Because of the limitations of the survey, the case study can 'flesh out' the picture in a way that is both crucial to our understanding, and not possible using more superficial techniques.[11]

These potential contributions of the case study counter the disapproving attitude described above. At the same time, this critical attitude can have validity, especially when a case study is standing alone, not integrated with other approaches to its subject matter and simply descriptive, or when more is claimed from its findings than the data can bear. Therefore, because of these criticisms, and because of the diversity within case study research, it seems especially important to be clear on the rationale behind the case study, and on its purpose(s). That means developing research questions to guide the study, either ahead of it or as focal points in the case become clear.

### 8.3.4 Preparing a case study

We can now summarize what has been said into a set of guidelines for preparing a case study. A case study research proposal would need to:

- be clear on what the case is, including identification of its boundaries
- be clear on the need for the study of this case, and on the general purpose(s) of this case study
- translate that general purpose into specific purposes and research questions (these may emerge during the early empirical work)
- identify the overall strategy of the case study, especially whether it is one case or multiple cases, and why
- show what data will be collected, from whom, and how
- show how the data will be analysed.

The last point will come up again in Chapter 10, especially when we look at levels of abstraction in the analysis of qualitative data. Similarly, the first point, on identifying and bounding the case, has implications for the unit of analysis in the study, and for the analysis of the study's data.[12]

## 8.4 **Ethnography**

This section has three parts. First, it summarizes the introduction to ethnography given by Hammersley and Atkinson in their well known textbook on the subject. Second, it identifies some important features of the ethnographic approach to research. Third, it makes some general comments about the place of ethnography in social research. Some enthnographic studies are summarized in Example 8.2. The term 'ethnography' itself comes from cultural anthropology. 'Ethno' means people or folk, while 'graphy' refers to describing something. Thus ethnography means describing a culture and understanding a way of life from the point of view of its participants; ethnography is the art and science of describing a group or culture (Fetterman, 1989; Neuman, 1994). Fielding (1996a) discusses the origins of ethnography, and surveys the history of its use in British colonial and American research.

---

*Translated Woman: Crossing the Border with Esperanza's Story* (Behar, 1993) is the life story of a Mexican Indian woman who was reputed to have bewitched her former husband for abusing her and leaving her for another woman. Rumours of her witchcraft powers were reinforced when her husband suddenly went blind.

**Example 8.2**
*Examples of ethnographies*

Charlesworth et al.'s (1989) study *Life among the Scientists: An Anthropological Study of an Australian Scientific Community* was carried out on a community of scientists at the Walter and Eliza Hall Institute of Medical Science in Melbourne, Australia. The book reveals what is actually done in concrete situations, as distinct from what scientists say they do and what philosophers and historians and sociologists of science theorize about what they do.

*When Prophecy Fails: A Social and Psychological Study of a Modern Group that Predicted the Destruction of the World*, a participant observation study by Festinger et al. (1964), was carried out opportunistically with two small groups who claimed to have received messages from a planet 'Clarion' predicting a catastrophic flood in three months. The researchers and some hired observers joined the group and conducted intensive investigations before the predicted disaster and afterwards during the period of disconfirmation.

*The National Front* (Fielding, 1981) is an ethnography of an extreme right racist organization. The researcher joined the group as a member and conducted participant observation at meetings and interviews with party officials and opponents of the party, as well as content analysis of party documents.

---

(Continued)

McLaren's (1986) ethnographic study *Schooling as a Ritual Performance: Towards a Political Economy of Educational Symbols and Gestures* is of an inner-city Catholic school in Toronto, Canada, where the school population is largely made up of Portuguese and Italian students. McLaren analyses body postures and gestures of students and generates a theoretical framework for conceptualizing embodied meaning and power.

**Example 8.2 (Continued)**

In *Nisa: The Life and Words of a !Kung Woman,* Shostak (1981) worked with a female key informant, Nisa, in her study of !Kung society. A life history approach is utilized in which the voices of the informant Nisa, the anthropologist putting Nisa's story in cultural perspective, and an American woman experiencing another world, are all recognized.

*The Forest People by Turnbull* (1968) is a classic work which describes the researcher's experiences while living with the Ba Mbuti pygmies in the Ituri Forest in the former Belgian Congo.

*The Man in the Principal's Office: An Ethnography* is Wolcott's (1973) inquiry into the behaviour of one elementary school principal. The researcher spent two years following a typical school principal in all of his professional and many of his private activities.

*The Rashaayda Bedouin: Arab Pastoralists of Eastern Sudan,* a case study by Young (1996) of a Bedouin culture, provides vivid descriptions of the daily life of these nomadic pastoralists. The way of life is described from the perspective of one who has lived it (including learning the language and wearing the costume) and who for a while has become a member of one family.

### 8.4.1 Introduction

Hammersley and Atkinson (1995: 1–10) take a fairly 'liberal' view of ethnography, whereby the ethnographer participates, overtly or covertly, in people's daily lives for an extended period of time, watching what happens, listening to what is said, asking questions and collecting any other relevant data. They point out ethnography's connection to naturalism, a way of doing social research developed by ethnographers in the face of the difficulties they saw with positivism. In naturalistic research, unlike other approaches, the social world is studied as far as possible in its natural state, undisturbed by the researcher. Research uses methods that are sensitive to the nature of the setting, and the primary aim is to describe what happens in the setting, and how the people involved see their own actions, others' actions, and the context.

Drawing especially on symbolic interactionism, but also on phenomenology and hermeneutics, naturalism sees social phenomena as quite different in character from physical phenomena. The basic ideas here are that human behaviour is based upon meanings which people attribute to and bring to situations, and that behaviour is not 'caused' in any mechanical way, but is continually constructed and reconstructed on the basis of people's interpretations of the situations they are in.

Therefore, to understand behaviour, we need an approach which gives access to the meanings that guide behaviour. It is the capacities we have all developed as social actors – the capacity to do participant observation – which can give us that access. As participant observers, we can learn the culture or subculture of the people we are studying, and learn to understand the world as they do. Classic anthropological studies demonstrate how this approach is used to study societies other than our own, but it can be used for the study of all societies, including our own. This is because there are many different layers of cultural knowledge within any society, especially modern industrialized society.

Thus ethnography

> exploits the capacity that any social actor possesses for learning new cultures, and the objectivity to which this process gives rise. Even where he or she is researching a familiar group or setting, the participant observer is required to treat this as 'anthropologically strange', in an effort to make explicit the presuppositions he or she takes for granted as a culture member. In this way, it is hoped, the culture is turned into an object available for study. Naturalism proposes that through marginality, in social position and perspective, it is possible to construct an account of the culture under investigation that both understands it from within and captures it as external to, and independent of, the researcher: in other words, as a natural phenomenon. Thus, the *description* of cultures becomes the primary goal. (1995: 9–10)

Hammersley and Atkinson then focus on the central theme of reflexivity in ethnographic work,[13] and the remainder of their book considers different aspects of the research process, advocating and illustrating the reflexive point of view.

This introduction makes clear that the concept of culture is central in ethnography. Culture can be thought of as a shared set of meanings, or a cognitive map of meanings (Spradley, 1980). The cultural knowledge that any group of people have is their knowledge of that map. Ethnography has developed within anthropology as the central strategy to study culture, and many anthropologists consider cultural interpretation to be ethnography's main contribution. A full discussion of the concept of culture is beyond our scope here, but useful references are Keesing (1976), Haviland (1990) and Howard (1993).

We can summarize this introduction to ethnography using the words of a prominent educational ethnographer:

> Ethnography means, literally, a picture of the 'way of life' of some identifiable group of people. Conceivably, those people could be any culture-bearing

group, in any time and place. In times past, the group was usually a small, intact, essentially self-sufficient social unit, and it was always a group notably 'strange' to the observer. The anthropologist's purpose as ethnographer was to learn about, record, and ultimately portray the culture of this other group. Anthropologists always study human behaviour in terms of cultural context. Particular individuals, customs, institutions, or events are of anthropological interest as they relate to a generalized description of the life-way of a socially interacting group. Yet culture itself is always an abstraction, regardless of whether one is referring to culture in general or to the culture of a specific social group. (Wolcott, 1988: 188)

### 8.4.2 Some main characteristics

The overarching characteristic of the ethnographic approach is its commitment to cultural interpretation. The point of ethnography is to study and understand the cultural and symbolic aspects of behaviour and the context of that behaviour, whatever the specific focus of the research. That specific focus is typically either some group of people, or a case (or a small number of cases), focusing on culturally significant behaviour. In addition to this central characteristic, we can identify six (related) important features of the ethnographic approach.

First, when studying a group of people, ethnography starts from the assumption that the shared cultural meanings of the group are crucial to understanding its behaviour. This is part of its commitment to cultural interpretation. As Goffman says: 'any group of persons – prisoners, primitives, pilots or patients – develop a life of their own that becomes meaningful, reasonable and normal once you get close to it' (1961: ix–x). The ethnographer's task is to uncover that meaning.

Second, the ethnographer is sensitive to the meanings that behaviour, actions, events and contexts have in the eyes of the people involved. What is needed is the insider's perspective on those events, actions and contexts. As Spindler and Spindler point out: 'Sociocultural knowledge held by social participants makes social behaviour and communication sensible. Therefore a major part of the ethnographic task is to elicit that knowledge from informant participants' (1992: 73). The ethnographic study will be designed, and its data collection techniques organized, in line with this.

Third, the group or case will be studied in its natural setting. A true ethnography therefore involves the researcher becoming part of that natural setting (Fielding, 1996a: 157). This explains why participant observation, discussed in Chapter 9, is the favoured method in ethnographic research. To understand any group, or any culturally significant act, event or process, it is necessary to study behaviour in its natural setting, with special reference to the symbolic world associated with that behaviour.

Fourth, an ethnography is likely to be an unfolding and evolving sort of study, rather than prestructured. As part of developing a focus for the study, it will not normally be clear what to study in depth until some fieldwork has been done. While specific research questions and hypotheses will be used in the research, they are more likely to develop as the study proceeds, rather than to be formulated ahead of the research. This point also applies to data collection procedures and to data.[14] Data collection in ethnography may use several techniques, but any structuring of the data or of data collection instruments will be generated *in situ* as the study unfolds.

Fifth, from the point of view of data collection techniques, ethnography is eclectic, not restricted. Any techniques might be used, but fieldwork is always central. An ethnographic fieldwork continuum would range from direct non-participant observation to participant observation, then to ethnographic interviewing with one or more informants, and then to the words of the people themselves (often called, in ethnographic writing, the 'voices of the natives'). Data collection may well range across this whole continuum in an ethnography, and it may be further supplemented by anything that gives a fuller picture of the live data, such as film or audio records, documents, diaries, and so on. It may also use structured and quantitative questionnaires, with scaled variables, though these would be developed as the study proceeds.

Sixth, ethnographic data collection will typically be prolonged and repetitive. There is both a general and a specific reason for this. The general reason is that the reality being studied – the meanings, symbolic significance and cultural interpretation – exists on several levels. It takes time for a researcher to gain access to the deeper and most important levels of this reality (Woods, 1992). The specific reason is that the ethnographic record needs to be comprehensive and detailed, and typically focuses on things that happen again and again. The ethnographer therefore needs to observe this a sufficient number of times. Closure is achieved by recognizing the point at which nothing new about its cultural significance is being learned.

### 8.4.3 General comments

While ethnography is a distinctive approach, there is no one design for an ethnographic study. Its design may overlap, in whole or in part, with other designs. Thus, for example, it may use elements of the case study or grounded theory approaches which are consistent with its orientation. It can also be used in combination with field experimentation and with surveys. Whatever the specific design, ethnography typically uses relatively unstructured empirical materials, a small number of cases, and a style of analysis and writing which stresses description and interpretation (Atkinson and Hammersley, 1994). Ethnography is also both process and product. 'Process' means that it is a particular approach to research and has a particular distinctive way of going about it. 'Product' means that a certain type of research report (sometimes called the ethnographic record, or a full ethnographic description) will be produced. The term 'an ethnography' illustrates the idea of ethnography as a product.

A full-scale ethnography means carrying out a detailed and demanding study, with fieldwork and data collection running over a long period of time. Where these demands exceed the time and resources of one project, there is nonetheless great value in bringing the ethnographic approach to the topic. Thus elements of the ethnographic approach, or 'borrowing ethnographic techniques' (Wolcott, 1988), will be used in many projects, rather than producing full-scale ethnographies.

When would the ethnographic approach be most appropriate? In general, when we need to understand the cultural context of behaviour, and the symbolic meaning and significance of the behaviour within that context. The ethnographic approach, being a method of discovery, is particularly useful when we are dealing with something new, different or unknown. It is an excellent way of gaining insight into a culture or a social process, particularly those in complex behavioural settings, and particularly those involving other cultures and subcultures, including those of organizations and institutions. The ethnographic approach can sensitize us to the cultural context and symbolic significance of behaviour we need to understand, in a way that other research approaches cannot. As Fielding points out, it is often pathbreaking, and, 'as a means of gaining a first insight into a culture or social process, as a source of hypotheses for detailed investigation using other methods, it is unparalleled' (1996a: 155).

## 8.5 Grounded Theory

As a research strategy, grounded theory is specific and different. At the same time it cuts across the other designs discussed in this chapter. Because it is different, and also because grounded theory is probably 'the most widely employed interpretive strategy in the social sciences today' (Denzin and Lincoln, 1994: 204), it needs special treatment here.[15] This need is accentuated because the grounded theory literature is somewhat difficult.

This book has two sections on grounded theory, one in this chapter and one in Chapter 10. This is because grounded theory is both a strategy for research, and a way of analysing data. In this chapter, we deal with grounded theory as a strategy under six headings:

* What is grounded theory?
* A short history of grounded theory.
* Theory generation versus theory verification.
* Data-collection/data-analysis relationships: theoretical sampling.
* The use of the literature in grounded theory.
* The place of grounded theory research.

Some grounded theory studies are summarized in Example 8.3, and more are noted in Chapter 10.

Using a database of 33 interviews with academic department chairpersons, Creswell and Brown (1992) in 'How chairpersons enhance faculty research: a grounded theory study' developed a grounded theory relating categories of chair influence to faculty scholarly performance.

**Example 8.3**
*Examples of grounded theory studies*

*Fresh Starts: Men and Women after Divorce* (Cauhape, 1983) describes the processes by which men and women rebuild their social worlds after mid-life divorce. Participants were upwardly mobile professional men and women, who were originally from non-professional backgrounds.

*Awareness of Dying* (Glaser and Strauss, 1965) was the first publication reporting the original grounded theory studies. Those studies (and this book) focus on the process of dying: what happens when people die in hospitals, how hospitals manage the situation, and the interaction between staff and patients. The research was carried out at six hospitals in San Francisco.

*Time for Dying* (Glaser and Strauss, 1968) was the second report of the grounded theory study. This book is based on intensive fieldwork combining observation and interviewing in the six hospitals. The focus again is on the organization of terminal care in hospitals, and the aim in the book is to describe the temporal features of dying, seeing dying itself as a social process.

*From Practice to Grounded Theory* (Chenitz and Swanson, 1986: Chapters 14 to 19) describes six grounded theory studies dealing with topics such as 'Getting around with emphysema' and 'Entry into a nursing home as status passage'.

The focus in Davis's (1973) study *Living with Multiple Sclerosis: A Social Psychological Analysis* was on patients with multiple sclerosis who, in certain circumstances, took the initiative in furthering the continuity of their care.

### 8.5.1 What is grounded theory?

The first point to make is that grounded theory is not a theory at all. It is a method, an approach, a strategy. Grounded theory is a research strategy whose purpose is to generate theory from data. 'Grounded' means that the theory will be generated on the basis of data; the theory will therefore be grounded in data. 'Theory' means that the objective of collecting and analysing the research data is to generate theory. The essential idea in grounded theory is that theory will be developed inductively from data.

Grounded theory, then, is an overall strategy for doing research. To implement that strategy, grounded theory has a particular set of techniques and procedures. As well as the grounded theory strategy, we can therefore talk also about grounded theory analysis – that style of analysis which uses procedures to develop a theory grounded in the data. This section is about the grounded theory approach; in Chapter 10, we will discuss grounded theory analysis.

### 8.5.2 A short history of grounded theory

A brief look at the history of grounded theory helps in understanding it, and in seeing its present place in social science research. That history is in fact quite short, and can be traced primarily through its five key publications. In the 1960s Glaser and Strauss began collaborative work in medical sociology, and published two landmark studies of dying in hospitals (Glaser and Strauss, 1965; 1968). These books had an important impact, and represented a different style of empirically based sociology. In response to numerous 'How did you do it?' requests from readers after *Awareness of Dying* was published, the authors wrote a book which detailed the methods they had developed and used in the dying studies. This book was published in 1967 under the title of *The Discovery of Grounded Theory*, and was the first description of the method, and the first key publication about grounded theory. According to Strauss and Corbin (1994: 275), *The Discovery of Grounded Theory* had three purposes: to offer the rationale for theory that was grounded, to suggest the logic for and specifics of grounded theories, and to legitimate careful qualitative research. In the years after its publication, first Glaser and then Strauss taught a grounded theory style seminar in qualitative analysis at the University of California in San Francisco.

While a good deal of research using grounded theory to investigate a variety of phenomena was published by numerous graduates of this programme, the next methodological work, and the second key publication, was *Theoretical Sensitivity*, by Glaser, in 1978, 11 years after *The Discovery of Grounded Theory*. Its purposes were to update methodological developments in grounded theory, and to help analysts develop theoretical sensitivity. Once again, while studies reporting grounded theory research continued to be published, it was another nine years before the next methodological statement. This was Strauss's *Qualitative Analysis for Social Scientists*, published in 1987, and the third key grounded theory publication. In this book, the focus is broadened to qualitative analysis in general, but grounded theory still plays the central role. It is described as 'a handbook of sorts for the better understanding of social phenomena through a particular style of qualitative analysis of data (*grounded theory*). That mode of doing analysis ... is designed especially for *generating and testing theory*' (1987: xi).

The fourth key publication was in 1990, with Strauss and Corbin's *Basics of Qualitative Research*, subtitled *Grounded Theory Procedures and Techniques*. It is addressed to researchers in various disciplines who aim to build theory through the qualitative analysis of data. It presents the analytic mode of grounded theory, and stresses that skill in this method of analysis is learnable by anyone who takes the trouble to study its procedures. This provokes, in response, the fifth key publication – Glaser's critique of the Strauss and Corbin book – titled *Basics of Grounded Theory Analysis*, subtitled *Emergence vs Forcing*, and published in 1992. In this book, Glaser sets out to correct what he takes to be the misconceptions about grounded theory evident in the Strauss and Corbin book.

These five publications give the basic history of the development of grounded theory. They are not the only methodological statements on grounded theory, but they are the main ones. Others which could be mentioned include those by Charmaz (1983) and by Chenitz and Swanson (1986), but they are more derivative statements, seeking to bring grounded theory to a wider audience rather than to advance the approach. Mention should also be made of two other works from Glaser – *Examples of Grounded Theory: A Reader* (1993) and *More Grounded Theory Methodology: A Reader* (1994) – which continue his critique of the Strauss and Corbin work. Finally, Strauss and Corbin (1994) give an overview of grounded theory methodology in a chapter in the Denzin and Lincoln *Handbook*. In that chapter, they comment on the developing nature of grounded theory methodology.

Grounded theory was developed by Glaser and Strauss doing research from a sociological perspective in organizational contexts. That is, it was developed as a method for the study of complex social behaviour. It was initially presented as a method for the analysis of qualitative data, and has inevitably become associated with qualitative research. But it is equally applicable to quantitative data, especially in Glaser's view.[16] While developed in sociology, grounded theory is in fact a general way of approaching research, and does not depend on particular disciplinary perspectives. It has therefore been used in a wide variety of research contexts. Some indication of the range of grounded theory studies is given by Strauss and Corbin (1990: 275–6) and by Glaser (1994).

### 8.5.3 Theory generation versus theory verification

Grounded theory has as its explicit purpose the generation of theory from data. This raises the contrast between research which aims to generate theory and research which aims to verify theory. As pointed out in Chapter 2, this contrast represents a difference in research styles. Traditionally, much research, especially quantitative research, has followed the theory verification model, as indicated in the importance it has traditionally given to the role of the hypothesis. Many research methods texts insisted that hypotheses were central to research and that, since the hypothesis was deduced from some more general theory, the point of the research was the testing of theory.

In the grounded theory approach, which aims to generate theory, no 'upfront' theory is proposed, and no hypotheses are formulated for testing ahead of the research. The research does not start with a theory from which it deduces hypotheses for testing. It starts with an open mind, aiming to end up with a theory. This emphasis was deliberately developed by Glaser and Strauss as a reaction against the exclusive insistence on theory verification research, especially in the American sociology of the 1950s.

It is useful to make this theory generation versus verification contrast sharply, in order to highlight the difference in research styles. But in fact, in practice, the distinction is not so sharp. For while we may start without a theory, and have the objective of creating one, it is not long into the theorizing process before we are also wanting to test theoretical ideas which are emerging. So, in fact, theory generation depends on progressive verification as well. Another way of saying this is that grounded theory is essentially an inductive technique, but it uses deduction as well. It stresses induction as the main tool for theory development, but, in developing the theory, deduction will also often be necessary.

### 8.5.4 Data-collection/data-analysis relationships: theoretical sampling

Grounded theory has a specific approach to this topic, which is different from many other approaches.[17] In the traditional view of research, data collection is a discrete stage in the research, to be completed before data analysis begins. In grounded theory, the pattern is different. Guided by some initial research questions, the researcher will collect a first set of data, preferably quite small. At that point, analysis of the data begins, using the procedures to be described in Chapter 10. The second set of data will be collected after the first analysis of data, guided by emerging directions in that analysis. This is the principle of theoretical sampling – the idea that subsequent data collection should be guided by theoretical developments that emerge in the analysis. This cycle of alternation between data collection and analysis will not stop at two repetitions. It continues until theoretical saturation is achieved – that is, until new data are not showing new theoretical elements, but are rather confirming what has already been found. This pattern is shown in Figure 8.1.

It is becoming more common to find this sort of data-collection/data-analysis relationship in qualitative research today. It is different from traditional research, but it resembles what we normally do in everyday life when we encounter a puzzling situation. Like much else in grounded theory, it models the way humans have always learned. In this respect, grounded theory is faithful to its philosophical roots in pragmatism (Glaser and Strauss, 1967).

**Figure 8.1**   *Theoretical sampling: data-collection/data-analysis relationships*

### 8.5.5 The use of the literature in grounded theory

Grounded theory has a different perspective on this matter from other research approaches. The difference lies in how the literature is dealt with, and when it is introduced, and follows from the stress that grounded theory places on theory generation.

If a satisfactory theory already exists on a particular topic, there is no point in mounting a study to generate a new theory about that topic. The rationale for doing a grounded theory study is that we have no satisfactory theory on the topic, and that we do not understand enough about it to begin theorizing. In that case, we will want to approach the data as open-mindedly as possible, guided by the research questions. The problem with reviewing the literature in advance of such a study is that it can strongly influence us when we begin working with the data.

As is detailed in Chapter 10, we want to begin the analysis by finding categories and concepts within the data, not by bringing them to the data, from the literature or anywhere else. In such a case, it makes sense to delay the literature reviewing stage of the work, at least until conceptual directions within the data have become clear. We will introduce the literature later than would normally be done, seeing the relevant literature as further data for the study. That is the key concept in using the literature in grounded theory: the literature is seen as further data to be fed into the analysis, but at a stage in the data analysis when theoretical directions have become clear. This use of the literature is consistent with the overall logic of grounded theory research. The whole approach is organized around the principle that theory which is developed will be grounded in data.

### 8.5.6 The place of grounded theory research

It is not surprising that grounded theory has become a widely used approach in qualitative research. I think there are five main reasons for this:

1  While much is said in the research methodology literature about the need to generate theory in research, very little is said about *how* to do that. Grounded theory explicitly addresses that question, as we will see in Chapter 10.
2  It represents a coordinated, systematic but flexible overall research strategy, in contrast to the *ad hoc* and uncoordinated approaches which have sometimes characterized qualitative research.
3  It brings a disciplined and organized approach to the analysis of qualitative data, again as is described in Chapter 10. In the qualitative research context, with its history of a lack of well formulated methods for the analysis of data, this has great appeal.
4  There are impressive demonstrations of what the grounded theory approach can produce in a research area. These began with the dying studies of

Glaser and Strauss, and have continued, especially in the area of medical sociology.[18]

5   There are issues to do with the identification of social research problems from professional practice, and from organizational and institutional contexts. In these situations, a traditional hypothesis testing approach is not appropriate. Many of these problems confronting social researchers, especially in applied areas, are substantively new, because they come from new developments in professional practice and/or from newly developing organizational contexts.[19] Empirical research, much of it qualitative, is needed in these areas, and the theory verification approach would be inappropriate. The theory generation approach of grounded theory has much to recommend it in these substantively new areas, where there is a lack of grounded concepts for describing and explaining what goes on. Grounded theory appeals because it concentrates on discovering concepts, hypotheses and theories.

## 8.6 Action Research

Early in *The Handbook of Action Research*, editors Reason and Bradbury (2001: 1) tell us that there is no short answer to the question 'What is action research?' Rather, the term is used for a family of related techniques which share certain important common ideas, while differing in details of their approach to the research. The differences have led to a variety of names by which such researchers describe their approach. Technical action research, practical action research, emancipatory action research, participatory action research and collaborative action research are examples, along with feminist action research (see Section 8.1.2), but the generic term 'action research' probably encompasses most of the approaches (Kemmis and McTaggart, 2000: 567). This section concentrates on the main common ideas behind the different strands of action research.[20]

The central idea is conveyed by the term 'action research' itself. Action and research are brought together: action researchers 'engage in careful, diligent inquiry, not for purposes of discovering new facts or revising accepted laws or theories, but to acquire information having practical application to the solution of specific problems related to their work' (Stringer, 2004: 3) Action research brings together the acting (or the doing) and the researching (or the inquiring). In contrast to the ideas of inquiry for its own sake and building knowledge for its own sake, action research aims to design inquiry and build knowledge for use in the service of action to solve practical problems. Therefore, in action research, the inquiry deliberately starts from a specific practical or applied problem or question. Its whole purpose is to lead to action to solve that practical problem or answer that practical question. As Reason and Bradbury say, action research 'seeks to bring together action and reflection, theory and practice, in participation with others, in the pursuit of practical solutions to issues of pressing concern to people' (2001: 1). And again: 'A primary purpose of action research is to produce practical knowledge that is useful to people in the everyday conduct of their lives' (2001: 2). In similar vein, Stringer's five-part action research sequence shows 'basic research' in four parts (research design, data gathering, data analysis, communication), with action research adding a fifth part – action – to those.

Stringer's five-part action research sequence shows clearly that research itself is central in the sequence. That is, systematic, disciplined inquiry – research – is brought to bear on a practical problem which requires a solution – action. All of this is done in a carefully organized framework. This systematic, disciplined inquiry – this research – is of course empirical. Therefore it draws on exactly the approaches to research covered in this book. Thus action research may involve quantitative data methods and designs, qualitative data methods and designs, or mixed-method data and designs. While action research is usually thought of as a qualitative approach, and is included here under qualitative research designs, it does not rely only on qualitative data. On the contrary, it uses quantitative data whenever they are appropriate and available. It is like case study research in this respect.

An important characteristic of action research, which sets it apart from other designs, is that it is usually cyclical in nature, reflecting the fact that people usually work towards solutions to their problems in cyclical, iterative ways. The words 'cycle', 'spiral' (and sometimes 'helix') are used by writers on action research to describe this. They convey the idea that the one piece of research leading to the one set of actions is not the end of the process, but rather the start of a cycle or spiral. The research produces outcomes which lead to the taking of action, but that in turn generates further questions for research, which in turn generates further action, and so on. Kemmis and McTaggart diagram the action research spiral, and write that, while it is difficult to describe the process as a series of steps, participatory action research is generally thought to involve a

> spiral of self-reflective cycles of
>
>> planning a change,
>> acting and observing the consequences of the change,
>> reflecting on these processes and consequences, and then
>> replanning,
>> acting and observing,
>> reflecting, and so on. (2000: 595–6)

Stringer begins with the action research cycle, then broadens that to the action research helix and then the spiral. Whichever version we consider, the main idea here is that action research is repetitive, continuing and cyclical.

For many people, the spiral of cycles of self-reflection, involving planning, acting and observing, reflecting, replanning and so on, has become the dominant feature of action research as an approach. For Kemmis and McTaggart, however, there are seven additional important features of participatory action research. It is a social process, participatory, practical and collaborative, emancipatory, critical, recursive, and it aims to transform both theory and practice.

Just as action research does not separate inquiring from doing, nor does it separate the researcher from the researched. An older version of action research, especially in educational research in the 1970s, located the two roles in the one person: the teacher became the action researcher. This led to credibility problems for action research, since most teachers did not have the research skills to communicate effectively to an often sceptical research community. Now the action and the research are seen as different roles, and are typically done by different people, but collaboration and participation between the different people are stressed. Stringer (2003) distinguishes practitioner research in education from action research in education on this very point. When the teacher steps back, reflects, collects information, observes classroom interaction, and so on, this is practitioner research. When the teacher engages others in the process of inquiry, with the intent of solving an educational work problem together, this is action research. Collaborative participation becomes central.

Similarly, Kemmis and McTaggart (2000: 595) believe that, while some action research depends on solitary processes of systematic self-reflection by the action researcher, the steps in the self-reflection spiral are best undertaken collaboratively by co-participants in the research process. This is why they prefer the term 'participatory action research'. Their formulation highlights the role of participation and collaboration in some types of action research. When participation and collaboration are involved, action research develops new research relationships, and often works towards building a community of learners. Whether that happens or not, the researcher and the researched become co-researchers, collaborating participants in the action research.

Action research has diverse origins. Many writers trace it back to the social experiments of Kurt Lewin in the 1940s, but Reason and Bradbury (2001: 2–4) identify other important influences as well. These include the contemporary critique of positivist science and scientism, Marxism ('the important thing is not to understand the world but to change it'), the liberating perspectives on gender and race, the practices of experiential learning and psychotherapy, and some types of spiritual practices. Kemmis and McTaggart (2000: 568) also note the connection of participatory research to liberation theology and Third World movements aimed at social transformation. In some professional areas – for example education – action research became popular in the 1970s, but then declined in popularity and credibility in the 1980s, only to resurface strongly in the 1990s. An indication of its present popularity in educational research is the vast literature on action research in education (Stringer, 2003). An indication of its present prominence in social research in general comes from the recent and already mentioned *Handbook of Action Research* (Reason and Bradbury, 2001).

## 8.7   REVIEW CONCEPTS

Feminism:
- rejection of positivism
- influence of gender relations
- science as value-laden
- liberation methodology, the politics of empowerment, feminist action research
- non-hierarchical research relationships
- feminist action research
- feminist empiricism, feminist standpoint epistemology, feminist postmodernism

Postmodernism:
- debunking grand narratives
- deconstruction
- discourse and text
- creating worlds by language

Common themes in the diversity of qualitative research:
- naturalistic
- lived experience
- holistic and in context
- 'from the inside'
- researcher as instrument
- data as words

Qualitative research design (see also Figure 5.1):
    data collected and analysed
- following what strategy?
- within what framework?
- data collected from whom and how?
- data analysed how?

Case studies:
- intrinsic case study
- instrumental case study
- collective (multiple) case study
- characteristics of case studies:
      the case as a bounded system
      the case as a case of something
      holistic, but requiring points of focus
      multiple data sources and multiple data collection methods

Ethnography
- culture as a shared set of meanings
- characteristics of ethnographies:
      uncovering cultural meaning
      insider's perspective
      natural settings
      evolving and unfolding
      multiple sources of data and data collection
      prolonged and repetitive data collection

*(Continued)*

---

### 8.7   REVIEW CONCEPTS (CONTINUED)

Grounded theory:
- grounded theory approach to research
- grounded theory analysis
- theory generation versus theory verification
- theoretical sampling
- using the literature

Action research:
- research for action, research to solve problems
- cyclical and iterative
- planning, acting, observing, reflecting; replanning, acting, observing; etc.
- researcher and researched as collaborative participants

---

## NOTES

1  We should be careful, however, about labelling all quantitative research positivistic, for two reasons. One is that the term 'positivism' has many different interpretations (Blaikie, 1993); the other is that some researchers (for example, Marsh, 1982) point out that some quantitative work is not positivist.

2  Also in the power of the researcher to set the agenda for the research, and to control the results (Sapsford and Abbott, 1996).

3  The failure of positivism, the value-ladenness of inquiry, the possibilities of critical social science, the politics of empowerment and the challenges of postmodernism. Hammersley (1995) also sees an emphasis on the validity of personal experience as opposed to the 'scientific method' as a major theme in feminist methodology.

4  Reinharz stresses that each type draws on all the techniques of the social sciences.

5  Reinharz (1992: 180–94) cites many examples of feminist action research, from a variety of countries and settings, and dealing with a variety of topics and research problems. In addition, Berden and Mies (1981) describe an action research project in a women's shelter in Cologne, and Mies (1991: 70–82) gives two examples, one with rural Indian women, the other as coordinator of a 'Women in development' programme in Holland.

6  And poststructuralism. Lather equates the two, but this is contentious for other writers.

7  Or 'metanarratives', the supposedly universal, absolute or ultimate truths that are used to legitimize various projects, political, religious or scientific.

8  Grounded theory is normally seen as an approach to data analysis in qualitative research, and is treated as that in Chapter 10. It is not a research design as such, but an overall way of thinking about and approaching research, and in that sense we can think of it as a research strategy. Thus there are two sections on grounded theory in this book, one on the overall approach in this chapter, and one on data analysis in Chapter 10.

9  Stake also reports a personal communication from Julian Stanley: 'When I want to find out something important for myself I often use the case study approach' (1988: 262). That is a statement worth bringing to the attention of critics of case study research, coming as it does from a prominent quantitative researcher and a major contributor to its literature.

10   A prominent example is the early study of organizational climate in management and administration (Halpin and Croft, 1963).

11   We should also note that the case study may be particularly appropriate in a student project or dissertation, where there are limited resources, including time.

12   Stake (1988: 271–3) gives a set of guidelines for doing a field observation case study.

13   'Reflexivity' refers to the fact that social researchers are part of the social world they study.

14   Becker's (1971) procedure of sequential analysis has similar ideas to these, and both relate closely to theoretical sampling, which is discussed under grounded theory.

15   Assessing that claim would have to take account of the selective application by some researchers of aspects of grounded theory: see Platt (1995).

16   There is some irony in this. The subtitle of *The Discovery of Grounded Theory* is *Strategies for Qualitative Research*. In fact, many of the examples used in that book are quantitative, and much of the reasoning of grounded theory analysis derives from principles which apply in quantitative analysis. Despite that, grounded theory has inevitably come to be seen as a qualitative technique.

17   It is not unique, however: see Hughes (1958) and Becker (1971).

18   One reason for the concentration of grounded theory studies in medical sociology was the original location of the Glaser and Strauss studies in the University of California at San Francisco. This campus functions as the medical school of the University of California.

19   Examples are how computers are integrated into classroom teaching and learning, the use of the internet in education, performance evaluation in health management, and so on.

20   Kemmis and McTaggart (2000: 568–72) identify seven approaches within the general area of participatory action research. They are: participatory research, critical action research, classroom action research, action learning, action science, soft systems approaches, and industrial action research.


## Further Reading

---

### Feminism and research methods

Fonow, M. and Cook, J. (eds) (1991) *Beyond Methodology*. Bloomington, IN: Indiana University Press.

Lather, P. (1991) *Getting Smart: Feminist Research and Pedagogy With/In the Postmodern*. New York: Routledge.

Reinharz, S. (1992) *Feminist Methods in Social Research*. New York: Oxford University Press.

Stanley, L. and Wise, S. (1983) *Breaking Out: Feminist Consciousness and Feminist Research*. London: Routledge and Kegan Paul.

Tom, W. (ed.) (1989) *The Effects of Feminist Approaches on Research Methodologies*. Waterloo: Wilfrid Laurier University Press.

### *Postmodernism*

Appignanesi, R. and Garratt, C. (1995) *Postmodernism for Beginners*. London: Icon.

Best, S. and Kellner, D. (1991) *Postmodern Theory: Critical Interrogations*. London: Macmillan.

Docherty, T. (ed.) (1992) *Postmodernism: A Reader*. London: Harvester Wheatsheaf.

Harvey, D. (1989) *The Condition of Postmodernity*. Oxford: Blackwell.

Lyotard, J.-F. (1992) *The Postmodern Condition: A Report on Knowledge*. Manchester: Manchester University Press.

Nicholson, L.J. (1990) *Feminism/Postmodernism*. London: Routledge.

Rosenau, P.M. (1992) *Postmodernism and the Social Sciences*. Princeton, NJ: Princeton University Press.

Ross, A. (ed.) (1988) *Universal Abandon: The Politics of Postmodernism*. Minneapolis: University of Minnesota Press.


### *Case studies*

Ragin, C.C. and Becker, H.S. (eds) (1992) *What is a Case? Exploring the Foundations of Social Inquiry*. New York: Cambridge University Press.

Stake, R.E. (1988) 'Case study methods in educational research: seeking sweet water', in R.M. Jaeger (ed.), *Complementary Methods for Research in Education*. Washington, DC: American Educational Research Association. pp. 253–300.

Stake, R.E. (1994) 'Case studies', in N.K. Denzin and Y.S. Lincoln (eds), *Handbook of Qualitative Research*. Thousand Oaks, CA: Sage. pp. 236–47.

Yin, R.K. (1989) *Case Study Research: Design and Methods*. Newbury Park, CA: Sage.


### *Ethnography*

Agar, M. (1986) *Speaking of Ethnography*. Beverly Hills, CA: Sage.

Atkinson, P. and Hammersley, M. (1994) 'Ethnography and participant observation', in N.K. Denzin and Y.S. Lincoln (eds), *Handbook of Qualitative Research*. Thousand Oaks, CA: Sage. pp. 248–61.

Fetterman, D.M. (1989) *Ethnography Step by Step*. Newbury Park, CA: Sage.

Hammersley, M. and Atkinson, P. (1995) *Ethnography: Principles in Practice*. 2nd edn. London: Routledge.

Spindler, G. and Spindler, L. (1992) 'Cultural process and ethnography: an anthropological perspective', in M.D. LeCompte, W.L. Millroy and J. Preissle (eds), *The Handbook of Qualitative Research in Education*. San Diego: Academic. pp. 53–92.

Wolcott, H.F. (1988) 'Ethnographic research in education', in R.M. Jaeger (ed.), *Complementary Methods for Research in Education*. Washington, DC: American Educational Research Association. pp. 187–249.


## Grounded theory
Glaser, B. (1978) *Theoretical Sensitivity*. Mill Valley, CA: Sociology Press.

Glaser, B. (1992) *Basics of Grounded Theory Analysis*. Mill Valley, CA: Sociology Press.

Glaser, B. and Strauss, A. (1967) *The Discovery of Grounded Theory: Strategies for Qualitative Research*. Chicago: Aldine.

Strauss, A. (1987) *Qualitative Analysis for Social Scientists*. New York: Cambridge University Press.

Strauss, A. and Corbin, J. (1990) *Basics of Qualitative Research: Grounded Theory Procedures and Techniques*. Newbury Park, CA: Sage.

Strauss, A. and Corbin, J. (1994) 'Grounded theory methodology: an overview', in N.K. Denzin and Y.S. Lincoln (eds), *Handbook of Qualitative Research*. Thousand Oaks, CA: Sage. pp. 273–85.


## Action research
Kemmis, S. and McTaggart, R. (2000) 'Participatory action research', in N.K. Denzin and Y.S. Lincoln (eds), *Handbook of Qualitative Research*. Thousand Oaks, CA: Sage. pp. 567–605.

Reason, P. and Bradbury, H. (eds) (2001) *Handbook of Action Research*. London: Sage.

Stringer, E. (1996) *Action Research: A Handbook for Practitioners*. Thousand Oaks, CA: Sage.

Stringer, E. (2003) *Action Research in Education*. Englewood Cliffs, NJ: Prentice-Hall.

# 9

# Collecting Qualitative Data

Qualitative researchers study spoken and written representations and records of human experience, using multiple methods and multiple sources of data. Several types of data collection might well be used in the one qualitative project. In this chapter, we deal with the main ways of collecting qualitative data: the interview, observation, participant observation and documents.

## 9.1 The Interview

The interview is one of the main data collection tools in qualitative research. It is a very good way of accessing people's perceptions, meanings, definitions of situations and constructions of reality. It is also one of the most powerful ways we have of understanding others. As Jones puts it:

> In order to understand other persons' constructions of reality, we would do well to ask them ... and to ask them in such a way that they can tell us in

their terms (rather than those imposed rigidly and *a priori* by ourselves) and in a depth which addresses the rich context that is the substance of their meanings. (1985: 46)

While interviewing is basically about asking questions and receiving answers, there is much more to it than that, especially in a qualitative research context. Consider this description:

> Interviewing has a wide variety of forms and a multiplicity of uses. The most common type of interviewing is individual, face-to-face verbal interchange, but it can also take the form of face-to-face group interviewing, mailed or self-administered questionnaires, and telephone surveys. Interviewing can be structured, semi-structured, or unstructured. It can be used for marketing purposes, to gather political opinions, for therapeutic reasons, or to produce data for academic analysis. It can be used for the purpose of measurement or its scope can be the understanding of an individual or a group perspective. An interview can be a one-time, brief exchange, say five minutes over the telephone, or it can take place over multiple, lengthy sessions, sometimes spanning days, as in life-history interviewing. (Fontana and Frey, 1994: 361)

In short, there are many different types of interviews.

### 9.1.1 Types of interviews

Much has been written on the topic of different types of interviews. For example, Patton (1980) distinguishes three main types of interview: the informal conversational interview, the general interview guide approach and the standardized open-ended interview. Minichiello et al. (1990) provide a useful continuum of interviewing methods, based on the degree of structure involved. It is shown in Figure 9.1, and is similar to the typology Fielding (1996b) describes, using the terms 'standardized', 'semi-standardized' and 'non-standardized'. Similarly, Fontana and Frey (1994) use a three-way classification of structured, semi-structured and unstructured interviewing, and they apply that to individual and group interviews. This section draws on their work.

| Structured interviews | Focused or semi-structured interviews | Unstructured interviews |
|---|---|---|
| Standardized interviews | In-depth interviews | In-depth interviews |
| Survey interviews | Survey interviews | Clinical interviews |
| Clinical history taking | Group interviews | Group interviews |
| | | Oral or life history interviews |

**Figure 9.1** *The continuum model for interviews*
*Source*: Minichiello et al., 1990: 89

Whichever typology we use, the main dimensions of this variation are the degree of structure in the interview, and how deep the interview tries to go. At the left-hand end of the continuum, interviews are tightly structured and standardized. Here, interview questions are planned and standardized in advance, precoded categories are used for responses, and the interview itself does not attempt to go to any great depth. At the right-hand end, by contrast, interviews are unstructured and open-ended. Interview questions are not pre-planned and standardized, but instead there are general questions to get the interview going and to keep it moving. Specific questions will then emerge as the interview unfolds, and the wording of those questions will depend upon the directions the interview takes. There are no pre-established categories for responding.

With so many different types, the interview is a data collection tool of great flexibility, which can be adapted to suit a wide variety of research situations. Different types of interview have different strengths and weaknesses, and different purposes in research. The type of interview selected should therefore be aligned with the strategy, purposes and research questions, as Fontana and Frey write:

> Clearly, different types of interviewing are suited to different situations. If we wish to find out how many people oppose a nuclear repository, survey research is our best tool, and we can quantify and code the responses and use mathematical models to explain our findings (Frey, 1993). If we are interested in opinions about a given product, a focus group interview will provide us with the most efficient results; if we wish to know and understand about the lives of Palestinian women in the resistance (Gluck, 1991), we need to interview them at length and in depth in an unstructured way. (1994: 373)

In short, we begin by recognizing that there are many different types of interview, and then we select the interview type based on research purposes and questions. The type of interview we select will influence the practical aspects of the interview, and how we manage the process.

### Structured interviews

In structured interviews the respondent is asked a series of pre-established questions, with preset response categories. There is little room for variation in response, though open-ended questions may sometimes be used. All respondents receive the same questions in the same order, delivered in a standardized manner. Flexibility and variation are minimized, while standardization is maximized. In this sort of interview, the interviewer attempts to play a neutral role, and a neutral manner and demeanour are encouraged in executing that role. The stimulus–response nature of this type of interview stresses rational rather than emotional responses (Fontana and Frey, 1994). The standardized interview schedule is described in detail by Wilson (1996), and Fielding (1996b) gives suggestions for developing structured and semi-structured interview schedules.[1]

### Group interviews: focus groups

Group interviewing is a general term, where the researcher works with several people simultaneously, rather than just one. The focus group was originally a particular type of group interview used in marketing and political research, but now the terms 'focus group interview' and 'group interview' are used more interchangeably. Group interviewing is now becoming popular in social research, though it is not new.

There are several different types of group interview, and like other interviews they can be unstructured, semi-structured or highly structured. Since different types of group interviews have different purposes, which type should be used in a particular research situation depends on the context and research purposes. Fontana and Frey (1994) tabulate the characteristics of five different types of group interviews, and Morgan (1988) and Stewart and Shamdasani (1990) also discuss the characteristics of different types of group interviews, along with their purposes, strengths and weaknesses.

The role of the researcher changes in a group interview, functioning more as a moderator or facilitator, and less as an interviewer. The process will not be one of alternate question and answer, as in the traditional interview. Rather, the researcher will be facilitating, moderating, monitoring and recording group interaction. The group interaction will be directed by questions and topics supplied by the researcher. This means particular skills are required of the group interviewer (Fontana and Frey, 1994; Merton et al., 1956).

Group interviews can make an important contribution in research. Writing about focus groups, Morgan points out that 'the hallmark of focus groups is the explicit use of the group interaction to produce data and insights that would be less accessible without the interaction found in a group' (1988: 12). Well facilitated group interaction can assist in bringing to the surface aspects of a situation which might not otherwise be exposed. The group situation can also stimulate people in making explicit their views, perceptions, motives and reasons. This makes group interviews an attractive data gathering option when research is trying to probe those aspects of people's behaviour. They are inexpensive, data-rich, flexible, stimulating, recall-aiding, cumulative and elaborative. But there can also be problems associated with group culture and dynamics, and in achieving balance in the group interaction (Fontana and Frey, 1994).

The data from group interviews are the transcripts (or other records) of the group's interaction. They might be used as the only data gathering technique in a study, or, frequently, in conjunction with other quantitative or qualitative techniques. It is becoming increasingly common today to see them used in conjunction with surveys, sometimes to assist in developing questionnaires, and sometimes used after the survey to 'flesh out' views and information on topics surveyed. The numerous specific practical issues which need to be considered in planning group interviews are dealt with in the two monographs by Morgan (1988) and by Stewart and Shamdasani (1990). The latter includes a useful typology of focus group questions.

### Unstructured interviews

There is a wide range indeed when it comes to unstructured interviewing. The traditional type of unstructured interview is the non-standardized, open-ended, in-depth interview, sometimes called the ethnographic interview. It is used as a way of understanding the complex behaviour of people without imposing any *a priori* categorization which might limit the field of inquiry. Fontana and Frey discuss seven aspects of unstructured interviewing, and use a variety of examples from the research literature to illustrate each aspect. These aspects provide a useful checklist of things to think about when planning data collection by unstructured interview:

* accessing the setting
* understanding the language and culture of respondents
* deciding on how to present oneself
* locating an informant
* gaining trust
* establishing rapport
* collecting the empirical materials.

How each is handled will vary with the nature of the situation and respondents. There is, and needs to be, flexibility in the unstructured interview situation (what Douglas, 1985, calls creative interviewing), especially for oral history and life history projects. The unstructured interview is a powerful research tool, widely used in social research and other fields, and capable of producing rich and valuable data. A successful in-depth interview has many of the characteristics of a prolonged and intimate conversation. Skill in this sort of interviewing does not come naturally, and most of us need specific training to develop that skill.

### 9.1.2 Feminist perspectives on interviewing

Feminist research makes great use of the semi-structured and unstructured interview: 'The use of semi-structured interviews has become the principal means by which feminists have sought to achieve the active involvement of their respondents in the construction of data about their lives' (Graham, quoted in Reinharz, 1992: 18).

Feminist research also redefines the interview in significant ways. This is because the feminist perspective sees traditional interviewing as a masculine paradigm, embedded in a masculine culture, stressing masculine traits and excluding sensitivity, emotionality and other traits culturally viewed as feminine. Oakley (1981) identifies the contradiction between scientific positivistic research requiring objectivity and detachment, and feminist interviewing requiring openness, emotional engagement, and the development of trust in a potentially long-term relationship.

A primary consideration for feminists concerns the researcher's role. We noted earlier the feminist preference for non-hierarchical research relationships. The traditional interview is seen not only as paternalistic, condescending in its attitudes towards women and not accounting for gendered differences, but also as based on a hierarchical relationship with the respondent in a subordinate position. As Fontana and Frey point out, there are both moral and ethical objections to this, and methodological ones as well: better data are at stake. Minimizing status differences between interviewer and respondent, and developing a more equal relationship based on trust which includes both self-disclosure by the researcher and reciprocity, can avoid the 'hierarchical pitfall' (Reinharz, 1992), enabling greater openness and insight, a greater range of responses, and therefore richer data. In this perspective, as Haig (1997) points out and as the above quote from Graham suggests, researcher and researched become co-creators of data through the interview. Feminist redefinition of the interview situation transforms interviewers and respondents into co-equals, who are carrying on a conversation about mutually relevant, often biographically critical, issues (Denzin and Lincoln, 1994: 354).

Reinharz (1992) points out that there is no single uniform perspective in feminism on such topics as researcher–interviewee relationships, and self-disclosure. Rather there is openness to different possible meanings of these things in different research situations. Feminist-based interview research has already modified social science concepts, and created important new ways of seeing the world:

> By listening to women speak, understanding women's membership in particular
> social systems, and establishing the distribution of phenomena accessible only
> through sensitive interviewing, feminist researchers have uncovered
> previously neglected or misunderstood worlds of experience. (Reinharz,
> 1992: 44)

Reinharz points out also that feminist researchers are likely to continue to refine and elaborate the method of interviewing, as more and more experience with it is built up.

Sharing some of the same concerns as feminists, postmodern ethnographers have been concerned with moral aspects of the traditional researcher–subject interview, with the controlling role of the interviewer, and with the influence of the interviewer on data and reporting. As well as gender, they stress the importance of race (Stanfield, 1985), and the perspectives of the decolonialized, the disadvantaged and the disempowered. Fontana and Frey note several directions in which postmodern researchers take account of these matters. They include polyphonic interviewing, interpretive interactionism, critical ethnography and oralysis, specialist topics beyond our scope in this book.

### 9.1.3 Practical aspects of interviewing

A major decision has been made once the type of interview has been selected, in accordance with the research strategy, perspective, purposes and questions of the study. Practical aspects of interviewing then include the selection of interview respondents, managing the interview, and recording.

#### Interview respondents
The main issues that need to be considered here are:

* Who will be interviewed and why?
* How many will be interviewed, and how many times will each person be interviewed?
* When and for how long will each respondent be interviewed?
* Where will each respondent be interviewed?
* How will access to the interview situation be organized?

All of these issues depend on the type of interview selected, where it falls on the structured–unstructured continuum shown in Figure 9.1, and the perspective from which the research is being conducted. The first two issues relate to the sampling plan for the project, which itself depends on the research questions and purposes. The next two questions, concerning time and location, are obvious things which need organizing, but their influence on the quality of the data can be decisive. Recognizing the importance of these questions, and careful consideration of the alternatives in any particular research situation, enable decisions to be made which maximize the quality of the data, in the light of ethical responsibilities towards those being interviewed. The last point concerns gaining access. Much is written on this (for example, Lofland and Lofland, 1984; Hammersley and Atkinson, 1995) and how it is done depends on the particular research project, its setting and context. How interviewers make contact with respondents, and organize access, can affect all stages of the interviewer–interviewee relationship, and with that the quality, reliability and validity of interview data.

#### Managing the interview
A general checklist for managing the interview includes:

* preparation for the interview: the interview schedule
* beginning the interview: establishing rapport
* communication and listening skills

- asking questions: the sequence and types of questions
- closing the interview.

The importance of each of these, and how each is handled, are determined by the type of interview selected. Thus, a highly structured interview requires a schedule, which will need developing and pretesting. If practical, trialling of the process and situation for this type of interview is also recommended, since the quality of the preparation will influence the quality of the data. On the other hand, an unstructured interview would have only a general sense of the questions or topics to be discussed and would be kept deliberately open-ended, and there would be no attempt at standardization.

The more unstructured the interview, the more communication skills in general, and listening in particular, are important. Considerable literature exists on this topic – see, for example, Woods (1986), Keats (1988) and McCracken (1988) – which is useful in developing the skills involved. In particular, Minichiello et al. (1990) show 16 subskills of listening which they recommend researchers practise in order to improve their listening competency.

Question asking is at the centre of interviewing, and has been analysed extensively in the research methods literature. This analysis includes the way questions are delivered, the wording that is used, and the sequence and types of questions that can be asked. This latter topic in particular has been the subject of classification systems. For example, Patton (1990) classifies questions into experience/behaviour, opinion/belief, feeling, knowledge, sensory and demographic/background. Patton also goes on to discuss and classify probing questions, providing a useful checklist of questions which will often be necessary at different stages during the interview. Other classifications are described by Sudman and Bradburn (1982) and by Foddy (1993). Finally, ways of closing the interview may also require attention, and six strategies for closing the interview are described by Minichiello et al. (1990). The applicability of these points, and of much of the literature cited, depends very much on the perspective, on the approach taken to interviewing in a particular project, and on the type of interview selected.

### Recording
How the interview data are to be recorded needs to be considered in planning the research. For highly structured interviews, which use precoded response categories, recording of responses is probably a simple matter of making checkmarks on a response sheet. For more open-ended interviews, the possibilities include tape recording, video recording, and/or note taking. Although the literature is not unanimous on the point (see, for example, Lincoln and Guba, 1985; Patton, 1980), there are important advantages to tape recording open-ended interviews, which are spelled out by Seidman (1991: 86–7). It may be that the situation dictates the recording method. If, for example, interviewing is being

done in the field, there may be no opportunity for electronic recording. But other situations will differ. The various possibilities need to be assessed in relation to the practical constraints of the situation, the cooperation and approval of the respondent, and the type of interview selected. Whatever recording method is chosen, some preparation work is involved. If electronic recording is involved, the researcher must be adept at working the equipment (Minichiello et al., 1990; Patton, 1987). If note taking is involved, note taking skills need to be developed. After the interview is completed, the data will need to be transcribed.

### 9.1.4 The analytic status of interview data: the role of language

The great variety and flexibility of the interview as a research tool give it wide applicability, with different types of interview suited to different situations. In some respects, however, interview data are problematic, since they are never simply raw, but are always situated and textual (Silverman, 1993):

> the interview is a conversation, the art of asking questions and listening.
> It is not a neutral tool, for the interviewer creates the reality of the interview
> situation. In this situation answers are given. Thus the interview produces
> situated understandings grounded in specific interactional episodes. This
> method is influenced by the personal characteristics of the interviewer,
> including race, class, ethnicity and gender. (Denzin and Lincoln, 1994: 353)

The analytic status of interview data is discussed by, among others, Mishler (1986), Silverman (1985; 1993) and Fielding (1996b). The discussion in this section follows mainly that of Fielding.

How should we interpret the responses received in the research interview? On a technical level, this is an issue about the validity of interview responses, aspects of which include the possibility of interviewer bias and effects, the accuracy of respondents' memories, people's response tendencies, dishonesty, self-deception and social desirability. The special situations of cross-cultural research raise further problems in interpreting interview responses. But, as Fielding points out, these technical issues can usually be countered by careful design, planning and training. The more difficult problem concerns the correspondence between verbal responses and behaviour, the relationship between what people say, what they do and what they say they do, and the assumption that language is a good indicator of thought and action.

What is the relation between interviewees' accounts and the worlds they describe, and are such accounts potentially true or false, or do these concepts not apply? Silverman (1993: 90–8) describes the positivist answer to these questions (where interview data are seen as giving access to facts about the social world) and the symbolic interactionist answer (where the interview is seen as a social event based on mutual participant observation, and the primary issue is to generate data, using no fixed format or questions, which give authentic insight into people's experiences). There are other theoretical positions as well on this issue of the analytic status of interview data. However, some researchers are so doubtful about the status of such data that they abandon any concern with the content of response in favour of examining its form. Thus, for ethno-methodologists, interview data are not a report on external reality, but a reality constructed by both parties as they contrive to accomplish an interview, and can be studied as such. In focusing on form rather than content, they treat interview data as a topic, not as a resource (Fielding, 1996b; see also Silverman, 1993; Hammersley and Atkinson, 1995).[2]

Another aspect of this issue centres on language itself. An older view of language is that it represents a transparent medium to reality, that the words are used to transmit information about the world 'out there', based on a cor-respondence between the words used, their meanings, and the aspects of the world they describe. That view is no longer tenable, since a number of important ideas have changed the way we see language and especially its relation to social life (Wooffitt, 1996). These ideas have come from philo-sophy, linguistics and sociology. Wittgenstein, in particular, emphasized the importance of language use, showing that the meaning of words derives largely from their use, and that language is a central feature of the socio-cultural situation in which it is used, not merely a system of symbols to represent the world 'out there'. Similarly, the linguist Saussure stresses that the signs of language, like all signs, derive meaning from their relation with other signs. A correspondence view of language is thus replaced by a rela-tional view. Language use is itself a form of social action, and descriptions are actions: they do not merely represent the world, they do specific tasks in the world (Wooffitt, 1996: 297).

This change in the way of seeing language, and especially seeing language use itself as a form of social action, has opened up important new perspectives in qualitative analysis. Examples include conversation analysis in sociology (with its connections to ethnomethodology), discourse analysis, semiotics and deconstruction. Conversation analysis concentrates on oral talk, but the others can be applied as much to written language as to spoken language (and, for that matter, to all types of verbal and textual material). Whether applied to spoken or written language, the transcript or text is not reduced to a secondary status in the research. We return to these topics in Chapter 10.

Language is obviously central in qualitative research, with data primarily in the form of words. Talk is the primary medium of social interaction, and language is the material from which qualitative social research is constructed. Qualitative field data are linguistic in character: observations, texts and interviews all focus and rely on language (Silverman, 1993). Language permeates those aspects and phenomena which are central to social research (Wooffitt, 1996), and cultural categories are organized and defined through language (Coffey and Atkinson, 1996). An emphasis on the point that social reality is constructed through language has produced the 'linguistic turn' in social theory (Manning and Cullum-Swan, 1994). Recognition of the centrality of language has produced important developments in qualitative research, and this theme will occur again in Chapters 10 and 12.

## 9.2 Observation

Observation has a long tradition in the social sciences: for example, it has been extensively employed by psychologists (Irwin, 1980; Brandt, 1981; Liebert, 1995) and by educational researchers (Foster, 1996b). Looking from a more sociological perspective, Adler and Adler (1994) review five 'observational paradigms' which can be distinguished in the way observational methods have been used, and give several examples of each. Their classification is used here to show the variety of observational approaches.

*Formal sociology* traces back to Simmel, who studied the forms, structures and patterns in social interaction based on his own direct observation: 'If society is conceived as interaction among individuals, the description of the forms of this interaction is the task of the science of society' (1950: 21–2). Contemporary practitioners of formal sociology often incorporate symbolic interactionist principles, and prefer to use full videotaped recordings of observations, often in such contrived situations as laboratories.

*Dramaturgical sociology* became popular with Goffman, who described his method as 'unsystematic naturalistic observation' in order to study how people interact, form relationships, accomplish meaning in their lives, and, especially, construct their self-presentations and carry them off in front of others. Researchers in the dramaturgical tradition have been more attentive to the observational method than Goffman, but have still relied mainly on unstructured, naturalistic recording techniques, whether working individually or in teams. The method has obvious similarities with participant observation.

*Studies of the public realm* extend the dramaturgical approach, and have developed into a research area in its own right. They address a wide range of issues, cover a wide range of public places, and use observational strategies which vary in researcher involvement, researcher openness, the use of teams and gender issues.

In *auto-observation*, sociologists study themselves and their companions. The use of self as a research tool goes back to the origins of sociology, and can be seen in the writings of Dilthey and Weber. Existential sociology has developed from this line of thinking. This observational approach offers great depth, yielding insights about core meanings and experiences, while raising questions about the role of the observer-researcher.

In *ethnomethodology*, the focus is on how everyday life is constructed. Since much of the interest is in processes below the surface of conscious awareness, at the taken-for-granted level, many ethnomethodologists favour observational techniques over interview and self-report data. Observation includes listening as well as looking, and everyday face-to-face interaction depends heavily on both verbal and visual behaviour. Therefore, alongside observation, contemporary ethnomethodologists have directed much of their attention to conversation analysis, since they see language as the fundamental base of communication and social order. Using audio- and videotaping, they gather data that can be analysed later, and repeatedly, in minute detail, and the techniques of conversation analysis have been extended to interaction analysis (Heath and Luff, 1996). Compared with observations made from the interpretive perspective (as in participant observation), ethnomethodological observation is more structural and objective, and less mediated by the subjective perspective of the researcher.

### 9.2.1 Structured and unstructured approaches to observation

In naturalistic observation, observers neither manipulate nor stimulate the behaviour of those whom they are observing, in contrast to some other data gathering techniques. The situation being observed is not contrived for research purposes. This is pure or direct or non-participant observation, in contrast with participant observation, which we discuss in Section 9.3.[3]

In the literature on observation as a data collection technique, the terms 'quantitative' and 'qualitative' are frequently used. The terms 'structured' and 'unstructured' are more appropriate in this book, because observational data can be highly structured without necessarily being turned into numbers. The issue is not whether the observational data will be turned into numbers, but rather how much structure the observations will involve.

Quantitative approaches tend to be highly structured, and to require predeveloped observation schedules, usually very detailed. If this approach is chosen, decisions will be required from the researcher as to whether already existing observational schedules will be used, or whether an observation schedule will be specially developed. This is similar to the decision in Chapter 6 about whether to use already existing measuring instruments, or to develop them specifically for a study, and similar considerations to those given in Chapter 6 can guide the choice here.[4]

Qualitative approaches to observation are much more unstructured. In this case, the researcher does not use predetermined categories and classifications, but makes observations in a more natural open-ended way. Whatever the recording technique, the behaviour is observed as the stream of actions and events as they naturally unfold. The logic here is that categories and concepts for describing and analysing the observational data will emerge later in the research, during the analysis, rather than be brought to the research, or imposed on the data, from the start.

When the observational strategy is unstructured, the process of observation typically evolves through a series of different activities. It begins with selecting a setting and gaining access to it, then starting the observing and recording. As the study progresses, the nature of the observation changes, typically sharpening in focus, leading to ever clearer research questions which require more selected observations. The observational data gathering continues until theoretical saturation is reached (Adler and Adler, 1994). Silverman (1993) suggests five stages in organizing an initially unstructured observational study: beginning the research (where a set of very general questions is proposed), writing field notes (usually beginning with broad descriptive categories, but later developing more focused codes and categories), looking as well as listening, testing hypotheses and making broader links.

Where focus and structure emerge during the fieldwork, the analogy of the funnel is useful (Spradley, 1980; Silverman, 1993):

> Ethnographic research should have a characteristic 'funnel' structure, being progressively focused over its course. Over time the research problem needs to be developed or transformed and eventually its scope is clarified and delimited and its internal structure explored. In this sense, it is frequently well into the process of inquiry that one discovers what the research is really 'about', and not uncommonly it turns out to be about something rather different from the initial foreshadowed problems. (Hammersley and Atkinson, 1995: 206)

This theme of structure which is imposed or structure which emerges is familiar. In this case, it also illustrates the specific point made in Chapter 6, about holistic and reductionist approaches to data. Structured observation, based on predetermined categories, breaks behaviour up into small parts. Unstructured observation, by contrast, can focus on the larger patterns of behaviour, more holistically and more macroscopically. There are advantages and disadvantages in both approaches. With smaller units of behaviour, you lose the larger picture, but recording and analysing are easier and more standardized. The more holistic approach keeps the larger picture in view, but the logistics of recording and, especially, of analysing the data will be more demanding. As with other issues, this does not need to be an either–or matter. Combinations of the two approaches are possible, depending on the research purposes and context.

### 9.2.2 Practical issues in observation

There are two main practical issues in planning the collection of observational data: approaching observation, and recording.

Approaching observation (Foster, 1996b) means establishing the focus of the observations, selecting the cases for observation and, as appropriate, selecting within cases for observation. In other words, the researcher has to decide what will be observed, and why. These are sampling decisions, and they need to be made with reference to the research questions. The issue of structure applies here too. At the highly structured end, approaching the observation in terms of focus and cases is organized ahead of data collection. In unstructured observation, focus and cases may only become clear as observations are made. Gaining access is also part of the practical business of approaching observation. In some settings, this will involve negotiation with gatekeepers, and different types of research may well require different types of negotiation and access.

The general possibilities for recording observational data range from the use of video and audiovisual equipment to the use of field notes.[5] There may be advantages to combining these different methods. The choice here is influenced by the extent to which the data are structured or unstructured – although increasingly, with today's sophisticated recording equipment, there is value in recording everything and, even if structured observation schedules are involved, using those in the analysis stage. These different recording methods each have their strengths and their limitations (Foster, 1996a; 1996b). The observational researcher's task is the usual one of analysing these in relation to the purposes and context of the research, and to choose accordingly. Earlier, we saw the connections between observation, ethnomethodology and conversation analysis. The primary sources of data for ethnomethodological observation studies are audio and audiovisual recordings of naturally occurring interactions, sometimes supplemented by field observation.

Before leaving observation and moving to participant observation, a central method for data collection in ethnography, we should note the importance of observation in ethnography. 'The requirement for direct, prolonged on-the-spot observation cannot be avoided or reduced. It is the guts of the ethnographic approach. This does not always mean participant observation' (Spindler and Spindler, 1992: 63). And again: 'Above all else is the requirement that the ethnographer observe directly. No matter what instruments, coding devices, recording devices or techniques are used, the primary obligation is for the ethnographer to be there when the action takes place, and to change that action as little as possible by his or her presence' (1992: 64). Thus direct observation, as well as participant observation, is important in ethnography.[6]

At the same time, ethnographic observation, as distinct from direct observation, has a special flavour, the flavour of ethnography itself. As Wolcott puts it:

> We are ethnographic observers when we are attending to the cultural context
> of the behaviour we are engaging in or observing, and when we are looking
> for those mutually understood sets of expectations and explanations that

enable us to interpret what is occurring and what meanings are probably being attributed by others present. (1988: 193)

Data collection techniques in ethnography need to be aligned with this viewpoint. This means that it is not only the behaviour, or situation, itself which is of interest in ethnography. It is also, and centrally, the meaning of that behaviour or situation as seen by the people we are studying which is the focus.

## 9.3 Participant Observation

The main characteristics of ethnography were described in Chapter 8. The essential idea is captured again in this quote from Spradley:

> The essential core of ethnography is this concern with the meaning of actions and events to the people we seek to understand. Some of these meanings are directly expressed in language; many are taken for granted and communicated only indirectly through word and action. But in every society people make constant use of these complex meaning systems to organize their behavior, to understand themselves and others, and to make sense out of the world in which they live. These systems of meaning constitute their culture; ethnography always implies a theory of culture. (1980: 5)

Participant observation is the central ethnographic data collection technique. It differs from direct or non-participant observation in that the role of the researcher changes from detached observer of the situation, to both participant in and observer of the situation. This raises a general question about the role of the researcher in observation research: how far distant or removed will the researcher be from the behaviour being studied? Or, to what extent will the researcher be involved in the behaviour? There is a continuum of possibilities here, as summarized in the literature by the frameworks of Gold (1958), Adler and Adler (1994) and Wolcott (1988).

Gold's analysis cross-classifies participant and observer, as shown in Figure 9.2. Adler and Adler modify that, and describe three membership roles for the observer-researcher: the complete member-researcher, the active member-researcher, and the peripheral member-researcher. Wolcott distinguishes between the researcher's opportunity to be an active participant, a privileged observer or a limited observer. Whichever classification is used, these possibilities for the researcher have different consequences for the level of obtrusiveness or unobtrusiveness involved in ethnographic data collection. This refers to the extent to which the researcher intrudes into the situation during data collection. This in turn influences the level of reactivity in the observation or participant observation data.[7]

|  | • Complete participant |
| Mainly participant | |
|  | • Participant as observer |
| --- | --- |
|  | • Observer as participant |
| Mainly observer | |
|  | • Complete observer |

**Figure 9.2**   *Typology of naturalistic research roles*
*Source*: Gold, 1958

These frameworks help us to think about the role of the researcher in participant observation, and possible effects of that role on the data. The actual fieldwork role in research may be a blending of these possibilities. Whatever the role, full-scale participant observation – 'prolonged immersion in the life of a group, community or organization in order to discern people's habits and thoughts as well as to decipher the social structure that binds them together' (Punch, 1994: 84) – is a demanding and specialized form of data collection. To take the role of the other, to 'go native', to obtain the insider's perspective by becoming part of the natural setting, is not straightforward, and raises a number of issues. They include the ethical issues associated with this method of data collection; the conceptual issues of the importance of the researcher's prior picture and the role of exploration and inspection in participant observation (Blumer, 1969); and the more practical issues of gaining access to the situation, overt versus covert observation, 'front management' or the researcher's presentation of self, and how to record what is being observed (Fielding, 1996b).

It is difficult to codify the steps involved in participant observation, but Spradley's framework is useful. He analyses participant observation (and ethnography) into a sequence of 12 developmental tasks (his developmental research sequence), the end product of which is a written ethnography (Spradley, 1980). For Spradley, participant observation together with ethnographic interviewing produce ethnographic description. Ethnographic interviewing uses questions designed to discover the cultural meanings people have learned. Spradley shows how descriptive questions, structural questions and contrast questions are used in this way, as part of the step-by-step account he gives of participant observation. On the other hand, Hammersley and Atkinson (1983) are less directive: ethnographers do not decide beforehand the questions they want to ask, though they may enter the interview with a list of issues to be covered.

Wolcott (1988) writes more generally about seven types of interviews anthropologists may use, in conjunction with participant observation.[8] Much of that has been covered in Section 9.1, but key informant interviewing and life history interviewing require a brief comment. Empirical work in anthropology and sociology has often depended on the key informant – 'an individual in whom one invests a disproportionate amount of time because that individual appears to be particularly well informed, articulate, approachable or available' (1988: 195). It is an approach which can often be adapted for applied social research. In ethnography, key informant interviewing is appropriate because people differ also in their cultural sensitivity, and therefore in their ability to contribute culturally meaningful data. Life history interviewing, where it is possible, can help greatly with understanding how the social context gets played out in individual lives. The depth of data possible in such an interview helps in getting a full understanding of the participant's view of the world (Fetterman, 1989).

## 9.4 Documentary Data

Documents, both historical and contemporary, are a rich source of data for social research. A distinguishing feature of our society may well be the vast array of 'documentary evidence' which is routinely compiled and retained, yet much of this is neglected by researchers, perhaps because the collection of other sorts of social data (experiments, surveys, interviews, observations) has become more fashionable. This is ironic, since the development of social science depended greatly on documentary research (MacDonald and Tipton, 1996: 187). For example, in sociology, Marx, Durkheim and Weber worked primarily from documents; similarly, Chicago School sociology was often based on written documents (Hammersley and Atkinson, 1995: 158).

Documentary sources of data might be used in various ways in social research. Some studies might depend entirely on documentary data, with such data the focus in their own right.[9] In other research, for example case studies or grounded theory studies, documentary data may be collected in conjunction with interviews and observations. In conjunction with other data, documents can be important in triangulation, where an intersecting set of different methods and data types is used in a single project (Denzin, 1989). Finally, documentary products are especially important for the ethnographer, providing a 'rich vein for analysis' (Hammersley and Atkinson, 1995: 173). The ethnographer will make use of all manner of written resources, and of any other materials which will help in documenting either the immediate natural and detailed behaviour of participants (Spindler and Spindler, 1992: 74), or the cultural and symbolic context and significance of that behaviour. Sociologists point out that documentary evidence does not only mean words; it can also include audio and visual evidence.

The range of documents which might be used by social scientists includes diaries, letters, essays, personal notes, biographies and autobiographies, institutional memoranda and reports, and government pronouncements and proceedings (Jupp, 1996). And this list does not include documentary quantitative evidence, such as files, statistics and records, which are also of interest. Writers have classified this bewildering variety (Hammersley and Atkinson, 1995: 159).

For example, MacDonald and Tipton (1996) use a broad four-way classification of public records, the media, private papers and visual documents. Other distinctions used are primary–secondary sources, direct–indirect uses (Finnegan, 1996), classification according to referent, and whether or not the document(s) was produced with this research in mind – the witting–unwitting distinction. 'Unwitting' documents are a type of unobtrusive measure, where the observer is removed from the interactions or events being studied (Jupp, 1996; Webb et al., 1966).[10]

Scott's two-way typology of documents is based on authorship and access (Scott, 1990; Jupp, 1996). Authorship refers to the origin of the document (in three categories: personal, official-private, official-state), while access refers to the availability of documents to people other than the authors (in four categories: closed, restricted, open-archival and open-published). The resulting 12-cell typology suggests four key questions in evaluating documentary data (Jupp, 1996: 303): its authenticity (whether it is original and genuine), its credibility (whether it is accurate), its representativeness (whether it is representative of the totality of documents of its class) and its meaning (what it is intended to say).

MacDonald and Tipton (1996: 199) stress that, in documentary research, nothing can be taken for granted, and they recommend Denzin's triangulation framework to ensure that everything is checked from more than one angle. Finnegan (1996: 146–9) points out that thinking about and checking how documents have come into existence generates eight other useful questions:

1  Has the researcher made use of the existing sources relevant and appropriate for his or her research topic?
2  How far has the researcher taken account of any 'twisting' or selection of the facts in the sources used?
3  What kind of selection has the researcher made in her or his use of the sources, and on what principles?
4  How far does a source which describes a particular incident or case reflect the general situation?
5  Is the source concerned with recommendations, ideals or what ought to be done?
6  How relevant is the context of the source?
7  With statistical sources: what were the assumptions according to which the statistics were collected and presented?
8  And, finally, having taken all the previous factors into account, do you consider that the researcher has reached a reasonable interpretation of the meaning of the sources?

For ethnographers, documentary products provide a rich source of analytic topics, which include: how are documents written? How are they read? Who writes them? Who reads them? For what purposes? On what occasions? With what outcomes? What is recorded? What is omitted? What does the writer seem to take for granted about the reader(s)? What do readers need to know in order to make sense of them (Hammersley and Atkinson, 1995: 173)? Such questions as these point ahead to textual analysis, the analysis of documentary data,[11] outlined in Chapter 10. How the document has come into existence – its social production – is one of its main themes. Others are the social organization of the document and the analysis of its meaning.

## 9.5 Data Collection Procedures

Whether qualitative data collection involves interviews, observation, participant observation or documents, there are four common-sense things we can do to maximize the quality of the data:

- Think through the rationale and logistics of the proposed data collection, and plan carefully for data collection.
- Anticipate and simulate the data collection procedures; this will show the value of pilot testing any instruments (if appropriate) and the procedures for using them.
- When approaching people for data collection, ensure that the approach is both ethical and professional.
- Appreciate the role of training in preparing for data collection, both for ourselves and for others. For example, if we are doing unstructured interviews, we should not just assume we will be good at this, but prepare for it, undertaking activities designed to develop the skills involved. If others are to be involved, they will need training for the data collection. If special equipment is involved (for example for recording), we should ensure that the appropriate skills have been mastered.

Very often, the point of a qualitative study is to look at something holistically and comprehensively, to study it in its complexity, and to understand it in its context. These points correspond to three criticisms of quantitative social research: that it is too reductionist in its approach to the study of behaviour, thereby losing sight of the whole picture; that it oversimplifies social reality, in its stress on measurement; and that it strips away context from the data. For the qualitative researcher, the 'truth' about human social behaviour is not independent of context; it is not context-free. Therefore it is important for the qualitative researcher to be able to convey the full picture. The term often used to capture this is 'thick description'. There are two parts to this idea. First, the description (of the group or the case, event or phenomenon) must specify everything a reader needs to know in order to understand the findings. Second, the research report needs to provide sufficient information about the context of the research so that a reader can judge the transferability or generalizability of its findings (Lincoln and Guba, 1985). The exact nature of the thick description will vary from project to project, but both parts of this idea acknowledge and emphasize the context around any project and its findings. But we cannot *give* the full picture unless we *have* the full picture. This is an important aspect of the quality of data in qualitative research.

## 9.6 Sampling in Qualitative Research

Sampling is as important in qualitative research as it is in quantitative research: as noted earlier, we cannot study everyone everywhere doing everything. Sampling decisions are required not only about which people to interview or which events to observe, but also about settings and processes. Even a case study, where the case selection itself may be straightforward, will require sampling within the case. We cannot study everything about even one case. A qualitative study based on documents will also, in all probability, face sampling issues.

However, there is a major difference in sampling in the two approaches. In quantitative research, the focus tends to be on people sampling. The basic concept most often is probability sampling directed at representativeness: measurements of variables are taken from a sample, which is chosen to be representative of some larger population. Because of the representativeness, findings from the sample will then be inferred back to the population. Qualitative research would rarely use probability sampling, but rather would use some sort of deliberate sampling. 'Purposive sampling' is the term often used; it means sampling in a deliberate way, with some purpose or focus in mind.

There are no simple summaries of strategies for sampling in qualitative research, because of the great variety of research approaches, purposes, and settings. Thus Miles and Huberman (1994) show 16 qualitative sampling strategies in a typology, and refer to more in their discussion. Patton (1980), Johnson (1990) and Janesick (1994) contribute still others. The basic ideas behind the specific sampling strategies vary considerably, and reflect the purposes and questions guiding the study. For example, a maximum variation sampling plan would deliberately seek as much variation as possible, whereas a homogeneous sampling plan would seek to minimize variation. Some research situations would require the former, some the latter. Similarly, there are some situations where convenience sampling would be appropriate, where advantage is taken of cases, events, situations or informants which are close at hand. Others would require extreme-case sampling, for example when the strategy is to learn from unusual or negative manifestations of the phenomenon. In ethnography and participant observation research especially, informant sampling will be involved, and this may be sequential in the sense that several steps might be needed to locate information-rich informants. In case study research, qualitative sampling involves identifying the case(s) and setting the boundaries, where we indicate the aspects to be studied, and constructing a sampling frame, where we focus selection further. After that, however, general descriptions of sampling are difficult, because there is great variability. As another example, within-case sampling involves selection of focus within the case being studied, whereas multiple case sampling is directed more at replication across similar and contrasting cases.

Across the various qualitative sampling strategies, there is a clear principle involved, which concerns the overall validity of the research design, and which stresses that the sample must fit in with the other components of the study. There must be an internal consistency and a coherent logic, across the study's components, including its sampling. The sampling plan and sampling parameters (settings, actors, events, processes) should line up with the purposes and the research questions of the study. If it is not clear which cases, aspects or incidents to study, it is usually worth devoting more work to developing the research questions. If the research purposes and questions do not provide any direction at all about sampling, they probably require further development.

This principle is helpful when we are prespecifying the sampling plan. But what about when the sampling plan evolves during the course of the study? Here again there needs to be a logical basis to the way it evolves, and the same principle applies. Decisions about the sampling directions must be coherent, and consistent with the study's logic, rather than arbitrary or *ad hoc*. A clear example of this principle in operation as a study's sampling plan evolves is theoretical sampling, as was discussed in Section 8.5.4. Theoretical sampling is:

> the process of data collection for generating theory, whereby the analyst
> jointly collects, codes and analyses his data and decides what data to collect
> next and where to find them, in order to develop his theory as it emerges.
> The process of data collection is controlled by theoretical sampling according
> to the emerging theory. (Glaser, 1992: 101)

Both theoretical sampling as a study develops, and theory-driven sampling ahead of the research, are examples of the more general concept of purposive sampling.

Miles and Huberman (1994: 34) suggest six general questions against which to check a qualitative sampling plan. The first of these is the one we have just considered:

* Is the sampling relevant to your conceptual frame and research questions?
* Will the phenomena you are interested in appear? In principle, can they appear?
* Does your plan enhance generalizability of your findings, through either conceptual power or representativeness?

* Can believable descriptions and explanations be produced, ones that are true to real life?
* Is the sampling plan feasible, in terms of time, money, access to people and your own work style?
* Is the sampling plan ethical, in terms of such issues as informed consent, potential benefits and risks, and the relationship with informants?

Finally, as with quantitative research, we should note also the growing importance of secondary analysis with qualitative data, as primary research becomes more and more expensive: in the UK, for example, the Qualidata archive has been set up (ESDS, 2004). A discussion of secondary analysis, with directions to further reading, was given in Section 6.12.

---

### 9.7   REVIEW CONCEPTS

Interviews:
* structured, semi-structured, unstructured
* standardized, semi-standardized, unstandardized
* in-depth interviews
* focus group interviews
* ethnographic interviews
* life history interviews
* key informant interviews

Managing the interview:
* type of interview
* preparation for the interview
* recording the interview
* beginning the interview (rapport)
* communication and listening skills
* asking questions
* closing the interview

Interview data as a topic versus interview data as a resource

Observation:
* structured (quantitative), semi-structured, unstructured (qualitative)
* ethnographic observation
* participant observation

Continuum for participant observation:

| complete participant | _____ | participant as observer | _____ | observer as participant | _____ | complete observer |

Documentary data

Sampling in qualitative research

---

## NOTES

1 The highly structured interview, especially when response alternatives are also highly structured, is more like a quantitative data collection technique (see also Chapter 4, note 15). To show the interview as a qualitative data collection technique (as here) is to stress the more unstructured, open-ended type of interview.

2 This point applies not only to interview data, but to any accounts by people of their world. These accounts can be advocated, deconstructed, or subjected to the same 'topic versus resource' distinction noted here (Hammersley and Atkinson, 1995: 124–6). The analytic status of interview data is an example of the analytic status of qualitative data generally.

3 Not all observation in research is naturalistic or non-interventionist. For example, data collection in an experiment may well involve observation. Such observation is both interventionist and non-naturalistic. The focus here is on naturalistic, non-interventionist observation, which is more likely to be found in qualitative research.

4 Examples of highly structured observation schedules are shown in Foster (1996a: 52–60).

5 Making and taking field notes raises questions of what to record, when and how. For the 'what', Spradley (1980) suggests a basic checklist to guide field notes, using nine headings (space, actor, activity, object, act, event, time, goal and feeling). The 'when' and 'how' of making field notes in observation and participant observation research are discussed by Hammersley and Atkinson (1995: 175–86).

6 These comments are in line with the views of Silverman (1993) about the dangers of replacing direct observation with data about perceptions.

7 These issues, and especially the connection between obtrusiveness and reactivity, were highlighted in the book by Webb et al. (1966). They are considered again in Chapter 11.

8 They are key informant interview, life history interview, structured or formal interview, informal interview, questionnaire, projective techniques, and standardized tests and related measuring techniques.

9 For example, the exercise suggested by MacDonald and Tipton (1996: 200), where students are asked to research financial scandals in the twentieth century using documentary sources.

10 Finnegan (1996: 140) also gives a summary of types of sources for UK documentary data.

11 Jupp (1996: 299) distinguishes between the document (the medium on which the message is stored) and the text (the message that is conveyed through the writing).

## *Further Reading*

Adler, P.A. and Adler, P. (1994) 'Observational techniques', in N.K. Denzin and Y.S. Lincoln (eds), *Handbook of Qualitative Research*. Thousand Oaks, CA: Sage. pp. 377–92.

Atkinson, P. and Hammersley, M. (1994) 'Ethnography and participant observation', in N.K. Denzin and Y.S. Lincoln (eds), *Handbook of Qualitative Research*. Thousand Oaks, CA: Sage. pp. 248–61.

Babbie, E. (1992) *The Practice of Social Research*. 6th edn. Belmont, CA: Wadsworth.

Brenner, M., Brown, J. and Canter, D. (1985) *The Research Interview: Uses and Approaches*. London: Academic.

Denzin, N.K. (1989) *The Research Act*. 3rd edn. Englewood Cliffs, NJ: Prentice-Hall.

Fielding, N. (1996) 'Qualitative interviewing', in N. Gilbert (ed.), *Researching Social Life*. London: Sage. pp. 135–53.

Finnegan, R. (1992) *Oral Traditions and the Verbal Arts: A Guide to Research Practices*. London: Routledge.

Finnegan, R. (1996) 'Using documents', in R. Sapsford and V. Jupp (eds), *Data Collection and Analysis*. London: Sage. pp. 138–51.

Foddy, W. (1993) *Constructing Questions for Interviews and Questionnaires: Theory and Practice in Social Research*. Cambridge: Cambridge University Press.

Fontana, A. and Frey, J.H. (1994) 'Interviewing: the art of science', in N.K. Denzin and Y.S. Lincoln (eds), *Handbook of Qualitative Research*. Thousand Oaks, CA: Sage. pp. 361–76.

Foster, P. (1996) Observing *Schools: A Methodological Guide*. London: Chapman.

Greenbaum, T.L. (1998) The *Handbook for Focus Group Research*. Thousand Oaks, CA: Sage.

Hammersley, M. and Atkinson, P. (1995) *Ethnography: Principles in Practice*. 2nd edn. London: Routledge.

Krueger, R.A. and Casey, M.A. *Focus Groups: A Practical Guide for Applied Research*. 3rd edn. Thousand Oaks, CA: Sage.

Kvale, S. (1996) Interviews: *An Introduction to Qualitative Research Interviewing*. Newbury Park, CA: Sage.

MacDonald, K. and Tipton, C (1996) 'Using documents', in N. Gilbert (ed.), *Researching Social Life*. London: Sage. pp. 187–200.

Minichiello, V., Aroni, R., Timewell, E. and Alexander, L. (1990) *In-Depth Interviewing: Researching People*. Melbourne: Longman Cheshire.

Morgan, D.L. (1988) *Focus Groups as Qualitative Research*. Newbury Park, CA: Sage.

Plummer, K. (1983) Documents of Life. London: Allen and Unwin.

Scott, J. (1990) *A Matter of Record: Documentary Sources in Social Research*. Cambridge: Polity.

Silverman, D. (1985) *Qualitative Methodology and Sociology*. Farnborough: Gower.

Silverman, D. (1993) *Interpreting Qualitative Data: Methods for Analyzing Talk, Text and Interaction*. London: Sage.

Spradley, J.P. (1979) *The Ethnographic Interview*. New York: Holt, Rinehart and Winston.

Spradley, J.P. (1980) *Participant Observation*. New York: Holt, Rinehart and Winston.

Stewart, D. and Shamdasami, P. (1990) *Focus Groups: Theory and Practice*. Newbury Park, CA: Sage.

# 10
# The Analysis of Qualitative Data

In Chapter 8, the diversity of qualitative research was noted. Perhaps nowhere is that diversity more apparent than in approaches to the analysis of qualitative data. Indeed, the term 'data analysis' itself has different meanings among qualitative researchers, and these interpretations lead to different methods of analysis. We begin this chapter by looking at the present-day diversity in qualitative analysis.

## 10.1 Diversity in Qualitative Analysis

Qualitative research concentrates on the study of social life in natural settings. Its richness and complexity mean that there are different ways of analysing social life, and therefore multiple perspectives and practices in the analysis of qualitative data: 'There is variety in techniques because there are different questions to be addressed and different versions of social reality that can be elaborated' (Coffey and Atkinson, 1996: 14). The different techniques are often interconnected, overlapping and complementary, and sometimes mutually exclusive – 'irreconcilable couples' (Miles and Huberman, 1994: 9). But whether complementary or contrasting, there are good reasons for the existence of the many analytic strategies, since any set of qualitative data can be looked at from different perspectives. A repertoire of analytic techniques thus characterizes qualitative research today, and different techniques can be applied to the same body of qualitative data, illuminating different aspects of it (Example 10.1).

| | |
|---|---|
| Feldman (1995) applies the four techniques of ethnomethodology, semiotics, dramaturgical analysis and deconstruction to the one body of qualitative data, drawn from a single study of a university housing office. The different techniques illuminate different aspects of the data. | **Example 10.1** *Different analytic techniques* |

Despite this variety, some writers have sought to identify the common features of qualitative data analysis. For example, Miles and Huberman (1994: 9) suggest a 'fairly classic set' of six moves common across different types of analysis. Similarly, Tesch (1990: 95–7), while concluding that no characteristics are common to all types of analysis, nevertheless identifies 10 principles and practices which hold true for most types of qualitative analysis. But Tesch also identifies no fewer than 26 different approaches to the analysis of qualitative data in her survey.

This variety and diversity in approaches underlines the point that there is no single right way to do qualitative data analysis – no single methodological framework. Much depends on the purposes of the research, and it is important that the method of analysis is integrated from the start with other parts of the research, rather than being an afterthought. In the expanding literature on qualitative analysis, terms such as 'transforming', 'interpreting' and 'making sense of' qualitative data are prominent, and it is the different ways of doing these things that lead to the diversity in methods of analysis. This diversity is valuable, but scholarly rigour and discipline are also important. In their book

*Making Sense of Qualitative Data*, Coffey and Atkinson stress: 'What links all the approaches is a central concern with transforming and interpreting qualitative data – in a rigorous and scholarly way – in order to capture the complexities of the social worlds we seek to explain' (1996: 3). A similar point about the need for discipline is made by Silverman (1993: 211).

These recent concerns for disciplined methods of analysis echo this well known quote from some 25 years ago:

> The most serious and central difficulty in the use of qualitative data is that methods of analysis are not well formulated. For quantitative data, there are clear conventions the researcher can use. But the analyst faced with a bank of qualitative data has very few guidelines for protection against self-delusion, let alone the presentation of unreliable or invalid conclusions to scientific or policy-making audiences. How can we be sure that an 'earthy', 'undeniable', 'serendipitous' finding is not, in fact, wrong? (Miles, 1979: 591)

Methods for the analysis of data need to be systematic, disciplined and able to be seen (and to be seen through, as in 'transparent') and described. A key question in assessing a piece of research is: how did the researcher get to these conclusions from these data? If there is no answer to that question – if the method of analysis cannot be described and scrutinized – it is difficult to know what confidence to have in the findings put forward.

All empirical research has to deal with this problem. One strength of quantitative research is that methods for the analysis of its data are well known and transparent. That enables reproducibility in the analysis: a second analyst, working with the same quantitative data and using the same statistical operations as the first, should get the same results.[1] For qualitative research, the relevance of the criterion of reproducibility is a matter of debate in the literature. But there have been great developments in the analysis of qualitative data in the last 20 years,[2] and the concept of the 'audit trail' through the data analysis is now realistic for much qualitative research.[3]

For the individual researcher, this problem comes alive at the point of sitting down in front of the qualitative data – perhaps interview transcripts, and/or field notes from observations and discussions, and/or documents. At this point, what, exactly, does the researcher do? Deciding what to do can cause bewilderment, as Feldman's (1995: 1) vivid description shows. And when data have been analysed, is the researcher able to say how the conclusions were reached? Important progress has been made on this question in the last 20 or so years.

Despite this progress, it would be wrong to assume that all developments in qualitative analysis have been directed at this issue. For one thing, there are researchers who would reject the view of knowledge on which the ideas of reproducibility and the audit trail are based – for example, those devoted to a relativist epistemology rooted in a postmodernist and constructivist philosophy (Kelle, 1995). For another, some more recent developments in qualitative analysis have taken the field in quite new directions, where this criterion has seemed both less central and less problematic. This will be seen in later sections of this chapter.

To deal in detail with all current approaches to the analysis of qualitative data is not possible in the space we have. Therefore a choice was required for this chapter: to sketch all approaches, or to concentrate in detail on some? I have chosen the latter, concentrating on those approaches which are most similar in logic to the way quantitative data analysis works. That means the Miles and Huberman approach, and, especially, grounded theory. But these are not the only approaches, and others are also outlined later in the chapter.

Therefore the remainder of this chapter has three main parts: a short description of analytic induction preceding an overview of the Miles and Huberman approach; a detailed discussion of grounded theory; and an overview of some of the more interpretive and linguistic approaches to qualitative analysis. This division is similar to the three-way classification used by Tesch (1990) in her survey of methods of qualitative analysis. But I stress again that there are other approaches than these,[4] that this selection of content is not meant to imply that these approaches are somehow better, and that there is no single methodological framework or prescription for the analysis of qualitative data.

## 10.2 Analytic Induction

In the search for regularities in the social world, induction is central. Concepts are developed inductively from the data and raised to a higher level of abstraction, and their interrelationships are then traced out. But while induction is central, deduction is needed also, since, as noted in Chapter 8, theory generation involves theory verification as well. This sort of qualitative data analysis is a series of alternating inductive and deductive steps, whereby data-driven inductive hypothesis generation is followed by deductive hypothesis examination for the purpose of verification (Kelle, 1995).

The fact that much qualitative analysis depends on induction suggests 'analytic induction' as a useful general term. But this term also has a more specific meaning. Analytic induction was developed by Znaniecki (1934), and was originally identified with the search for 'universals' in social life.[5] Today, it is often used to refer to the systematic examination of similarities between cases to develop concepts or ideas (Example 10.2). It has been described by, for example, Lindesmith (1968), Cressey (1950; 1971) and Hammersley and Atkinson. This is the description given by Hammersley and Atkinson (1995: 234–5):

---

- Bloor (1978) used analytic induction in his study of surgeons; the study is summarized in Silverman (1993).
- Cressey (1950) used analytic induction to study 'trust violation'.
- Lindesmith (1947) used analytic induction to study drug addiction.

Example 10.2
*Analytic induction*

---

1 An initial definition of the phenomenon to be explained is formulated.
2 Some cases of this phenomenon are investigated, documenting potential explanatory features.
3 A hypothetical explanation is framed on the basis of analysis of the data, designed to identify common factors across the cases.
4 Further cases are investigated to test the hypothesis.
5 If the hypothesis does not fit the facts from these new cases, either the hypothesis is reformulated or the phenomenon to be explained is redefined (so that the negative cases are excluded).
6 This procedure of examining cases, reformulating the hypothesis, and/or redefining the phenomenon is continued until new cases continually confirm the validity of the hypothesis, at which point it may be concluded that the hypothesis is correct (though this can never be known with absolute certainty).

Ragin (1994) believes that it is better to see analytic induction today as directing researchers to study evidence that challenges or disconfirms concepts or ideas they are developing, paying particular attention to the negative cases, or exceptions. This is done by comparing incidents or cases, establishing similarities and differences in order to define categories and concepts. Analytic induction shares common features with the two approaches to qualitative analysis now described.

## 10.3 The Miles and Huberman Framework for Qualitative Data Analysis

*Qualitative Data Analysis*, by Miles and Huberman, is a comprehensive sourcebook, describing analysis which is directed at tracing out lawful and stable relationships among social phenomena, based on the regularities and sequences that link these phenomena (1994: 4). They label their approach 'transcendental realism', and their analysis has three main components:

- data reduction
- data display
- drawing and verifying conclusions.

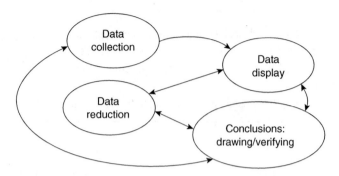

**Figure 10.1**   *Components of data analysis: interactive model*
*Source*: Miles and Huberman, 1994: 12

They see these as three concurrent streams or activities, interacting throughout the analysis, as shown in Figure 10.1.

1   *Data reduction*. Data reduction occurs continually throughout the analysis. It is not something separate from the analysis, it is part of the analysis. In the early stages, it happens through editing, segmenting and summarizing the data. In the middle stages, it happens through coding and memoing, and associated activities such as finding themes, clusters and patterns. In the later stages, it happens through conceptualizing and explaining, since developing abstract concepts is also a way of reducing the data. In the need to reduce data, qualitative analysis is not different from quantitative analysis, and the parallels in conceptual structure are shown in the levels of abstraction diagram in Figure 10.2. In both quantitative and qualitative analysis, the objective of data reduction is to reduce the data without significant loss of information. In qualitative analysis, an additional important component of not losing information is not to strip the data from their context.

2   *Data display*. Data displays organize, compress and assemble information. Because qualitative data are typically so voluminous, bulky and dispersed, displays help at all stages in the analysis. Miles and Huberman regard displays as essential, often using the phrase 'You know what you display.' They have no doubt that better displays are a major avenue to valid qualitative analysis (1994: 11). There are many different ways of displaying data – graphs, charts, networks, diagrams of different types (Venn diagrams, causal models, etc.) – and any way that moves the analysis forward is appropriate. Displays are used at all stages, since they enable data to be organized and summarized, they show what stage the analysis has reached, and they are the basis for further analysis. The message is clear: good qualitative analysis involves repeated and iterative displays of data. The same point is made in the grounded theory literature.

3 *Drawing and verifying conclusions.* The reasons for reducing and displaying data are to assist in drawing conclusions. While drawing conclusions logically follows reduction and display of data, in fact it takes place more or less concurrently with them. Thus possible conclusions may be noted early in the analysis, but they may be vague and ill-formed at this stage. They are held tentative pending further work, and sharpened during it. They are not finalized until all the data are in, and have been analysed. Conclusions will be in the form of propositions, and once they have been drawn, they need to be verified.

These three components are interwoven and concurrent throughout the data analysis. The first two, data reduction and display, rest mainly on the operations of coding and memoing, which are discussed below. For each part of the third component, drawing and then verifying conclusions, Miles and Huberman present a list of tactics to use in developing propositions. These three components – data reduction, data display and drawing conclusions – give an overall view of data analysis. They involve three main operations: coding, memoing and developing propositions.

Coding and memoing are the two basic operations which get the analysis going. I discuss them here in general terms, and deal with them separately. In practice, they happen together and are closely related.

### 10.3.1 Coding

Coding is the starting activity in this sort of qualitative analysis, and the foundation for what comes later. For analysis directed at discovering regularities in the data, coding is central.

What is coding? The literature is a little confusing about this. On the one hand, coding is analysis. On the other hand, coding is the specific and concrete activity which starts the analysis. Both are correct, in the sense that coding both begins the analysis, and also goes on at different levels throughout the analysis. Codes are tags, names or labels, and coding is therefore the process of putting tags, names or labels against pieces of the data (Example 10.3). The pieces may be individual words, or small or large chunks of the data. The point of assigning labels is to attach meaning to the pieces of data, and these labels serve a number of functions. They index the data, providing a basis for storage and retrieval. The first labels also permit more advanced coding, which enables the summarizing of data by pulling together themes, and by identifying patterns. In view of the volume and complexity of much qualitative data, these early labels become an essential part of subsequent analysis. So basic coding is both the first part of the analysis, and part of getting the data ready for subsequent analysis. Advanced coding is the same activity – labelling and categorizing – applied at higher levels of abstraction with the data. This is what is meant by saying that coding is analysis.

---

- Coffey and Atkinson (1996: 33–44) illustrate coding using an interview with an academic anthropologist.
- Miles and Huberman (1994: 55–72) give coding examples from several different studies and settings, and show some coding frameworks and lists.

Example 10.3
*Coding*

---

There are two main types of codes: descriptive codes, and inferential (or pattern) codes. Early labels may be descriptive codes, requiring little or no inference beyond the piece of data itself. These are especially valuable in getting the analysis started, and in enabling the researcher to get a 'feel' for the data. Glaser and Strauss use the term *in vivo* codes in the same way, in grounded theory coding. First-level coding mainly uses these descriptive, low-inference codes, which are very useful in summarizing segments of data, and which provide the basis for later higher-order coding. Later codes may be more interpretive, requiring some degree of inference beyond the data. Thus second-level coding tends to focus on pattern codes. A pattern code is more inferential, a sort of 'meta-code'. Pattern codes pull together material into smaller and more meaningful units. A good way to understand pattern codes is by analogy with factor analysis in quantitative research. A factor is a concept at a higher level of abstraction, which brings together less abstract variables. Similarly, a pattern code is a more abstract concept which brings together less abstract, more descriptive codes.

There is the usual range of possibilities when it comes to bringing codes to the data or finding them in the data. At one end of the continuum, we can have prespecified codes or more general coding frameworks. At the other end, we can start coding with no prespecified codes, and let the data suggest initial codes. This decision is not independent of other such decisions concerning research questions, conceptual frameworks and the structuring of data generally. Nor, as before, does it need to be an either–or decision. Thus, even when guided by an initial coding scheme, we can be alert to other labels and categories suggested by the data. Similarly, we might start with a *tabula rasa*, derive a first set of codes from the data, and then draw on a coding scheme after the initial analysis.

There is another similarity, in this sort of coding of data, with quantitative research. It concerns operational definitions:

> Whether codes are prespecified or developed along the way, clear operational definitions are indispensable, so they can be applied by a single researcher over time and multiple researchers will be thinking about the same phenomena as they code. (Miles and Huberman, 1994: 63)

Operational definitions, in a quantitative context, mean the definition of a variable in terms of the operations necessary to measure it. This quote makes clear the applicability of the concept in this style of qualitative analysis. There must be clear links between data indicators and the conceptual labels (or codes) given to the data. These links enable check coding, and tests of inter-coder reliability in qualitative analysis. They are important in establishing the audit trail through the analysis.

In summary, coding is the concrete activity of labelling data, which gets the data analysis under way, and which continues throughout the analysis. Initial coding will typically be descriptive and of low inference, whereas later coding will integrate data by using higher-order concepts. Thus there are two main types of codes: low-inference descriptive codes, and higher-inference pattern codes. While coding is central, basic to all analysis, and goes on throughout the analysis, analysis is not only coding. It also involves memoing.

### 10.3.2 Memoing

Memoing is the second basic operation, but this does not imply that it is the second stage. The operations are not sequential: memoing begins at the start of the analysis, along with coding.

While coding, at whatever level, the analyst will have all sorts of ideas. These become the stuff of memos, which record the ideas. Glaser's definition of a memo is widely used:

> A memo is the theorizing write-up of ideas about codes and their
> relationships as they strike the analyst while coding … it can be a sentence,
> a paragraph or a few pages … it exhausts the analyst's momentary ideation
> based on data with perhaps a little conceptual elaboration. (Miles and
> Huberman, 1994: 72; Glaser, 1978: 83–4)

These memos can cover many things. They may be substantive, theoretical, methodological or even personal (Example 10.4). When they are substantive and theoretical, these memos may suggest still deeper concepts than the coding has so far produced. Thus they may point towards new patterns, and a higher level of pattern coding. They may also elaborate a concept or suggest ways of doing that, or they may relate different concepts to each other. This last type of memo produces propositions.

---

- Miles and Huberman (1994: 72–5) show several memos taken from different projects.
- Corbin (1986: 102–20) shows a series of memos developed in an observation study in a paediatric ward.

**Example 10.4**
*Memoing*

The important thing about substantive and theoretical memos is that they have conceptual content and are not simply describing the data. They help the analyst move from the empirical to the conceptual level. They are therefore especially important in induction, since they move the analysis towards developing propositions. Memoing links coding with the developing of propositions. It is important in qualitative analysis to balance discipline with creativity, and it is in memoing where creativity comes in. We can think of coding as the systematic and disciplined part of the analysis (though creativity and insight also are needed to see patterns and connections), whereas memoing is the more creative-speculative part of the developing analysis. That speculative part of course needs verification.

Together, coding and memoing provide the building blocks for this style of qualitative analysis. While the initial analysis might be mainly concerned with coding, it is not long before memoing is involved. We have said earlier that the analysis of qualitative data cannot be reduced to rules. But there is one exception to this, one rule (Glaser, 1978: 83): record all ideas, as they happen, as memos. When an idea occurs during coding, stop the coding and record the idea. Later, the memos can be indexed for storage and subsequent use.

Conclusion drawing and verifying is the third part of this analysis. It involves developing propositions, and is conceptually distinct from the other stages, but again is likely to happen concurrently with them. Miles and Huberman give a list of 13 tactics for drawing meaning and conclusions from displayed data. Since conclusions need also to be verified, they give a second list of 13 tactics for testing and confirming findings.

This stage in the analysis is the most difficult to describe, because it typically involves a number of different analytical processes, which may be used simultaneously rather than sequentially, and which cut across and combine with each other. In other words, several things are going on at once. This work starts from a point where ordering and integration of the previous analysis are required. After coding and memoing, there are many labels, at different levels of abstraction, and piles of memos of various kinds. The aim of this stage is to integrate what has been done into a meaningful and coherent picture of the data. The two lists of tactics give an overview of the activities involved, and are shown in Appendix 2.

In summary, the Miles and Huberman view of qualitative analysis has the three components of reduction, display and drawing conclusions, and the three operations of coding, memoing and drawing conclusions. Their framework gives a useful general picture of this style of qualitative analysis, and a good background against which to look at grounded theory analysis. There are many connections between the two approaches. Two of the main ones are through abstracting and comparing.

## 10.4 Abstracting and Comparing

The sort of qualitative analysis so far described requires many different intellectual tools and activities, but two stand out as fundamental – abstracting and comparing.

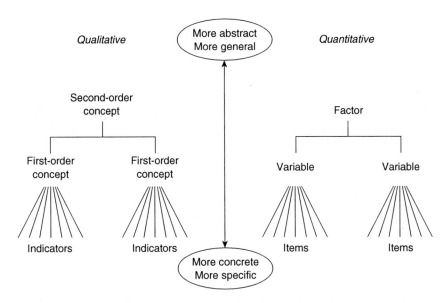

**Figure 10.2**   *Levels of abstraction in data analysis*

### *Abstracting*

The essential point here is that some concepts are at a higher level of abstraction than others. The terms 'concrete' and 'abstract' describe this continuum of abstraction, as do the terms 'specific' and 'general'. Figure 10.2 shows this idea, as did Figure 2.1.

Figure 10.2 shows the levels of abstraction in both the qualitative and quantitative contexts, and the close similarities between the two. At the lowest level of abstraction, the most concrete or specific or descriptive level, we have indicators (qualitative) and items (quantitative). At the next level, the first level of abstraction, we have first-order concepts (qualitative) and variables (quantitative). As shown in Chapter 6, latent trait theory in measurement formalizes this idea. At the next level, the second order of abstraction, we have second-order concepts (qualitative) and factors (quantitative). Again, factor analysis and cluster analysis in quantitative work formalize this idea. The process of abstraction does not need to stop there. Still more abstract and general concepts are possible, in both approaches, but two levels of abstraction show the idea, and encompass most of what we do.

Two things stand out from this diagram. First, the conceptual structure, in terms of the continuum from concrete to abstract and from specific to general, is similar in both approaches. Therefore, the general nature of this sort of analysis, developing higher-order concepts to summarize and integrate more concrete levels of data, is also similar in both approaches. Second, quantitative analysis has formalized the way it moves from one level to the next to a much greater extent than qualitative analysis. Thus quantitative analysis aggregates items into variables, to move to the first level of abstraction, and derives factors from variables, to move to the second level of abstraction. By the nature of its data, qualitative analysis cannot be formalized to the same extent.

### Comparing

Comparison is fundamental to all systematic inquiry, whether the data are quantitative or qualitative. In quantitative research, we don't often think explicitly about comparison, since comparison is built into all stages of quantitative inquiry. Thus measurement encapsulates the concept of comparison, quantitative design is developed to permit comparison, and the various data analysis techniques are based on comparison. So we are comparing automatically when we use the techniques of quantitative research.

Comparison is not so automatically integrated into qualitative analysis, and it therefore needs stressing. Comparing is essential in identifying abstract concepts, and in coding. At the first level of coding, it is by comparing different indicators in the data that we arrive at the more abstract concepts behind the empirical data. Thus it is comparison which leads to raising the level of abstraction, to the 'one-upping' (Glaser, 1978) so essential to conceptual development. The same is true for coding at a higher level. Comparing concepts and their properties at a first level of abstraction enables us to identify more abstract concepts. The systematic and constant making of comparisons is therefore essential to conceptual development at all levels in the analysis of qualitative data.

Tesch (1990), in her comprehensive survey of methods used in qualitative data analysis, sees comparison as the central intellectual activity in analysis. Glaser and Strauss (1967), co-founders of grounded theory, saw comparison as so important that they described grounded theory analysis as the 'constant comparative method'. Thus comparing is at the heart of grounded theory analysis.

## 10.5 Grounded Theory Analysis

In Chapter 8, grounded theory was defined as both an overall approach to research and a set of procedures for developing theory through the analysis of data. The approach was described in Chapter 8. This section deals with the basic ideas of grounded theory analysis. This analysis aims directly at generating abstract theory to explain what is central in the data. All of its procedures are oriented to that aim, and from the start of its coding it recognizes both the central role of conceptual abstraction and the hierarchical structure of theoretical knowledge.

How does the analyst go about generating theory from data? What follows now is an overview of grounded theory analysis, then a description of open, axial and selective coding, then a summary of the key concepts of grounded theory analysis. This material is based on the five key grounded theory publications referred to in Section 8.5.2.

### 10.5.1 Overview

The essential idea in discovering a grounded theory is to find a core category, at a high level of abstraction but grounded in the data, which accounts for what is central in the data. Grounded theory analysis does this in three steps. The first is to find conceptual categories in the data, at a first level of abstraction. The second is to find relationships between these categories. The third is to conceptualize and account for these relationships at a higher level of abstraction. This means there are three general types of codes: substantive codes, which are the initial conceptual categories in the data; theoretical codes, which connect these categories; and the core code, which is the higher-order conceptualization of the theoretical coding, around which the theory is built.

Thus the first objective is to find the substantive codes in the data. These are categories generated from the empirical data, but at a more abstract level than the data themselves. In this first level of analysis, some of these substantive codes will appear as more central in the data than others. The second objective is to bring the main substantive codes together, to interconnect them using theoretical codes. These statements of interconnection are propositions or hypotheses about the data, to be integrated in the third stage into the grounded theory. The third objective is thus to find a higher-order, more abstract construct – the core category – which integrates these hypotheses into a theory, and which describes and explains them.

At the heart of grounded theory analysis is coding: open coding, axial coding and selective coding. These are not necessarily done sequentially: rather, they are likely to be overlapping and done concurrently. But they are conceptually distinct operations. Open coding finds the substantive codes. Axial coding uses theoretical codes to interconnect the main substantive codes. Selective coding isolates and elaborates the higher-order core category.

### 10.5.2 Open coding

Open coding constitutes a first level of conceptual analysis with the data. The analyst begins by 'fracturing' or 'breaking open' the data. This is why the term 'open' in open coding is used. The idea is to open up the theoretical possibilities in the data. The purpose is to use the data to generate abstract conceptual categories – more abstract than the data they describe – for later use in theory building. These are the substantive codes. Open coding necessarily involves a close examination of (some of) the data, identifying conceptual categories implicit or explicit in the data, and the theoretical possibilities the data carry. What makes grounded theory analysis different from other forms of qualitative

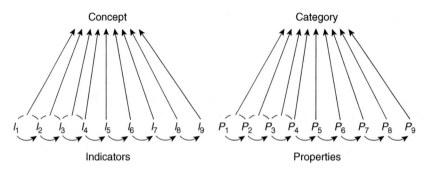

**Figure 10.3**   *Concept–indicator diagram*
*Source*: Glaser, 1978: 62

analysis is its insistence, from the start, on generating abstract conceptual categories to account for the data being studied. Therefore its coding is *not* centrally concerned with simple description, thematic analysis or interpretation of the data, though these may assist the analyst in the open coding. It *is* centrally concerned with 'rendering the data theoretically' (Glaser) or 'converting the data analytically' (Strauss). Those phrases mean using the data to generate more abstract categories. The focus is on generating grounded abstract concepts, which can become the building blocks for the theory.

The key to understanding open coding, and grounded theory analysis in general, is the concept-indicator model. It is shown in Figure 10.3. It is the same model we saw earlier, both in latent trait measurement (Figure 6.1) and in the discussion of levels of abstraction (Figure 10.2). As Glaser (1978: 62) points out, this model directs the coding of empirical indicators in the data.

The central idea behind this model is that a concept can have many different possible empirical indicators. When we infer a concept from an indicator in the data, we are abstracting – going upwards from a piece of empirical data to a more abstract concept. Because a concept has many indicators, the indicators are interchangeable with each other for the purposes of inferring the concept. This means that $I_1$ (indicator $I_1$) is an indicator of the concept, and so is $I_2$ (and $I_3$, $I_4$, etc.). We compare indicator with indicator, assessing their similarities and differences, in order to infer the concept. We also ask, constantly, what concept this piece of empirical data indicates.

As the diagram shows, the terms 'categories' and 'properties' are also equivalent, respectively, to concepts and indicators. Thus the grounded theory phrase 'elaborating a category in terms of its properties' is equivalent to specifying additional indicators of a concept. To ask what concept this piece of empirical data indicates is to ask what category this property indicates.

The process of labelling in open coding is guided by two main activities: making comparisons and asking questions. The first means that different pieces of data are constantly compared with each other to help generate abstract categories. For the second, one type of question is constantly asked which is distinctive of grounded theory.

It has three forms:

* What is this piece of data an example of? Or,
* What does this piece of data stand for, or represent? Or,
* What category or property of a category does this piece of data indicate?

These two activities – making comparisons and asking this sort of question – focus directly on abstracting, on raising the conceptual level in the data, on one-upping the data. This quote from Strauss and Corbin describes the process:

> Open coding is the part of analysis that pertains specifically to the naming and categorizing of phenomena through close examination of data … During open coding the data are broken down into discrete parts, closely examined, compared for similarities and differences, and questions are asked about the phenomena as reflected in the data. While various questions are asked, the key question is the one above – 'What is this piece of data an example of?' (1990: 62)

Open coding, like all coding, is labelling, putting labels on pieces of data. Sometimes these labels will be descriptive, low-inference labels, and sometimes they will be *in vivo* labels, but mostly they will be labels which involve a first level of inference. In grounded theory open coding, the labelling is guided by the model and questions shown above. Sometimes a piece of data is a word or phrase, sometimes a line, sometimes a paragraph, sometimes more, depending on the data and on what constitutes indicators (or units) in the data. It is the indicators in the data which are constantly being compared in the open coding. For Glaser (1978; 1992), it is primarily incidents which are compared, but indicators and units are broader terms. It is essential to code some of the data in great detail, line by line, especially parts which are rich. Intensive coding also helps to learn about grounded theory analysis, but not all data in a project will be coded at this level of intensity.

Codes (labels) at this early stage of the analysis are provisional, and any piece of data may have several labels. Closure on final codes is delayed until substantial coding has been done, and until the analyst has a stable view of what is central in the data. Potentially central categories are also being noted as the open coding proceeds, but closure is delayed here also.

Open coding is about using the data to generate conceptual labels and categories for use in theory building. Its function is to expose theoretical possibilities in the data. It is not about bringing concepts to the data, and no *a priori* coding scheme is used. Using only concepts and categories generated by the data ensures that they are grounded in the data, and that any concepts to be used in the theory have earned their conceptual status. Thus the analyst starts with no preconceived conceptual categories, but uses only those generated by the data. Open coding is not centrally concerned with summarizing data, or with describing data, or with finding synonyms for words in the data or with interpreting data. It may do these things indirectly, or as part of generating abstract categories, but these things are not the objective; the objective is to conceptualize the data.

The emphasis in grounded theory open coding is on the theoretical possibilities that all data carry, but which are frequently overlooked in analysis. In order not to miss these possibilities, the advice is to 'hasten slowly' through the early coding, in order to let all possibilities emerge. Specific techniques for enhancing theoretical sensitivity ensure that we open up our thinking about the phenomena we are studying. These techniques are described in Glaser (1978) and Strauss and Corbin (1990), and reflect the importance of theoretical sensitivity as a concept in grounded theory analysis.

Open coding, like most of grounded theory analysis, is best done in a small group. This helps keep the analysis on track and grounded, and helps to ensure theoretical sensitivity. It is easy to miss the theoretical possibilities in data, to ignore the requirement that our categories be grounded, or more generally to lose sight of the purpose of open coding in grounded theory. The best defence against these difficulties is a small group of analysts working together with a set of data (Example 10.5).

---

- Strauss and Corbin (1990: 61–74) illustrate open coding using observational data from a restaurant setting.
- Strauss (1987: 40–64 and 82–108) demonstrates open coding in a seminar with students, with himself as leader, using observational data from a study of pain management in a cardiac recovery unit.
- Corbin (1986: 102–20) describes open coding on observational data from a nurse in a paediatric unit studying children's responses to hospitalization.

**Example 10.5**
*Open coding*

---

Successful open coding generates many provisional labels quickly from even a small amount of data, but this sort of coding does not go on indefinitely. The objective of open coding is not the endless generation of conceptual labels throughout the data. This process of labelling therefore needs to be balanced by two other processes. One is to keep an overview of the data in mind, and to keep looking broadly across the data, rather than only to do the intensive coding. This is what Glaser (1992) calls 'dip and skip', where you intensively code some parts (dip), while at the same time skimming the data using comparisons to look for possible conceptual patterns, and for concepts which tie together different pieces of the data and different incidents in the data (skip). The other is deliberately to step back from the data and to make judgements about what seems to be central and basic in the data, over and above all the coding labels generated. This judgement is made by stepping back and focusing on such questions as: what centrally seems to be going on here? What are these data mainly about?

In grounded theory analysis, it is important to find and focus on what is central in the data. The whole process is about successively integrating the data into a smaller set of more abstract concepts and categories. Therefore the focus is on possible integrating concepts right from the start. Ultimately, a grounded theory will be built around a core category, which accounts for most of the variation in the data, and integrates other parts of the data around it. Therefore coding procedures at all stages are aligned with this purpose of reducing the data through abstracting, of seeking to discover the conceptually central aspects of the data. The outcome of open coding is a set of conceptual categories generated from the data. There will also be some ordering and classification of these categories, and some sense of what is central in the data. There may be some initial views of possible core categories, but whether this has happened or not at this stage, a small number of important categories will have emerged.

### 10.5.3 Axial (or theoretical) coding

Grounded theory analysis is a process of abstracting across two levels, first from data to first-order concepts, and then from first-order concepts to higher-order concepts. In this process there are three stages. In the first stage, open coding produces a set of first-order categories from the data, raised already to one level of abstraction. In the second stage, these categories are interconnected with each other, producing a set of propositions. In the third stage, selective coding is applied to these propositions, raising the level of abstraction again, and producing the core category, around which the theory is written and the data are integrated.

Axial coding is the name given to the second stage, where the main categories which have emerged from open coding of the data are interconnected with each other (Example 10.6). The word 'axial' is used by Strauss and Corbin, and is intended to denote the idea of putting an axis through the data, where an axis connects the categories identified in open coding. Glaser (1978) uses the more general term 'theoretical coding' to describe this stage. Its meaning is made clear below.

---

- Strauss and Corbin (1990: 96–115) illustrate axial coding using pain management data.
- Strauss (1987: 64–8) demonstrates axial coding around the category 'monitoring', in a study of medical technology in a cardiac care unit.
- Swanson (1986: 121–32) gives several examples of developing categories in axial coding, using as data nurses' accounts of their learning experiences.

**Example 10.6**
*Axial coding*

---

If open coding breaks the data apart or 'runs the data open' (Glaser, 1978), in order to expose their theoretical possibilities and categories, axial coding puts categories back together again, but in conceptually different ways. Thus axial coding is about interrelating the substantive categories which open coding has developed.

How is this done? To do the interrelating, we will need some concepts which connect things to each other. These connecting concepts are called theoretical codes, which is why Glaser uses the term 'theoretical coding' rather than 'axial coding'. Strauss and Corbin also use the term 'coding paradigm' to describe the set of concepts used for making the connections between things. All of these terms mean the same thing.

We know from quantitative analysis that there are many different ways in which connections between things can occur. For example, causes and consequences is one way; seeing things as different aspects (or dimensions or properties) of a common category is another; seeing things as parts or stages of a process is a third; a stimulus–response association is a fourth; and so on. Some of the ways things can be connected are covered by Miles and Huberman, in their list of tactics noted earlier, and two comprehensive treatments of this topic are by Glaser and Rosenberg. Glaser (1978: 72–82) discusses 18 ways these connections between things can occur; he calls them 'coding families'. Rosenberg (1968: 1–21), writing more from the quantitative perspective, classifies relationships between variables (the quantitative equivalent of connections between things) into three main types (symmetrical, reciprocal and asymmetrical) and then gives several subtypes within each of these classifications.

Strauss and Corbin (1990: 99–107) write exclusively about the interactionist coding paradigm. This identifies causal conditions, phenomenon, context, intervening conditions, action/interaction strategies, and consequences, as a way of interrelating categories in the data; these are theoretical concepts used to interconnect the data. Thus, if the interactionist paradigm is used, the outcome of axial coding is an understanding of the central phenomenon in the data in terms of the conditions which give rise to it, the context in which it is embedded, the action/interaction strategies by which it is handled, managed or carried out, and the consequences of those strategies.

In true grounded theory analysis, theoretical codes, like all other codes, should emerge from the data, and should not be forced upon the data. One of the major criticisms made by Glaser of the Strauss and Corbin book is that, by using only the interactionist coding paradigm described above, they are forcing theoretical codes on the data rather than letting these codes emerge from the data. Theoretical codes, like all other parts of the theory, must earn their status in grounded theory. For Glaser, this is done by trusting in the emergence of theoretical codes as the analysis proceeds, not by forcing such codes on the data.[6]

This idea of theoretical codes is important, but not esoteric: it is about the ways in which things are interconnected with each other. We saw in quantitative analysis (Chapter 7) that there are two conceptually distinct stages in studying relationships between variables. One is finding and describing the relationship. The other is interpreting the relationship, or saying how the relationship has come about, or giving meaning to the relationship. It is the same here in qualitative analysis. The three sources indicated above – Glaser (1978), Rosenberg (1968) and Miles and Huberman (1994) – together give a comprehensive description of possible ways things can be related. These descriptions overlap, and all draw upon ideas on this topic from quantitative research.

### 10.5.4 Selective coding

Selective coding is the third stage in grounded theory analysis. The term 'selective' is used because, for this stage, the analyst deliberately selects one aspect as a core category, and concentrates on that. When that selection is made, it delimits the theoretical analysis and development to those parts of the data that relate to this core category, and open coding ceases. The analysis now proceeds around the core category, and the core category becomes the centrepiece of the grounded theory.

Selective coding builds on the propositions produced by axial coding:

> In axial coding you developed the basis for selective coding. You now have categories worked out in terms of their salient properties, dimensions and associated paradigmatic relationships … You should also have begun to note possible relationships between major categories along the lines of their properties and dimensions. Furthermore, you have … begun to formulate some conception of what your research is all about … The question is: How do you take that which is in rough form, and hopefully in your diagrams and memos, and systematically develop it into a picture of reality that is conceptual, comprehensible, and above all grounded? (Strauss and Corbin, 1990: 117)

In selective coding, therefore, the objective is to integrate and pull together the developing analysis. The theory to be developed must have a central focus, around which it is integrated. This will be the core category of the theory. It must be a central theme in the data, and must also be seen as central by the participants whose behaviour is being studied (Example 10.7). In order to integrate the other categories in the data, the core category will have to be at a higher level of abstraction. Potential core categories are noted right from the start of the analysis, though final decisions about the core category should not be made too early in the analysis.

> - Strauss and Corbin (1990: 116–42) illustrate the steps involved in selective coding using data about how women with chronic illness manage pregnancy.
> - Strauss (1987: 69–75) illustrates selective coding using nursing work in a cardiac recovery unit.
> - Corbin (1986: 102–20) illustrates selective coding using memos relating to pregnancy in situations of chronic illness.

Example 10.7
*Selective coding*

Selective coding is aimed at developing the abstract, condensed, integrated and grounded picture of the data referred to in the quote above. For Strauss and Corbin, the key concepts are the core category and the story line: the core category is the central phenomenon around which other categories are integrated, and the story line is a descriptive narrative about this central phenomenon. The story line is seen as a device which gets you started in selective coding, equivalent to a description of what the axial coding has produced. When analysed, it becomes your core category. What does 'analyse' mean? It means moving from a description of the story line to a conceptualization of the story line. It means telling the story analytically, not descriptively. It means finding a conceptual category abstract enough to encompass what has been described in the story.

Thus selective coding uses the same techniques as the earlier open and axial coding, but at a higher level of abstraction. The focus now is on finding a higher-order concept, a central conceptual category at the second level of abstraction. For Glaser (1992), in true grounded theory analysis, that category will emerge from the constant comparisons which have driven the earlier coding. Once that category is clear, it is elaborated in terms of its properties, and systematically related to other categories in the data. Relationships are then validated against the data. This stage also shows those categories where further data are required, and thus directs further theoretical sampling. In grounded theory language, this stage is called the systematic densification and saturation of the theory.

### 10.5.5 Key concepts of grounded theory analysis

Grounded theory analysis emphasizes the conceptualization of the data, and the generation of conceptually abstract categories grounded in the data. It insists on getting above the empirical level in analysing data, and on working towards a condensed, abstract and emerging interpretation of what is central in the data. It uses the power of abstract theory to transcend the empirical data, and to connect seemingly disparate phenomena. Put simply, the outcome of grounded theory analysis is an abstract but grounded concept (the core category) the development of which constitutes a substantive theory of the phenomenon being studied.

In grounded theory, we start with data generated from some initial research questions. The objective is to discover and develop theory, grounded in what is central in those data. In this approach, theory is seen as a set of propositions which show the connections between concepts which are at a higher level of abstraction than the data themselves. Therefore grounded theory analysis involves the identification of categories, as first-order abstractions, and the inductive development of a higher-order concept (the core category), at a second level of abstraction, from those categories. Once that is done, the core category is elaborated through its interconnection with other first-order concepts in the data.

The objective is to construct abstract theory about the data, which is grounded in the data. The concepts which the theory will use are not brought to the data and are not obvious in the data. They need to be inferred from the data by induction. This inductive inference is the process of abstraction. By showing a particular piece of data to be an example of a more abstract (first-order) concept, the analyst raises the conceptual level of the data. By showing that first-order concept to be a particular instance, or property, of a more general second-order concept, the conceptual level of the data is raised again. Thus this abstracting is done twice, following the conceptual structure shown in the levels of abstraction diagram in Figure 10.2.

By way of summary, a diagrammatic representation of grounded theory analysis is shown in Figure 10.4, and the key grounded theory terms and

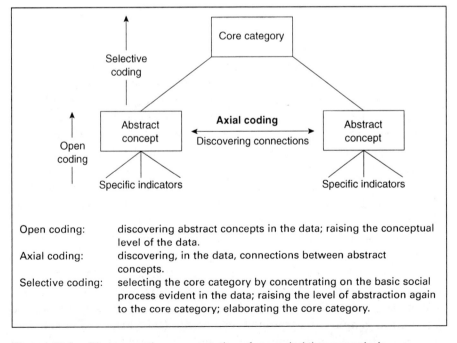

**Figure 10.4**  *Diagrammatic representation of grounded theory analysis*

**Table 10.1**  *Key concepts in grounded theory analysis*

| 1 **Overall processes** | Constant comparative method |
| --- | --- |
|  | Coding – memoing – elaborating |
|  | Theoretical sorting and integrating |

| 2 **Types of coding** | Coding: | Codes: |
| --- | --- | --- |
|  | Open | – Substantive |
|  | Axial | – Theoretical |
|  | Selective | – Core |

3 **Model**

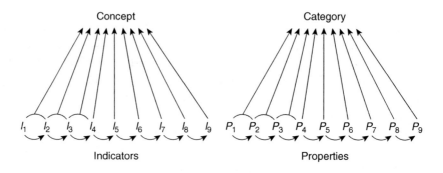

4 **Guidelines**        Theoretical sensitivity
                Theoretical sampling
                Theoretical saturation

5 **Other**           Basic social problem
                Basic social process

concepts are listed in Table 10.1. Three items in the table require further comment. The first is the term 'elaborating'. To elaborate a category is to specify and compare its additional properties. Just as a concept has many indicators, so a category has many properties. We find additional properties of a category by finding additional indicators of the concept, and we continue doing that until saturation. Elaborating a category also means to develop and examine its variation systematically. We know from quantitative research that a key to understanding a concept is to study its variation. The same idea is used here. The analytic device used to do this in grounded theory analysis is to elaborate the category by specifying, comparing and developing its properties.[7]

The second is the three 'theoretical' terms 'sensitivity', 'sampling' and 'saturation'. Theoretical sensitivity stresses that the analyst must counter a natural tendency to take data for granted, thus failing to see their theoretical possibilities. The point of opening up the data, as in open coding, is to open up thinking about the theoretical possibilities in what is being studied. Theoretical sampling describes the relationship (the 'dialectical interaction') between data collection and data analysis in grounded theory research. Theoretical saturation is reached when further data produce no new theoretical development. Saturation is necessary to ensure that the theory is conceptually complete.

The third concerns the terms 'basic social problem' and 'basic social process'. A basic social problem refers to what, in the view of the people being studied, is their main concern or problem. A basic social process refers to what, essentially, they do in dealing with that basic problem. For something to qualify as a process, it must occur over time, and must involve changes and stages over time. The core category in a grounded theory study will often (though not always) be a basic social process. This is because grounded theory studies set out to discover and model the patterns which emerge in the processes people use for dealing with their main problems in particular situations.[8] As well as useful ideas in understanding grounded theory, these are helpful ways of thinking about research in general in many different behavioural situations.

The description in this chapter has not covered all aspects of grounded theory analysis. Among topics not dealt with here, but covered in the grounded theory literature, are the difference between substantive and formal theories, densification of a grounded theory, and the implications of the grounded theory approach for the study of social processes (Example 10.8). Another direction for further reading concerns the criticism by Glaser (1992) of the Strauss and Corbin (1990) book. That criticism is essentially that the book forces concepts on the data, rather than trusting in their emergence, and that the method Strauss and Corbin describe is not grounded theory at all, but what Glaser calls 'full conceptual description'. For Glaser, the function of grounded theory is not to provide full conceptual description of all of the data. Rather, it is the discovery and development of theory about what is central in the data – theory which is condensed, abstract and selective.

---

- *Grounded Theory in Practice* (Strauss and Corbin, 1997) is an edited collection of readings of grounded theory studies, from former students of Strauss. The editors provide commentaries for each paper.

  Example 10.8
  *Grounded theory*

- *Examples of Grounded Theory: A Reader* (Glaser, 1993) is an edited collection of 25 grounded theory papers from both quantitative and qualitative projects.

---

Grounded theory is widely used today, and techniques similar to those described in this section are also widely used, but it is not without its critics. Lonkila (1995), for example, points out that there is intense ongoing debate about grounded theory in qualitative analysis, with more to come. Silverman (1993) notes criticisms of its failure to acknowledge implicit theories which guide the early analysis. He also points out that it is clearer about the generation of theories than about their test, and that it can degenerate into fairly empty empiricism. Further criticisms (Lonkila, 1995) are that some of its terms are not defined clearly, and that its rhetoric and language can often be misleading.[9] Glaser (1992), too, warns that the attempt by Strauss and Corbin to codify the procedures of grounded theory analysis is against the spirit of the method as originally developed. Like other analytic approaches which stress induction, grounded theory has a particular view of theory, and of theory generation. But this is not the only path to theorizing (see, for example, Coffey and Atkinson, 1996): there are different types of theories with which qualitative researchers may be concerned (especially in ethnography: see Hammersley and Atkinson, 1995), and, in any case, not all qualitative research is concerned with theory building, refining and testing.

These points, and others, are made by Denzin (1988) in his review of Strauss's (1987) book on qualitative analysis and grounded theory. Denzin points out that searching for theory, as in grounded theory analysis, may displace the goal of actually writing the theory of interpretation that exists in the social worlds being studied (Lonkila, 1995: 49). He also points out that the book marked a turning point in the history of qualitative research in American sociology:

> At the very moment that this work finds its place in the libraries of scholars
> and students, it is being challenged by a new body of work coming from the
> neighbouring fields of anthropology and cultural studies ... [They] are
> proposing that postmodern ethnography can no longer follow the guidelines
> of positivist social science. Gone are words like theory, hypothesis, concept,
> indicator, coding scheme, sampling, validity, and reliability. In their place
> comes a new language; readerly texts, modes of discourse, cultural poetics,
> deconstruction, interpretation, domination, the authority of the text, the
> author's voice, feminism, genre, grammatology, hermeneutics, inscription,
> master narrative, narrative structures, otherness, postmodernism, redemptive
> ethnography, semiotics, subversion, textuality, tropes. (Denzin, 1988: 432)

## 10.6 Other Approaches in Qualitative Analysis

The dilemma of grounded theory, according to Denzin, is how to be subjective, interpretive and scientific at the same time (Lonkila, 1995: 46). The difficulty of doing this may be one reason for the development of other approaches in qualitative analysis. We will now look briefly at five of these, the first more interpretive, and the other four more focused on language.

### 10.6.1 Narratives and meaning

Data analysis approaches based on segmenting, coding and categorization are valuable in attempts to find and conceptualize regularities in the data. But they by no means exhaust the data, or possibilities for their exploration. Also, they break the data into small pieces, fostering a 'culture of fragmentation' (Atkinson, 1992). In doing this, they can also decontextualize the data. Coffey and Atkinson write:

> Our interview informants may tell us long and complicated accounts and reminiscences. When we chop them up into separate coded segments, we are in danger of losing the sense that they are accounts. We lose sight, if we are not careful, of the fact that they are often couched in terms of stories – as narratives – or that they have other formal properties in terms of their discourse structure. Segmenting and coding may be an important, even an indispensable, part of the research process, but it is not the whole story. (1996: 52)

Both Miles and Huberman and the grounded theory writers are aware of the problem of fragmentation and decontextualization, and both suggest ways of recombining and of recontextualizing the data.[10] But other approaches (such as the analysis of narratives and stories) deal more holistically with qualitative data right from the start. Many social science data occur 'naturally' in story form (for example, in participant observation research), and qualitative data can also be solicited and collected in story form, as in oral and life histories and biographical interviewing. Even where data are not explicitly solicited in story form, they will often come with storied characteristics, as in unstructured interviews, where people may give narrative responses to an interviewer's questions. Thus there is a storied character to much qualitative data, and thinking about stories in the data can enable us to think creatively about collecting and interpreting data (Coffey and Atkinson, 1996).

Narratives and stories are also valuable in studying lives and lived experience, as is often demonstrated in studies concerned with empowerment. Contemporary anthropology and feminism often emphasize the study of lives from the narrator's viewpoint, with data seen as a shared production with the researcher (Manning and Cullum-Swan, 1994). Using stories as a way to capture the lived experience has occurred in many research settings: in medical and illness studies (Brody, 1987; Coles, 1989), in studies of major life events and trauma (Riessman, 1993), in studies in education from both students' points of view (Delamont, 1989; 1990; Measor and Woods, 1984) and teachers' points of view (Goodson, 1992), and in studies of life in organizations (Martin, 1990) (Example 10.9). Narratives of this sort can give a uniquely rich and subtle understanding of life situations, and the story is often a feasible way of collecting data just because it is such a common device in everyday interaction.[11]

---

- Coffey and Atkinson (1996: 54–81) give examples of narrative analysis using interviews with social anthropologists.

  Example 10.9
  *Narrative*
  *analysis and*
  *meaning*

- Silverman (1993: 72–9) discusses the organization of systems of narration using a study of the folk tale.
- Riessman (1993) discusses the topics of locating narrative, practical models for analysis and doing narrative analysis.
- Coffey and Atkinson (1996: 89–105) give an extensive example of domain analysis using the anthropological folk term 'fieldwork', showing how metaphors reveal meaning.

---

How can qualitative data in narrative and story form be explored and analysed? The following brief description draws mainly on the writing of Coffey and Atkinson (1996), who use Denzin's framework from interpretive biography for thinking about narratives. They describe formal approaches to narrative analysis, where the focus is on identifying the structural features of narratives and their arrangement: here, narrative analysis tends towards semiotics (Manning and Cullum-Swan, 1994).[12] They show also how narratives can be studied from the point of view of their function, using function as the unit of analysis. To illustrate the functional properties of narratives, they take the examples of success stories and moral tales, and of narratives as chronicles. The latter lead naturally to oral and life histories, and to biographies, autobiographies and personal experience methods generally (Clandinin and Connelly, 1994). Further avenues for the analysis of narratives are opened up by thinking about whose voices are telling the stories – in any storytelling context, the voices are differentiated and stratified – and by the social and cultural context in which the stories are told. In a general sense, stories are part of the representation of social reality as text, and narratives are therefore social constructions located within power structures and social milieux. In this respect, narrative analysis overlaps with discourse analysis.

In narrative analysis, form and content can be studied together, and a concern with narrative can illuminate how informants use language to convey particular meanings and experiences. How people convey their meanings through language can be looked at from a variety of complementary perspectives. We can examine, for example, how language is used figuratively. Coffey and Atkinson show how analysis can explore participants' use of imagery, and how such devices as metaphors reveal shared meanings and understandings. The more general exploration of the use of linguistic symbols to convey shared cultural meanings is referred to as 'domain analysis' (Coffey and Atkinson, 1996; Spradley, 1980).

People use metaphors constantly as a way of making sense of experience, and of expressing and conveying its meaning. Qualitative analysts will often do the same thing in making sense of data. Miles and Huberman (1994: 250–2) indicate some of the useful properties of metaphors in qualitative analysis: for example, they are data reducing devices, pattern making devices, decentring devices, and ways of connecting findings to theory. Metaphors are one important way that people use language figuratively. They are a major type of trope (or literary device), comparing two things using their similarities but ignoring their differences. Other tropes often used are irony (the view from the opposite, sometimes incongruous or paradoxical side), synecdoche (linking instances to a larger concept) and metonymy (representing a whole in terms of one of its parts: Miles and Huberman, 1994: 287). Focusing on these concepts in analysing data for meaning links this sort of qualitative analysis with semiotics, as Coffey and Atkinson point out, and as is shown in Section 10.6.4.

Chapter 9 discussed the analytic status of interview data and the central role of language in qualitative research. That focus, together with the view of language as a form of social action rather than as a neutral medium for 'making pictures of the world out there', provides a convenient way to approach the following types of qualitative analysis.[13]

### 10.6.2 Ethnomethodology and conversation analysis

Sociological interest in the study of language was stimulated by ethnomethodology, pioneered by Garfinkel (1967). Ethnomethodology sets out to understand 'folk' (ethno) methods (methodology) for organizing the world (Silverman, 1993). The fundamental assumption of ethnomethodology is that people within a culture have procedures for making sense of their daily life. For ethnomethodologists, culture thus consists not of a stable set of things that members are supposed to know, but of processes for figuring out or giving meaning to the actions of members. The primary focus is on how central features of a culture, its shared meanings and social norms, are developed, maintained and changed, rather than on the content of those meanings and norms (Feldman, 1995: 8).

This focus on how the shared common world is created leads the ethnomethodologist to study activities that ordinary people engage in, often without thinking.[14] Most of the time, especially when joint action and interaction is involved, language is central to these everyday activities. With so much of social life mediated through written and especially spoken communication, the study of language is at the heart of ethnomethodology. Thus conversation analysis becomes a central concern, as ethnomethodologists seek to understand people's methods for producing orderly social interaction (Example 10.10).

---

- Silverman (1993: 125–43) discusses conversational openings, obligations to answer, the structure of turn-taking and institutional talk.
- Wooffitt (1996: 287–305) refers to data from various sources in discussing linguistic repertoires, the organization of descriptive sequences and assembling descriptions.
- Heath and Luff (1996: 306–26) demonstrate the interdependence of visual and vocal conduct using video recordings of controllers in the London Underground.

*Example 10.10*
*Ethnomethodology and conversation analysis*

---

As an indication of its importance, Heath and Luff (1996) refer to a 1990 bibliography of ethnomethodological/conversation-analytic studies which contains more than 1400 citations to articles in five different languages. The general purpose of such studies is to understand the social organization of ordinary, naturally occurring human conduct, in which talk is a primary vehicle for the production and intelligibility of human actions. Where talk only is analysed, verbatim transcripts of actual conversations are used. If the data include all interaction including conversation, a video recording is more likely to be used, as in interaction analysis (Heath and Luff, 1996).

Silverman (1993: 125) summarizes Heritage's account of three fundamental assumptions of conversation analysis. They concern the structural organization of talk, the sequential organization of talk, and the need for the empirical grounding of the analysis. Following these assumptions, and using specialized transcription conventions, conversation analysis studies the situated production and organization of talk (or action), developing a 'bottom-up' understanding of how context influences participants' production of the social reality. For example, with respect to sequential organization, a part of that context is the immediately preceding utterance (or action). The next utterance is produced with respect to the immediately preceding utterance, and itself forms part of the context for the subsequent utterance(s). In this turn-taking, the conduct of participants in interaction is doubly contextual, both context-shaped and context-renewing (Heritage, 1984). Some of the tools and techniques used in conversation analysis are described by Coulthard (1985) and McCarthy (1991).

In this way, conversation analysis, like ethnomethodology generally, aims systematically to uncover and analyse the foundations of social life. Silverman (1993: 127–33) lists some of the features discovered so far in this microscopic analysis of ordinary talk. He concludes that conversation analysis, as an empirically based activity grounded in a basic theory of social action, generates significant implications from the analysis of previously unnoticed interactional forms, and goes on to show how conversation analysis can help in analysing and understanding the talk which occurs in organizations and institutions. Similarly, Heath and Luff (1996: 324) conclude that the naturalistic analysis of conversation and interaction has developed a substantial body of findings which delineate the interlocking social organization of a wide range of ordinary social actions and activities.

### 10.6.3 Discourse analysis

Another view of language looks above its words, sentences and linguistic features and focuses attention on the way language is used, what it is used for, and the social context in which it is used. The term 'discourse' captures this broader focus, and refers to the general framework or perspective within which ideas are formulated (Sapsford and Abbott, 1996). Discourse inextricably permeates social life, since everything people do is framed within some sort of discourse: thus an ideology is framed within a discourse, so are accounts and descriptions (Wooffitt, 1996), and so is science itself (Gilbert and Mulkay, 1984).

Jupp cites Worrall's use of the term:

> 'Discourse embraces all aspects of a communication – not only its content, but its author (who says it?), its authority (on what grounds?), its audience (to whom?), its objective (in order to achieve what?)' (Worrall, 1990: 8). 'Discourse' encompasses ideas, statements or knowledge that are dominant at a particular time among particular sets of people ... and which are held in relation to other sets of individuals ... Implicit in the use of such knowledge is the application of power ... discourse involves all forms of communication, including talk and conversation. In the latter, however, it is not restricted exclusively to verbalized propositions, but can include ways of seeing, categorizing and reacting to the social world in everyday practices. (1996: 300)

Discourse analysis is not a unified body of theory, method and practice. Rather, it is conducted within various disciplines, with different research traditions, and with no overarching unifying theory common to all types; being heterogeneous, it is difficult to define (Gee et al., 1992). Edley (2001: 189) notes that discourse analysis has become an umbrella term for a wide variety of different analytical principles and practices. In Taylor's view (2001: 5) it is best understood as a field of research rather than a single practice.

Coulthard (1985) gives an overview of its historical development, and shows the various disciplines which have contributed to it, while Potter and Wetherell (1994: 47) list at least four types of work that use the label 'discourse analysis'. The first is influenced by speech act theory, and is directed at accounts of the organization of conversational exchanges.[15] The second, more psychological, focuses on discourse processes, such as the effect of discourse structure on recall and understanding. The third was developed from a sociology of knowledge perspective, studying specifically how scientists construct their talk and texts to present and validate their work and their actions. The fourth derives from European social philosophy and cultural analysis, and attempts to show how institutions, practices and even the individual person can be understood as produced through the workings of a set of discourses. A similar classification is given by Gee et al. (1992),[16] and McCarthy (1991) identifies some differences between British and American discourse analysis. Our interest here is on the third and fourth types described by Potter and Wetherell – on discourse analysis for qualitative social research.

Despite the diversity and the many disciplinary perspectives, writers point to some fundamental principles and common features of discourse analysis. At the most general level, three principles inform all studies of discourse (Gee et al., 1992: 228): (1) human discourse is rule-governed and internally structured; (2) it is produced by speakers who are ineluctably situated in a socio-historical matrix, whose cultural, political, economic, social and personal realities shape the discourse; (3) discourse itself constitutes or embodies important aspects of that socio-historical matrix. In other words, discourse reflects human experience and, at the same time, constitutes important parts of that experience. Thus, discourse analysis may be concerned with any part of human experience touched on or constituted by discourse.

At a similar general level, Jupp (1996: 305) identifies three features of discourse analysis as used by Foucault. First, discourse is social, which indicates that words and their meanings depend on where they are used, by whom and to whom. Consequently, their meaning can vary according to social and institutional settings and there is, therefore, no such thing as a universal discourse. Second, there can be different discourses which may be in conflict with one another. Third, as well as being in conflict, discourses may be viewed as being arranged in a hierarchy. The notions of conflict and of hierarchy link closely with the exercise of power. The concept of power is vital to discourse analysis by way of the theoretical connection between the production of discourses and the exercise of power. The two are very closely interwoven and, in some theoretical formulations, are viewed as one and the same.

More specifically, Potter and Wetherell point to three features which make the sort of discourse analysis they describe especially pertinent for qualitative research:

> First, it is concerned with talk and texts as social practices; and as such it pays close attention to features which would traditionally be classed as linguistic *content* – meanings and topics – as well as attending to features of linguistic *form* such as grammar and cohesion. Indeed, once we adopt a discourse analytic approach, the distinction between content and form becomes problematic; content is seen to develop out of formal features of discourse and vice versa. Put more generally, the discourse analyst is after the answers to social or sociological questions rather than to linguistic ones.

Second, discourse analysis has a triple concern with action, construction and variability (Potter and Wetherell, 1987). People perform actions of different kinds through their talk and their writing, and they accomplish the nature of these actions partly through constructing their discourse out of a range of styles, linguistic resources and rhetorical devices.

A third feature of discourse analysis is its concern with the rhetorical or argumentative organization of talk and texts. Rhetorical analysis has been particularly helpful in highlighting the way discursive versions are designed to counter real or potential alternatives (Billig, 1991). Put another way, it takes the focus of analysis away from questions of how a version relates to some putative reality and asks instead how this version is designed successfully to compete with an alternative. (1994: 48)

Gee et al. (1992) discuss two main stances within discourse-analytic research in education: one emphasizes the study of discourse structure for its own sake, using analytic tools from linguistics (discourse as structure); the other studies discourse as it relates to other social, cognitive, political or cultural processes and outcomes (discourse as evidence). Potter and Wetherell (1994) distinguish two different complementary emphases in their style of discourse analysis. One studies the resources used to construct discourse and enable the performance of particular actions, and maps out the broad systems or 'interpretive repertoires' which sustain different social practices. The other studies the detailed procedures through which versions are constructed and made to appear factual. These different stances towards discourse analysis are often combined in research, but they produce different types of research questions, as shown in Example 10.11.

---

- Discourse as structure: Gee et al. (1992: 229a) list eight types of question which involve the study of discourse structure for its own sake.
- Discourse as evidence: the same authors list seven types of questions researchers have used in the study of discourse in relation to social and cognitive processes (1992: 230).
- A discourse-analytic research agenda from a critical perspective: Jupp (1996: 306) lists 12 questions which might guide a critical analysis of documents, using discourse analysis.
- Silverman (1993) shows how a discourse-analytic perspective can change research questions dramatically.

**Example 10.11**
*Research questions in discourse analysis*

---

Potter and Wetherell (1994: 55–63) point out that it is difficult to describe and codify explicit procedures that are used in discourse analysis, but they list five considerations which do recur, and they illustrate how each can operate in analysis. They are: using variation as a lever, reading the detail, looking for rhetorical organization, looking for accountability and cross-referencing discourse studies. Gee et al. (1992) indicate some of the ways the analysis might proceed in the discourse-as-structure and discourse-as-evidence stances noted above, listing some of the tools linguists use when analysing discourse structure,[17] and showing the categories they find useful in studying the social location of texts. Tonkiss (1998: 250–60) discusses 'doing discourse analysis' under the three broad headings of selecting and approaching data, sorting, coding and analysing the data, and presenting the analysis. Under the second heading – sorting, coding and analysing data – she adds two considerations to the list of five given by Potter and Wetherell above: using key words and themes, and attending to silences.

Discourse analysis is an important development in qualitative research, starting as it does from the assumption that discourse at all levels, including people's accounts, are an important resource:

> In our view, people's texts are not trivial outcomes of communicative needs. Rather, they function at many levels and are the product of a person's entire set of political and psychological conditions and entities. Humans are constant creators of complex and multifaceted meanings. (Gee et al., 1992: 233)

Discourse analysis is sensitive to how spoken and written language is used, to how accounts and descriptions are constructed, and to the complex processes for producing social meanings (Tonkiss, 1998). At the microscopic level it shares much in common with conversation analysis, and some writers (Coulthard, 1985; McCarthy, 1991) see conversation analysis as a particular type of discourse analysis. In a more macroscopic perspective, discourse analysis emphasizes the interrelationships between accounts and hierarchies, power and ideology. Two important directions for this latter type of discourse analysis are critical discourse analysis (Blommaert and Bulcaen, 2000) and Foucauldian discourse analysis (Gubrium and Holstein, 2000). Critical discourse analysis aims to show 'non-obvious ways in which language is involved in social relations of power and domination, and in ideology' (Fairclough, 2001: 229). Foucault examines how historically and culturally located systems of power/knowledge construct subjects and their world. For Foucault, power operates in and through discourse as the other face of knowledge: thus the term power/knowledge. Discourse not only puts words to work, but gives them their meanings, constructs and perceptions and formulates understanding and ongoing courses of interaction (Gubrium and Holstein, 2000: 493–5). At this level, discourse analysis is similar to deconstruction, in dismantling constructed accounts to show connections with power and ideology. It has grown into a wide-ranging and heterogeneous discipline, which finds its unity in the description of language above the level of the sentence, and an interest in systems of meaning and in the context and cultural influences which affect language in use (Example 10.12).

---

- Gee et al. (1992: 253–81) describe three examples of discourse analysis: sharing time in a first-grade class-room, reading with story books at home, and verbal analogy items in standardized test-taking.

  **Example 10.12**
  *Discourse analysis*

- Potter and Wetherell (1994) use five extracts from their case study of the con-struction of a TV current affairs programme about cancer charities to illustrate discourse analysis.
- Jupp (1996) gives four case studies of discourse analysis, using different kinds of documents.
- Coulthard (1985) has many examples of micro-level discourse analysis in the language teaching context.

---

### 10.6.4 Semiotics

Language can be seen as a symbolic sign system, where a sign is something that stands for something else. In language, obviously, the signs are words. Semiotics,[18] or the science of signs, lays out assumptions, concepts and meth-ods for the analysis of sign systems. There are many sign systems (for example, mathematics, music, etiquette, symbolic rites, street signs) to which semiotics can be applied, and Eco (1976) points out that semiotics is concerned with everything that can be taken as a sign. At the same time, semiotics is based squarely on language, in line with the view that human linguistic communi-cation can be seen as a display of signs, or a 'text to be read' (Manning and Cullum-Swan, 1994).

The Swiss linguist Saussure, and the American philosopher Pierce, were the founders of semiotics. Pierce's basic point is that anything can be a sign. For Saussure, being a sign entails being part of a code, and he generated a method which showed that structures and words are inseparable (Silverman, 1993). Semiotics has thus been associated with the structural tradition in literary crit-icism, but the apparatus of semiotics also provides a way of thinking about any sign-mediated social activity.

An essential idea in semiotics is that surface manifestations derive their meanings from underlying structures (Feldman, 1995). This makes semiotics especially useful in the analysis of language and of texts. Semioticians identify mechanisms by which meaning is produced (the most common ones are metaphor, metonymy and opposition), and have devised techniques using these mechanisms for interpreting qualitative data. Feldman (1995: 22–39) illustrates three of those techniques (semiotic clustering, semiotic chains and semiotic squares) in her analysis of data from her university housing office study. She provides an example of how the use of these techniques helped her to see relationships in the data that she was not otherwise aware of, thereby illuminating her data in a powerful way. As a rather different example, Manning and Cullum-Swan (1994) present a semiotic reading of the menus at McDonald's (Example 10.13).

---

- McRobbie (1978; 1991) demonstrates semiotic analysis using a magazine aimed at teenage girls.   **Example 10.13**
- Feldman (1995: 21–41) discusses semiotic cluster analysis using the example of 'buildings'.   *Semiotic analysis*
- Manning and Cullum-Swan (1994) present a semiotic analysis of a McDonald's menu.

---

Semiotics can also be used for the analysis of texts, and we have noted already Silverman's (1993) use of semiotics to analyse narrative structures. With its focus on linguistic structures and categories, it can be used to develop a theory of texts and their constituent elements. This takes text analysis well past the earlier quantitative content analysis (Berelson, 1952) in an effort to get to the deeper meaning. Such meaning is to be found not only in words and phrases, but in the system of rules that structures the text as a whole. It is therefore this underlying structure and the rules it embodies that can tell the researcher what its cultural and social message is. While this semiotic emphasis is valuable, MacDonald and Tipton (1996) remind us that there are limits to the understanding we can develop using only the texts. A text also needs to be studied in its social context.

### 10.6.5 Documentary and textual analysis

We noted in Chapter 9 the richness of documentary data for social research. The analysis of such data shares characteristics with the approaches just described, but it also has some distinctive themes.

One theme focuses on the social production of the document, starting with how the document came into being. All documentary sources are the result of human activity, produced on the basis of certain ideas, theories or commonly accepted, taken-for-granted principles, and these are always located within the constraints of particular social, historical or administrative conditions and structures (MacDonald and Tipton, 1996; Finnegan, 1996). Words and their meanings depend on where they are used, by whom and to whom. Thus, as discourse analysts point out (for example, Jupp, 1996: 305), meaning varies according to social and institutional setting. Therefore documents and texts studied in isolation from their social context are deprived of their real meaning. Thus an understanding of the social production and context of the document affects its interpretation. Similar considerations apply also to the social production of an archive: what is kept, where and for how long, and what is thrown away (MacDonald and Tipton, 1996: 189).

A second related theme is the social organization of the document. We saw these questions from Hammersley and Atkinson (1995: 173) in Section 9.4: how are documents written? How are they read? Who writes them? Who reads them? For what purposes? On what occasions? With what outcomes? What is recorded? What is omitted? What does the writer seem to take for granted about the reader(s)? What do readers need to know in order to make sense of them? Silverman (1993: 63) uses these questions to study the social organization of documents, irrespective of their truth or error. Thus he shows how even such apparently 'objective' documents as organizational files are 'artfully constructed with a view to how they may be read'. He cites the work of Cicourel and Kitsuse in education, Garfinkel with coroners, and Sudnow in hospital deaths and criminal statistics to show how the sociological analysis of statistics and files raises fundamental questions about the processes which produce them, quite apart from questions of the truth or error of the statistics themselves. In the same light, he also considers public records and visual images (Example 10.14).

---

- Silverman (1993: 61–71) applies textual analysis to files, statistical records, records of official proceedings and images, and includes illustrations from the work of others.
- Woods (1979) analyses school reports, and shows the concepts and categories teachers use to make normative judgements about pupils.

**Example 10.14**
*Analysis of the social organization of documents*

---

A third theme concerns the more 'direct' analysis of text for meaning, this time including questions of truth and error. This analysis can focus on the surface or literal meaning, or on the deeper meaning, and the multilayered nature of meaning is now much more widely understood and accepted (Finnegan, 1996: 149). The surface meaning has often concerned historians, whereas sociologists have been more interested in ways of uncovering deeper meaning. Methods used range from interpretive understanding following the ideas of Dilthey (MacDonald and Tipton, 1996: 197) to more structural approaches, especially semiotics, as described above.

A fourth theme would be the application of different theoretical perspectives to the analysis of texts and documents. As an example, Jupp (1996) describes the critical analysis of documents, seeing documents as media for discourses, and thus drawing on discourse analysis. Deconstruction is an approach which also has applicability in such a context. Thus, as Silverman points out, there are many ways of thinking about textual analysis, and many different theoretical perspectives that can be applied. Silverman (1993: 89) is convinced also that sociologists make too little use of the great potential of texts as rich data, especially in light of their (often) relatively easy accessibility.

### 10.7 Computers in the Analysis of Qualitative Data[19]

While the use of a computer is not appropriate for all of the approaches to analysis described, there are a number of programs to assist the qualitative researcher today. Computer assisted qualitative data analysis is known among researchers as CAQDAS.

In choosing among the numerous packages available, several websites provide useful information. Thus, for example, Sage, through its Scolari imprint, publishes a number of commercial CAQDAS packages (http://www. scolari.com). The website Text Analysis Info Page (Klein, http://www.text analysis.info) has a comprehensive list of different sorts of packages available. The Computer Assistance of Qualitative Data Analysis Scheme (http://www. soc.surrey.ac.uk/caqdas) maintains a most useful site to investigate.

There are several factors to consider and questions to ask when a researcher is choosing among the packages. For example:

- *Compatibility with my analytic approach.* Does this package enable me to do the sort of analysis I want to do?
- *Ease of use.* Do I have the sense that I can master this software and work with it in ways that will promote my creativity?
- *Product support and upgrade path.* Is this product well supported by a strong company, and likely to be further developed and enhanced? This means that the product will continue to grow as my understanding and practice of qualitative research develops and as I grow as a researcher.

  Does the product have previous versions?

  Can I download and try out a trial copy? How does this trial cope and feel with some of my data?

  Is the company active in its engagement with research and researchers?

- *Is there a supportive learning community?*

  Does the product have good quality tutorials?

  Are there opportunities for training, workshops?

  Is the product supported by a website and is there a discussion forum available?

Do people actively use this product around me in my context?
Does the research community in my area use this product? Are there
frequent mentions of the product in the recent literature?

- *Costs of the software.* Not all the costs are in the purchase price.
  Does it require specialized or higher-grade hardware?
  Does the ongoing licence require further costs?
  Are training and support expensive?
  Who buys this software, or does my institution provide a copy?

Whatever the choice of package, it needs to be remembered that CAQDAS is
a tool which can help in qualitative data analysis, but which cannot do the
analysis. The researcher's input and creativity will always be required. In addition, it is important to consider the analysis tool when planning the research,
rather than as an afterthought once data are ready for analysis. The choice of
analysis package will be likely to influence the way data are transcribed and
input for analysis (and perhaps also collected). Appendix 1 contains a brief
description of QSR N6, one of the most prominent packages in use today to
assist in the analysis of qualitative data.

---

### 10.8   REVIEW CONCEPTS

Audit trail through the analysis of data

Analytic induction

The Miles and Huberman framework:
- data collection
- data display
- drawing and verifying conclusions

Coding:
- descriptive codes
- inferential (pattern) codes

Memoing:
- substantive memos
- theoretical memos
- methodological memos

Abstracting: levels of abstraction

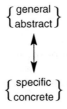

---

**10.8   REVIEW CONCEPTS** (Continued)

Comparing:
  • similarities
  • differences

Grounded theory analysis: the concept-indicators model
  coding:     ◄─────►  codes:
    open      ◄─────►     substantive
    axial     ◄─────►     theoretical
    selective ◄─────►     core

    theoretical    • sensitivity
                   • sampling
                   • saturation

Narratives: meaning
Ethnomethodology: conversation analysis
Discourse analysis
Semiotics
Documentary and textual analysis

---

## NOTES

1  There is still, however, the question of the interpretation of those findings: this comment applies only to the statistical analysis operations performed on the data.

2  Huberman and Miles (1994: 428) give a summary of the very substantial progress on this matter in the last 20 years.

3  Procedures for setting up an audit trail are described by Schwandt and Halpern (1988); see also Lincoln and Guba (1985).

4  Among those not considered here are phenomenology, phenomenography, hermeneutics, deconstruction and dramaturgy, and the writings of Wolcott (1994) and Dey (1993).

5  Universals are properties that are invariant: 'If all upper middle-class white males over the age of fifty in the US voted for the Republican Party, then this would constitute a universal' (Ragin, 1994: 93).

6  This is why Glaser's (1992) critique of the Strauss and Corbin (1990) book is subtitled *Emergence vs Forcing*.

7  Sometimes, by developing the dimensions of each property: see Strauss and Corbin (1990: 72). However, Glaser (1992: 47) underlines the difference between conceptual elaboration and grounded empirical elaboration.

8  Since much grounded theory research has focused on what people do in trying to deal with situations and problems, 'ing' words are common in the conclusions and titles of grounded theory studies: for example, 'cultivating', 'normalizing', 'centring', 'highlighting', and so on. See Glaser (1992) and also Miles and Huberman (1994: 252).

9  Lonkila (1995: 50) notes some of the literature devoted to discussion and criticism of grounded theory.

10  Similarly, Dey (1993) writes on reducing fragmentation in qualitative analysis.

11 At the same time, the stories, while seen as real, are sometimes seen to have a 'tenuous grip on a consensually defined social reality which can be reliably and validly reproduced by social scientists': see Manning and Cullum-Swan (1994: 465).

12 Similarly, Silverman (1993) shows the value of semiotics and the structuralist approach in the analysis of 'stories', ranging from Russian fairytales to contemporary political documents.

13 It is not only through a focus on language that these approaches have developed, and there are other philosophical and theoretical issues involved. Thus ethnomethodology, for example, does not have to be looked at by way of language, but it is convenient to do so here.

14 As Feldman (1995: 4) points out, ethnomethodologists are interested in two apparently diametrically opposed situations: breakdowns, and situations where norms are so internalized that breakdowns are nearly impossible. Breakdowns are similar to Garfinkel's original concept of breaching.

15 This type is similar to conversation analysis.

16 They identify four types of discourse analysis: an emphasis on linguistics, the analysis of talk from a sociological perspective, anthropological and socio-linguistic approaches, and discourse analysis in the explication of social, cultural and political institutions and relations.

17 Further descriptions of some of the linguistic tools can be found in Coulthard (1985), Brown and Yule (1984) and McCarthy (1991).

18 Semiosis is the process whereby something comes to stand for something else, and thus acquires the status of a sign (Anward, 1997).

19 Like section A1.2 in Appendix 1 (pp. 283–5), this section was contributed by Dr Roger Vallance of the University of Notre Dame, Australia.

## *Further Reading*

### *Narratives and meaning*
Bauman, R. (1986) *Story, Performance and Event: Contextual Studies of Oral Narrative.* Cambridge: Cambridge University Press.

Cortazzi, M. (1991) *Primary Teaching, How It Is: A Narrative Account.* London: Fulton.

Fernandez, J.W. (1991) *Beyond Metaphor: The Theory of Tropes in Anthropology.* Stanford, CA: Stanford University Press.

Lakoff, G. and Johnson, M. (1980) *Metaphors We Live By.* Chicago: University of Chicago Press.

Plummer, K. (1995) *Telling Sexual Stories: Power, Change and Social Worlds.* London: Routledge and Kegan Paul.

Polkinghorne, D.E. (1988) *Narrative Knowing and Human Sciences.* Albany, NY: State University of New York Press.

Riessman, C.K. (1993) *Narrative Analysis.* Newbury Park, CA: Sage.

### Ethnomethodology and conversation analysis

Atkinson, J.M. and Heritage, J. (eds) (1984) *Structures of Social Action: Studies in Conversation Analysis*. Cambridge: Cambridge University Press.

Button, G. (ed.) (1991) *Ethnomethodology and the Human Sciences*. Cambridge: Cambridge University Press.

Garfinkel, H. (1967) *Studies in Ethnomethodology*. Englewood Cliffs, NJ: Prentice-Hall.

Gilbert, G.N. and Mulkay, M. (1980) *Opening Pandora's Box: A Sociological Analysis of Scientists' Discourse*. Cambridge: Cambridge University Press.

Heritage, J. (1984) *Garfinkel and Ethnomethodology*. Cambridge: Polity.

Psathas, G. (1994) *Conversation Analysis*. Thousand Oaks, CA: Sage.

Wooffitt, R. (1996) 'Analysing accounts', in N. Gilbert (ed.), *Researching Social Life*. London: Sage. pp. 287–305.


### Discourse analysis

Boden, D. and Simmerman, D.H. (1991) *Talk and Social Structure*. Cambridge: Polity.

Coulthard, M. (1985) *Discourse and Social Change*. Cambridge: Polity.

Fairclough, N. (1992) *Discourse and Social Change*. Cambridge: Polity.

Gee, J.P., Michaels, S. and O'Connor, M.C. (1992) 'Discourse analysis', in M.D. LeCompte, W.L. Millroy, and J. Preissle (eds), *The Handbook of Qualitative Research in Education*. San Diego: Academic. pp. 227–91.

Jupp, V. (1996) 'Documents and critical research', in R. Sapsford and V. Jupp (eds), *Data Collection and Analysis*. London: Sage. pp. 298–316.

Potter, J. and Wetherell, M. (1987) *Discourse and Social Psychology: Beyond Attitudes and Behaviour*. London: Sage.

Potter, J. and Wetherell, M. (1994) 'Analyzing discourse', in A. Bryman and R.G. Burgess (eds), *Analyzing Qualitative Data*. London: Routledge. pp. 47–66.

Tonkiss, F. (1998) 'Analysing discourse', in C. Seale (ed.), *Researching Society and Culture*. London: Sage. pp. 245–60.

van Dijk, T. (ed.) (1985) *Handbook of Discourse Analysis*. Orlando, FL: Academic.

Wetherell, M., Taylor, S. and Yates, S.J. (eds) (2001) *Discourse as Data: A Guide for Analysis*. London: Sage.

### Semiotics

Barley, S.R. (1983) 'Semiotics and the study of occupational and organizational culture', *Administrative Science Quarterly,* 28: 393–413.

Eco, V. (1979) *A Theory of Semiotics.* Bloomington, IN: University of Illinois Press.

Feldman, M.S. (1995) *Strategies for Interpreting Qualitative Data.* Newbury Park, CA: Sage.

Fiol, C.M. (1989) 'A semiotic analysis of corporate language: organizational boundaries and joint venturing', *Administrative Science Quarterly,* 34: 277–303.

Manning, P.K. (1987) *Semiotics and Fieldwork.* Newbury Park, CA: Sage.


### Documentary and textual analysis

Hodder, I. (1994) 'The interpretation of documents and material culture', in N.K. Denzin and Y.S. Lincoln (eds), *Handbook of Qualitative Research.* Thousand Oaks, CA: Sage. pp. 393–402.

Jupp, V. (1996) 'Documents and critical research', in R. Sapsford and V. Jupp (eds), *Data Collection and Analysis.* London: Sage. pp. 298–316.

Jupp, V. and Norris, C. (1993) 'Traditions in documentary analysis', in M. Hammersley (ed.), *Social Research: Philosophy, Politics and Practice.* London: Sage. pp. 37–51.

MacDonald, K.M. (1989) 'Building respectability', *Sociology,* 2(3): 55–80.

Silverman, D. (1993) *Interpreting Qualitative Data: Methods for Analyzing Talk, Text and Interaction.* London: Sage.

# 11
# Mixed Methods and Evaluative Criteria

This chapter has two main parts. The first deals with combining quantitative and qualitative approaches in social research, while the second presents general evaluative criteria for assessing empirical research.

## 11.1 Combining Quantitative and Qualitative Approaches

### 11.1.1 Similarities in the two approaches

The quantitative and qualitative approaches to research have important differences, and the quantitative–qualitative distinction has been an organizing principle for this book. Despite this, the two approaches also share many similarities. Indeed, a basic premise of this book has been that some of the same logic drives both types of empirical inquiry, and that is why the two approaches have been dealt with under the same general headings. The main differences emphasized here between the two approaches lie in the nature of their data, and in methods for collecting and analysing data. However, these differences should not obscure the similarities in logic which make combining the approaches possible.

There is also more overlap between the purposes behind the two approaches than is sometimes recognized. For example, quantitative research is thought to be more concerned with the deductive testing of hypotheses and theories, whereas qualitative research is more concerned with exploring a topic, and with inductively generating hypotheses and theories. While this is often true, those stereotypes can be overdone. There is, overall, a correlation between the approach (quantitative or qualitative) and the purpose (for example, theory testing or theory generating), but that correlation is neither perfect nor necessary. While quantitative research may be mostly used for testing theory, it can also be used for exploring an area and for generating hypotheses and theory. Similarly, qualitative research can certainly be used for testing hypotheses and theories, even though it is the most favoured approach for theory generation. As Miles and Huberman say: 'Both types of data can be productive for descriptive, reconnoitering, exploratory, inductive, opening up purposes. And both can be productive for explanatory, confirmatory, hypothesis-testing purposes' (1994: 42). We do not need to be restricted to stereotypes in our thinking about the purposes of the two approaches. Each approach can be used for various purposes.

Taking this point further, stereotyped distinctions between the two approaches can also be overdone. Hammersley (1992), in particular, argues that seven dichotomies typically used to differentiate quantitative and qualitative approaches are overdrawn. Five of the dichotomies he discusses bring together many of the points we have covered in previous chapters, and reflect some of the emphases of this book. They are:

- qualitative versus quantitative data
- the investigation of natural versus artificial settings
- a focus on meanings rather than behaviour
- an inductive versus a deductive approach
- the identification of cultural patterns as against seeking scientific laws.[1]

For each of these, Hammersley argues that it is more a matter of a range of positions than a simple contrast; that a position on one does not necessarily imply a position on another; and that selection among these positions should depend more on the purposes and circumstances of the research than on philosophical considerations.

Each of these points (the similarity of logic, the overlap of purposes and the weakening of traditional dichotomies) blurs the sharpness of the quantitative–qualitative distinction, making the contrast between them less stark. The same holds true for the argument about the respective merits of the two approaches. The position taken here is that the argument is unnecessary, for three reasons. First, neither approach is always superior to the other. Each approach has its strengths and its weaknesses, and over-reliance on any one method is not appropriate. Second, both approaches are needed in social research. Our task is to understand the strengths and weaknesses of each, to analyse any particular research situation in the light of those strengths and weaknesses, and to select the approach, or combination of approaches, on the basis of that analysis. Third, while there are connections of each approach to paradigm considerations, those connections are not emphasized in this book. Questions of approach and method can be dealt with independent of those paradigm considerations, and decisions about methods can be governed by the research context, purposes and practicalities as well as by paradigms.

Instead of starting from paradigms, I have tried to focus in this book on research which starts from a more pragmatic position, stressing what the research is trying to find out. I have then argued that matters of method follow from that. The important thing is that the research questions and the methods are matched to each other. Sometimes it is not clear what the research questions are in advance of the research, or it is not appropriate to try to establish those firmly during the planning stage. Then, the specific focus and research questions emerge during the inquiry, rather than ahead of it. But even when this happens, the connections between questions and methods remain important.

When research adopts this pragmatic position, and whether research questions are fully prespecified or emerge, a different perspective on methods opens up, compared with that which follows from a particular paradigm position. Once we have a clear view of the questions we want to answer in the research, we can then ask what data are necessary to answer them, and how such data will be collected and analysed. This allows a less stereotyped view of methods, and opens up the possibility of both approaches. Sometimes quantitative methods and data will be required to answer the questions we have asked; sometimes qualitative methods and data will be required; sometimes both will be required; sometimes either approach might be used. This reinforces the need to understand the basic characteristics of both approaches, which has been the focus of this book. The next section summarizes these basic characteristics.

### 11.1.2 Basic characteristics of the two approaches

A good way to overview the central characteristics of the two approaches is to compare, as Huberman and Miles do, variables and cases.

*A crucial distinction: variables and cases*

Consider a typical study, one trying to predict the decision to attend college, with a sample of 300 adolescents and the following set of predictors: gender, socioeconomic status, parental expectations, school performance, peer support, and decision to attend college.

In a variable-oriented analysis, the predictor variables are intercorrelated and the key dependent variable, 'decision to attend college', is regressed on the six others. This might show us that deciding to attend college is mainly influenced by school performance, with additional influences from parents' expectations and SES. We see how the variables as concepts are related, but we do not know the profile of any one individual.

In a case-oriented analysis, we would look more closely into a particular case, say, Case 005, who is female, middle-class, has parents with high expectations, and so on. These are, however, 'thin' measures. To do a genuine case analysis, we need to look at a full history of Case 005: Nynke van der Molen, whose mother trained as a social worker but is bitter over the fact that she never worked outside the home, and whose father wants Nynke to work in the family florist shop. Chronology is also important: two years ago, Nynke's closest friend decided to go to college, just before Nynke began work in a stable and just before Nynke's mother showed her her scrapbook from social work school. Nynke then decided to enrol in veterinary studies.

These and other data can be displayed in matrix form (see Miles and Huberman, 1994), where the flow and configuration of events and reactions leading to Nynke's decision would come clear. It would also help to 'incarnate' what the five predictors look like singly and how they interact collectively. That, in turn, would surface recurrent patterns, 'families' or 'clusters' of cases with characteristic configurations.

As Ragin (1987) notes, such a case-oriented approach looks at each entity, then teases out configurations *within* each case and subjects them to comparative analysis. In these comparisons (of a smaller number of cases), underlying similarities and systematic associations are sought out with regard to the main outcome variable. From there, a more explanatory model can be explicated, at least for the cases under study.

Each approach has its pluses and minuses. Variable-oriented analysis is good for finding probabilistic relationships among variables in a large population, but has difficulties with causal complexities, or dealing with subsamples. Case-oriented analysis is good at finding specific, concrete, historically grounded patterns common to small sets of cases, but its findings remain particularistic, although several case writers speciously claim greater generality. (1994: 435–6)

The quantitative approach conceptualizes reality in terms of variables, and relationships between them. It rests on measurement, and therefore prestructures data, and usually research questions, conceptual frameworks and design as well. Samples are typically larger than in qualitative studies, and generalization through sampling is usually important. It does not see context as central, typically stripping data from their context, and it has well developed and codified methods for data analysis. Its methods in general are more unidimensional and less variable than qualitative methods. It is therefore more easily replicable.

On the other hand, the qualitative approach deals more with cases. It is sensitive to context and process, to lived experience and to local groundedness, and the researcher tries to get closer to what is being studied. It aims for in-depth and holistic understanding, in order to do justice to the complexity of social life. Samples are usually small, and its sampling is guided by theoretical rather than probabilistic considerations. Prestructuring of design and data is less common, and its methods are less formalized than those in the quantitative approach. They are also more multidimensional, more diverse and less replicable. It therefore has greater flexibility.

There are different strengths and advantages to each approach. Quantitative data enable standardized, objective comparisons to be made, and the measurements of quantitative research permit overall descriptions of situations or phenomena in a systematic and comparable way. This means we can sketch the contours or dimensions of these situations or phenomena. That is often what we want to do, either independent of deeper-level qualitative inquiry, or in conjunction with it. Procedures for the analysis of quantitative data, being well developed and codified, bring objectivity to the research, in the sense that they increase the chances that the results of the analysis do not depend on the researcher doing the analysis. The quantitative approach means that certain types of important questions can be systematically answered, opening the way to the development of useful knowledge.

On the other hand, there are important strengths and advantages to the qualitative approach. Qualitative methods are flexible, more so than quantitative methods. Therefore they can be used in a wider range of situations and for a wider range of purposes. They can also be more easily modified as a study progresses. Because of their great flexibility, they are well suited for studying naturally occurring real-life situations. Moreover, they accommodate the local groundedness of the things they study – specific cases embedded in their context. Qualitative methods are the best way we have of getting the insider's perspective, the 'actor's definition of the situation', the meanings people attach to things and events. This means they can be used to study the lived experience of people, including people's meanings and purposes. Qualitative data have a holism and richness, and are well able to deal with the complexity of social phenomena. This is what is meant when qualitative researchers talk about data providing thick descriptions. Qualitative research, especially grounded theory, is well suited to investigating process.[2]

Two things follow from these summaries. First, we need to be clear on what we are trying to find out. Second, we cannot find out everything we might want to know using only one approach, and we can often increase the scope, depth and power of research by combining the two approaches. That is the topic for

Section 11.1.4. Before that, however, we need to consider the situation where a topic could be approached either quantitatively or qualitatively.

### 11.1.3 Quantitative or qualitative?

This section focuses on those situations where a particular research area or topic could be approached, in any one study, either way. The question is: should we take a quantitative approach to this topic or a qualitative approach? It is a common question from beginning researchers. I do not try to lay down rules for making such decisions, but we can identify six factors which need to be considered when we are faced with this question.

The first, as always, takes us back to the research questions. Faced with this situation, it is especially useful to ask: what, exactly, are we trying to find out? In this situation, there is very likely to be interaction between the questions and the methods. The model established earlier, where content and research questions come first, and methods come later, is valuable as a guiding principle, and works for many research topics. But in clarifying situations like this, where either approach could be taken, content and methods are more interdependent. This means that the specific research questions differ when the detailed implications of the two different approaches are considered, even though it is the same research area or topic.

In the question 'What exactly are we trying to find out?', the word 'exactly' is important. At a general level, it often seems that a question could be tackled quantitatively or qualitatively. But when we make that question more specific, focusing on exactly what we are trying to find out, we often start to see the interaction between the question on the one hand, and the design and method on the other. This opens up the point that different questions require different methods to answer them. Some questions can only be answered using quantitative methods, and some can only be answered using qualitative methods. Thus question affects method. But it can also work the other way: to propose certain methods is to imply certain types of questions. Thus method can also affect questions. The important thing is the matching of question with method – using quantitative methods for quantitative questions, and qualitative methods for qualitative questions. However, while the reciprocal interaction between question and method needs to be kept in mind, it is useful to focus on the main direction of influence as being from question to method. Otherwise we run the risk of starting with methods, and adapting research questions to them. Focusing on questions before methods therefore brings us full circle, back to the importance of the research questions. What exactly are we trying to find out here?

The second consideration follows from the first, and goes back to the summaries of the two approaches in Section 11.1.2. Are we interested in making standardized and systematic comparisons, sketching contours and dimensions, or (for example) in accounting for variance? Or do we really want to study this phenomenon or situation in detail, holistically and in its context, finding out about the interpretations it has for the people involved, and about their meanings and purposes, or trying to see what processes are involved?

The third factor is the literature. There are two questions here. First, what guidance on the issue of a quantitative or qualitative approach to this topic do we find in the research literature? How have other researchers dealt with this topic? Second, to what extent (and why) do we wish to align this project with that literature? These questions should be routinely asked in planning a project. In the case of this decision, they can often help.

The fourth factor is practical considerations, including resources. There will sometimes be widely different consequences, in practical and resource terms, between the two approaches, and these can be decisive. These may involve time, money, the availability of samples and data, the researcher's familiarity with the situation being studied, access to situations, gaining the cooperation of others, and so on. The circumstances and context of the research are as important as more theoretical issues.

The fifth factor is 'knowledge payoff'. The question here is: will we learn more about this topic using the quantitative approach or the qualitative approach? Which approach will produce more useful knowledge? Which will do more good? These are not necessarily easy questions to answer, but they are useful questions nonetheless, and it is good discipline to try to answer them. They focus attention on the costs of the research in relation to its benefits.

The sixth factor can be loosely described as 'style'. Some people prefer, for a variety of reasons, one approach over the other. This may involve paradigm and philosophical issues, but there is often also a subconscious temperament factor at work. This usually comes down to different images about what a good piece of research looks like. Students will often express that by saying that they 'like this way better'.

The question 'quantitative or qualitative?' is commonly asked, especially by beginning researchers. Often, they are putting the 'methods cart' before the 'content horse'. The best advice in those cases is to step back from questions of method, and give further consideration to the purposes and research questions, bearing in mind that the way questions are asked influences what needs to be done to answer them. But when that has been done, and the question still remains, the above factors help in making the decision. Of course, a reasonable decision in any study might be to combine the two approaches. We now turn to that situation.

### 11.1.4 Quantitative and qualitative

Methodological justification for bringing quantitative and qualitative methods together is provided by Bryman (1988).[3] At a general level, the reasons for combining are to capitalize on the strengths of the two approaches, and to compensate for the weaknesses of each approach. At the same time, the specific reasons for combining the approaches should be considered in particular situations[4] in the light of the practical circumstances and context of the research. As this section will show, there are various ways it can be done.

There is more to this issue of combining the two approaches than first meets the eye. First there is the question of what 'combine' here might mean. The possibilities include adding one approach on to the other, interweaving the two approaches, integrating the two approaches and linking the two approaches. These different meanings lead to different models for combining the two approaches, some of which are considered below. Second, there is the distinction between combining methods, combining data and combining findings. There is a continuum of complexity here. At the simpler end, combining findings means that the quantitative and qualitative data and methods are not combined, only the results from the two sorts of inquiry. Next, combining data means that the two types of data are brought together during the analysis, and contribute to the findings. At the more complex end, studies which combine methods, data and findings can be described as full multi-method studies, of the type described by Brewer and Hunter (1989). Their book is about synthesizing what they see as the four main styles of social research (fieldwork, surveys, experiments and non-reactive studies). They see the synthesis at all stages of the research, from formulating research questions through to drawing conclusions. Multimethod studies are also covered by Fielding and Fielding (1986). In addition to multimethod, the term 'mixed method' is also used to describe different types of combinations of the quantitative and qualitative approaches.

As noted, there are various ways in which the two approaches might be combined, and we will look briefly at some literature on this topic. Some examples of mixed-method studies are noted in Example 11.1. In considering how they might be combined, three general questions are important:

* Will the two approaches be given equal weight?
* Will they be interactive or separate?
* How will they be sequenced?

Combining the two approaches has been written about by Brannen (1992), Brewer and Hunter (1989), Bryman (1992), Creswell (1994), Mathison (1988), Miles and Huberman (1994), and Morse (1991). A comprehensive treatment of the topic is given by Bryman, in full in Bryman (1988) and summarized in Bryman (1992: 59–61). Eleven approaches to combining are identified, and that summary is reproduced here:

1   *Logic of triangulation.* The findings from one type of study can be checked against the findings deriving from the other type. For example, the results of a qualitative investigation might be checked against a quantitative study. The aim is generally to enhance the validity of findings.

2　*Qualitative research facilitates quantitative research.* Qualitative research may: help to provide background information on context and subjects; act as a source of hypotheses; and aid scale construction.

3　*Quantitative research facilitates qualitative research.* Usually, this means quantitative research helping with the choice of subjects for a qualitative investigation.

4　*Quantitative and qualitative research are combined in order to provide a general picture.* Quantitative research may be employed to plug the gaps in a qualitative study which arise because, for example, the researcher cannot be in more than one place at any one time. Alternatively, it may be that not all issues are amenable solely to a quantitative investigation or solely to a qualitative one.

5　*Structure and process.* Quantitative research is especially efficient at getting to the 'structural' features of social life, while qualitative studies are usually stronger in terms of 'processual' aspects. These strengths can be brought together in a single study.

6　*Researchers' and subjects' perspectives.* Quantitative research is usually driven by the researcher's concerns, whereas qualitative research takes the subject's perspective as the point of departure. These emphases may be brought together in a single study.[5]

7　*Problem of generality.* The addition of some quantitative evidence may help to mitigate the fact that it is often not possible to generalize (in a statistical sense) the findings deriving from qualitative research.

8　*Qualitative research may facilitate the interpretation of relationships between variables.* Quantitative research readily allows the researcher to establish relationships among variables, but is often weak when it comes to exploring the reasons for those relationships. A qualitative study can be used to help explain the factors underlying the broad relationships that are established.

9　*Relationship between macro and micro levels.* Employing both quantitative and qualitative research may provide a means of bridging the macro–micro gulf. Quantitative research can often tap large-scale, structural features of social life, while qualitative research tends to address small-scale, behavioural aspects. When research seeks to explore both levels, integrating quantitative and qualitative research may be necessary.

10　*Stage in the research process.* Quantitative and qualitative research may be appropriate to different stages of a longitudinal study.

11　*Hybrids.* The chief example tends to be when qualitative research is conducted within a quasi-experimental (i.e. quantitative) research design.

A more general overview is given by Miles and Huberman (1994). They prefer the term 'linkage', and describe four general designs which link quantitative and qualitative data. In the first, there is the integrated collection of both types of data. In the second, a multiwave survey is conducted in parallel with continuous fieldwork. Their third design alternates the two, with exploratory fieldwork leading to quantitative instruments, and the quantitative data collection and analysis being followed by further qualitative work. The fourth design also alternates the two, with a survey followed by in-depth close-up qualitative work, which then leads to an experiment to test some hypotheses.

Creswell (1994) simplifies the possibilities down to three models of combined designs. The first is the two-phase design, where the quantitative and qualitative phases are kept quite separate.[6] The second is the dominant/ less-dominant design, where the researcher conducts a study within a single dominant paradigm, with one small component drawn from the alternate paradigm. The third is the mixed-methodology design, where aspects of the two approaches are mixed at all stages of the research. This is the full multi-method design referred to above.

Thus there are many models for combining the two approaches, and no one right way. How they are combined should be determined by the reasons for doing so, set against the circumstances, context and practical aspects of the research. Common sense should stand behind these decisions, as it should behind the way research is evaluated.

---

In 'Neither socialization nor recruitment: the avocational careers of old car enthusiasts', Dannefer (1981) conducted field research with old car buffs and blended this research with quantitative principles. Dannefer examined how people became involved in this activity and the ways they became involved.

**Example 11.1**
*Examples of mixed-method studies*

In 'A quantitative and qualitative inquiry into attitudes toward science of nonscience college students', Gogolin and Swartz (1992) studied the attitude toward science of 102 non-science and 81 science majors in a college. They measured six attitudinal variables by using the Attitudes Towards Science Inventory and collected interview data.

In 'Impact of newspaper crime reports on fear of crime: multimethodological investigation', Heath (1984) used multimethod research in a study of the impact of newspaper crime report on fear of crime. She conducted a telephone survey of 326 randomly selected readers of newspapers with different styles of crime reporting to determine readers' fears of crime in various situations. A quasi-experiment was then conducted in which the same conceptual variables were examined under controlled conditions.

Hofstede et al. (1990), in 'Measuring organizational cultures: a qualitative and quantitative study across twenty cases', studied organizational cultures in 20 units from 10 different organizations in Denmark and the Netherlands. Phase one of the study involved in-depth interviews while phases two and three consisted of surveys involving extensive statistical hypothesis testing.

*(Continued)*

*The Lives of Teachers* (Huberman, 1993) is a classic study of 160 Swiss secondary school teachers. The study charts the complexity of the professional life cycles of teachers and utilizes both surveys and in-depth interviewing.

Example 11.1
*(Continued)*

Kushman (1992), in 'The organizational dynamics of teacher workplaces', studied two types of teacher workplace commitment in 63 urban elementary and middle schools: organizational commitment and commitment to student learning. Phase one of the study explored statistical relationships between teacher commitment and organizational antecedents and outcomes in elementary and middle schools. Phase two investigated specific schools using case study methods to understand better the dynamics of teacher commitment.

In *Immigrant Entrepreneurs: Koreans in Los Angeles, 1965–1982,* Light and Bonacich (1988) trace how changes in Korean society led to an increase in Korean migration to the United States, and explore how small businesses owned by immigrants fit into the larger US economy. The authors use many types of data: survey research, existing statistics, field research, government documents, international reports and historical records.

In 'The blending of qualitative and quantitative methods in understanding child-bearing among welfare recipients', Rank (1992) conducted a study of families receiving public assistance in which both qualitative and quantitative data were gathered. The quantitative analysis of case record data was longitudinal and designed for statistical modelling of various events, while the in-depth interviews and fieldwork provided greater understanding of these and other events.

Sandelowski et al. (1992), in 'Using qualitative and quantitative methods: the transition to parenthood of infertile couples', describe the transition to parenthood of infertile couples. A naturalistic research design was chosen to explore this complex and sensitive phenomenon. The focal groups of study were infertile couples expecting a child conceived spontaneously or through biotechnical means or those waiting to adopt a child. A comparison group consisted of couples with no history of fertility impairment who were also expecting a child. Interviewing and observational inventories were used in the data collection phases.

*The Chinese Laundryman: A Study of Social Isolation* is a 20-year study by a Chinese-American researcher. Siu (1987) studied the 'Chinese laundryman' using participant observation. The study is placed in the context of the history of Chinese immigration to the United States, and maps, graphs and tables are provided to document the number of Chinese immigrants, the sex ratio of Chinese people in the US and the spread of Chinese laundry establishments in the Chicago area.

## 11.2 General Evaluative Criteria

In this book, we have now overviewed the basic ideas and concepts of quantitative research (Chapters 5, 6 and 7) and qualitative research (Chapters 8, 9 and 10), stressing the logic and the essentials of the two approaches, and using the same broad headings. This chapter has looked at the similarities and overlap between the two approaches, and has considered their combination. Since there are similarities in the logic of inquiry in both approaches, there is a set of general principles which can be applied to both. These are equivalent to general evaluative criteria for all empirical research. This section deals with those criteria.[7]

Ever increasing amounts of research are done and published in today's world, and this can be expected to continue, since the idea of research as the way we answer questions and solve problems is deeply embedded in our culture. This applies as much to social research as to any other field. As readers of research, we need to know what confidence we can have in its findings and conclusions; we need to be able to judge its quality. What criteria should be used? How do we answer the question: how good is this piece of work?

We need first to distinguish between general evaluative principles and specific evaluative criteria. We will deal here with the former. Literature listing specific evaluative criteria is mostly written from within either the quantitative or the qualitative approach, rather than to apply across them. Mostly, also, it gets down to technical issues in the form of detailed checklists for evaluating research proposals and reports. In line with the overall approach of this book, we concentrate more here on general criteria, both because the similarities between quantitative and qualitative empirical research are at a general level, and because it is also more helpful. At more specific levels, the technical differences between the two approaches can obscure their similarities.

Before getting to the general evaluative criteria, revisiting two concepts helps to establish a background to this question of evaluation. They are the two concepts of disciplined inquiry, and of the fit between the different parts of research. We deal with the more general of the two (disciplined inquiry) first.

### 11.2.1 Disciplined inquiry

The term 'disciplined' has been used frequently throughout this book, to indicate that good research is a disciplined form of inquiry. Thus disciplined inquiry provides a convenient way to begin this section, and a background for thinking about general evaluative principles. What follows draws on the work of Shulman (1988) in the field of education. Shulman (1988), who refers to the earlier work of Cronbach and Suppes (1969), is quoted here at some length:

When we speak of research, we speak of a family of methods which share the characteristics of *disciplined inquiry*. Cronbach and Suppes (1969) attempted to define disciplined inquiry a number of years ago ... Here are some of the definitions of disciplined inquiry they suggest:

> Disciplined inquiry has a quality that distinguishes it from other sources of opinion and belief. The disciplined inquiry is conducted and reported in such a way that the argument can be painstakingly examined. The report does not depend for its appeal on the eloquence of the writer or on any surface plausibility (p. 15).

Cronbach and Suppes continue:

> Whatever the character of a study, if it is disciplined the investigator has anticipated the traditional questions that are pertinent. He institutes control at each step of information collection and reasoning to avoid the sources of error to which these questions refer. If the errors cannot be eliminated he takes them into account by discussing the margin for error in his conclusions. Thus, the report of a disciplined inquiry has a texture that displays the raw materials entering the argument and the logical processes by which they were compressed and rearranged to make the conclusion credible (pp. 15–16).

The definition of disciplined inquiry could be misconstrued to imply that the appropriate application of research methods in education always leads to a sterile, ritualized, and narrowly conceived form of investigation. This is not the case. As Cronbach and Suppes observe subsequently:

> Disciplined inquiry does not necessarily follow well established, formal procedures. Some of the most excellent inquiry is free-ranging and speculative in the initial stages, trying what might seem to be bizarre combinations of ideas and procedures, or restlessly casting about for ideas (p. 16).

What is important about disciplined inquiry is that its data, arguments, and reasoning be capable of withstanding careful scrutiny by another member of the scientific community.

These quotes capture the essence of what it means to conduct disciplined inquiry, and show the fundamental requirements that need to be met for a piece of research to be taken seriously. They are also excellent general ideas to keep in mind when planning and writing a project, and they reappear in more specific form in the evaluative principles which follow. One thing they stress is the idea of a piece of research as a structured and coherent argument. That argument is strengthened when the different parts of a project fit together well.

### 11.2.2 The fit between the component parts of a research project

The world of social research today is much more complex and multidimensional than it was 20 or 30 years ago. There are different paradigms, two main different approaches, variations within those two main approaches, different methods and different combinations of methods. This complexity makes it important that the various components of a project fit together, and are aligned with each other.

The point of view stressed throughout this book is that in most cases the best way to do that is to get the research questions clear, and then align the design and methods with those. We have noted the reciprocal influence between question and methods, and limitations as to what can be done in terms of design and method impose limitations on questions that can be asked, but the argument is that this direction of influence should be minimized. The main influence should be from questions to methods.

This point about the fit between a study's components is really about the overall validity of the research. A project whose components do not fit together has questionable validity. This is because we can have little confidence in the answers put forward to research questions on the basis of a design and methods which do not fit with each other, or with the questions. In that case, it is not the stated questions, but some other questions, which have been answered. Under these circumstances, the argument behind the research falls down. That is what validity in this overall sense means. When the questions, design and methods fit together, the argument is strong and the research has validity. When they do not fit together, the argument is weakened and the research lacks validity.

This point is illustrated by the discussion in Chapter 10 about the variety of approaches in qualitative data analysis. With the numerous analytic alternatives available, the need for the method of analysis to fit with the research questions is even stronger, and this generalizes to the other components: 'Whatever research strategy is being followed, research problems, research design, data collection methods and analytic approaches should all be part of an overall methodological approach and should all imply one another' (Coffey and Atkinson, 1996: 11).

These concepts of research as disciplined inquiry and the fit between the component parts of a project give two general standards for assessing the quality of a piece of research. Against this background, we can now consider evaluative criteria.

### 11.2.3 Criteria for evaluation

Evaluative criteria are considered here at a general rather than specific level. They are presented in terms of a finished research project and report. With slight modifications, what is said can be applied to proposals as well as to reports.

The evaluative criteria are presented as general questions for each of five main areas:

- the set-up of the research
- the empirical procedures used in the research (design, data collection, sample and data analysis)
- the quality of the data
- the findings and conclusions reached in the research
- the presentation of the research.

### The set-up of the research

There are four general questions about the set-up of the research, and each is briefly discussed:

1  Is it clear what position the research is 'coming from'?
2  Is the topic area clearly identified?
3  Are the research questions appropriate?
4  Is the research appropriately set in context?

***Is it clear where the research is coming from?***    Social research today is characterized by multiple approaches, methods and paradigms. A reader of such research has to keep that in mind. But the writer, correspondingly, has to accept the responsibility to make clear what position the research takes. A project may or may not take a particular paradigm position; it may aim at theory verification or theory generation; it may or may not mix methods; it may be a tightly structured design or an emerging design; it may take a particular approach in the analysis of its data, especially if the data are qualitative. Any of these positions is acceptable, and each can be justified, but the writer needs to make clear what position is behind the research. This is part of its set-up, and making this clear is the best way of avoiding confusion and mistaken expectations on the part of the reader. As will be discussed in Chapter 12, a research project normally involves many different decisions, with most of the time no right or wrong criteria applying to those decisions. But they need to be made from some consistent base ('principled choices': Coffey and Atkinson, 1996), as implied in the discussion of validity in Section 11.2.2. The writer needs to inform the reader about that base.

***Is the topic area clearly identified?***    Whether the planning for the research proceeded deductively from topic area to research questions, or inductively from research questions to topic area, there needs to be a clear identification of the topic area early in the report (or proposal).

***Are the research questions appropriate?***    In Chapter 4 it was pointed out that good research questions organize a project, and are:

- *Clear.* They can be easily understood, and are unambiguous.
- *Specific.* Their concepts are at a specific enough level to connect to data indicators.
- *Answerable.* We can see what data are required to answer them, and how the data will be obtained.
- *Interconnected.* They are related to each other in some meaningful way.
- *Substantively relevant.* They are interesting and worthwhile questions for the investment of research effort.

These characteristics enable us to judge the research questions. In Chapter 4 we put special emphasis on the empirical criterion (the third point), which gives a specific principle for judging research questions: is it clear what evidence will be required to answer them? In a finished report, it does not matter whether the questions were fully prespecified or emerged during the study. In a proposal, the position of the research on this matter should be made clear.

**Is the research set in context?**   This means two things. First, is the relevance of the research either to some theoretical concern, or to some practical or professional concern, made clear? Second, has the connection of this study to the relevant literature been made, and handled appropriately? There are two main ways in which this connection to the literature can be handled. One is for a full literature review to be carried out ahead of this project. If this is the case, it is necessary for that review to be critical, and for this project to be connected to that review. Too often we see the required literature review, but the study itself is not integrated with that review. The other way, as in a grounded theory study, is for consideration of some of the relevant literature to be delayed until a certain stage is reached in the empirical work. The literature is then introduced into the study as further data. There are of course variations on these two main approaches, but whichever way is chosen, it needs to be explained.

### Empirical procedures

Empirical procedures means the design of the study, and the tools and techniques it uses for its data collection and data analysis. These matters are the focus of three of the questions in this section. In addition to those three, the first question concerns the level of information given about the procedures, and the fifth question concerns the study sample. The five questions are:

1   Are the design, data collection and data analysis procedures reported in sufficient detail to enable the research to be scrutinized and reconstructed?
2   Is the design of the study appropriate for the research questions?

3  Are the data collection instruments and procedures adequate and appropriate for the research questions?
4  Is the sample appropriate?
5  Are the data analysis procedures adequate and appropriate for the research questions?

Again, brief comments are given for each question.

***Are the design, data collection and data analysis procedures reported in sufficient detail to enable the research to be scrutinized and reconstructed?*** The section on disciplined inquiry stressed that the research needs to be conducted and reported in such a way that all stages of it can be thoroughly examined. Therefore the reader needs to be able to follow the full sequence of steps, and each should be described in sufficient detail to enable the audit trail through the study to be followed.

***Is the design of the study appropriate for the research questions?*** The function of research design is to connect the research questions to the empirical procedures and to data. The design situates the researcher in the empirical world. It answers these general overarching questions:

* Who or what will be studied?
* What strategies of inquiry will be used?
* What methods will be used for collecting and analysing empirical materials?

The design gives the overall framework for the empirical procedures, showing what they are and how they fit together. Therefore it is important that the design be reported in detail, and that it fits with the study's research questions.

A major consideration in the design is the overall approach: will the research be quantitative, qualitative or both? If quantitative, is the design experimental, quasi-experimental or survey? Is the focus on relationships between variables or accounting for variance? If qualitative, what cases were studied, and from what perspective? If combined, in what way and why? In both approaches, but especially in qualitative studies, there is often the additional question of a prespecified versus emerging design. Like the research questions, it does not matter in a finished report whether the design was prespecified, emerged, or was some mixture of the two. In a proposal, that matter needs consideration. If the design is prespecified, the accompanying conceptual framework should also be shown. Whatever the design chosen, it should fit with the research questions. This fit is part of the integrity or overall validity of the research. The design itself is about the internal logic, or internal validity, of the research. Internal validity is discussed later in this chapter.

***Are the data collection instruments and procedures adequate and appropriate for the research questions?***    This question leads directly to the question of the quality of data, discussed in the next section. In quantitative studies, measuring instruments are involved. Either they are already existing instruments, or they were developed for this study. If already existing, the criteria given in Chapter 6 apply, especially reliability and validity. If they were developed, the steps in doing that should be shown, along with the consideration of these same criteria. Qualitative research, depending on its orientation, may involve similar instruments – for example, interview schedules. In this case, the technical criteria of reliability, validity and reactivity apply.

Whatever the instruments, data collection procedures are also involved. They were described in some detail in Chapter 6 for quantitative data and Chapter 9 for qualitative data. The issue here is that the procedures are appropriate for the study, tailored to the circumstances to maximize the quality of the data, and reported in appropriate detail. If more than one person was involved in data collection, the way in which data collection procedures were standardized needs to be described.

***Is the sample appropriate?***    For any empirical study, the logic of the sample should be congruent with the overall logic of the study, and of the research questions. The sample needs to be properly described, and the basis for its selection made clear. In a quantitative study, the size and structure of the sample need to be described, along with its logic, its method of selection and the claims made for its representativeness. The last point needs to take account of the response rate, if a survey design is used. In a qualitative study, if purposive or theoretical sampling is used, the logic behind that needs to be made clear, and its connections with the research questions demonstrated.

In addition, it needs to be demonstrated that data were collected across the full range of conditions indicated in the research questions. This is important in both quantitative and qualitative studies, and in both theory testing and theory generating studies. It also influences the generalizability or transferability of the findings.

***Are the data analysis procedures adequate and appropriate for the research questions?***    Again, this overlaps with the quality of data, discussed in the next section. 'Adequate' here relates to the audit trail through the data analysis itself. It also means transparent. We need to be able to see how the researcher got from the data to the findings and conclusions, in order to know what confidence to have in the findings. This is important in both approaches, though historically it has been easier to demonstrate in quantitative research. With the procedures now available for the analysis of qualitative data, it is equally important for qualitative researchers to show how they got from data to conclusions. 'Appropriate' here means consistent with the research questions.

### The quality of the data

The findings and conclusions of empirical research are only as good as the data on which they are based. 'Quality control of data' in empirical research is therefore important. It is discussed first in terms of procedures in the collection of the data, and then in terms of three technical aspects of the quality of the data: reliability, validity and reactivity. Each of the latter issues is discussed in both the quantitative and qualitative contexts.

***Procedures in the collection of the data***   Care, control and thoroughness in the procedures for data collection were stressed in both quantitative and qualitative contexts. In Chapter 6, we saw what this means both in the development of a measuring instrument, and in the procedures by which it is used. In Chapter 9, we looked at the same matters in qualitative data collection. In both cases, the points raised are more common sense than technical and esoteric, but they are important nonetheless. They come down to careful thinking and planning, anticipation and pilot testing (where appropriate), and thorough preparation. They have a major impact on the more technical aspects of the quality of data.

***Reliability***   In Chapter 6, reliability of measurement was defined in terms of consistency, in the sense of both stability over time and of internal consistency. Procedures for estimating each type of reliability were described, and its interpretation in terms of error variance was given. The reliability of measurement data should be reported. For qualitative data, there is some translation of the concept of reliability, in line with the rethinking associated with newer paradigms. Thus, for example, the term 'dependability' is proposed to parallel reliability in the constructivist paradigm (Lincoln and Guba, 1985). But the basic idea is similar, and the concept of reliability has relevance for qualitative data in two respects. First, the same questions can be asked of qualitative data as of quantitative data: how stable are these data over time? And if multiple data sources are used, are they internally consistent? That is, to what extent do the data converge or diverge? Second, to what extent is there inter-observer agreement when observation data are involved? A related question concerns the early processing and analysis of qualitative data: does the check coding show inter-coder agreement?[8]

***Validity***   Validity here means the validity of the data. In Chapter 6, the validity of measurement data was discussed. The usual form of the validity question in that context is: how do we know this instrument measures what we think it measures? We discussed there the three main forms of quantitative validation: content, criterion-related and construct validity. A broader version of the validity question makes it directly applicable to all empirical research, quantitative and qualitative. The question 'How valid are the data?' really means, in this broader version: how well do the data represent the phenomena for which they stand?

In measurement, because of latent trait theory, the validity question in the first instance concerns the inference from items to variables, and in the second instance from variables to factors. With qualitative data, the first level of analysis concerns the inference from indicators to first-order concept, and the second level the inference from first-order to second-order concept. Because of the similarity in conceptual structure, the question about the validity of data is virtually identical in the two approaches. The research report needs to consider this question. Quantitative data are validated as above. Qualitative data are validated, in this technical sense, through the use of check coding, and by following the audit trail through the analysis.

*Reactivity*   Reactivity concerns the extent to which the process of collecting the data changes the data. It is a common issue in research, applying not only in the social sciences. Thus, in quantitative research, reactivity of measurement means the extent to which the act of measuring something changes that thing. Attitude scales, for example, may provoke or influence the attitude in question, changing it in some way. Reactivity is also a clear possibility in structured observation. The same sorts of possibilities exist in collecting qualitative data. A participant observer's presence may change the behaviour of those being observed, or there may be interviewer effects in the data as a result of the presence or style of a particular interviewer.

The evaluative question concerns whether the possibility of reactivity in the data has been considered, reported and taken into account, and what steps have been taken to minimize its effects.[9] In a general sense, reactivity concerns both the reliability and the validity of the data, and the sampling of the data. The question is whether the data obtained in the research are a true sample of the data. Would these be the data if the research were not being done? Has the research process itself, and specifically the collection of data, somehow influenced the data, or even created the data? This question applies in both approaches. Associated questions, which also apply in both approaches, concern respondents' or informers' knowledgeability (Are these people really able to answer these questions, or provide this information?) and the possibilities of deceit (Are they telling me the truth?) and of social desirability (Are they telling me what they think I want to hear, or what they think makes them look good?).

Reliability, validity and reactivity are technical issues about the quality of data in empirical research, and the ideas behind them apply to both approaches. For qualitative data, however, there is one other issue, as noted in Chapter 9. A strength of qualitative data, and often a reason for adopting a qualitative approach, is to see a phenomenon in its context, to study it both holistically and in detail. If the aim of the research is to obtain rich, holistic data, then it needs to be asked, and demonstrated, how well that was done. The central issue is: did the research provide a sufficient description of the context to enable the reader to judge both the validity and the transferability of the study's findings?[10]

### The findings and conclusions reached in the research

As noted earlier, we can see findings as answers to research questions, and conclusions as what can be said on the basis of those findings. There are three questions here:

1   Have the research questions been answered?
2   How much confidence can we have in the answers put forward?
3   What can be concluded from the research on the basis of what was found?

The first question requires little comment. The objective of the research is to answer its research questions (or test its hypotheses, if it is a theory verification study). The report should contain answers to these questions (or tests of these hypotheses). These answers are the findings of the research.[11]

Answers to the second and third questions depend in part on the evaluative criteria we have already considered, but they also go further than that. These two questions overlap, and come together in assessing the way evidence has been used to answer questions and draw conclusions, and in assessing the generality and applicability of the findings and conclusions. These two points correspond, respectively, to the technical concepts of internal validity and external validity.

*Internal validity*    Internal validity refers to the internal logic and consistency of the research. If research is seen as an argument (where questions are asked, and data are systematically collected and analysed to answer those questions) then internal validity is about the logic and internal consistency of that argument. Internal validity is most clearly defined in the quantitative context. There it means the extent to which the relationships between the variables are correctly interpreted. It has been well studied in that context, and the reference by Campbell and Stanley (1963) lists the various threats to internal validity which accompany different quantitative designs.

The same idea applies in the qualitative context, but it needs broadening in view of the greater range of purposes and designs in qualitative research. Denzin and Lincoln give a very broad definition: internal validity refers to 'the isomorphism of findings with reality' (1994: 114). This means the extent to which the findings faithfully represent and reflect the reality which has been studied, and it has two aspects. The first is whether the research has internal consistency. This means both, whether all the parts of the research fit together, as discussed in Section 11.2.2, and whether the findings themselves have internal consistency and coherence. The second is whether the ways in which propositions have been developed and confirmed are described, including the elimination of rival hypotheses, the consideration of negative evidence, and the cross-validation of findings with other parts of the data. In quantitative research, progressively more complex designs have been developed to counter the various threats to internal validity. This is the same thing as eliminating rival hypotheses. The same idea applies in qualitative studies, especially those whose purpose is explanation. The objective of theoretical sampling in qualitative research, including the systematic study of negative cases, is to incorporate these aspects into the study.

Qualitative designs sometimes incorporate another feature which is not typical in quantitative research, but which is part of internal validity. It is 'member checking'. It means checking with the people who are being studied, and who gave the data. It is not appropriate in all situations, and its use and limitations need to be assessed. When appropriate, it can be applied first to the data, whereby an interview transcript, for example, is taken back to the interviewee before analysis to check that the record is accurate. Second, it can be applied to the analysis as it develops. Here, it means taking the developing products of the research – its concepts, its propositions, the emerging cognitive map – back to the people being studied, for confirmation, validation and verification. When the purposes of a qualitative study are interpretive, and centred on meanings and symbolic significance as in an ethnographic description, the developing description can be checked by the members at different stages. When the purposes are more abstract, as in conceptualizing and explaining, the same thing can be done as the analysis proceeds. Thus member checking is often important in grounded theory studies.

The questions about internal validity are therefore: how internally consistent is this study? What threats are there to its internal validity, and how have those threats been taken into account?

**External validity**   External validity is the question of generalizability. How far are the findings of this study generalizable? For quantitative studies, part of this generalizability is 'people generalization', based on probability sampling. Bracht and Glass (1968) label this 'population validity', and acknowledge its importance. But they also make clear that this is not the only aspect of quantitative generalization: there is also the question of 'ecological validity'[12] when generalizing from a quantitative study.

With the qualification given in Chapter 8 (that there are some studies where generalization is not the objective), the question of generalizability can also be asked of findings in a qualitative study. How far can these findings be generalized? Are the conclusions transferable to other settings and contexts? The concept of transferability is often preferred to generalizability in qualitative writing, and in that context we can focus the question on three aspects. First, on the sampling itself: is it theoretically diverse enough, or does it capture enough variation, to encourage transfer of the findings to other situations?

Second, on the context: is the context thickly described, so that the reader can judge the transferability of findings to other situations? Third, on the level of abstraction of the concepts in the data analysis: are they at a sufficient level of abstraction to permit their application to other settings?

The questions regarding external validity are therefore: what claims can be made for the generalizability of these findings (if appropriate)? What possible threats are there to their generalization, and have those threats been taken into account? Does the report suggest how the generalizability of these findings could be assessed in other situations?

### Presentation

Finally, there is the written report of the research (or the written proposal). Research writing is discussed in the next chapter.

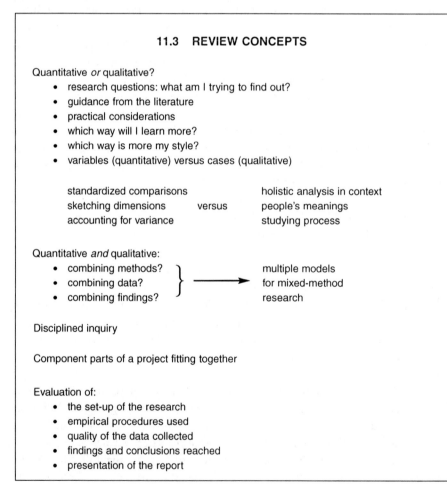

## 11.3   REVIEW CONCEPTS

Quantitative *or* qualitative?
- research questions: what am I trying to find out?
- guidance from the literature
- practical considerations
- which way will I learn more?
- which way is more my style?
- variables (quantitative) versus cases (qualitative)

| standardized comparisons | | holistic analysis in context |
| sketching dimensions | versus | people's meanings |
| accounting for variance | | studying process |

Quantitative *and* qualitative:
- combining methods?
- combining data?          →   multiple models for mixed-method research
- combining findings?

Disciplined inquiry

Component parts of a project fitting together

Evaluation of:
- the set-up of the research
- empirical procedures used
- quality of the data collected
- findings and conclusions reached
- presentation of the report

## NOTES

1   The others discussed by Hammersley are the adoption or rejection of natural science as a model, and idealism versus realism.

2   A summary of the strengths and weaknesses of the two approaches is given by Bryman (1988: 94). A summary of the criticisms and weaknesses of the quantitative approach (which they call the 'received view') is given in Guba and Lincoln (1994: 106–7). They see five main internal criticisms: context stripping, exclusion of meaning and purpose, grand theories not fitting local contexts, inapplicability of general data to individual cases, and excluding discovery. To these we could add simplification and reductionism. They also see four main external criticisms: the theory-ladenness of facts, the under-determination of theory, the value-ladenness of facts, and the interaction between the researcher and the researched.

3   Despite the increasing interest in combining methods in different areas of social research, the view that the two types of research are not compatible is still held in some quarters. Guba and Lincoln (1994: 116) point out that it is most closely associated with the critical theory and constructivist paradigms. On this question, it is interesting to note that some feminist researchers advocate combining the two approaches: see, for example, Jayaratne and Stewart (1991: 102) and Reinharz (1992: 197–213).

4   Various possible reasons are given by Sieber (1973), Rossman and Wilson (1985), and Greene et al. (1989). The reasons are important, since there is no intrinsic merit in combining methods. The point of doing so is to strengthen the research, preferably by using methods with complementary strengths.

5   Here is an example of this. A survey with standardized questions makes comparisons between subgroups of people easier and more systematic. This is an advantage, but such standardized questions risk using 'researcher-imposed constructs' rather than respondents' constructs. This is a disadvantage. A two-stage design can help overcome this disadvantage while retaining the advantage. In the first stage, respondents' perceptions and constructs are elicited, using whatever means seem suitable. This stage is complete when no further new constructs are forthcoming. The survey questions are then developed in the second stage, using those constructs.

6   As an extension of this, it is becoming increasingly common to see 'studies within a study'. Instead of a project being one overall study, it might be two or three smaller studies, all on the same topic, but coming at it from different angles, and using different approaches. This can be a pragmatic solution if the problem of integrating and interweaving the methods is difficult. In this case, the interweaving and integrating is left to the findings and conclusions stage.

7   An indication of the complexity of the question of evaluative criteria in contemporary qualitative research is given in Part V of the Denzin and Lincoln *Handbook* (1994: 479–557). Modifying Hamersley (1992), they describe four basic positions on the question of evaluative criteria: positivism, postpositivism, postmodernism and poststructuralism. (They also list the criteria important to constructivists, critical theorists and feminists.) In this book, where quantitative and qualitative research are brought together within the pragmatic question–method framework suggested, the criteria presented in this chapter fit best with the positivist and postpositivist positions they describe.

8   See Kirk and Miller (1986) and Silverman (1993: 145–9) for a discussion of reliability with qualitative data.

9   Hammersley and Atkinson (1995: 18) point out another perspective on reactivity, in their discussion of reflexivity. Reactivity can be a source of information: how

people respond to the presence of the researcher may be as informative as how they respond to other situations.

10   Miles and Huberman (1994: 279) suggest three specific questions for this: how context-rich and meaningful are the descriptions? Does the account ring true, make sense, seem convincing or plausible, enable a vicarious presence for the reader? Is the account rendered a comprehensive one, respecting the configuration and temporal arrangement of elements in the local context?

11   There may be other findings as well, which have come up during the research, but which were not phrased as research questions. Also, of course, questions may be incompletely or only partly answered, and consideration of findings and conclusions will almost always generate further questions for subsequent research.

12   Under what conditions (settings, treatments, experimenters, dependent variables, etc.) can the same results be expected?

## *Further Reading*

Brannen, J. (ed.) (1992) *Mixing Methods: Qualitative and Quantitative Research*. Aldershot: Avebury.

Brewer, J. and Hunter, A. (1989) *Multimethod Research: A Synthesis of Styles*. Newbury Park, CA: Sage.

Bryman, A. (1988) *Quantity and Quality in Social Research*. London: Unwin Hyman.

Creswell, J.W. (1994) *Research Design: Qualitative and Quantitative Approaches*. Thousand Oaks, CA: Sage.

Fielding, N.G. and Fielding, J.L. (1986) *Linking Data*. Beverly Hills, CA: Sage.

Jaeger, R.M. (1988) *Complementary Methods for Research in Education*. Washington: American Educational Research Association.

Miles, M.B. and Huberman, A.M. (1994) *Qualitative Data Analysis*. Thousand Oaks, CA: Sage.

Tashakkori, A. and Teddie, C. (eds) (2002) *Handbook of Mixed Methods in Social and Behavioral Research*. Thousand Oaks, CA: Sage.

# 12
## Research Writing

Knowledge is a social creation, and writing is one of the main ways in which knowledge is shared (Gilbert, 1996). It is also an important part of research. Getting a project started usually means taking it from ideas to a written proposal, and a project is not complete until it is shared, through writing. Thus, a written proposal is very often required for the project to commence, and a written record is almost certainly required after the project. It follows that the quality of research is judged in part by the quality of the written document (proposal or report).

The first part of this chapter gives some background to the topic of research writing, by looking briefly at writing in the quantitative tradition and at the much greater range of writing choices in qualitative research, and by using the 'analytical mix' as a device for thinking about quantitative and qualitative writing together. The second part then deals in some detail with research proposals and, in less detail, with abstracts and dissertations. Final sections then discuss briefly the distinction between writing to report and writing to learn, the choices facing the researcher when it comes to writing, and some of the ethical issues involved in social research.

## 12.1 Background

### 12.1.1 The quantitative tradition

The conventional format for reporting (or proposing) quantitative research has such headings as these (Miles and Huberman, 1994: 298):

- statement of the problem
- conceptual framework
- research questions
- method
- data analysis
- conclusions
- discussion.

A still briefer form used by some journals[1] has just four headings: introduction and problem, method, results, discussion. For much quantitative research reporting, this framework of headings is still quite appropriate: Gilbert (1996), for example, describes the conventional (quantitative) sociological paper with similar headings. But many qualitative researchers today would find such headings too constraining. The headings are still relevant to much of what we do, but we would often have different and broader expectations, for a qualitative research report especially, than can be met by these headings. Once again this reflects the range of perspectives in qualitative research in contrast with the relative homogeneity of most quantitative research.

### 12.1.2 Qualitative research writing

Throughout this book I have used the timing of structure continuum (Figure 2.2) to stress the range of social research, especially qualitative research. Writing about quantitative research has typically been a relatively straightforward matter, with conventional models and structures such as those in the previous section to guide the writer. Writing for qualitative research, however, like the research itself, is much more varied and diverse, and not at all monolithic (Coffey and Atkinson, 1996). Thus, towards the right-hand end of that continuum, there is a greater range of writing models, strategies and possibilities. Some of the perspectives of contemporary qualitative research (such as feminism and postmodernism, especially in ethnography) broaden that range even further.

The rethinking of research which has accompanied both the paradigm debates and the emergence of new perspectives has included research writing – how the research is to be put into written form, and communicated. Especially when seen in a discourse analysis or sociology of knowledge perspective, this rethinking has brought awareness of the choices about writing, identifying the conventional quantitative writing model as just one of those choices. The

**Table 12.1**   *Terms in the analytic mix*

| Quantitative | Qualitative |
| --- | --- |
| Variable oriented | Case oriented |
| Categorizing | Contextualizing |
| Analytical | Synthetic |
| Etic | Emic |
| Variance theory | Process theory |

appreciation of a wider range of choices has meant also the freeing up of some of the restrictions about writing, and is encouraging experimentation with newer forms of writing.

As a result, there is a proliferation of forms of writing in qualitative research, and older models of reporting are being mixed with other approaches:

> The reporting of qualitative data may be one of the most fertile fields going; there are no fixed formats, and the ways data are being analyzed and interpreted are getting more and more various. As qualitative data analysts, we have few shared canons of how our studies should be reported. Should we have normative agreement on this? Probably not now – or, some would say, ever. (Miles and Huberman, 1994: 299)

### 12.1.3 The analytical mix

In this chapter, I discuss research writing for both quantitative and qualitative approaches, keeping in mind but not overemphasizing their differences, and keeping in mind also those studies which combine both approaches. Adapting Miles and Huberman's 'analytic mix' (1994: 301–2) is a helpful device in doing this, since it brings key elements of the two approaches together.

One part of this analytic mix was used in Chapter 11, where variable-oriented research (quantitative) was contrasted with case-oriented research (qualitative). As Table 12.1 shows, other writers have used slightly different terms. Miles and Huberman write about this mix from within qualitative research, expressing strongly the view that good qualitative research and reporting require both elements from the mix. We can keep it in mind as a framework for all research writing.

The framework echoes the two tensions within qualitative research described by Nelson et al. (1992) in discussing cultural studies, and paraphrased by Denzin and Lincoln (1994: 4). On the one hand, qualitative research is drawn to a broad, interpretive, postmodern, feminist and critical sensibility. On the other, it is drawn to more narrowly defined positivist, postpositivist, humanistic and naturalistic conceptions of human experience and its analysis. These latter conceptions correspond more to the left-hand side of Table 12.1, whereas the former conceptions are closer to the right-hand side.

Miles and Huberman note that Vitz (1990) reflects these two views, seeing conventional data analysis, involving propositional thinking, as the fruit of abstract reasoning, leading to formal, theoretical interpretations. Figural genres, such as narratives, entail more concrete, holistic reasoning; they are 'stories' retaining the temporal configurations of the original events.

When it comes to writing, Miles and Huberman recommend a mixture of these two ways of seeing the world. As they see it, the problem is that:

> Stories without variables do not tell us enough about the meaning and larger import of what we are seeing. Variables without stories are ultimately abstract and unconvincing – which may explain certain scrupulous rules for reporting quantitative studies, as well as the familiar comment, 'I couldn't really understand the numbers until I looked at the open-ended data.' (1994: 302)

The challenge therefore is to:

> combine theoretical elegance and credibility appropriately with the many ways social events can be described; to find intersections between the propositional thinking of most conventional studies and more figurative thinking. Just as good analysis nearly always involves a blend of variable-oriented, categorizing, 'paradigmatic' moves, and case-oriented, contextualizing, narrative ones, so does good reporting. (1994: 299)

These ideas of the range of styles, and of mixing and blending them, are a useful background against which to consider proposals, abstracts and dissertations.

## 12.2 Research Documents

There are two main types of research documents: proposals and reports (which can be dissertations, journal articles[2] or reports for other purposes). Since this book is an introduction to research, with much focus on getting the research started, most attention here is on proposals. Much of what is said carries over naturally to dissertations and articles. Abstracts and titles are also briefly considered in this section.

### 12.2.1 Proposals

This section summarizes my views on research proposals. A full description of these views is given in Punch (2000), where all of the points made below are described in detail, and where two exemplary proposals are presented in full.

What is a research proposal? In one sense, the answer is obvious: the proposal describes what the proposed research is about, what it is trying to achieve and how it will go about doing that, and what we will learn from that and why it is worth learning. In another sense, the dividing line between the proposal and the research itself is not so obvious. The proposal describes what will be done, and the research itself is carried out after approval of the proposal. But preparing the proposal itself may also involve considerable research.

The three most basic questions shown in Chapter 3 are useful in guiding development of the proposal:

- What? What is the purpose of this research? What are we trying to find out?
- How? How will the proposed research answer these questions?
- Why? Why is this research worth doing (or funding)? Or, what will we learn, and why is it worth knowing?

The first question (what) is dealt with in Chapters 3 and 4. The second question (how) is dealt with in Chapters 5, 6 and 7 for quantitative research, and Chapters 8, 9 and 10 for qualitative research. The third question (why) is discussed later in this section.

Maxwell stresses that the form and structure of the proposal are tied to its purpose: 'to explain and justify your proposed study to an audience of nonexperts on your topic' (1996: 100–1). *Explain* means that your readers can clearly understand what you want to do. *Justify* means that they not only understand what you plan to do, but why. *Your proposed study* means that the proposal should be mainly about your study, not mainly about the literature, your research topic in general or research methods in general. *Non-experts* means that researchers will often have readers reviewing their proposals who are not experts in the specific area.

The proposal itself is an argument. Chapter 11 stressed that a finished research report can be seen as an argument. It is the same with the proposal – the document which represents both a report on the early stages of the research, and the plan for what will be done subsequently. Seeing it as an argument means stressing its line of reasoning, its internal consistency and the interrelatedness of its different parts. It means making sure that the different parts fit together, and showing how the research will be a piece of disciplined inquiry, as described in Chapter 11. As an argument, it should explain the logic behind the proposed study, rather than simply describing the study. In so doing, it should answer the question of why this design and method is chosen for this study.

What follows now is a suggested set of guidelines for developing a research proposal, shown in Table 12.2. Because no prescription is appropriate, but certain content is expected, and because there are both similarities and differences in quantitative and qualitative proposals, it seems best to present a full checklist of possible sections and headings. Some clearly apply to both quantitative and qualitative research, whereas some are more applicable to one

**Table 12.2**  *Checklist of possible sections for research proposals*

| | |
|---|---|
| 1 | Title and title page |
| 2 | Abstract |
| 3 | Introduction:   area and topic |
| |                     background and context |
| |                     statement of purpose |
| 4 | Research questions:   general and specific |
| 5 | Conceptual framework, theory, hypotheses (if appropriate) |
| 6 | The literature |
| 7 | Methods:   design – strategy and framework |
| |                sample and sampling |
| |                data collection – instruments and procedures |
| |                data analysis |
| 8 | Significance |
| 9 | Limitations and delimitations (if appropriate) |
| 10 | Consent, access and human participants' protection |
| 11 | References |
| 12 | Appendices (e.g. timetable, budget, instruments, etc.) |

approach. Not all would be required in any one proposal, and they can be used as appropriate. They are things to think about in proposal preparation and presentation, and they are useful in developing full versions of the proposal; where shorter versions are required, a good strategy is to prepare the full version, then summarize it.

Many of these headings (for example, general and specific research questions) do not now require comment, because of what has already been said in previous chapters. Where this is the case, the reader is referred to appropriate parts of the book. Where new points need to be made, or earlier ones reinforced, or where important distinctions apply between quantitative and qualitative approaches, brief comments are made. I stress that these are suggested guidelines. As with writing a report or dissertation, there is no fixed formula for a proposal. There are different ways to present the material, and different orders the sections can follow.

It is easier in many respects to suggest proposal guidelines for a quantitative study, since there is greater variety in qualitative studies, and many qualitative studies will be unfolding rather than prestructured. An emerging study cannot be as specific in the proposal about its research questions, or about details of the design. When this is the case, the point needs to be made in the proposal. A discussion of qualitative proposals follows this section.

### *Title and title page*
### *Abstract*
Abstracts and titles are discussed in Section 12.2.4.

### Introduction and context

There are many ways a topic can be introduced, and all topics have a background and a context. These need to be dealt with in the introduction, which sets the stage for the research. A strong introduction is important to a convincing proposal. Its purpose is not to review the literature, but rather to show generally how the proposed study fits into what is already known, and to locate it in relation to present knowledge and practice. In the process of doing this, there should be a clear identification of the topic area, and a general statement of purpose, and these can lead later into the research questions. Specific features of the proposed study can also be identified here, as appropriate: for example, if personal knowledge or experience form an important part of the context, or if preliminary or pilot studies have been done, or if the study will involve secondary analysis of existing data (Maxwell, 1996).

For qualitative proposals, two other points apply here. One is the first general evaluative question given in Chapter 11: what is the position behind this research? This can be answered in general terms, to orient the reader early in the proposal. The other is more specific: where on the structure continuum is the proposed study? This strongly influences later sections of the proposal. If a tightly structured qualitative study is planned, the proposal can proceed along similar lines to the quantitative proposal. If a more emergent study is planned, where focus and structure will develop as the study proceeds, this point should be made clearly. In the former case, there will be general and specific research questions. In the latter case, there will only be general orienting research questions.

### Research questions

These were discussed in detail in Chapters 3 and 4. In the proposal outline suggested, they can follow from the general statement of purpose given in the introduction.

### Conceptual framework, theory and hypotheses

There is wide variation in the applicability of this section. If it applies, it is a matter of judgement whether the conceptual framework goes here, or in the methods section later in the proposal. Theory and hypotheses are included if appropriate, as explained in Chapter 3. If theory is involved, it may be included in the literature review section, rather than here. The role of theory in the research should be made clear here, however.

### The literature

The proposal needs to be clear on the position taken with respect to the literature in the proposed study. As discussed in earlier chapters, there are three main possibilities:

- The literature is reviewed comprehensively in advance of the study, and that review is included as part of the proposal.
- The literature will be reviewed comprehensively ahead of the empirical stage of the research, but that review will not be done until the proposal is approved. In this case, the nature and scope of the literature to be reviewed should be indicated.
- The literature will deliberately not be reviewed prior to the empirical work, but will be integrated into the research during the study, as in grounded theory. In this case too, the nature and scope of the literature should be indicated.

For some qualitative proposals, the literature may be used in sharpening the focus of the study, and to give structure to its questions and design. If so, this should be indicated, along with how it is to be done. In all cases, the researcher needs to connect the proposed study to the literature.[3]

### Methods

**Design, strategy and framework**   The basic quantitative designs we have discussed are the experimental, quasi-experimental, and correlational survey designs. For these designs or variations of them, the conceptual framework may be shown here instead of earlier. In qualitative studies, the location of the study along the structure continuum is particularly important for its design. As noted in Chapter 8, qualitative designs such as case studies (single or multiple, cross-sectional or longitudinal), ethnography or grounded theory may overlap, and elements of these strategies may be used separately or together. This means it will be difficult to compartmentalize the study neatly. That is not a problem, but it should be made clear that the proposed study uses elements of different strategies. Qualitative studies vary greatly on the issue of predeveloped conceptual frameworks, and the position of the study on this matter should be indicated. A fully or partly predeveloped framework should be shown. Where one will be developed, it needs to be indicated how that will be done. This will interact with data collection and analysis, and may be better dealt with there.

**Sample**   As shown in Chapter 6, the three key sampling issues for quantitative research are the size of the sample, how it is to be selected and why, and what claims are made for its representativeness. The qualitative proposal should deal with the questions of who or what will be studied, and why. The sampling strategy is important for both types of studies, and its logic needs to be clear. Where the sampling strategy itself is emergent, as in theoretical sampling, this needs to be explained.

*Data collection*   The two matters here are the instruments (if any) which will be used for data collection, and the procedures for administering the instruments. If a quantitative study proposes to use instruments which already exist, and information about their psychometric characteristics is available, it should be reported. If the instruments are to be developed, the steps for developing them should be shown. If a qualitative study proposes to use instruments (for example, observation schedules, structured interviews), the same comments apply. Less structured qualitative data collection techniques should be indicated and discussed, especially in terms of the quality of data issues shown in Section 11.2.3. For both quantitative and qualitative studies, the procedures proposed for data collection should also be described, and the description should show why these data collection activities have been chosen. Possible threats to the validity of data can also be indicated here.

*Data analysis*   Quantitative proposals should indicate the statistical procedures by which the data will be analysed. Similarly, the qualitative proposal needs to show how its data will be analysed, and how the proposed analysis fits with the other components of the study. If applicable, both types of proposal should indicate what computer use is planned in the analysis of the data.

### Significance

The particular topic and its context will determine the study's significance.[4] There are three general areas for the significance and contribution of the study: to knowledge in the area, to policy considerations and to practitioners (Marshall and Rossman, 1989). The first of these, contribution to knowledge, is closely tied to the literature in the area. One function of the literature review is to indicate gaps in the knowledge in the area, and to show how this study will contribute to filling those gaps. This has to be set against the position taken on the literature, as discussed above.

### Limitations and delimitations

Any study has limitations, and they should be noted in the proposal, which should argue nonetheless for the importance of this work. Delimitation means the drawing of boundaries around a study, and showing clearly what is and is not included. This is sometimes useful in avoiding misunderstanding by the reader.

### Consent, access and human participants' protection

These are dealt with in Section 12.5 on ethical issues.

### References

This is a list of the references cited in the proposal.

*Appendices*

This section may include any of the following: a timetable for the research, letters of introduction or permission, consent forms, measuring instruments, questionnaires, interview guides, observation schedules, examples of pilot study or other relevant work already completed (Maxwell, 1996).

### 12.2.2 Qualitative proposals

Qualitative studies vary greatly, and in many, the design and procedures will evolve. This obviously means that the writer cannot specify exactly what will be done in advance, in contrast with many quantitative proposals. When this is the case, there is a need to explain the flexibility the study requires and why, and how decisions will be made as the study unfolds. Together with this, as much detail as possible should be provided. Review committees have to judge the quality, feasibility and viability of the proposed project, and the ability of the researcher to carry it out. The proposal itself, through its organization, coherence and integration, attention to detail and conceptual clarity can inspire confidence in the researcher's ability to execute the research. In addition, where specialized expertise is involved, it helps for the researcher to indicate how that expertise will be acquired.[5]

Marshall and Rossman (1989) stress the need for the qualitative proposal to reassure the reader as to the academic merit and discipline of the proposed research. That need is less pronounced today, when there is very much greater recognition and acceptance of qualitative research. However, there are two main ways the qualitative proposal can provide that reassurance. One is by giving information about the technical issues of the research, under research methods, as is routinely done in quantitative proposals. This means the sampling plan, the data collection and quality of data issues, and the proposed methods of analysis. The other applies to an unfolding qualitative study. Its proposal should indicate that focus will be developed as the study proceeds, and how that focus will be developed during the early empirical work.

Contrasting design and proposals at different ends of the structure continuum in qualitative research, Denzin and Lincoln write:

> The positivist, postpositivist, constructionist, and critical paradigms dictate, with varying degrees of freedom, the design of a qualitative research investigation. This can be looked at as a continuum, with rigorous design principles on one end and emergent, less well structured directives on the other. Positivist research designs place a premium on the early identification and development of a research question and a set of hypotheses, choice of a research site, and establishment of sampling strategies, as well as a specification of the research strategies and methods of analysis that will be employed. A research proposal may be written that lays out the stages and phases of the study. These phases may be conceptualized in terms of those

outlined by Janice Morse in Chapter 13 (reflection, planning entry, data collection, withdrawal from the field, analysis, and write-up). This proposal may also include a budget, a review of the relevant literature, a statement concerning protection of human subjects, a copy of consent forms, interview schedules, and a timeline.[6] Positivist designs attempt to anticipate all of the problems that may arise in a qualitative study. Such designs provide rather well defined road maps for the researcher. The scholar working in this tradition hopes to produce a work that finds its place in the literature on the topic being studied.

In contrast, much greater ambiguity is associated with postpositivist and nonpositivist designs – those based, for example, on the constructivist or critical theory paradigms or the ethnic, feminist, or cultural studies perspectives. In studies shaped by these paradigms and perspectives there is less emphasis on formal grant proposals, well-formulated hypotheses, tightly defined sampling frames, structured interview schedules, and predetermined research strategies and methods and forms of analysis. The researcher follows a path of discovery, using as a model qualitative works that have achieved the status of classics in the field (1994: 200).

Thus, for some types of qualitative research especially, we do not want to constrain too much the structure of the proposal, and we need to preserve flexibility. On the other hand, several writers (Silverman, 1993; Coffey and Atkinson, 1996) point out that this should not be taken to mean that 'anything goes'. Eisner writes in the same vein about qualitative research in education:

> Qualitative research proposals should have a full description of the topic to be investigated, a presentation and analysis of the research relevant to that topic, and a discussion of the issues within the topic or the shortfalls within the research literature that make the researcher's topic a significant one. They should describe the kinds of information that are able to be secured and the variety of methods or techniques that will be employed to secure such information. The proposals should identify the kinds of theoretical or explanatory resources that might be used in interpreting what has been described, and describe the kind of places, people, and materials that are likely to be addressed.

> The function of proposals is not to provide a watertight blueprint or formula the researcher is to follow, but to develop a cogent case that makes it plain to a knowledgeable reader that the writer has the necessary background to do the study and has thought clearly about the resources that are likely to be used in doing the study, and that the topic, problem, or issue being addressed is educationally significant.

Lest these comments be interpreted by some to mean that no planning is necessary in conducting qualitative research, or that 'anything goes', as they say, I want to make it clear that this is not how my words should be interpreted. Planning is necessary. Nevertheless, it should not and cannot function as a recipe or as a script. Evidence matters. One has a responsibility to support what one says, but support does not require measured evidence. Coherence, plausibility, and utility are quite acceptable in trying to deal with social complexity. My point is not to advocate anarchy or to reduce the study of schools and classrooms to a Rorschach projection, it is to urge that the analysis of a research proposal or a research study should employ criteria appropriate to the genre. Professors who make such assessments should understand, as should graduate students, the nature of the genre, what constitutes appropriate criteria, and why they are appropriate. (1991: 241–2)

### 12.2.3 Examples of proposals

The recent literature contains some very useful examples of research proposals: two are shown in Punch (2000). A detailed treatment of proposals of different types is given by Locke et al., (1993). They present four examples of research proposals in full, and they give a detailed critical commentary on the different sections and aspects of each. They have chosen the proposals to illustrate different designs and styles of research, and using topics drawn from different areas. The four proposals are:

1  An experimental study ('The effects of age, modality, complexity of response and practice on reaction time'). This study proposes a two-factor design with repeated measures, to test 14 hypotheses about reaction times.
2  A qualitative study ('Returning women students in the community college'). This study proposes the use of in-depth interviewing to explore the meaning of experience of older women returning as students to a community college.
3  A quasi-experimental study ('Teaching children to question what they read: an attempt to improve reading comprehension through training in a cognitive learning strategy'). This study proposes a quasi-experimental design to test three hypotheses about the acquisition of reading in children.
4  A funded grant proposal ('A competition strategy for worksite smoking cessation'). This renewal grant proposal also uses a quasi-experimental design, to assess the effectiveness of competition/facilitation on recruiting employees into a self-help smoking cessation programme, and on the outcomes of that programme.

In addition to these examples, Maxwell (1996: 116–37) presents a qualitative proposal entitled 'How basic science teachers help medical students learn: the students' perspective', and he too gives a detailed commentary on the proposal. The research he describes proposes to use a case study of four exceptional teachers to answer six specific research questions about how teachers help medical students learn. Classroom participant observation and student and teacher interviews are the main sources of data, supplemented by relevant documentary data. Finally, Chenitz (1986) does not include an example of an actual proposal, but writes about the preparation of a proposal for a grounded theory study.

### 12.2.4 Abstracts and titles

An abstract is a brief summary, whether of a proposal or a finished study. Abstracts play an important role in the research literature, and they are required in proposals (usually), in dissertations and in research articles in most refereed journals. Abstracts and titles are at the heart of the hierarchical indexing system for the research literature, which becomes more and more important as the volume of research continues to build. This indexing system enables researchers first to scan a title, to see if they need to go further into a project. If so, they can go to the abstract, which will tell them more, and perhaps enough. If they need to go still further, the last chapter (for example, of a dissertation) will often contain a summary of the study and its findings, in more detail than the abstract. They can then go to the full report if they need still more detail about the research.

Good abstract writing requires the skill of saying as much as possible in as few words as possible. For a proposal, the abstract needs to deal with two main issues: what the study is about and aims to achieve (usually best stated in terms of its research questions), and how it intends to do that. For a report, the abstract would need three main sections: these two, and a third which summarizes what was found. The abstract should give an overview not just of the study itself, but also of the argument behind the study, and this should run through these sections. For most of us, abstract writing is a skill which needs to be developed, since we typically use many superfluous words when we speak and write. Together with the title, the abstract is written last, since it is difficult to summarize what has not yet been written.

Titles also have importance in the research literature indexing process, as indicated. Therefore a title should not just be an afterthought, nor should it use words or phrases which obscure rather than reveal meaning. Extending the point about abstract writing, the title should convey as much information as possible in as few words as possible. Titles and their role are discussed by Locke et al. (1993).

### 12.2.5 Dissertations (and projects)

Much of the focus in this book has been on getting research started, so the emphasis in this chapter is on writing the research proposal. Completed research is reported in several forms, and dissertations are one of the main forms. Because I have emphasized proposals, there is not a detailed description of the dissertation here, or guidelines for its structure and writing. There is a considerable literature on that topic, and directions into that literature are given in the suggestions for further reading in this chapter. Instead, this section includes comments about three aspects of a dissertation: about the general content a dissertation should cover, about how a dissertation might be seen, and about the nature of dissertation writing.

Whatever its specific structure, certain basic content is expected in a dissertation. This content includes:

- the research area and the topic
- a statement of purpose(s) and research questions
- a setting of the study in context including its relationship to relevant literature
- a description of methods including design, sample, and the collection and analysis of data
- a clear statement of the findings and a consideration of what can be concluded from those findings.

These headings are general enough to cover quantitative and most qualitative work. They are similar to Miles and Huberman's (1994: 304) minimum guidelines for the structure of a qualitative research report:

1  The report should tell us what the study was about or came to be about.
2  It should communicate a clear sense of the social and historical context of the setting(s) where data were collected.
3  It should provide us with what Erickson (1986) calls the 'natural history of the inquiry,' so we see clearly what was done, by whom, and how. More deeply than in a sheer 'methods' account, we should see how key concepts emerged over time; which variables appeared and disappeared; which codes led to important insights.
4  A good report should provide basic data, preferably in focused form (vignettes, organized narrative, photographs, or data displays) so that the reader can, in parallel with the researcher, draw warranted conclusions. (Conclusions without data are a sort of oxymoron.)
5  Finally researchers should articulate their conclusions, and describe their broader meaning in the worlds of ideas and action they affect.

How the material is divided up into chapters and sections is a matter for the dissertation writer. In doing that, it is useful to remember that a dissertation is essentially the report of a piece of research, where that research constitutes an argument. Empirical research (quantitative, qualitative or both) systematically introduces empirical evidence into that argument, as its way of answering questions, testing hypotheses or building understanding. In line with that, one way to look at research, including dissertation research, is as a series of decisions. Especially in planning and designing the project, the researcher faces choices, many of which have been the subject of this book. Therefore the completed project itself is a combination of those choices, and the dissertation is the report of that. It is very often not the case that there is a right and wrong choice in the face of these many decisions. As I have stressed frequently in this book, it is rather a case of assessing each situation in the research, along with its alternative choices and their inevitable strengths and weaknesses, and of making each decision based on that analysis, in the light of the circumstances of the research, and of the need for the parts of the project to fit together.

To reflect this perspective in the writing of the dissertation, the writer can say what the choices were at each point, what choice was made, and why. Seeing a dissertation this way makes it clear that there is no one way to do a piece of research, and that any piece of research will have its critics. Recognizing that, the objective is to produce a thorough report of a carefully reasoned set of consistent choices, after consideration of the alternatives. In the written report, the writer is, among other things, telling the reader about the decision path taken through the research, and taking the reader down that path. The writing indicates why that path was chosen, the alternatives considered and the decisions taken. Presenting it this way conveys the impression of a thorough and careful project, well planned, well executed and well reported.

Much has been written on the topics of tactics and style in dissertation and academic writing, and both topics are covered in the further reading indicated. The comments here concern the need for clarity, the role of shortening, and the modular and iterative nature of research writing.

Whether proposal or report, research writing needs to communicate clearly and effectively, and striving for clarity is part of the writer's responsibility. Clarity is required in the structure of the document (the sections it will have, the order in which they appear, and how they are connected to each other), and in the words, sentences and paragraphs which make up the sections. Clear guidelines help on these matters in quantitative research, but it is rather more difficult to balance clarity with 'fidelity' in the qualitative context. Quoting Berger and Kellner (1981), Webb and Glesne (1992) point out that we have a moral obligation to reflect stories of human meanings as faithfully as possible. Reflecting the style of qualitative analysis emphasized in Chapter 10 of this book,[7] with abstractions from the data to first-order and then to second-order constructs, they write:

> The second order constructs that social scientists use to make sense of
> people's lives must grow from and refer back to the first order constructs
> those same people use to define themselves and fill their lives with meaning.

> Moving gracefully between first and second order constructs in social science writing is difficult. We have suggested that students have a moral obligation to be clear; otherwise the reader is separated from the lives of the people under study and from the researcher's analysis. We are not suggesting that students should 'dumb-down' their text or simplify what is complex just to make reading easier. (1992: 804)

One general strategy to help in being clear is to put oneself (as writer) in the position of reader. What will make most sense to the reader? What will ensure that the reader is easily able to follow the argument and does not 'get lost' in the document? In this way, the writer tries to anticipate reader expectations and reactions. It is useful to remember also that the research document (proposal or report) will, in the end, be a stand-alone document. This means that the writer will not be there to interpret it for the reader, when it is being read.

Shortness is important because it often promotes clarity. There are various pressures today to restrict length: thus research journals restrict article length because of space considerations, and universities place upper limits on the length of dissertations. Ways to achieve shortness include getting straight to the point, cutting out unnecessary padding, not using long words when short ones will do, and keeping sentences short. The problem is that shortening requires reworking, which takes time. Every researcher discovers that lack of time is a problem in making the writing short (and clear). The message is, if possible, to leave adequate time to do the shortening.

The organization and structure of a dissertation (or proposal) usually require that it be segmented into sections. It is useful to see these as modules, to organize these modules into chapters, and to write the dissertation by writing these modules. By breaking it up, this makes the task less formidable. It is also important to write the different sections, or at least to keep full notes and draft the sections, as the stages of the research are being carried out. So many issues and decisions arise during a research project that it is impossible to remember all of them when it comes to 'writing time' without full notes of the various discussions, readings and so on. Wolcott (1990) goes even further with his advice: 'You cannot begin writing early enough.' The strategy of 'writing as you go' helps in making ideas explicit (Miles and Huberman, 1994), and it also exploits the value of writing as a part of the learning.

## 12.3 Writing to Report versus Writing to Learn: Writing as Analysis

In the traditional model of research writing, the write-up does not get done until the research is completed, and everything is figured out: 'I've done all the research, now I am writing it up.' Implicit in this is the idea that I don't start the writing until I have 'got it all worked out'. This is writing to report.

A different view sees writing as a way of learning, a way of knowing, a form of analysis and inquiry. This is the idea of 'writing in order to work it out'. In this view, I don't delay the writing until I have it all figured out. On the contrary, I use the process of writing itself to help me figure it out, since I learn by writing. Writers interpret, so writing is a way of learning, through discovery and analysis (Richardson, 1994). Thus writing becomes an integral part of the research, and not just an add-on once the 'real' research is completed. This is writing to learn.

Writing to learn is more likely in qualitative research. However, it can also have a role in quantitative studies: for example, when the researcher is interpreting the results from the analysis of complex data sets, as in a multivariable correlational survey. In these cases, building an overall picture of the results, integrating and interpreting them, is similar to describing the emerging picture which accompanies some forms of qualitative data analysis (such as the Miles and Huberman type). At the same time, this model of writing is especially appropriate for some types of qualitative analysis, where the researcher is constructing a map or theoretical picture of the data, which emerges as the analysis proceeds. The process of writing can be a great help in developing this emerging picture. A practical implication of this view is that a useful tactic, when stuck or confused in developing the picture, is to do some writing about it.

Qualitative researchers are therefore more likely to stress that writing is analysis, not separated from it. In the 'analytic work of writing' (Coffey and Atkinson, 1996), writing is part of thinking, analysing and interpreting. The 'crisis of representation' (Denzin and Lincoln, 1994) has also brought shifts in conceptions of how to represent the 'reality' with which qualitative social science (especially) has to deal, particularly the world of lived real experience. Together, these two points bring a new focus on the form of the written research report:

> The net effect of recent developments is that we cannot approach the task of 'writing up' our research as a straightforward (if demanding) task. We have to approach it as an analytical task, in which the form of our reports and representations is as powerful and significant as their content. (Coffey and Atkinson, 1996: 109)

This view, particularly prominent in recent writing about ethnography (Hammersley, 1995; Coffey and Atkinson, 1996), leads to a realization of the many choices involved in the production of research documents.

## 12.4 Writing Choices

Webb and Glesne (1992: 803) order the writing choices facing the researcher, especially the qualitative researcher, on three levels. Macro questions are about power, voice and politics in research; middle-range issues concern authorial authority, the marshalling of evidence, and the relationship between the researcher and the researched; micro issues are about whether or not a piece should be written in the first person, whether or not its tone changes when the author moves from data to theory, and how the story is told. Miles and Huberman (1994: 298–306) also identify a series of choices about reports and reporting, stressing choices rather than a fixed set of ideas. They include choices about the report's audiences and its hoped-for effects on them, the voice or genre of the report, its writing style, and its structure and format. To go with this array of choices (and, in a way, to summarize them) Denzin and Lincoln (1994: 479) add that the process of writing is itself an interpretive, personal and political act.

These writing choices in fact apply across the whole range of research approaches, quantitative and qualitative, though it is the developments in qualitative research in the last 20 years which have demonstrated that most clearly. The further reading indicated, especially in qualitative research writing, includes discussions and examples of these choices.

## 12.5 Ethical Issues

All social research involves ethical issues. This is because the research involves collecting data from people, and about people. A thorough research proposal will have anticipated the ethical issues involved, and will show how they will be dealt with.

The substantial literature on ethical issues in social science is of two main types. There are the codes of ethical and professional conduct for research, put out by the various social science organizations. Examples are those of the American Psychological Association (1992), the American Sociological Association (1989), the American Educational Research Association (1992), and the handbook for the American Anthropological Association (Cassell and Jacobs, 1987). The other type of literature is the various commentaries on ethical issues, sometimes across social research in general, and sometimes specific to particular social science areas. Examples are the writings of Miles and Huberman (1994) and Punch (1986; 1994). Both types of literature are valuable. The first type offers researchers guidelines for ethical conduct, and checklists of points to consider. The second type of literature describes what issues have come up for different researchers, and how they have been handled.

Ethical issues can arise in both approaches, but they are more likely and more acute in some qualitative approaches. This is because, while all social research intrudes to some extent into people's lives, qualitative research often intrudes more. Some qualitative research deals with the most sensitive, intimate and innermost matters in people's lives, and ethical issues inevitably accompany the collection of such information. With the growth of interest in qualitative methods, recognition and consideration of ethical issues have become a bigger feature of the social science research literature. Ethical issues saturate all stages of the research process, beginning with the researcher's choice of topic (Why is this research worthwhile? Who benefits from this research?). Fetterman (1989) describes the various ethical issues which can arise during the different stages of a research project, using the life cycle terms of 'inception and prenatal care', 'gestation and birth', 'childhood', 'adolescence and adulthood', and 'retirement and last rites'.

The second type of literature mentioned above discusses many of the ethical issues which can arise in research. Punch (1994) summarizes the main ones as harm, consent, deception, privacy and confidentiality of data. Miles and Huberman (1994: 290–7) have a broader list of 11 ethical issues that typically need attention before, during and after qualitative studies, though many apply to quantitative studies also. Each issue is briefly outlined as a series of relevant questions.

Issues arising early in a project:

1  *Worthiness of the project.* Is my contemplated study worth doing? Will it contribute in some significant way to a domain broader than my funding, my publication opportunities, my career?
2  *Competence boundaries.* Do I have the expertise to carry out a study of good quality? Or, am I prepared to study, to be supervised, trained or consulted, to get that expertise? Is such help available?
3  *Informed consent.* Do the people I am studying have full information about what the study will involve? Is their consent to participate freely given? Does a hierarchy of consent (e.g. children, parents, teachers, administrators) affect such decisions?
4  *Benefits, costs, reciprocity.* What will each party to the study gain from having taken part? What do they have to invest in time, energy or money? Is the balance equitable?

Issues arising as the project develops:

5  *Harm and risk.* What might this study do to hurt the people involved? How likely is it that such harm will occur?
6  *Honesty and trust.* What is my relationship with the people I am studying? Am I telling the truth? Do we trust each other?
7  *Privacy, confidentiality and anonymity.* In what ways will the study intrude, come closer to people than they want? How will information be guarded? How identifiable are the individuals and organizations studied?
8  *Intervention and advocacy.* What do I do when I see harmful, illegal or wrongful behaviour by others during a study? Should I speak for anyone's interests besides my own? If so, whose interests do I advocate?

Issues arising later in, or after, the project:

9 *Research integrity and quality.* Is my study being conducted carefully, thoughtfully and correctly in terms of some reasonable set of standards?
10 *Ownership of data and conclusions.* Who owns my field notes and analyses: myself, my organization, my funders? And once my reports are written, who controls their diffusion?
11 *Use and misuse of results.* Do I have an obligation to help my findings be used appropriately? What if they are used harmfully or wrongly?

As Miles and Huberman point out, these issues typically involve dilemmas and conflicts, and negotiated trade-offs are often needed, rather than the application of rules. But heightened awareness of all these issues is an important starting point.

Feminist approaches to research have contributed further perspectives on the ethical issues involved. Thus, Mauthner et al. (2002) point out that ethical debates in society in general are increasingly wide-ranging, and these authors show that ethical concerns in research are similarly more wide-ranging than can be covered by sets of rules. Their key themes are responsibility and accountability in applied feminist research practice based on personal experience methods. Some of the ethical issues their analysis exposes are questions of intention underlying research, the many meanings of participation, and the idea that consent may need to be ongoing and renegotiated throughout a research project.

Directions to literature on ethical issues are given in the suggestions for further reading.

---

### 12.6   REVIEW CONCEPTS

Proposal as argument
Writing to report
Writing to learn
Ethical issues

---

### NOTES

1   For example, those with a strong behaviourist leaning in psychology and education.
2   I do not deal with writing journal articles here, but the topic is discussed by Gilbert (1996).
3   There are various ways this can be done: see, for example, Marshall and Rossman (1989), Locke et al. (1993), Maxwell (1996).
4   Other terms for this might be the 'justification', 'importance' or 'contribution' of the study. They all address the third of the earlier overarching questions: why is this study worth doing?

5  This point might apply to both research approaches: for example, advanced statistical analysis in a quantitative study, or grounded theory analysis in a qualitative study.
6  Morse (1994: 208) suggests a list of the components of a qualitative research proposal.
7  The type of analysis used in qualitative studies will affect writing choices.

## *Further Reading*

### *Academic writing in general*
Broadley, L. (1987) *Academic Writing in Social Practice*. Philadelphia: Temple University Press.

Mullins, C.J. (1977) *A Guide to Writing and Publishing in the Social and Behavioural Sciences*. New York: Wiley.

Strunk, W. Jr and White, E.B. (1979) *The Elements of Style*. 3rd edn. New York: Macmillan.

Zinsser, W. (1976) *On Writing Well*. New York: Harper and Row.

### *Qualitative writing*
Atkinson, P. (1990) *The Ethnographic Imagination: Textual Constructions of Reality*. London: Routledge.

Becker, H.S. (1986) *Writing for Social Scientists: How to Finish your Thesis, Book, or Article*. Chicago: University of Chicago Press.

Clifford, J. and Marcus, G.E. (1986) *Writing Culture: The Poetics and Politics of Ethnography*. Berkeley, CA: University of California Press.

Geertz, C. (1983) *Works and Lives: The Anthropologist as Author*. Cambridge: Polity.

van Maanen, J. (1988) *Tales of the Field: On Writing Ethnography*. Chicago: University of Chicago Press.

Wolcott, H.F. (1990) *Writing up Qualitative Research*. Newbury Park. CA: Sage.

### *Proposals and dissertations*
Behling, J.H. (1984) *Guidelines for Preparing the Research Proposal*. Lanham, MD: University Press.

Krathwohl, D.R. (1988) *How to Prepare a Research Proposal*. 3rd edn. Syracuse, NY: Syracuse University Press.

Lauffer, A. (1983) *Grantsmanship.* Beverly Hills, CA: Sage.

Locke, L.F., Spirduso, W.W. and Silverman, S.J. (1993) *Proposals that Work: A Guide for Planning Dissertations and Grant Proposals.* 3rd edn. Newbury Park, CA: Sage.

Long, T.J., Convey, J.J. and Chwalek, A.R. (1991) *Completing Dissertations in the Behavioural Sciences and Education.* San Francisco: Jossey-Bass.

Madsen, D. (1992) *Successful Dissertations and Theses.* 2nd edn. San Francisco: Jossey-Bass.

Phillips, M. and Pugh, D.S. (1987) *How to Get a PhD.* Milton Keynes: Open University Press.

Punch, K.F. (2000) *Developing Effective Research Proposals.* London: Sage.

Rudestam, K.E. and Newton, R.R. (1992) *Surviving your Dissertation: A Comprehensive Guide to Content and Process.* Newbury Park, CA: Sage.

Sternberg, D. (1981) *How to Complete and Survive a Doctoral Dissertation.* New York: St Martin's.

### Ethical issues

Burgess, R.G. (ed.) (1989) *The Ethics of Educational Research.* Lewes: Falmer.

Mauthner, M., Birch, M., Jessop, J. and Miller, T. (2002) *Ethics in Qualitative Research.* London: Sage.

Miles, M.B. and Huberman, A.M. (1994) *Qualitative Data Analysis.* Thousand Oaks, CA: Sage.

Punch, M. (1986) *The Politics and Ethics of Fieldwork.* Beverly Hills, CA: Sage.

Punch, M. (1994) 'Politics and ethics in qualitative research', in N.K. Denzin and Y.S. Lincoln (eds), *Handbook of Qualitative Research.* Thousand Oaks, CA: Sage. pp. 83–97.

Sapsford, R. and Abbott, P. (1996) 'Ethics, politics and research', in R. Sapsford and V. Jupp (eds), *Data Collection and Analysis.* London: Sage. pp. 317–42.

Sieber, J.E. (1982) *Planning Ethically Responsible Research: A Guide for Students and Internal Review Boards.* Newbury Park, CA: Sage.

# Appendix 1: Computer Software in Quantitative and Qualitative Analysis

This appendix contains additional information on computer programs for the analysis of data. It follows on from Section 7.8 for quantitative analysis and Section 10.7 for qualitative analysis. It deals with two of today's most widely used programs: SPSS (Statistical Package for the Social Sciences) for quantitative analysis and N6 for qualitative analysis.

## A1.1 Quantitative Analysis: SPSS (www.spss.com)

Now in its 11th release, SPSS is an extremely comprehensive statistical package for the analysis of quantitative data. It has the following general features and main functions.

### General features of SPSS

- *Data retrieval.* Ability to read and analyse complex file and record structures such as index, nested, or hierarchical files.
- *Data and file management.* Extensive file management capabilities including the ability to split files, save files, and match and merge multiple files.
- *Data storage and transformation.* Extended data management capabilities including the ability to define and manipulate long-string variables, do conditional data transformations, and perform a wide variety of numeric functions.
- *Data display.* Great latitude in data display, incorporating report as standard feature.
- *Basic and advanced statistics.* Wide range of statistical analysis routines.
- *Non-parametrics.* Large array of non-parametric tests, e.g. Friedman, Kruskal–Wallis, Mann–Whitney, and Wilcoxon.
- *Graphics.* Presentation style graphics, graph editing, plots, scatterplot matrix, charts and histograms.

### Main functions of SPSS

- data transformations
- contingency tables
- *t*-tests
- regression
- discriminant analysis
- probit analysis
- forecasting, time series
- data examination
- reliability tests
- ANOVA
- non-linear regression
- factor analysis
- survival analysis
- non-parametric analysis
- descriptive statistics
- correlation
- MANOVA
- logistic regression
- cluster analysis
- multidimensional scaling
- graphics and graphical interface

## Instructions for using SPSS

The following step-by-step guide to analysing data using SPSS focuses only on the statistical techniques described in Chapter 7. It was compiled by Dr John West of the Graduate School of Education at The University of Western Australia.

### Descriptive statistics
1 Select **Descriptive Statistics** and then **Descriptives** from the **Analyze** menu.
2 Move the desired variable(s) to the **Variable(s)** window.
3 Click on **Options**. Use the mouse to select the types of descriptive statistics that you require.
4 Click **Continue** and then **OK**.

### Frequency distribution plot
1 Select **Descriptive Statistics** and then **Frequencies** from the **Analyze** menu.
2 Move the desired variable(s) to the **Variable(s)** window.
3 Click on **Statistics**. Select any descriptive statistics you require and click on **Continue**.
4 Click on **Charts**. Select the type of chart you require.
5 Click **Continue** and then **OK**.

### One-way ANOVA
1 Select **Compare Means** and then **One-Way ANOVA** from the **Analyze** menu.
2 Move the dependent variable to the **Dependent List** window.
3 Move the independent variable to the **Factor** window.
4 Click on **Options** and select **Descriptive Statistics**.

If multiple comparisons are required:

5 Click on **Post Hoc** and then select the type of multiple comparisons you wish to perform. Click **Continue**.
6 Click **Continue** and then **OK**.

### Two-way ANOVA
1 Select **General Linear Model** and the **Univariate** from the **Analyze** menu.
2 Move the dependent variable to the **Dependent Variables** window.
3 Move the two independent variables to the **Fixed Factor(s)** window.
4 Click on **Options** and move the variables from the **Factor(s) and Factor Interactions** window to the **Display Means** window.
5 Click **Continue** and then **OK**.

### Correlation coefficient
1 Select **Correlate** and then **Bivariate** from the **Analyze** menu.
2 Move the two variables to be correlated into the **Variable(s)** window.
3 Select **Pearson** correlation.
4 Click **OK**.

### Intercorrelation matrix
1 Select **Correlate** and then **Bivariate** from the **Analyze** menu.
2 Move the two variables to be correlated into the **Variable(s)** window
3 Click **OK**.

### Simple linear regression
1. Select **Regression** and then **Linear** from the **Analyze** menu.
2. Move the criterion variable to the **Dependent** window.
3. Move the predictor variable to the **Independent(s)** window.
4. Click **Continue** and then **OK**.

### Multiple linear regression
1. Select **Regression** and then **Linear** from the **Analyze** menu.
2. Move the criterion variable to the **Dependent** window.
3. Move the predictor variable(s) to the **Independent(s)** window.
4. Click on **Method** to select the method by which variables are entered or removed from the analysis. The options are **Enter, Remove, Forward, Backward** and **Stepwise**.
5. Click on **Statistics** and make sure **Regression Coefficient Estimates, Model Fit** and **R Squared Change** are selected.
6. Click **Continue** and then **OK**.

### $2 \times 2$ contingency table analysis
1. Select **Descriptive Statistics** and then **Crosstabs** from the **Analyze** menu.
2. Move the row variable to the **Row(s)** window.
3. Move the column variable to the **Column(s)** window.
4. Click on **Statistics** and select **Chi-square**.
5. Click **Continue** and then **OK**.

### Factor analysis
1. Select **Data Reduction** and then **Factor** from the **Analyze** menu.
2. Move the variables to be analysed to the **Variable(s)** window.
3. Click on **Extraction** if you wish to select the method of factor extraction.
4. Click on **Rotation** if you wish to select the method of factor rotation.
5. Click **Continue** and then **OK**.

## A1.2 Qualitative Analysis

This section was contributed by Dr Roger Vallance of the University of Notre Dame, Australia.

In 1994, QSR International commenced marketing NUD•IST.[1] This qualitative data analysis package became known as N4, and the present product, QSR N6, is a further development of that software. QSR market other software for qualitative analysis, notably NVivo and XSight (QSR, 2004).

In the last decade, N6 has grown to be the predominant qualitative computer package in university research.[2] This section briefly describes some features of the QSR N6 software for the analysis of qualitative data. XSight has been developed specifically to meet the needs of market researchers who gather different types of qualitative data from most academic researchers.

The approach that underlies N6 is similar to the types of qualitative data analysis (the Miles and Huberman type, and grounded theory analysis) given most emphasis in Chapter 10 of this book, in that the researcher is encouraged to break the data open to reveal ideas that underlie what is being said or reported. These ideas are labelled (as in open coding), and reflect an abstraction from the data to a higher-order concept. As the relationships between codes emerge through the process of analytic induction, the researcher can begin to build a hierarchy of codes and categories. Thus a 'tree structure' is formed as the researcher works toward development of a theory. Such trees are based on the structure shown in Figures 10.2 and 10.3.

At the same time, N6 does not help with only one method of qualitative analysis. As well as grounded theorists and inductive analysts, ethnographers, phenomenologists and hermeneuticists all use N6. They use it because it expands their creativity, extends their research skills and facilitates their analytic engagement with their data. This reflects the fact that N6 was constructed by qualitative researchers for qualitative researchers.

N6 uses text units. A text unit is the smallest portion of text that can be retrieved by the system. Naturally, more than the minimum is always able to be retrieved. Preparation for use of N6 means that word processor documents should be saved in ASCII format. In MSWord™ the command sequence is **File/Save As/Save as Type**: **Text Only** (txt); then choose the **MSDOS** option to save as text without line breaks. Then the file can be imported into N6. This is a simple process which needs to be done once only for each document imported into N6.

Once you have your documents in N6 you are ready to start. Indeed, with a bit of experience, you can work quite quickly. Basically you work by reading the text and selecting the piece of text that relates to your research question. You then code that text to a node.

A node is a flag or category name. It becomes a place holder or container for text which you judge to be relevant to your research questions. Nodes can be organized in a tree or left free. Free nodes are without connections to other nodes, although you can later move nodes into the tree structure or out of the tree structure as the needs of your analysis require. In this way, N6 helps to organize your ideas, as your thinking about the project is being developed and mapped out in the node structure.

The two main ways of searching a body of data are called text search and node search. Text search is a powerful tool to find strings of words or whole phrases. By default each search operates on all your documents, but you can tailor any search to just a subset in which you are interested. Text search even allows you to develop lists of alternative words or phrases. Because there can be more than one way of expressing an idea, just searching for a single word might not capture all the expressions of the meaning. This is why alternative phrase searches are powerful. Each text search becomes a node itself. Of course, qualitative data is about meaning. The wise qualitative researcher will never be restricted to just searching for specific words, or even to a lot of alternative ways of expression. The experienced researcher knows that there is no substitute for a close personal reading of the text to engage with the meanings being communicated. This is why node searches are important.

Node searches involve relationships between nodes. The researcher asks whether there is any text in common with node A and node B. The search immediately presents the researcher with all text coded in common. The search find then becomes a new node. When you have found the text you want, what do you do? You simply highlight the text and copy it to the Windows clipboard and then paste it into your word processor.

Some of the reasons N6 is helpful to qualitative researchers are:

* *N6 is a very robust piece of software*. Rarely will one see the 'blue death' of a major fault. And N6 constantly saves its files. It is a database and so every major change to the database – new document or node, text coded or searches done – initiates a save operation. You can easily back up your project to another medium (another drive or removable disk).
* *N6 helps document your research journey*. Each document and node can have an attached memo which is like a file describing what it does and why it is used. You might

use such memos to describe how you understand certain concepts (nodes) and other memos might be your reflective research journal. As you move and develop nodes, perform searches and reorganize your node tree, N6 date stamps what you did and creates a brief record of your actions. N6 even allows you to annotate parts of your documents – a bit like a coloured Post-it note that many use to mark important parts. All this is kept together and updated and saved with the project.

- *N6 has logical closure.* This means that everything you do in N6 becomes part of N6 and can be utilized in N6. Each and every search produces a node which can itself be searched, moved into the organizational tree and even be made a free node. Memos can also become part of the N6 data. A report produced in N6 can be copied and pasted to a word processor and it is also a node and can be further manipulated in N6.
- *N6 is inclusive.* By default all documents (or nodes) are part of document (or node) searches. You have full control to change this, so you can restrict searches to particular documents (or nodes). Versatility is a strength of N6.
- Perhaps most importantly, *N6 enables better analysis.* It keeps you close to your data. It encourages the creative question by making node searches speedy, convenient and definitive – because it immediately shows you the data as the results of the search. This means that you can ask a 'What if?' type question and get a split-second response. You can also try out multiple conjectures and explore lines of tentative inquiry quickly, efficiently and conclusively. As your analysis progresses you can grow or prune your node structure to reflect your theoretical structures. You might be wise to save copies of your project before major pruning so that you can come back to a previous construction.

N6 comes with the *Reference Manual* (QSR, 2002) and another text to guide your learning (Morse and Richards, 2002). These are easy-to-read and complete documents. The N6 online help is very good. It is also context sensitive, so the help mirrors where you are in the program.

## NOTES

1 NUD·IST stands for Non-numerical Unstructured Data: Indexing, Searching and Theorizing.
2 NVivo is also widely used today. NVivo is a companion product to N6, not its successor or replacement. NVivo does a different sort of qualitative analysis. NVivo's strengths lie in its use of rich text (rtf files rather than txt or ASCII files), data documents other than word (e.g. pictures and sound), and its very fine-grained analysis of the data. NVivo has several limitations that N6 does not suffer: it has no command or auto-program facilities, and does not offer the wide user base that N6 enjoys.

# Appendix 2: Drawing and Verifying Conclusions in Qualitative Analysis

This appendix contains the two lists of tactics given by Miles and Huberman (1994), the first for generating meaning in qualitative analysis, and the second for testing or confirming findings. All tactics in both lists are described and discussed in the Miles and Huberman book.

Both sets of tactics fit within the set of six 'fairly classic' analytic moves noted by Miles and Huberman (1994: 8) as common general features of different approaches to qualitative analysis:

- affixing codes to a set of field notes drawn from observations or interviews
- noting reflections or other remarks in the margins
- sorting and sifting through these materials to identify similar phrases, relationships between variables, patterns, themes, distinct differences between subgroups, and common sequences
- isolating these patterns and processes, commonalities and differences, and taking them out to the field in the next wave of data collection
- gradually elaborating a small set of generalizations that cover the consistencies discerned in the databases
- confronting those generalizations with a formalized body of knowledge in the form of constructs or theories.

## A2.1 Tactics for Generating Meaning

These tactics are numbered from 1 to 13. They are arranged roughly from the descriptive to the explanatory, and from the concrete to the more conceptual and abstract. They are briefly overviewed and then listed.

Noting patterns, themes (1), seeing plausibility (2), and clustering (3) help the analyst see 'what goes with what'. Making metaphors (4), like the preceding three tactics, is a way to achieve more integration among diverse pieces of data. Counting (5) is also a familiar way to see 'what's there'.

Making contrasts/comparisons (6) is a pervasive tactic that sharpens understanding. Differentiation sometimes is needed, too, as in partitioning variables (7).

We also need tactics for seeing things and their relationships more abstractly. These include subsuming particulars into the general (8); factoring (9), an analogue of a familiar quantitative technique; noting relations between variables (10); and finding intervening variables (11).

Finally, how can we systematically assemble a coherent understanding of data? The tactics discussed are building a logical chain of evidence (12) and making conceptual/theoretical coherence (13).

The 13 tactics are:

1   noting patterns, themes
2   seeing plausibility
3   clustering
4   making metaphors
5   counting
6   making contrasts/comparisons
7   partitioning variables
8   subsuming particulars into the general
9   factoring
10  noting relations between variables
11  finding intervening variables
12  building a logical chain of evidence
13  making conceptual/theoretical coherence (1994: 245–62)

## A2.2 Tactics for Testing or Confirming Findings

These tactics are also numbered from 1 to 13, beginning with those aimed at ensuring the basic quality of the data, then moving to those that check findings by examining exceptions to early patterns. They conclude with tactics that take a sceptical, demanding approach to emerging explanations.

Data quality can be assessed through checking for representativeness (1); checking for researcher effects (2) on the case, and vice versa; and triangulating (3) across data sources and methods. These checks also may involve weighting the evidence (4), deciding which kinds of data are most trustable.

Looking at 'unpatterns' can tell us a lot. Checking the meaning of outliers (5), using extreme cases (6), following up surprises (7), and looking for negative evidence (8) are all tactics that test a conclusion about a 'pattern' by saying what it is not like.

How can we really test our explanations?  Making if–then tests (9), ruling out spurious relations (10), replicating a finding (11), and checking out rival explanations (12) are all ways of submitting our beautiful theories to the assault of brute facts, or to a race with someone else's beautiful theory.

Finally, a good explanation deserves attention from the very people whose behaviour it is about – informants who supplied the original data. The tactic of getting feedback from informants (13) concludes the list.

The 13 tactics are:

1   checking for representativeness
2   checking for researcher effects
3   triangulating
4   weighting the evidence
5   checking the meaning of outliers
6   using extreme cases
7   following up surprises
8   looking for negative evidence
9   making if–then tests
10   ruling out spurious relations
11   replicating a finding
12   checking out rival explanations
13   getting feedback from informants (1994: 262–77).

# Glossary

Readers using this book to support the Open University course EK310 ('Research with Children and Young People'), may also want to refer to the booklet *Key Research Terms* (2004) prepared by the course team. Where a term is in this glossary and also in the *Key Research Terms* booklet, page numbers to the latter entry are given below after the abbreviation 'KRT'.

**Accounting for variance** – a central strategy in quantitative research; accounting for the variation in a dependent variable through studying its relationship with independent variables.

**Action research** – using empirical procedures, in iterative cycles of action and research, to solve practical problems. (KRT: 2)

**Analysis of covariance** – a statistical technique for investigating the difference between groups on some dependent variable after controlling for one or more covariates. (KRT: 2–3)

**Analysis of variance** – a statistical technique for investigating differences between groups on some dependent variable. (KRT: 3–4)

**Audit trail** (through the data) – showing how the data were analysed to arrive at conclusions.

**Axial coding** – discovering connections in the data between abstract concepts; used in grounded theory analysis; produces theoretical codes. (KRT: 5)

**Case study** – a research strategy which focuses on the in-depth, holistic and in-context study of one or more cases; will typically use multiple sources of data.

**Chi square** – a statistical technique with many uses; a common use is to see whether variables in a cross-tabulation are related to each other. (KRT: 5–6)

**Coding** – placing labels or tags on pieces of qualitative data. (KRT: 7–8)

**Conceptual framework** – a framework showing the central concepts of a piece of research, and their conceptual status with respect to each other; often expressed as a diagram.

**Contingency table** – uses cross-tabulation to see if the distribution of one variable is related to (or contingent upon) the other variable. (KRT: 10)

**Continuous variable** – a variable which varies in degree rather than in kind (e.g. height, level of income, level of achievement); synonym is measured variable.

**Control variable** – a variable whose effect we want to rule out, or control; synonym is covariate. (KRT: 11)

**Correlation** – a statistical technique for showing the strength and direction of the relationship between two variables. (KRT: 12)

**Correlational survey** – a quantitative survey where the focus is on studying the relationships between variables.

**Covariate** – see control variable. (KRT: 12)

**Cross-tabulation** – two variables are cross-tabulated against each other. (KRT: 13–14)

**Data collection questions** – the actual questions asked to collect the data; examples are survey questions in quantitative research, and interview questions in qualitative research; data collection questions follow logically from specific research questions.

**Deduction** – moving downward in levels of abstraction, from more general and abstract to more specific and concrete; opposite of induction.

**Definitions** – *conceptual* definition: the definition of a concept (or variable) in terms of other abstract concepts. This brings the need to find observable activities which are indicators of the concept. Those activities constitute the *operational* definition of the concept. Construct validity is enhanced when there are tight logical links between the conceptual and operational definitions.

**Deliberate** (or purposive) sampling – the sample is drawn from the population in a deliberate or targeted way, according to the logic of the research.

**Dependent variable** – the variable seen as the 'effect' in a cause–effect relationship. Synonyms are: outcome variable in experimental design; criterion variable in a correlational survey. (KRT: 14)

**Discourse** – a system of language which draws on a particular terminology and which encodes specific forms of knowledge; often used to refer to systems of knowledge and their associated practices (Seale, 1998; Tonkiss, 1998). (KRT: 14–15)

**Discrete variable** – a variable which varies in kind, not degree; its variance is in categories (e.g. eye colour, religious affiliation, country of birth); synonyms are categorical variable, discontinuous variable.

**Empirical** – based on direct experience or observation of the world.

**Empirical criterion** (for a research question) – is it clear what data are needed to answer this research question? If yes, the research question satisfies the empirical criterion. If no, further development of the research question is necessary.

**Empiricism** – philosophical term to describe the epistemological theory that sees experience as the foundation or source of knowledge.

**Ethnography** – the preferred research strategy of anthropologists; seeks to understand the symbolic significance of behaviour, in its cultural context, to the participants; aims for a full cultural description of the way of life of some group of people. (KRT: 15–16)

**Ethnomethodology** – examines how people produce orderly social interaction in ordinary everyday situations; exposes the taken-for-granted 'rules' which constitute the infrastructure making everyday social interaction possible. (KRT: 16)

**Experiment** – a predominantly quantitative research design where [a] one or more independent variables are manipulated to study their effect on a dependent variable and [b] participants are randomly assigned to treatment or comparison groups. (KRT: 16)

**Factor analysis** – a family of statistical techniques for reducing the number of variables without loss of information.

**Fact–value gap** – the view that statements of fact and statements of value have no *logical* connection between them.

**Focus group** (interview) – a powerful method of qualitative data collection where a small group (6–8) of people are interviewed as a group. (KRT: 17–18)

**Frequency distribution** – a table or diagram showing the distribution of a set of scores. (KRT: 19)

**Grounded theory** – a distinctive strategy for research which aims to generate explanatory theory grounded in data. (KRT: 20)

**Grounded theory analysis** – specific procedures in the analysis of data for generating explanatory theory; focuses essentially on raising the conceptual level of (i.e. reconceptualizing) the data.

**Hierarchy of concepts** – a useful tool in planning and organizing research; the hierarchy is area-topic-general research questions-specific research questions-data collection questions.

**Hypothesis** – a predicted answer to a research question; in theory verification research the hypothesis follows from the theory by deduction.

**Hypothetico-deductive model** – the central strategy of theory verification research which stresses the empirical testing of hypotheses deduced from theory. A *hypothesis* is *deduced* from a *theory* and then tested against data.

**Independent variable** – the variable seen as the 'cause' in a cause–effect relationship. (Synonyms are: treatment variable in experimental design; predictor variable in a correlational survey). (KRT: 20)

**Induction** – moving upwards in levels of abstraction, from more specific and concrete to more general and abstract; opposite of deduction.

**Interaction** – a technical term in quantitative research design; two (or more) independent variables may interact in their effect on a dependent variable. (KRT: 21)

**Latent trait** – the trait (or variable) we want to measure is hidden; we measure it by inference from its observable indicators.

**Measurement** – the operation which turns data into numbers.

**Member checking** – the qualitative researcher checks the data and the analysis as it develops with the people being studied, who gave the data; typical in grounded theory research.

**Memoing** – pausing, in qualitative analysis especially, to write down ideas about the data as they occur during coding and analysis.

**Mixed-method research** – empirical research which brings together quantitative data (and methods) and qualitative data (and methods); there are many models for doing this.

**Multiple causation** – the idea that a particular 'effect' has multiple causes which are usually interrelated.

**Multiple linear regression** – a quantitative design and data analysis strategy with several independent variables and one dependent variable; aims to account for variance in the dependent variable.

**Multivariate** – more than one dependent variable.

**Naturalism** – the social world is studied in its natural state, rather than contrived for research purposes. (KRT: 31)

**Negative correlation** – high scores on one variable go with low scores on the other variable (and vice versa); as one variable goes up, the other variable goes down.

**Open coding** – concentrates on raising the conceptual level of the data; guided by the question: what is this piece of data an example of? Used in grounded theory analysis; produces substantive codes. (KRT: 31)

**Operationalism** – in quantitative research, the idea that the meaning of a concept is given by the set of operations necessary to measure it (see definitions – operational).

**Paradigm** – a set of assumptions about the social world, and about what constitute proper techniques and topics for inquiring into that world; a set of basic beliefs, a world view, a view of how science should be done (ontology, epistemology, methodology).

**Participant observation** – the preferred strategy for doing ethnography; the researcher aims to be both observer of and participant in the situation being studied, in order to understand it. (KRT: 34)

**Population** – the target group, usually large, about whom we want to develop knowledge, but which we cannot study directly; therefore we sample from that population.

**Positive correlation** – high scores on one variable go with high scores on the other variable (and vice versa); the two variables go up or down together. (KRT: 34)

**Positivism** – in a loose sense, has come to mean an approach to social research that emphasizes the discovery of general laws, and separates facts from values; it often involves an empiricist commitment to naturalism and quantitative methods (Seale, 1998: 328).

**Purposive** (or deliberate sampling) – the sample is drawn from the population in a deliberate or targeted way, according to the logic of the research.

**Quasi-experiment** – naturally occurring treatment groups permit comparisons between the groups approximating those of true experimental design. (KRT: 38)

**Reactivity** – the idea that the data being collected might be somehow changed or influenced by the data collection process itself.

**Regression** – a statistical technique for predicting scores on one variable from scores on another variable. (KRT: 40–1)

**Reliability** (of data) – in quantitative research, the consistency of measurement: [a] consistency over time – test-retest reliability; [b] consistency within indicators – internal consistency reliability. In qualitative research, the dependability of the data. (KRT: 41)

**Representative sampling** – a sampling strategy where each unit of the population has an equal chance of being selected in the sample; directed at generalization. (KRT: 41)

**Research questions** – organize the research by showing its purposes. General research questions guide the research by showing the general questions the research aims to answer; too general themselves to be answered directly; need to be made more specific. Specific research questions make the general research questions more specific; connect the general research questions to the data.

**Sample** – a smaller group which is actually studied, drawn from a larger population; data are collected (and analysed) from the sample, and inferences are then made to the population. (KRT: 41–3)

**Science as method** – an empirical method for building knowledge where the objective is to develop and test theory to explain data. Theory generation research-generating theory from data; theory verification research – testing theory against data.

**Secondary analysis** – the re-analysis of previously collected and analysed data.

**Selective coding** – used in grounded theory analysis; identifies the core category of a grounded theory, and raises the conceptual level of the analysis a second time. (KRT: 43)

**Semiotics** – the science of signs; focuses on the process whereby something comes to stand for something else.

**Sensitivity** (of measurement) – the ability of a measuring instrument to produce (reliable) variance, to differentiate between the people being measured.

**Statistical inference** – a set of decision making rules to assess the accuracy of the inference made from sample to population.

**Statistically significant** – using inferential statistics to conclude that a particular result is very unlikely to have occurred by chance; such a result is therefore taken as real. (KRT: 44, 46–7)

**Structured interview** – interview questions are pre-established and have pre-set response categories. (KRT: 47)

**T test** – a statistical technique for investigating differences between two groups on some dependent variable; a special case of analysis of variance. (KRT: 48)

**Theoretical sampling** – consecutive cycles of data collection are guided by the theoretical directions emerging from the ongoing analysis (see Figure 8.1); typically used in grounded theory research. (KRT: 47–8)

**Theoretical saturation** – the 'end-stage' of theoretical sampling in grounded theory research, when new data are not showing new theoretical elements, but rather confirming what has already been found.

**Theoretical sensitivity** – a term used in grounded theory; being alive and sensitive to the theoretical possibilities in the data; the ability to 'see', with theoretical and analytic depth, what is in the data.

**Theory** – explanatory theory – a set of propositions which explain the data; the concepts in the propositions of the explanatory theory are more abstract than those in the data.

**Theory generation research** – empirical research where the objective is discovering or constructing theory to explain data; starts with data, ends with theory.

**Theory verification research** – empirical research where the objective is testing theory against data; starts with theory, uses data to test the theory (see hypothetico-deductive method).

**Thick description** – the emphasis in qualitative research on capturing and conveying the full picture of behaviour being studied – holistically, comprehensively and in context.

**Triangulation** – using several kinds of methods or data to study a topic; the most common type is data triangulation, where a study uses a variety of data sources. (KRT: 49)

**Univariate** – only one dependent variable.

**Unstructured interview** – interview questions and response categories are not pre-established; interview questions are deliberately open-ended. (KRT: 49–50)

**Validity** – a complex term with many meanings, both technical and general; three important technical meanings are: the validity of a measuring instrument; the validity of a research design (internal validity); the truth status of a research report. (KRT: 50)

**Validity** (of measurement) – the extent to which a measuring instrument measures what it is supposed to measure.

    **Content (or face) validity**: How well does the measuring instrument sample from all areas of content in the conceptual description?

    **Criterion related validity**:

        *Concurrent validity*: How does the measuring instrument compare with another measure of the same construct?

        *Predictive validity*: How well does the measuring instrument predict later behaviour?

    **Construct validity**: How well does the measuring instrument conform with theoretical expectations?

**Value judgements** – moral or ethical judgements; judgements of what is good or bad, right or wrong etc.; usually made as terminal values – ends in themselves.

# References

Ackoff, R. (1953) *The Design of Social Research*. Chicago: University of Chicago Press.

Adler, P.A. and Adler, P. (1994) 'Observational techniques', in N.K. Denzin and Y.S. Lincoln (eds), *Handbook of Qualitative Research*. Thousand Oaks, CA: Sage. pp. 377–92.

American Educational Research Association (1992) 'Ethical standards of the American Educational Research Association', *Educational Researcher*, 21 (7): 23–6.

American Psychological Association (1992) 'Ethical principles of psychologists and code of conduct', *American Psychologist*, 47 (12): 1597–628.

American Sociological Association (1989) *Code of Ethics*. Washington, DC: ASA.

Anastasi, A. (1988) *Psychological Testing*. 6th edn. New York: Macmillan.

Andrich, D. (1988) *Rasch Models for Measurement*. Newbury Park, CA: Sage.

Andrich, D. (1997) 'Rating scale analysis', in J.P. Keeves (ed.), *Educational Research, Methodology, and Measurement: An International Handbook*. 2nd end. Oxford: Elsevier. pp. 874–80.

Anward, J. (1997) 'Semiotics in educational research', in J.P. Keeves (ed.), *Educational Research, Methodology, and Measurement: An International Handbook*. 2nd edn. Oxford: Elsevier. pp. 106–11.

Apple, M. (1991) 'Introduction', in P. Lather, *Getting Smart: Feminist Research and Pedagogy With/In the Postmodern*. New York: Routledge.

Asch, S.E. (1955) 'Opinions and social pressure', *Scientific American*, 193: 31–5.

Asher, H.B. (1976) *Causal Modeling*. Beverly Hills, CA: Sage.

Atkinson, J.M. (1978) *Discovering Suicide: Studies in the Social Organization of Sudden Death*. London: Macmillan.

Atkinson, P. (1992) *Understanding Ethnographic Texts*. Newbury Park, CA: Sage.

Atkinson, P. and Hammersley, M. (1994) 'Ethnography and participant observation', in N.K. Denzin and Y.S. Lincoln (eds), *Handbook of Qualitative Research*. Thousand Oaks, CA: Sage. pp. 248–61.

Ball, S.J. (1981) *Beachside Comprehensive: A Case Study of Secondary Schooling*. Cambridge: Cambridge University Press.

Bardack, N.R. and McAndrew, F.T. (1985) 'The influence of physical attractiveness and manner of dress on success in a simulated personnel decision', *Journal of Social Psychology*, 125: 777–8.

Barker, R.G. and Gump, P.V. (1964) *Big School, Small School: High School Size and Student Behavior*. Stanford, CA: Stanford University Press.

Bean, J. and Creswell, J.W. (1980) 'Student attrition among women at a liberal arts college', *Journal of College Student Personnel*, 3: 320–7.

Becker, H. (1971) *Sociological Work*. London: Allen Lane.

Behar, R. (1993) *Translated Woman: Crossing the Border with Esperanza's Story*. Boston: Beacon.

Berden, M. and Mies, M. (1981) 'Experimenting with a new methodological approach: "Fieldwork"', in *Women's Studies, Institute of Social Studies, 1979–81*. The Hague: Institute of Social Studies.

Berelson, B. (1952) *Content Analysis in Communication Research*. New York: Hafner.

Berger, P.L. and Kellner, H. (1981) *Sociology Reinterpreted: An Essay on Method and Vocation*. Garden City, NY: Anchor/Doubleday.

Berger, P.L. and Luckman, T. (1967) *The Social Construction of Reality*. Harmondsworth, Middlesex: Allen Lane.

Billig, M. (1991) *Ideologies and Beliefs*. London: Sage.

Blaikie, N. (1993) *Approaches to Social Enquiry*. Cambridge: Polity.

Blau, P.M. and Duncan, O.D. (1967) *The American Occupational Structure*. New York: Wiley.

Blommaert, J. and Bulcaen, C. (2000) 'Critical discourse analysis', *Annual Review of Anthropology*, 29: 447–66.

Bloor, M. (1978) 'On the analysis of observational data: a discussion of the worth and uses of inductive techniques and respondent validation', *Sociology*, 12 (3): 545–52.

Blumer, H. (1969) *Symbolic Interactionism: Perspective and Method*. Englewood Cliffs, NJ: Prentice-Hall.

Bracht, G.H. and Glass, G.V. (1968) 'The external validity of experiments', *American Educational Research Journal*, 5 (4): 437–74.

Brandt, R.M. (1981) *Studying Behavior in Natural Settings*. Washington, DC: University Press of America.

Brannen, J. (ed.) (1992) *Mixing Methods: Qualitative and Quantitative Research*. Aldershot: Avebury.

Brewer, J. and Hunter, A. (1989) *Multimethod Research: A Synthesis of Styles*. Newbury Park, CA: Sage.

Brodbeck, M. (ed.) (1968) *Readings in the Philosophy of the Social Sciences*. London: Macmillan.

Brody, H. (1987) *Stories of Sickness*. New Haven, CT: Yale University Press.

Broudy, H.S., Ennis, R.H. and Krimerman, L.I. (1973) *Philosophy of Educational Research*. New York: Wiley.

Brown, G. and Yule, G. (1984) *Discourse Analysis*. Cambridge: Cambridge University Press.

Bryman, A. (1988) *Quantity and Quality in Social Research*. London: Unwin Hyman.

Bryman, A. (1992) 'Quantitative and qualitative research: further reflections on their integration', in J. Brannen (ed.), *Mixing Methods: Qualitative and Quantitative Research*. Aldershot: Avebury. pp. 57–78.

Burns, R.B. (1995) *Introduction to Research Methods*. Melbourne: Longman.

Calder, J. and Sapsford, R. (1996) 'Multivariate analysis', in R. Sapsford and V. Jupp (eds), *Data Collection and Analysis*. London: Sage. pp. 262–381.

Campbell, D.T. and Ross, H.L. (1968) 'The Connecticut crackdown on speeding: time-series data in quasi-experiment analysis', *Law and Society Review*, 3: 33–53.

Campbell, D.T. and Stanley, J.C. (1963) *Experimental and Quasi-Experimental Designs for Research*. Chicago: Rand McNally. pp. 37–64.

Campbell, J.P., Daft, R.L. and Hulin, C.L. (1982) *What to Study: Generating and Developing Research Questions*. Beverly Hills, CA: Sage.

Cassell, J. and Jacobs, S.E. (1987) *Handbook on Ethical Issues in Anthropology*. Washington, DC: American Anthropological Association.

Cauhape, E. (1983) *Fresh Starts: Men and Women after Divorce*. New York: Basic.

Charlesworth, M., Farrall, L., Stokes, T. and Turnbull, D. (1989) *Life among the Scientists: An Anthropological Study of an Australian Scientific Community*. Melbourne: Oxford University Press.

Charmaz, K. (1983) 'The grounded theory method: an explication and interpretation', in R. Emerson (ed.), *Contemporary Field Research*. Boston: Little Brown. pp. 109–26.

Charters, W.W. Jr (1967) 'The hypothesis in scientific research'. Unpublished paper, University of Oregon, Eugene.

Chenitz, W.C. (1986) 'Getting started: the research proposal for a grounded theory study', in W.C. Chenitz and J.M. Swanson (eds), *From Practice to Grounded Theory: Qualitative Research in Nursing*. Menlo Park, CA: Addison-Wesley.

Chenitz, W.C. and Swanson, J.M. (eds) (1986) *From Practice to Grounded Theory: Qualitative Research in Nursing*. Menlo Park, CA: Addison-Wesley.

Clandinin, D.J. and Connelly, F.M. (1994) 'Personal experience methods', in N.K. Denzin and Y.S. Lincoln (eds), *Handbook of Qualitative Research*. Thousand Oaks, CA: Sage. pp. 413–27.

Coakes, Sheridan, J. and Steed, Lyndall, G. (2003) *SPSS Analysis without Anguish: Version for Windows*. Milton, Queensland: Wiley.

Cochran, W.G. (1977) *Sampling Techniques*. 3rd edn. New York: Wiley.

Coffey, A. and Atkinson, P. (1996) *Making Sense of Qualitative Data: Complementary Research Strategies*. Thousand Oaks, CA: Sage.

Coleman, J.S., Campbell, E.Q., Hobson, C.J., McPartland, J., Mood, A.M., Weinfeld, F.D. and York, R.L. (1966) *Equality of Educational Opportunity*. Washington, DC: US Government Printing Office.

Coles, R. (1989) *The Call of Stories*. Boston: Houghton Mifflin.

Converse, J.M. and Presser, S. (1986) *Survey Questions: Handcrafting the Standardized Questionnaire*. Beverly Hills, CA: Sage.

Corbin, J. (1986) 'Coding, writing memos and diagramming', in W.C. Chenitz and J.M. Swanson (eds), *From Practice to Grounded Theory: Qualitative Research in Nursing*. Menlo Park, CA: Addison-Wesley. pp. 102–20.

Coulthard, M. (1985) *An Introduction to Discourse Analysis*. 2nd edn. London: Longman.

Cressey, D.R. (1950) 'The criminal violation of financial trust', *American Sociological Review*, 15: 738–43.

Cressey, D.R. (1971) *Other People's Money: A Study in the Social Psychology of Embezzlement*. 2nd edn. Belmont, CA: Wadsworth.

Creswell, J.W. (1994) *Research Design: Qualitative and Quantitative Approaches*. Thousand Oaks, CA: Sage.

Creswell, J.W. and Brown, M.L. (1992) 'How chairpersons enhance faculty research: a grounded theory study', *The Review of Higher Education*, 16 (1): 41–62.

Cronbach, L.J. (1951) 'Coefficient alpha and the internal structure of tests', *Psychometrika*, 16: 297–334.

Cronbach, L.J. (1957) 'The two disciplines of scientific psychology', *American Psychologist*, 12: 671–84.

Cronbach, L.J. and Suppes, P. (eds) (1969) *Research for Tomorrow's Schools: Disciplined Inquiry for Education*. New York: Macmillan.

Dale, A., Arber, S. and Procter, M. (1988) *Doing Secondary Analysis*. London: Unwin Hyman.

Dannefer, D. (1981) 'Neither socialization nor recruitment: the avocational careers of old car enthusiasts', *Social Forces*, 60: 395–413.

Davis, J.A. (1985) *The Logic of Causal Order*. Beverly Hills, CA: Sage.

Davis, M.Z. (1973) *Living with Multiple Sclerosis: A Social Psychological Analysis*. Springfield, IL: Thomas.

DeCasper, H.S. (1988) 'Use of the Georgia eighth grade criterion-referenced test: reports by ninth grade teachers', in R.M. Jaeger (ed.), *Complementary Methods for Research in Education*. Washington, DC: American Educational Research Association. pp. 341–87.

de Vaus, D.A. (1991) *Surveys in Social Research*. 3rd edn. London: Allen and Unwin.

de Vaus, D.A. and McAllister, I. (1987) 'Gender differences in religion: a test of structural location theory', *American Sociological Review*, 52: 472–81.

Delamont, S. (1989) 'The nun in the toilet: urban legends and educational research', *International Journal of Qualitative Studies in Education*, 2 (3): 191–202.

Delamont, S. (1990) *Sex Roles and the School*. 2nd edn. London: Routledge and Kegan Paul.

Denzin, N.K. (1983) 'Interpretive interactionism', in G. Morgan (ed.), *Beyond Method: Strategies for Social Research*. Beverly Hills, CA: Sage. pp. 129–46.

Denzin, N.K. (1988) 'Qualitative Analysis for Social Scientists: book review', Contemporary Sociology, 17 (3): 430–2.

Denzin, N.K. (1989) The Research Act: A Theoretical Introduction to Sociological Methods. 3rd edn. New York: McGraw–Hill.

Denzin, N.K. and Lincoln, Y.S. (eds) (1994) Handbook of Qualitative Research. Thousand Oaks, CA: Sage.

Derrida, J. (1984) 'Deconstruction and the Other', in R. Kearney (ed.), Dialogues with Contemporary Continental Thinkers. Manchester: Manchester University Press. pp. 107–26.

Dey, I. (1993) Qualitative Data Analysis: A User-Friendly Guide for Social Scientists. London: Routledge.

Douglas, J.D. (1985) Creative Interviewing. Beverly Hills, CA: Sage.

Durkheim, E. (1951) Suicide: A Study in Sociology. Trans. J. Spaulding and G. Sampson. Glencoe, IL: Free Press.

Eco, U. (1976) A Theory of Semiotics. Bloomington, IN: Indiana University Press.

Edley, N. (2001) 'Analysing masculinity: interpretive repertoires, ideological dilemmas and subject positions', in M. Wetherell, S. Taylor and S.J. Yates (eds), Discourse as Data: A Guide for Analysis. London: Sage. pp. 189–228.

Edwards, A.L. (1957) Techniques of Attitude Scale Construction. New York: Appleton-Century-Crofts.

Eichler, M. (1986) 'The relationship between sexist, nonsexist, woman-centred and feminist research', Studies in Communication, 3: 37–74.

Eisner, E.W. (1991) The Enlightened Eye: Qualitative Inquiry and the Enhancement of Educational Practice. New York: Macmillan.

Ekman, P., Friesen, W.V., O'Sullivan, M., et al. (1987) 'Universals and cultural differences in the judgments of facial expressions of emotion', Journal of Personality and Social Psychology, 53: 712–17.

Enns, C.Z. and Hackett, G. (1990) 'Comparison of feminist and non-feminist women's reactions to variants of non-sexist and feminist counseling', Journal of Counseling Psychology, 37 (1): 33–40.

Erickson, F. (1986) 'Qualitative methods in research on teaching', in M.C. Wittrock (ed.), Handbook of Research on Teaching. 3rd edn. New York: Macmillan. pp. 119–61.

ESDS (2004) ESDS Qualidata website. Economic and Social Data Service. http://www.esds.ac.uk/qualidata/about/introduction.asp

Fairclough, N. (2001) Language and Power. 2nd edn. London: Longman.

Feldman, M. (1995) Strategies for Interpreting Qualitative Data. Thousand Oaks, CA: Sage.

Festinger, L., Riecken, H.W. and Schachter, S. (1964) When Prophecy Fails: A Social and Psychological Study of a Modern Group that Predicted the Destruction of the World. New York: Harper Torchbooks.

Fetterman, D.M. (1989) Ethnography Step by Step. Newbury Park, CA: Sage.

Fielding, N. (1981) The National Front. London: Routledge and Kegan Paul.

Fielding, N. (1996a) 'Ethnography', in N. Gilbert (ed.), Researching Social Life. London: Sage. pp. 154–71.

Fielding, N. (1996b) 'Qualitative interviewing', in N. Gilbert (ed.), Researching Social Life. London: Sage. pp. 135–53.

Fielding, N.G. and Fielding, J.L. (1986) Linking Data. Beverly Hills, CA: Sage.

Finnegan, R. (1996) 'Using documents', in R. Sapsford and V. Jupp (eds), Data Collection and Analysis. London: Sage. pp. 138–51.

Firestone, W.A. (1993) 'Alternative arguments for generalizing from data as applied to qualitative research', Educational Researcher, 22 (4): 16–23.

Foddy, W. (1993) Constructing Questions for Interviews and Questionnaires: Theory and Practice in Social Research. Cambridge: Cambridge University Press.

Fonow, M.M. and Cook, J.A. (eds) (1991) *Beyond Methodology: Feminist Scholarship as Lived Research.* Bloomington, IN: Indiana University Press.

Fontana, A. and Frey, J.H. (1994) 'Interviewing: the art of science', in N.K. Denzin and Y.S. Lincoln (eds), *Handbook of Qualitative Research.* Thousand Oaks, CA: Sage. pp. 361–76.

Foster, P. (1996a) 'Observational research', in R. Sapsford and V. Jupp (eds), *Data Collection and Analysis.* London: Sage. pp. 57–93.

Foster, P. (1996b) *Observing Schools: A Methodological Guide.* London: Chapman.

Foucault, M. (1980) *Power/Knowledge: Selected Interviews and Other Writings 1972–1977.* Brighton: Harvester.

Frey, J.H. (1993) 'Risk perceptions associated with a high-level nuclear waste repository', *Sociological Spectrum,* 13: 139–51.

Friedenberg, L. (1995) *Psychological Testing: Design, Analysis and Use.* Boston: Allyn and Bacon.

Garfinkel, H. (1967) *Studies in Ethnomethodology.* Englewood Cliffs, NJ: Prentice-Hall.

Gee, J.P., Michaels, S. and O'Connor, M.C. (1992) 'Discourse analysis', in M.D. LeCompte, W.L. Millroy and J. Preissle (eds), *The Handbook of Qualitative Research in Education.* San Diego, CA: Academic. pp. 227–91.

Gilbert, G.N. and Mulkay, M.J. (1984) *Opening Pandora's Box: A Sociological Analysis of Scientists' Discourse.* Cambridge: Cambridge University Press.

Gilbert, N. (1996) 'Writing about social research', in N. Gilbert (ed.), *Researching Social Life.* London: Sage. pp. 328–44.

Glaser, B. (1978) *Theoretical Sensitivity.* Mill Valley, CA: Sociology Press.

Glaser, B. (1992) *Basics of Grounded Theory Analysis: Emergence vs Forcing.* Mill Valley, CA: Sociology Press.

Glaser, B. (ed.) (1993) *Examples of Grounded Theory: A Reader.* Mill Valley, CA: Sociology Press.

Glaser, B. (ed.) (1994) *More Grounded Theory Methodology: A Reader.* Mill Valley, CA: Sociology Press.

Glaser, B. and Strauss, A. (1965) *Awareness of Dying.* Chicago: Aldine.

Glaser, B. and Strauss, A. (1967) *The Discovery of Grounded Theory: Strategies for Qualitative Research.* Chicago: Aldine.

Glaser, B. and Strauss, A. (1968) *Time for Dying.* Chicago: Aldine.

Glass, G.V., Cahen, L.S., Smith, M.L. and Filby, N.N. (1982) *School Class Size: Research and Policy.* Beverly Hills, CA: Sage. pp. 33–50.

Glass, G.V. (1988) 'Quasi-experiments: the case of interrupted time series', in R.M. Jaeger (ed.), *Complementary Methods for Research in Education.* Washington, DC: American Educational Research Association. pp. 445–61.

Gluck, S.B. (1991) 'Advocacy oral history: Palestinian women in resistance', in S.B. Gluck and D. Patai (eds), *Women's Words: The Feminist Practice of Oral History.* London: Routledge. pp. 205–20.

Goffman, E. (1961) *Asylums: Essays on the Social Situation of Mental Patients and Other Inmates.* Harmondsworth, Middlesex: Penguin.

Gogolin, L. and Swartz, F. (1992) 'A quantitative and qualitative inquiry into attitudes toward science of nonscience college students', *Journal of Research in Science Teaching,* 29 (5): 487–504.

Gold, R.L. (1958) 'Roles in sociological field observations', *Social Forces,* 36: 217–23.

Goldman, B.A. and Mitchell, D.F. (eds) (1996) *Directory of Unpublished Experimental Mental Measures.* Vol. 6. Washington, DC: American Psychological Association.

Goode, W.J. and Hatt, P.K. (1952) 'The case study', in W.J. Goode and P.K. Hatt (eds), *Methods of Social Research.* New York: McGraw-Hill. pp. 330–40.

Goodson, I. (1992) *Studying Teachers' Lives.* London: Routledge and Kegan Paul.

Gordon, V. (1992) 'Treatment of depressed women by nurses', in P.A. Abbott and R.J. Sapsford (eds), *Research into Practice: A Reader for Nurses and the Caring Professions*. Buckingham: Open University Press.

Greene, J.C., Caracelli, V.J. and Graham, W.F. (1989) 'Towards a conceptual framework for mixed-method evaluation designs', *Educational Evaluation and Policy Analysis*, 11 (3): 255–74.

Greenwood, E. (1968) 'The practice of science and the science of practice', in W.G. Bennis, K.D. Benne and R. Chin (eds), *The Planning of Change*. New York: Holt, Rinehart and Winston. pp. 73–82.

Guba, E.G. and Lincoln, Y.S. (1994) 'Competing paradigms in qualitative research', in N.K. Denzin and Y.S. Lincoln (eds), *Handbook of Qualitative Research*. Thousand Oaks, CA: Sage. pp. 105–17.

Gubrium, J.F. and Holstein, J.A. (2000) 'Analyzing interpretive practice', in N.K. Denzin and Y.S. Lincoln (eds), *Handbook of Qualitative Research*. 2nd edn. Thousand Oaks, CA: Sage. pp. 487–508.

Haig, B.D. (1997) 'Feminist research methodology', in J.P. Keeves (ed.), *Educational Research, Methodology, and Measurement: An International Handbook*. 2nd edn. Oxford: Elsevier. pp. 180–5.

Hakim, C. (1982) *Secondary Analysis in Social Research*. London: Allen and Unwin.

Halfpenny, P. (1982) *Positivism and Sociology: Explaining Social Life*. London: Allen and Unwin.

Halpin, A.W. and Croft, D.B. (1963) *The Organizational Climate of Schools*. Chicago: Chicago Midwest Administration Center.

Hammersley, M. (1992) 'Deconstructing the qualitative–quantitative divide', in J. Brannen (ed.), *Mixing Methods: Qualitative and Quantitative Research*. Aldershot: Avebury. pp. 39–55.

Hammersley, M. (ed.) (1993) *Social Research: Philosophy, Politics and Practice*. London: Sage.

Hammersley, M. (1995) *The Politics of Social Research*. London: Sage.

Hammersley, M. and Atkinson, P. (1995) *Ethnography: Principles in Practice*. 2nd edn. London: Routledge.

Harding, S. and Hintikka, M.B. (eds) (1983) *Discovering Reality: Feminist Perspectives on Epistemology, Metaphysics, Methodology and Philosophy*. Dordrecht: Reidel.

Hardy, M.A. (1993) *Regression with Dummy Variables*. Newbury Park, CA: Sage.

Haviland, W.A. (1990) *Cultural Anthropology*. 6th edn. Fort Worth, TX: Holt, Rinehart and Winston.

Heath, C. and Luff, P. (1996) 'Explicating face-to-face interaction', in N. Gilbert (ed.), *Researching Social Life*. London: Sage. pp. 306–26.

Heath, L. (1984) 'Impact of newspaper crime reports on fear of crime: multi-methodological investigation', *Journal of Personality and Social Psychology*, 47: 263–76.

Heritage, J. (1984) *Garfinkel and Ethnomethodology*. Cambridge: Polity.

Hesse, E. (1980) *Revolutions and Reconstructions in the Philosophy of Science*. Bloomington, IN: Indiana University Press.

Hofstede, G., Neuijen, B., Ohayv, D.D. and Sanders, G. (1990) 'Measuring organizational cultures: a qualitative and quantitative study across twenty cases', *Administrative Science Quarterly*, 35: 286–316.

Howard, M.C. (1993) *Contemporary Cultural Anthropology*. 4th edn. New York: Harper Collins.

Huberman, M. (1993) *The Lives of Teachers*. Trans. J. Neufeld. London: Teachers College Press.

Huberman, A.M. and Miles, M.B. (1994) 'Data management and analysis methods', in N.K. Denzin and Y.S. Lincoln (eds), *Handbook of Qualitative Research*. Thousand Oaks, CA: Sage. pp. 428–44.

Hughes, E.C. (1958) *Men and Their Work*. Chicago: Free Press.

Irwin, D.M. (1980) *Observational Strategies for Child Study*. New York: Holt, Rinehart and Winston.

Jaeger, R.M. (1984) *Sampling in Education and the Social Sciences*. New York: Longman.

Jaeger, R.M. (1988) 'Survey methods in educational research', in R.M. Jaeger (ed.), *Complementary Methods for Research in Education*. Washington, DC: American Educational Research Association. pp. 301–87.

Jaeger, R.M. (1990) *Statistics as a Spectator Sport*. 2nd edn. Beverly Hills, CA: Sage.

Janesick, V.J. (1994) 'The dance of qualitative research design: metaphor, methodolatry, and meaning', in N.K. Denzin and Y.S. Lincoln (eds), *Handbook of Qualitative Research*. Thousand Oaks, CA: Sage. pp. 209–19.

Jayaratne, T.E. and Stewart, A.J. (1991) 'Quantitative and qualitative methods in the social sciences: current feminist issues and practical strategies', in M.M. Fonow and J.A. Cook (eds), *Beyond Methodology: Feminist Scholarship as Lived Research*. Bloomington, IN: Indiana University Press. pp. 85–106.

Johnson, J.C. (1990) *Selecting Ethnographic Informants*. Newbury Park, CA: Sage.

Jones, S. (1985) 'Depth interviewing', in R. Walker (ed.), *Applied Qualitative Research*. Aldershot: Gower. pp. 45–55.

Jupp, V. (1996) 'Documents and critical research', in R. Sapsford and V. Jupp (eds), *Data Collection and Analysis*. London: Sage. pp. 298–316.

Kaufman, H. (1981) *The Administrative Behavior of Federal Bureau Chiefs*. Washington, DC: Brookings Institution.

Keats, D.M. (1988) *Skilled Interviewing*. Melbourne: Australian Council for Educational Research.

Keesing, R.M. (1976) *Cultural Anthropology: A Contemporary Perspective*. New York: Holt, Rinehart and Winston.

Kelle, U. (ed.) (1995) *Computer-Aided Qualitative Data Analysis: Theory, Methods and Practice*. London: Sage.

Kemmis, S. and McTaggart, R. (2000) 'Participatory action research', in N.K. Denzin and Y.S. Lincoln (eds), *Handbook of Qualitative Research*. 2nd edn. Thousand Oaks, CA: Sage. pp. 567–605.

Kerlinger, F.N. (1973) *Foundations of Behavioral Research*. New York: Holt, Rinehart and Winston.

Kerr, A.W., Hall, H.K. and Kozub, S.A. (2002) *Doing Statistics with SPSS*. London: Sage.

Kiecolt, K.J. and Nathan, L.E. (1985) *Secondary Analysis of Survey Data*. Beverly Hills, CA: Sage.

Kincheloe, J.L. and McLaren, P.L. (1994) 'Rethinking critical theory and qualitative rersearch', in N.K. Denzin and Y.S. Lincoln (eds), *Handbook of Qualitative Research*. Thousand Oaks, CA: Sage. pp. 138–57.

Kirk, J. and Miller, M.L. (1986) *Reliability and Validity in Qualitative Research*. Beverly Hills, CA: Sage.

Kirk, R.E. (1995) *Experimental Design: Procedures for the Behavioral Sciences*. 3rd edn. Belmont, CA: Brooks/Cole.

Kushman, J.W. (1992) 'The organizational dynamics of teacher workplaces', *Educational Administration Quarterly*, 28 (1): 5–42.

Lather, P. (1991) *Getting Smart: Feminist Research and Pedagogy With/In the Postmodern*. New York: Routledge.

LeCompte, M.D. and Preissle, J. (1993) *Ethnography and Qualitative Design in Educational Research*. 2nd edn. San Diego, CA: Academic.

Lewins, F. (1992) *Social Science Methodology*. Melbourne: Macmillan.

Liebert, R.M. (1995) *Science and Behavior: An Introduction to Methods of Psychological Research*. Englewood Cliffs, NJ: Prentice-Hall.

Liebow, E. (1967) *Tally's Corner*. Boston: Little Brown.

Light, I. and Bonacich, E. (1988) *Immigrant Entrepreneurs: Koreans in Los Angeles, 1965–1982*. Berkeley, CA: University of California Press.

Lincoln, Y.S. and Guba, E.G. (1985) *Naturalistic Inquiry*. Beverley Hills, CA: Sage.

Lindesmith, A. (1947) *Opiate Addiction*. Bloomington, IN: Principia.

Lindesmith, A. (1968) *Addiction and Opiates*. Chicago: Aldine.

Little, D. (1991) *Varieties of Social Explanation: An Introduction to the Philosophy of Social Science*. Boulder, CO: Westview.

Locke, L.F., Spirduso, W.W. and Silverman, S.J. (1993) *Proposals That Work*. 3rd edn. Newbury Park, CA: Sage.

Lofland, J. and Lofland, L.H. (1984) *Analyzing Social Settings*. 2nd edn. Belmont, CA: Wadsworth.

Lonkila, M. (1995) 'Grounded theory as an emerging paradigm for computer-assisted qualitative data analysis', in U. Kelle (ed.), *Computer-Aided Qualitative Data Analysis: Theory, Methods and Practice*. London: Sage. pp. 41–51.

Lyotard, J.-F. (1984) *The Postmodern Condition: A Report on Knowledge*. Trans. G. Bennington and G. Masumi. Manchester: Manchester University Press.

MacDonald, K. and Tipton, C. (1996) 'Using documents', in N. Gilbert (ed.), *Researching Social Life*. London: Sage. pp. 187–200.

Manning, P.K. and Cullum-Swan, B. (1994) 'Narrative, content, and semiotic analysis', in N.K. Denzin and Y.S. Lincoln (eds), *Handbook of Qualitative Research*. Thousand Oaks, CA: Sage. pp. 463–83.

Marsh, C. (1982) *The Survey Method: The Contribution of Surveys to Sociological Explanation*. London: Allen and Unwin.

Marshall, C. and Rossman, G.B. (1989) *Designing Qualitative Research*. Newbury Park, CA: Sage.

Martin, J. (1990) 'Deconstructing organizational taboos', *Organization Science*, I: 339–59.

Mathison, S. (1988) 'Why triangulate?', *Educational Researcher*, 17 (2): 13–17.

Matocha, L.J. (1992) 'Case study interviews: caring for persons with AIDS', in J.F. Gilgun, K. Daly and G. Handel (eds), *Qualitative Methods in Family Research*. Newbury Park, CA: Sage. pp. 66–84.

Mauthner, M., Birch, M., Jessop, J. and Miller, T. (2002) *Ethics in Qualitative Research*. London: Sage.

Maxwell, J.A. (1996) *Qualitative Research Design: An Interactive Approach*. Thousand Oaks, CA: Sage.

McCarthy, M. (1991) *Discourse Analysis for Language Teachers*. Cambridge: Cambridge University Press.

McCracken, G. (1988) *The Long Interview*. Beverly Hills, CA: Sage.

McLaren, P. (1986) *Schooling as a Ritual Performance: Towards a Political Economy of Educational Symbols and Gestures*. London: Routledge and Kegan Paul.

McRobbie, A. (1978) '*Jackie*: an ideology of adolescent femininity'. Birmingham: Centre for Contemporary Cultural Studies.

McRobbie, A. (1991) *Feminism and Youth Culture: From Jackie to Just Seventeen*. London: Macmillan.

Measor, L. and Woods, P. (1984) *Changing Schools*. Milton Keynes: Open University Press.

Menard, S. (1991) *Longitudinal Research*. Newbury Park, CA: Sage.

Merton, R.K., Fiske, M. and Kendall, P.L. (1956) *The Focused Interview*. Glencoe, IL: Free Press.

Mies, M. (1991) 'Women's research or feminist research? The debate surrounding feminist science and methodology', in M.M. Fonow and J.A. Cook (eds), *Beyond Methodology: Feminist Scholarship as Lived Research*. Bloomington, IN: Indiana University Press. pp. 60–84.

Miles, M.B. (1979) 'Qualitative data as an attractive nuisance: the problem of analysis', *Administrative Science Quarterly*, 24: 590–601.

Miles, M.B. and Huberman, A.M. (1994) *Qualitative Data Analysis*. 2nd edn. Thousand Oaks, CA: Sage.

Milgram, S. (1974) *Obedience to Authority*. New York: Harper and Row.

Miller, D.C. (1991) *Handbook of Research Design and Social Measurement*. 5th edn. Newbury Park, CA: Sage.

Mills, C.W. (1959) *The Sociological Imagination*. New York: Oxford University Press.

Minichiello, V., Aroni, R., Timewell, E. and Alexander, L. (1990). *In-Depth Interviewing: Researching People*. Melbourne: Longman Cheshire.

Mishler, E. (1986) *Research Interviewing*. Cambridge, MA: Harvard University Press.

Morgan, D.L. (1988) *Focus Groups as Qualitative Research*. Newbury Park, CA: Sage.

Morse, J.M. (1991) 'Approaches to qualitative–quantitative methodological triangulation', *Nursing Research*, 40 (1): 120–3.

Morse, J.M. (1994) 'Designing funded qualitative research', in N.K. Denzin and Y.S. Lincoln (eds), *Handbook of Qualitative Research*. Thousand Oaks, CA: Sage. pp. 220–35.

Morse, J.M. and Richards, L. (2002) *Readme First for a Users' Guide to Qualitative Methods*. Thousand Oaks, CA: Sage.

Moser, C.A. and Kalton, G. (1979) *Survey Methods in Social Investigation*. 2nd edn. Hants: Gower.

Nagel, E. (1961) *The Structure of Science: Problems in the Logic of Scientific Explanation*. New York: Harcourt, Brace and World.

Nelson, C., Treichler, P.A. and Grossberg, L. (1992) 'Cultural studies', in L. Grossberg, C. Nelson and P.A. Treichler (eds), *Cultural Studies*. New York: Routledge. pp. 1–16.

Neuman, W.L. (1994) *Social Research Methods: Qualitative and Quantitative Approaches*. 2nd edn. Boston: Allyn and Bacon.

Neustadt, K.E. and Fineberg, H. (1983) *The Epidemic That Never Was: Policy-Making and the Swine Flu Affair*. New York: Vintage.

Oakley, A. (1974) *The Sociology of Housework*. Oxford: Martin Robertson.

Oakley, A. (1981) 'Interviewing women: a contradiction in terms', in H. Roberts (ed.), *Doing Feminist Research*. London: Routledge and Kegan Paul. pp. 30–61.

O'Connor, D.J. (1957) *An Introduction to the Philosophy of Education*. London: Routledge and Kegan Paul.

Olesen, V. (1994) 'Feminisms and models of qualitative research', in N.K. Denzin and Y.S. Lincoln (eds), *Handbook of Qualitative Research*. Thousand Oaks, C.A: Sage. pp. 158–74.

Oppenheim, A.N. (1992) *Questionnaire Design, Interviewing and Attitude Measurement*. London: Pinter.

Osgood, C., Suci, G. and Tannenbaum, P. (1957) *The Measurement of Meaning*. Urbana, IL: University of Illinois Press.

Pallant, J. (2001) *SPSS Survival Manual: A Step by Step Guide to Data Analysis Using SPSS*. Crows Nest, NSW: Allen & Unwin.

Parker, I., Georgaca, E., Harper, D., McLaughlin, T. and Stowell-Smith, M. (1995) *Deconstructing Psychopathology*. London: Sage.

Patton, M.Q. (1980) *Qualitative Evaluation Methods*. Newbury Park, CA: Sage.

Patton, M.Q. (1987) *How to Use Qualitative Methods in Evaluation*. Newbury Park, CA: Sage.

Patton, M.Q. (1990) *Qualitative Evaluation and Research Methods*. 2nd edn. Newbury Park, CA: Sage.

Peaker, G.F. (1971) *The Plowden Children Four Years Later*. London: National Foundation for Educational Research in England and Wales.

Peters, T.J. and Waterman, R.H. Jr (1982) *In Search of Excellence: Lessons from America's Best-Run Companies*. New York: Harper and Row.

Platt, J. (1995) 'Research methods and the second Chicago School', in G.A. Fine (ed.), *A Second Chicago School? The Development of a Postwar American Sociology*. Chicago: University of Chicago Press. pp. 82–107.

Popper, K. (1959) *The Logic of Scientific Discovery*. London: Hutchinson.

Potter, J. and Wetherell, M. (1987) *Discourse and Social Psychology: Beyond Attitudes and Behaviour*. London: Sage.

Potter, J. and Wetherell, M. (1994) 'Analyzing discourse', in A. Bryman and R.G. Burgess (eds), *Analyzing Qualitative Data*. London: Routledge. pp. 47–66.

Procter, M. (1996) 'Analysing other researchers' data', in N. Gilbert (ed.), *Researching Social Life*. London: Sage. pp. 255–86.

Punch, M. (1986) *The Politics and Ethics of Fieldwork: Muddy Boots and Grubby Hands*. Beverly Hills, CA: Sage.

Punch, M. (1994) 'Politics and ethics in qualitative research', in N.K. Denzin and Y.S. Lincoln (eds), *Handbook of Qualitative Research*. Thousand Oaks, CA: Sage. pp. 83–97.

Punch, K.F. (2000) *Developing Effective Research Proposals*. London: Sage.

Punch, K.F. (2003) *Survey Research: The Basics*. London: Sage.

QSR (2002) *N6 Reference Manual*. Melbourne: QSR International.

QSR (2004) QSR International website. http://www.qsrinternational.com/aboutus/company_profile.htm

Ragin, C.C. (1987) *The Comparative Method: Moving Beyond Qualitative and Quantitative Strategies*. Berkeley, CA: University of California Press.

Ragin, C.C. (1994) *Constructing Social Research*. Thousand Oaks, CA: Pine Forge.

Rank, M.R. (1992) 'The blending of qualitative and quantitative methods in understanding childbearing among welfare recipients', in J.F. Gilgun, K. Daly and G. Handel (eds), *Qualitative Methods in Family Research*. Newbury Park, CA: Sage. pp. 281–300.

Reason, P. and Bradbury, H. (eds) (2001) *Handbook of Action Research*. London: Sage.

Reeve, R.A. and Walberg, J.J. (1997) 'Secondary data analysis', in J.P. Keeves (ed.), *Educational Research, Methodology, and Measurement: An International Handbook*. 2nd edn. Oxford: Elsevier. pp. 439–44.

Reinharz, S. (1992) *Feminist Methods in Social Research*. New York: Oxford University Press.

Richardson, L. (1994) 'Writing: a method of inquiry', in N.K. Denzin and Y.S. Lincoln (eds), *Handbook of Qualitative Research*. Thousand Oaks, CA: Sage. pp. 516–29.

Riessman, C.J. (1993) *Narrative Analysis*. Newbury Park, CA: Sage.

Robinson, J.P. and Shaver, P.R. (1973) *Measures of Social Psychological Attitudes*. Ann Arbor, MI: Institute for Social Research.

Robinson, J.P., Athanasiou, R. and Head, K.B. (1969) *Measures of Occupational Attitudes and Occupational Characteristics*. Ann Arbor, MI: Institute for Social Research.

Roman, L.G. (1992) 'The political significance of other ways of narrating ethnography: a feminist materialist approach', in M.D. LeCompte, W.L. Millroy and J. Preissle (eds), *The Handbook of Qualitative Research in Education*. San Diego, CA: Academic. pp. 555–94.

Rosenberg, M. (1968) *The Logic of Survey Analysis*. New York: Basic.

Rosenberg, M. (1979) *Conceiving the Self*. New York: Basic.

Rossman, G.B. and Wilson, B.L. (1985) 'Numbers and words: combining quantitative and qualitative methods in a single large-scale evaluation study', *Evaluation Review*, 9 (5): 627–43.

Rutter, M., Maughan, B., Mortimore, P. and Ouston, J. (1979) *Fifteen Thousand Hours: Secondary Schools and their Effects on Children*. London: Open.

Sandelowski, M., Holditch-Davis, D. and Harris, B.G. (1992) 'Using qualitative and quantitative methods: the transition to parenthood of infertile couples', in J.F. Gilgun, K. Daly and G. Handel (eds), *Qualitative Methods in Family Research*. Newbury Park, CA: Sage. pp. 301–22.

Sapsford, R. and Abbott, P. (1996) 'Ethics, politics and research', in R. Sapsford and V. Jupp (eds), *Data Collection and Analysis*. London: Sage. pp. 317–42.

Savage, M., Watt, P. and Arber, S. (1990) 'The consumption sector debate and housing mobility', *Sociology*, 24 (1): 97–117.

Schachter, S. and Singer, J.E. (1962) 'Cognitive, social and physiological determinants of emotional state', *Psychological Review*, 69: 379–99.

Schwandt, T.A. and Halpern, E.S. (1988) *Linking, Auditing and Metaevaluating: Enhancing Quality in Applied Research*. Newbury Park, CA: Sage.

Scott, J. (1990) *A Matter of Record: Documentary Sources in Social Research*. Cambridge: Polity.

Seale, C. (ed.) (1998) *Researching Society and Culture*. London: Sage.

Seidman, I.E. (1991) *Interviewing as Qualitative Research: A Guide for Researchers in Education and the Social Sciences*. New York: Teachers College Press.

Selznick, P. (1949) *TVA and the Grass Roots: A Study of Politics and Organization*. Berkeley, CA: University of California Press.

Shaw, M.E. and Wright, J.M. (1967) *Scales for the Measurement of Attitudes*. New York: McGraw-Hill.

Sherif, M., Harvey, O.J., White, B.J., Hood, W.R. and Sherif, C.W. (1961) *Intergroup Conflict and Cooperation: The Robber's Cave Experiment*. Norman, OK: University of Oklahoma Book Exchange.

Shostak, M. (1981) *Nisa: The Life and Words of a !Kung Woman*. Cambridge, MA: Harvard University Press.

Shulman, L.S. (1988) 'Disciplines of inquiry in education: an overview', in R.M. Jaeger (ed.), *Complementary Methods for Research in Education*. Washington, DC: American Educational Research Association. pp. 3–17.

Sieber, S.D. (1973) 'Threat as a factor in authoritarianism: an analysis of archival data', *Journal of Personality and Social Psychology*, 28: 44–57.

Siegel, S. (1956) *Nonparametric Statistics for the Behavioural Sciences*. New York: McGraw-Hill.

Silverman, D. (1985) *Qualitative Methodology and Sociology*. Farnborough: Gower.

Silverman, D. (1993) *Interpreting Qualitative Data: Methods for Analyzing Talk, Text and Interaction*. London: Sage.

Simmel, G. (1950) *The Sociology of George Simmel*. Trans. K.H. Wolff. Glencoe, IL: Free Press.

Siu, P.C.P. (1987) *The Chinese Laundryman: A Study of Social Isolation*. Edited by John Kuo Wei Tchen. New York: New York University Press.

Smart, C. (1976) *Women, Crime and Criminology*. London: Routledge and Kegan Paul.

Snider, J.G. and Osgood, C.E. (eds) (1969) *Semantic Differential Technique: A Sourcebook*. Chicago: Aldine.

Spindler, G. and Spindler, L. (1992) 'Cultural process and ethnography: an anthropological perspective', in M.D. LeCompte, W.L. Millroy and J. Preissle (eds), *The Handbook of Qualitative Research in Education*. San Diego, CA: Academic. pp. 53–92.

Spradley, J.P. (1980) *Participant Observation*. New York: Holt, Rinehart and Winston.

Stake, R.E. (1988) 'Case study methods in educational research: seeking sweet water', in R.M. Jaeger (ed.), *Complementary Methods for Research in Education*. Washington, DC: American Educational Research Association. pp. 253–300.

Stake, R.E. (1994) 'Case studies', in N.K. Denzin and Y.S. Lincoln (eds), *Handbook of Qualitative Research*. Thousand Oaks, CA: Sage. pp. 236–47.

Stanfield, J. (1985) *Philanthropy and Jim Crow in American Social Sciences*. Westport, CT: Greenwood.

Stanley, L. and Wise, S. (1983) *Breaking Out: Feminist Consciousness and Feminist Research*. London: Routledge and Kegan Paul.

Stevens, S.S. (1951) 'Mathematics, measurement and psycho-physics', in S.S. Stevens (ed.), *Handbook of Experimental Psychology*. New York: Wiley.

Stewart, D.W. (1984) *Secondary Research: Information, Sources and Methods*. Beverly Hills, CA: Sage.

Stewart, D.W. and Shamdasani, P. (1990) *Focus Groups: Theory and Practice*. Newbury Park, CA: Sage.

Strauss, A. (1987) *Qualitative Analysis for Social Scientists*. New York: Cambridge University Press.

Strauss, A. and Corbin, J. (1990) *Basics of Qualitative Research: Grounded Theory Procedures and Techniques*. Newbury Park, CA: Sage.

Strauss, A. and Corbin, J. (1994) 'Grounded theory methodology: an overview', in N.K. Denzin and Y.S. Lincoln (eds), *Handbook of Qualitative Research*. Thousand Oaks, CA: Sage. pp. 273–85.

Strauss, A. and Corbin, J. (eds) (1997) *Grounded Theory in Practice*. Thousand Oaks, CA: Sage.

Stringer, E. (2004) *Action Research in Education*. Upper Saddle River, NJ: Pearson.

Sudman, S. and Bradburn, N.M. (1982) *Asking Questions: A Practical Guide to Questionnaire Design*. San Francisco: Jossey-Bass.

Swanson, J.M. (1986) 'Analyzing data for categories and description', in W.C. Chenitz and J.M. Swanson (eds), *From Practice to Grounded Theory: Qualitative Research in Nursing*. Menlo Park, CA: Addison-Wesley. pp. 121–32.

Taylor, S. (2001) 'Locating and conducting discourse analytic research', in M. Wetherall, S. Taylor and S.J. Yates (eds), *Discourse as Data: A Guide for Analysis*. London: Sage. pp. 5–48.

Tesch, R. (1990) *Qualitative Research: Analysis Types and Software Tools*. Basingstoke: Falmer.

Theodorson, G.A. and Theodorson, A.G. (1969) *A Modern Dictionary of Sociology*. New York: Crowell.

Thomas, R. (1996) 'Statistical sources and databases', in R. Sapsford and V. Jupp (eds), *Data Collection and Analysis*. London: Sage. pp. 121–37.

Tonkiss, F. (1998) 'Analyzing discourse', in C. Seale (ed.), *Researching Society and Culture*. London: Sage. pp. 245–60.

Turnbull, C.M. (1968) *The Forest People*. New York: Simon and Schuster.

Vitz, P.C. (1990) 'The use of stories in moral development: new psychological reasons for an old education method', *American Psychologist*, 45 (6): 709–20.

Wallen, N.E. and Fraenkel, J.R. (1991) *Educational Research: A Guide to the Process*. New York: McGraw-Hill.

Webb, E.J., Campbell, D.T., Schwartz, R.D. and Sechrest, L. (1966) *Unobtrusive Measures*. Chicago: Rand McNally.

Webb, R.B. and Glesne, C. (1992) 'Teaching qualitative research', in M.D. LeCompte, W.L. Millroy and J. Preissle (eds), *The Handbook of Qualitative Research in Education*. San Diego, CA: Academic. pp. 771–814.

Whyte, W.F. (1955) *Street Corner Society: The Social Structure of an Italian Slum*. Chicago: University of Chicago Press.

Willis, P. (1981) 'Cultural production is different from cultural reproduction is different from social reproduction is different from reproduction', *Interchange*, 12 (2–3): 48–67.

Wilson, M. (1996) 'Asking questions', in R. Sapsford and V. Jupp (eds), *Data Collection and Analysis*. London: Sage. pp. 94–120.

Wolcott, H.F. (1973) *The Man in the Principal's Office: An Ethnography*. Illinois: Waveland.

Wolcott, H.F. (1982) 'Differing styles of on-site research, or, "If it isn't ethnography, what is it?"', *The Review Journal of Philosophy and Social Science*, 7 (1 and 2): 154–69.

Wolcott, H.F. (1988) 'Ethnographic research in education', in R.M. Jaeger (ed.), *Complementary Methods for Research in Education*. Washington, DC: American Educational Research Association. pp. 187–249.

Wolcott, H.F. (1990) *Writing Up Qualitative Research*. Newbury Park, CA: Sage.

Wolcott, H.F. (1992) 'Posturing in qualitative inquiry', in M.D. LeCompte, W.L. Millroy and J. Preissle (eds), *Handbook of Qualitative Research in Education*. San Diego, CA: Academic. pp. 3–52.

Wolcott, H.F. (1994) *Transforming Qualitative Data*. Thousand Oaks, CA: Sage.

Woods, P.H. (1979) *The Divided School*. London: Routledge and Kegan Paul.

Woods, P.H. (1986) *Inside Schools: Ethnography in Educational Research*. London: Routledge and Kegan Paul.

Woods, P.H. (1992) 'Symbolic interactionism: theory and method', in M.D. LeCompte, W.L. Millroy and J. Preissle (eds), *The Handbook of Qualitative Research in Education*. San Diego, CA: Academic. pp. 337–404.

Wooffitt, R. (1996) 'Analysing accounts', in N. Gilbert (ed.), *Researching Social Life*. London: Sage. pp. 287–305.

Worral, A. (1990) *Offending Women*. London: Routledge.

Yin, R.K. (1984) *Case Study Research: Design and Methods*. Newbury Park, CA: Sage.

Young, W.C. (1996) *The Rashaayda Bedouin: Arab Pastoralists of Eastern Sudan*. USA: Harcourt Brace.

Zeller, R.A. (1996) 'Validity', in J.P. Keeves (ed.), *Educational Research, Methodology, and Measurement: An International Handbook*. 2nd edn. Oxford: Elsevier. pp. 822–9.

Zimbardo, P.G., Haney, C., Banks, W. and Jaffe, D. (1974) 'The psychology of imprisonment: privation, power and pathology', in Z. Rubin (ed.), *In Doing unto Others*. Englewood Cliffs, NJ: Prentice-Hall.

Znaniecki, F. (1934) *The Method of Sociology*. New York: Farrar and Rinehart.

Zuckerman, H. (1978) 'Theory choice and problem choice in science', in J. Gaston (ed.), *Sociology of Science*. San Francisco: Jossey-Bass. pp. 65–95.

# Index

Lightning Source UK Ltd.
Milton Keynes UK
UKOW010621160113

204913UK00001B/17/P